THE

ALLAH DELUSION

Sujit Das

With a Preface by Ali Sina

Publisher: Felibri.com
felibri@gmail.com
Publication date: June 2013
Distributed by Ingram Book Group

The Allah Delusion / by Sujit Das
ISBN 978-1-926800-09-7
1. Muhammad, Prophet, d. 632--Psychology.
2. Islam—Controversial literature. I. Title.

*****

Picture on the cover: An Afghan Muslim prays near Afghanistan's main top-security prison, *Pul-e-Charkhi* in Kabul, the capital city of Afghanistan (picture taken by Sarah Zahirudin). In this torn country, where death is cheaper than life, where children die before they are born, where chastity is molested day and night, where life cries and moan, and where hills, valleys and lakes glow in blood and fire; the Humanity is assassinated thousand times a day in the name of Allah. In spite of this oppression in the name of Islam, Allah is their sole savior. This is – **THE ALLAH DELUSION.**

*****

Also by Sujit Das

Islam Dismantled: The Mental Illness of Prophet Muhammad

*****

Dedicated to the victims of Islamic Jihad worldwide

Your sufferings are not forgotten

Contents

The methodology of this book

"Indeed, your Lord is ever watchful". (Q: 89.14)
"Allah warns you to be cautious of Him, the arrival is to Allah". (Q: 3.28)

My poetic response to the above two Qur'anic verses is,

Within logic lies the eternal truth
Who sees it all?
Allah may have thousand eyes
To watch over his critics
But I have only two – Science and Reason.

The methodology of Chapter 1 (The god who failed) and Chapter 2 (Allah under investigation) is mostly based on two logical principles – Law of Contradiction and Occam's razor. The Law of Contradiction states, a proposition cannot be true and false at the same time and in the same respect. Occam's razor (also called The Principle of Parsimony) was named after the fourteenth-century theologian William of Occam. This dictum states that one should neither multiply explanations nor increase their complexity beyond necessity. An explanation should be as simple and direct as possible, and any excess baggage should be discarded. Adler (1967, p. 143) explains the function of this principle as,

"Occam's razor is a two-edged instrument – one that works in opposite directions. It eliminates theoretical constructs, that cannot be shown to be necessary for explanatory purposes; but it also justifies the retention of theoretical constructs the need for which can be shown".

The simpler explanations are, other things being equal, generally better than more complex ones. The common form of the razor, used to distinguish between equally explanatory hypotheses, may be supported by the practical fact that simpler theories are easier to understand. Simply stated, Occam's razor is this – Get rid of redundant entities.

Throughout most of this book, we are concerned with one question and one question only – Should we accept Allah as a true God, or is he a redundant entity? In the final analysis (Chapter 7: The final conclusion), this is the only important question.

In Chapter 3 (Allah: The psychotic delusion of Muhammad), I have re-visited Allah and analyzed him from the perspective of psychiatry. In other three chapters; I went on to explore the ethical and social (Chapter 6: The cost of Allah delusion), psychological (Chapter 5: Allah: The virus of the mind), and psychiatric (Chapter 4: Human evil and dimensions of delusions) implications of a belief in Allah, but these areas are secondary to the basic issue of the truth. After the final conclusion, this document continues with two additional slightly off-topic chapters, as Addendum 1 (The delusion of Dr. Richard Dawkins) and Addendum 2 (Closing thoughts: Militant Islam and Militant Atheism – both failed). These two supplementary chapters criticize the idea of aggressive atheism that Dr. Dawkins promoted in his book *The God Delusion,* and focus on the demerits of militant atheism and Islam, and condemn both of them. Throughout this book, I have quoted extensively from other authors, and where I have not quoted, I have paraphrased, all with the proper acknowledgments in the references at the end.

This book is heavy reading. I ask for readers' patience on this.

Preface

By Ali Sina

Does God exist? This is probably the most asked and the least answered question of all times. It can't be answered because one can neither prove the existence of God nor disprove it.

The strongest evidence presented for the existence of God is that of Descartes. Descartes was a rationalist philosopher who rejected anything that could not be proven by reason. He thought that senses are unreliable. Discarding all the information that came to him through his senses, he found that he knew nothing. Everything that we know, he argued, comes through our senses. And since our senses can be deceptive, everything that seems real can be unreal. It was then that Descartes realized he must exist in order to doubt. The very fact that he could think was evidence of his existence. He expressed his discovery as *"cogito ergo sun"* – I think, therefore I am.

This discovery led Descartes to prove the existence of God. He realized that among things that he thinks about is the notion of a perfect being. He wondered why an imperfect being should have the thought of a perfect being. If such thought exists, it must have been put in him by the prefect being who must have wanted him to think of Him and discover His existence. Based on this idea he formulated the following syllogism.

1. I exist (Axiom)
2. I have in my mind the notion of a perfect being (Axiom, partly based on 1)
3. An imperfect being, like myself, cannot think up the notion of a perfect being (Axiom)
4. Therefore, the notion of a perfect being must have originated from the perfect being himself (from 2 & 3)
5. A perfect being would not be perfect if it did not exist (Axiom)
6. Therefore, a perfect being must exist (from 4 & 5)

There are problems with this argument. We can all agree that axiom 1 is true. But do all people have the notion of a perfect being in their mind? Descartes may have had, but those who don't believe in God don't have it. Did God fail to put his notion in the minds of everyone or maybe it is not as innate as Descartes had thought. In fact those who believe in God affirm that God cannot be conceived. If he can't be conceived then his notion is not congenial and the axiom 2 cannot be universally true.

When people want to speak to God they instinctively look up to the sky. However, since the Earth is spherical, the up for each person point to a different direction. Just because everyone believes that God is above his head, it does not mean it is so. If God is everywhere, then our innate notion of God being up is wrong.

Axiom 3 says an imperfect being cannot think-up of a perfect being. Why not? Humans can think of anything they want. The fact that we can think of something, does not imply it exists. Muhammad claimed that when he visited the heaven, he saw an angel larger than the entire world, with 70,000 heads; each head had 70,000 mouths, each mouth had 70,000 tongues and each tongue spoke in 70,000 different idioms singing endlessly the praises of the Most High. Such a creature cannot be envisioned or conceived. Does the fact that Muhammad was able to fancy it, an indication of its probable existence?

Something perfect must also be infinite. Does infinite exist? We can neither prove infinity nor disprove it. Mathematics fails when it comes to infinity. $2 \div \infty = 0$ and $5 \div \infty = 0$. Does this mean $2 = 5$? $\infty - 3 = \infty$. Can we conclude that $3 = 0$? Infinity may or may not exist, but that does not preclude us theorizing about it. We can't prove the existence of infinity. Likewise, we can't prove the existence of a perfect being, but we can have their notion in our mind.

A perfect being must also be good. If it is not good it can't be perfect. However, good and evil are entirely human concepts. Good to us is what benefits us and bad is what harms us. God and bad are anthropic concepts. Actually, they are egocentric concepts. If I get into fight with you and win, that is good for me, while the same outcome is bad for you, and vice-versa.

Every day, 2/3rd of animals kill in order to eat and feed their young. Is this good or bad? When a lion kills a baby deer, it is a tragedy for the calf and his mother, but it is a blessing for the lion and her cubs.

Sixty-six million years ago a large meteorite hit the Earth extinguishing 75% of the species of animals. This was a disaster of biblical proportion for those who went extinct, but a blessing for those who survived. The extinction of large dinosaurs allowed smaller mammals to evolve from relatively simple forms into a large group of diverse animals. We humans wouldn't be here if that calamity had not hit the earth. So was that destruction of life on Earth, in such a massive scale, a good thing or a bad thing? Good and bad are human concepts. If God is good and good doesn't exist outside human mind, doesn't this follow that God is a human concept?

A perfect being must also be just. Yet it is an observable fact that the foundation of the world is based on injustice. Turtles bury their eggs on sandy beaches. When the eggs hatch, hundreds of little turtles struggle to reach the ocean. Before they reach the water they are swooped by birds who feast on them. Their 100 years potential life is shortened to minutes. How can this be justice? There is no question of good or evil here. It's just how things are. And how things are is extremely cruel and unjust. How can a just God create a world so unjust?

Do the above arguments disprove the existence of God? No! They only disprove our old notion of God. When Galileo looked into his telescope, he did not reject the existence of the cosmos. He rejected people's understanding of it. New scientific evidences are emerging that force us to discard the old notion of God and give him a different interpretation.

The question whether God exists or not has been debated for thousands of years and we seem to be no closer to the answer. The last three - four centuries raised hope that reason and science may finally answer this question. Evermore powerful telescopes have been built and we looked into the sky searching for the heaven. We looked and looked and the more we looked the less we found it. We found infernally hot stars, perilous quasars, lethal Gama rays, crushing black holes and infernal planets where instead of water, molten iron rains. No heaven is on sight, but infernos abound. The only heaven we know of is our own tiny Earth.

Science has pushed aside most of the curtains of the universe, but found nobody behind them pushing any buttons. This big machine seems to operate on its own. It runs obeying the laws of physics. It is these laws that are immutable, eternal, encompassing and sovereign.

Then arrived the 20th century and we came to learn that atom is not atom (indivisible) at all. It is a universe on its own, made of particles that are made of sub particles, and at the core of everything there are strings that vibrate. The variety in matter is due to the differences in the vibration of these strings.

The strangest discovery was the principle of uncertainty. In the subatomic world of quanta, nothing has a definite position, a definite trajectory, or a definite momentum. This seems absurd, so absurd that Einstein refused to accept it and protested, God does not play dice.

This is not the craziest fact about the Quantum Physics. The mother of all crazy things is the fact that particles behave like wave when they are not observed and as discrete balls of energy when they are. Does this mean that the universe comes into being when we observe it or that there is someone, outside it that observed it? What if the universe is just a thought of someone? What is becoming more and more clear is that matter is intrinsically connected to consciousness.

Then entered the 21st century and all certainties were thrown out of the window. Leonard Susskind, a Professor in Theoretical Physics at Stanford University notes,

"The beginning of the 21st century is a watershed in modern science, a time that will forever change our understanding of the universe. Something is happening which is far more than the discovery of new facts or new equations. This is one of those rare moments when our entire outlook, our framework for thinking, and the whole epistemology of physics and cosmology are suddenly undergoing real upheaval."

Susskind is talking about the astounding fine-tuning of the principles of the universe. He says,

"There are a lot of puzzles in physics. Some of them are very, very deep, some of them are very, very strange, and I want to understand them. I want to understand what makes the world tick. Einstein said he wanted to know what was on God's mind when he made the world. I don't think he was a religious man, but I know what he means. The thing right now that I want to understand is why the universe was made in such a way as to be just right for people to live in it. This is a very strange story. The question is why certain quantities that go into our physical laws of nature are exactly what they are, and if this is just an accident. Is it an accident that they are finely tuned, precisely, sometimes on a knife's edge, just so that the world could accommodate us?"

The fundamental forces of Physics are gravity, electromagnetism, strong nuclear force (the force that holds the nucleus of the atom together), and weak nuclear force (the force that causes Beta decay). They are so fine-tuned that if they were slightly stronger or weaker the universe, as we know it, could not be formed and we could not exist.

If we give to the strength of the strong nuclear force the value of 1, the strength of electromagnetic force is equal to 1/137; the strength of the weak force is one million times weaker than the strong force and the strength of gravity is 6×10^{-36}. It means gravity is six over trillion, trillion, trillion times weaker that strong force. It is so weak that you need a mass the size of at least the Moon to barely feel it.

Scientists don't know why gravity is so weak, but one thing they know and that is if it were slightly stronger, even small objects like the Earth or the Moon could heat up and become stars. Bigger objects, the size of our Sun could become black holes. Planet masses would be scaled down. Irrespective of whether they could maintain steady orbits, the strength of gravity would have stunted the evolutionary potential on them. In a world like that nothing larger than insect could evolve and they too would need thick legs to support them. Galaxies would form much more quickly, and would be miniaturized. Stars would be so densely packed that close encounters would be frequent, precluding any stable planetary system as the orbits would be disturbed by passing stars. Stars would form and die before life having a chance to evolve on their planets. Depending on the magnitude of gravity, a star's life could be as short of a few million years to a few thousand years.

Conversely, if the gravity were weaker only the largest supernovae could become star and no heavy elements beyond iron would be formed, because inside the stars there would be not enough weight to transform lighter elements to heavier ones. As the result, the elements that are necessary for life would not exist.

If the strong nuclear force were a bit weaker, it would not be able to hold atomic nuclei together against the repulsion of the electromagnetic force. No atom could be formed and the universe would have been made of only particles.

If it were a bit stronger, the protons in the nucleus of atoms could stick together and all the hydrogen in the universe would have been burned to helium in the big bang. How a universe with no hydrogen could produce the complicated chemistry needed for life? There would be no water and without it there would be no life.

The most mind bugling example of fine-tuning is the strength of Dark Energy. This is the force we didn't know of until recently. Einstein had stipulated its existence and then discarded it. It was confirmed in 1998 when a number of observations showed that the universe is not only expanding; its expansion is speeding up. This force is so weak that its effect can only be felt between galaxies. For the first 5 billion years after the Big Bang, the universe was not large enough for it to be noticed. About 6 to 4 billion years ago its force has won over gravity and since then the universe has begun to accelerate its expansion. Dark Energy constitutes 75% of the universe.

It is estimated to be on the order of 10^{-29} g/cm3, or about 10^{-120} in reduced Planck units. Plank unit is the smallest unit of space and time. This is an extremely small number, but if it were a little stronger, the universe would have ended in a Big Rip, and if it were weaker, the gravitational pull of the matter would have forced the galaxies to pull together and end the universe in a Big Crunch.

There are about two dozen constants and each plays a crucial role in the stability of the universe. They are all extremely fine-tuned. Is it possible that these fine-tunings have happened by accident? Take the example of the cosmological constant that is fine-tuned to 10^{-120} in Planks unit. The chance of all these fine-tunings happening is almost one in infinity, or in other words zero. Susskind says,

"Everything seems to be on the knife edge, that if you changed the laws of physics even a little bit, the world as we know it wouldn't exist. The laws of physics, the laws of cosmology, the laws of how the universe evolved, seem to be very special. They are special in a way that they are very, very conducive to our own existence."

This notion that the fundamental physical constants are fine-tuned in such a way to be conducive to human existence is known as anthropic principle. It basically says that the universe was created with humans in mind. This argument is not scientific way of reasoning. It is very much religious. It requires stipulating that someone is setting the laws. Physicists want hardnosed facts and equations in order to explain everything.

There are two answers to this dilemma. Either God exists, or the fine-tuning of the cosmological constants is the result of accident. Believing in the supernatural, for a scientist is like embracing superstition. But the probability of accident is one in infinity. There is a famous quote from Sherlock Holmes who said, *"When you have eliminated the impossible, whatever remains, however improbable, must be the truth?"* We seem to have run out of the possibilities. Shall we accept the improbable and believe in a creator?

Einstein believed in a *"God who reveals Himself in the harmony of all that exists."* In his book, *Einstein: His Life and Universe*, the author Walter Isaacson writes, *"Einstein had a profound faith in, and reverence for the harmony and beauty of what he called the mind of God as it was expressed in the creation of the universe and its laws"*. In a dinner party, when Einstein had turned 50, a guest expressed a belief in Astrology. Einstein ridiculed the notion as pure superstition. Another guest stepped in and similarly disparaged religion. Belief in God, he insisted, was likewise a superstition. At this point the host tried to silence him by invoking the fact that even Einstein harbored religious beliefs. *"It isn't possible!"* the skeptical guest said, turning to Einstein to ask if he was, in fact, religious. *"Yes, you can call it that,"* Einstein replied calmly,

"Try and penetrate with our limited means the secrets of nature and you will find that, behind all the discernible laws and connections, there remains something subtle, intangible and inexplicable. Veneration for this force beyond anything that we can comprehend is my religion. To that extent I am, in fact, religious." [Einstein: His Life and Universe, by Walter Isaacson 2008]

When asked whether he believes in God, Einstein responded,
"I'm not an atheist. I don't think I can call myself a pantheist. The problem involved is too vast for our limited minds. We are in the position of a little child entering a huge library filled with books in many languages. The child knows someone must have written those books. It does not know how. It does not

11

understand the languages in which they are written. The child dimly suspects a mysterious order in the arrangement of the books but doesn't know what it is. That, it seems to me, is the attitude of even the most intelligent human being toward God. We see the universe marvelously arranged and obeying certain laws but only dimly understand these laws."

Note that Einstein's God has no resemblance to the anthropomorphic god of some religions. He did not believe in a god that intervenes in human affairs, breaks the laws of physics to perform miracles, sends prophets and answers prayers, as if humans could influence the mind of God and change the laws of the universe by supplicating. He described his belief in God as:

"A knowledge of the existence of something we cannot penetrate, of the manifestation of the profoundest reason and the most radiant beauty – it is this knowledge and this emotion that constitute the truly religious attitude; in this sense, and in this sense alone, I am a deeply religious man."

In another place he said,

"The insight into the mystery of life, coupled though it be with fear, has also given rise to religion. To know that what is impenetrable to us really exists, manifesting itself as the highest wisdom and the most radiant beauty which our dull faculties can comprehend only in their most primitive form — this knowledge, this feeling, is at the center of true religiousness, and in this sense only, I belong in the ranks of devoutly religious men. I cannot imagine a God who rewards and punishes the objects of his creation, whose purposes are modeled after his own — a God, in short, is but a reflection of human frailty. Neither can I believe that the individual survives the death of his body, although feeble souls harbor such thoughts through fear of ridiculous egotism."

Did Einstein believe that this *"something we cannot penetrate,"* is intelligent or intelligence itself? Did he envision it as a being or as a principle? Many physicists can't bring themselves to accept any notion of an intelligent being outside the universe. They believe the fine-tuning of the laws is the result of accident. If this means that the probability of accident is as low as one in infinity, then there must be infinite number of universes. It just happens that life can only appear in the one universe that can support it. That is why we are here. In other universes there is no one to ask this question. Our universe, however, is not the only one that supports life. Since there is infinite number of universes, there must also be infinite number of universes of each possible form, and consequently, infinite number of universes like ours.

Both hypotheses are difficult to accept. The belief in God and the multiverse are both based on the notion of infinity. Infinity cannot be demonstrated or comprehended. We can only observe a small portion of our own universe. The rest of it can never be seen because as the space is expanding the farthest galaxies get away from us faster than the speed of light. Their lights can never reach us. We can never know whether the universe is limited or infinite, let alone know whether there are universes beyond ours. The belief in the multiverse seems to be just as weak as the belief in God. Both arguments rely on infinity – something that cannot be proven.

Is infinity real? There is a number that is the most important of all numbers, without which complex mathematical calculations fail; all equations become unresolvable; all the discoveries in physics, cosmology and astronomy will be impossible, and this number does not exist. It is nothing and yet it is the foundation of everything. Only an Indian could have conjured the "zero." The same can be said about infinity. Infinity and zero are imaginary numbers. Neither has any reality. They only exist in human mind. In fact infinity is even less provable than zero. You can always assign the value zero to a point in space or time, but you can never know the location of infinity. The arguments that can be made for or against God can also be made for or against the multiverse. If infinity is the product of human imagination, so are God and the multiverse. Neither is more conceivable or convincing than the other.

Humans have tried to find an answer to the question of God since the dawn of their intelligence. They came with various answers, only to discard them later and find new ones. Gods were sought in the forces of the nature, in animals, in stars, in supernatural ghosts, and in natural laws. As our intellect expanded, our answers to God kept evolving. We may not be closer to the answer, but at least we know where not to look.

Throughout the history, our gods have always been the projection of our own self. Gods were the incarnation of our fears and hopes. They were the ideal towards which we aspired. Since humans are different, their thoughts, fears and aspirations are different, and so are their gods. Tell me who is your god and I'll tell you who you are.

The Aztec believed in Huitzilopochtli, a god of war. It is estimated that approximately 20,000 people were sacrificed by the Aztec royalty every year to appease this deity. Captives were taken to the top of pyramids where, upon a ritual flat stone table, they had their chests cut open and their hearts ripped out. Then the bodies of the victims were tossed down the steps of the pyramids.

The motivation behind the ritual sacrifices was the concept of tonalli, the "animating spirit." The tonalli in humans was believed to be located in the blood, which concentrates in the heart when one becomes frightened. This explains the gods' hunger for the heart. Without this sacrifice, all motion would stop, even the movement of the sun. So when the Aztecs made their sacrifices, as far as they were concerned, they were keeping the Sun from halting in its orbit.

The god of the Israelites played favoritism. He had chosen the Jews as his own people. The rationale behind this was that the Jews were living in captivity most of the time. Their captors mistreated them. In the past humans were crueler to each other than they are today. To compensate, their god liked them better. He would promise them victory at the end and severe punishment for their oppressors. He would assure them that their tribulations are only to purify them from their sins. Thanks to their faith the Jews endured great hardships and did not let go of hope. Redemption and glory were always around the corner.

The Hindu Goddess Kali represents time. Its name derives from the Sanskrit root word "Kal", which means time. Time creates, nurtures, and then destroys everything. When given an anthropic personality, it becomes a monstrous deity that gives birth and takes care of her children, only to devour them later. Thuggees (a group of Muslims, Hindus and Sikhs), chose Kali as their patron Goddess. It is estimated that they ceremoniously killed about 2,000,000 travelers, men and women, by deceiving them, and then strangulating them and robbing their possessions, to please this heartless and demonic deity.

For Zoroaster, God was the Light of Reason. Ahura means light and mazda means reason. Thus Ahura Mazda is the lord of light and wisdom, the creator and upholder of *Arta* (truth).

For Jesus, God was love. Jesus was a man of peace. He taught his followers to forgive each other's' sins, find the beam in their own eyes before looking for the speck in the eyes of others, to not throw stone when they are sinners themselves, to love their neighbors and even to turn the other cheek when they are slapped. His God is very much like him, a loving and forgiving God.

Muhammad was a narcissist. To him god was everything a narcissist wants to be. His Allah is omnipotent and a fearsome deity that demands respect, commands to be praised and orders to be worshiped. Muhammad's god is a wanton god who does as he pleases. He can make rules and break them at will and no one can question him. He can send pious people to hell and reward evildoers, if he so desires. Humans cannot be sure of their fate and cannot gain salvation through good deeds. What he cares most is submission. He is pleased when humans bow to him and worship him, and is hurt when they ignore him. Allah is a despot; his mind resembles the minds of Saddam Hussein, Hitler and Stalin. He is ruthless to those who defy his authority and magnanimous to those who praise him. He is a needy god desperate for his creatures' attention. To Muhammad, these qualities were supreme. His god is his own alter ego – a projection of his narcissistic mind.

Einstein's god was the god of natural laws. Einstein was a man of science. He believed that there is an order in the universe, beauty and harmony. He resented having his religious convictions misrepresented and clarified:

"It was, of course, a lie what you read about my religious convictions, a lie which is being systematically repeated. I do not believe in a personal God and I have never denied this but have expressed it clearly. If something is in me which can be called religious then it is the unbounded admiration for the structure of the world so far as our science can reveal it."

Great minds are religious and yet their religiosity is different from the religion of the common folks. Cosmologist and Mathematician Stephen Hawking who spoke of "the Mind of God," when asked by CNN's Larry King whether he believed in God answered: *"Yes, if by God is meant the embodiment of the laws of the universe."*

Each of us envisions God according to our understanding. The god we envision is the projection of our own self. It is by psychoanalyzing Allah that we can gauge the sickness of Muhammad's mind. This deity is truly evil, because his creator was a malignant narcissist.

Whether God exists or not, we may never know. The god we can envision is a figment of our imagination. Gods can be good or evil depending on who envisions them. All gods are human projections. The god of Jesus is good because Jesus was good. The god of Muhammad is evil, because Muhammad was evil.

During the last few years, scientists are beginning to believe that the universe is a hologram. All the objects in it are tridimensional projections of a two dimensional membrane that surrounds the universe. Objects are information. Everything can be reduced into bits of information, zeros and ones, like binary codes in a computer or dots and dashes in Morse code, and this information can be recorded in a magnetic disk or a piece of film. The information contained in the universe, does not exist in the universe. It is recorded on a two dimensional film that wraps around it.

This novel and fantastic idea is based on the fact that information is indestructible, a knowledge gained through our understanding of black holes. Since the universe is like a black hole in reverse, i.e. instead of objects falling into it, they fall out of it, the same rules that apply to black holes must also apply to the universe.

The conservation of information reveals a very strange reality, that we are immortal. Our body can be destroyed; it can disintegrate and its atoms scattered. But the information that constitutes us cannot be destroyed. My body is only a projection of the information that is me. That information is my reality and it is out of me; it is out of this universe. Since information cannot be destroyed, it follows that I am indestructible.

The word spirit brings to mind a world of superstitions. Now replace it with "information" and suddenly the spiritual gobbledygook enters into the domain of science. Pierre Teilhard de Chardin had reason to believe, we are spiritual beings, having a physical experience.

If our reality is information, something that can be written in bits on a computer disk, and what we experience in our daily life is a hologram, a projection of that information, then that information must be real, not matter – what we perceive as real with our senses.

This idea of a holographic universe opens a Pandora box and it may force us to redefine everything, from the survival of our consciousness after our death, to reincarnation, telepathy and psychic ability. It may also redefine our understanding of ourselves and our relationship to each other and the world. Are we really separate individuals or different projections of the same reality? Whatever the answer, it's not yet known. But maybe, just maybe, science is finally removing the curtains from a world, hitherto dismissed as occult and religious mumbo jumbo.

We don't know the truth about God, at least not yet. But we can know the lies that are told about him/it. By identifying these lies and rejecting them we will be one step closer to the truth. This is what Sujit Das has undertaken in this book. Das does not dismiss the existence of God. His goal is to unveil the fallacies and expose the deceptions that are promoted as god. We can't know the true God. We don't know even if He exists. But it is very easy to know what God is not. We can remove the mask from false gods and impostors and identify the false prophets and charlatans. Chapter after chapter, page after page, Das unveils the truth about Muhammad and his bogus Allah until all doubts are removed and the reader becomes convinced that Islam is no religion and Allah is no God. This deity is evil, because his creator was evil. Allah is the figment of the mind of a very sick man.

The Allah Delusion dissects the Quran and reveals its secrets. It shows the patent contradictions of a book claimed to be the word of God. It reveals its scientific, mathematical, historical and other mistakes. Then it moves to disprove the claims made in the Quran, such as hell, with logical arguments. It covers the story of Satanic Verses, a clear case that shows Muhammad was making up his revelations to suit his agenda. It unveils the ungodly characteristics of Allah, unmasks him as a deceptive, treacherous and greedy deity with satanic attributes.

Sujit Das is an analytical thinker. He tackles garbled subjects that litter the Quran and makes them clear and easy to read and to understand. He explains the errors and the absurdities of Muhammad's book that have eluded Muslim scholars for centuries with such clarity that one wonders why Muslims fail to see them.

Alas, those who will benefit most from this book will be the last to read it. Muslims live in a world of darkness. They fear to step out of it. The fear of hell overcomes their natural inquisitiveness. They are warned, to "*ask not about things which, if revealed to you, would cause you trouble,*" (Q. 5:101). Those who question and doubt will go to hell. As the result Muslims have shut themselves in a dark cave of ignorance and will never step out of it. If any Muslim dares to read this book, he will lose his faith, the very thought of which sends fear down their spine and will stop them from touching it.

This book however, gives the reader a great insight into the Quran and can be a wonderful reference book for those who like to debate Muslims. The arguments presented here are cogent, clear and irrefutable. I am glad to have a digital copy of it on my files. It will make my search on Islamic topics much easier.

Ali Sina is the founder of Faith Freedom International, the grassroots movement of ex-Muslims. He is also the author of *Understanding Muhammad: A Psychobiography of Allah's Prophet*, the book that inspired many Muslims to awake and question their cherished faith.

A note to the readers

"Follow the evidence, wherever it leads."
Socrates

The belief that Allah guided and helped humankind through the Qur'anic revelations is the central importance to development of Muhammad's religion. But the problem is at the sources. Allah's guidance to mankind is only a "belief", not a concrete proof. Even before this argument arises, according to me, there is a need for deeper understanding that must be settled first. **Does Allah exist?** Is he really the one true God as Muhammad claimed? In the realm of philosophy, logic and science the question of truth has been an important issue. If Allah is a myth then obviously Allah's guidance to mankind is also a myth.

There are three ways to justify religious beliefs – Revealed Theology (appeal to revelation), Philosophical Theology (analyses the meaning rather than proving the truth of religious belief), and Natural Theology (appeal to reason and perception). Islam is strictly a revealed theology. Muslims justify their belief in Allah by an appeal to revelation. Since we can only know Allah to the extent that he reveals himself to us, we can only justify our beliefs about him in the light of this revelation. This is the trouble with Islam. Here the clerics and the common Muslims base their religious truth claims on grounds not accessible to everybody, but only to Muhammad who is believed to have the privileged access to divine revelation.

Since Allah in this way transcends our human concepts, belief in Allah also transcends the rules of general logic and has a special paradoxical logic of his own. The result is an extreme form of confusion that I do not suppose the defenders of Islamic faith set out to achieve in the first place!

Muslims are inclined to believe Muhammad even when all other historical evidence contradicts him. The five oldest and most trusted Islamic sources do not portray Muhammad a superior being or any kind of mercy of God among mankind. The sources reveal that he was a thief, a liar, an assassin, a pedophile, a shameless womanizer, a promiscuous husband, a rapist, a mass-murderer, a desert pirate, a warmonger, a spineless coward and a calculating and ruthless tyrant. It is certainly not the character profile of the founder of a true religion. Critics often wonder how a true God can choose an illiterate criminal as his Prophet. When there are no substantiating items of evidence supporting Muhammad's view, it is much more reasonable to believe that Muhammad was wrong rather than right when he claimed his prophethood. From the standpoint of a test of truth, the claim of Muslims is incoherent, therefore, to be considered false.

Many critics have observed that Muslims have a real problem when it comes to the issue of truth. By simply claiming that something is true because Muhammad said it closes the Muslim mind to any rational objective consideration of truth. In effect, Islam has to reject the major tests of truth because of its acceptance of Muhammad as the arbiter of truth. Truth is a fact, not judgment. Either Allah stands on reason or he does not stand at all. This basic principle cannot be compromised – to surrender it by an inch is to surrender it in total.

In this literature I want to call the validity of Muhammad's religious truth-claim into question. I want to reach the truth through science and logic. I will not accept anything on faith; I need evidence. An all-knowing Allah knows the evidence I need to be convinced of his existence, and the all-powerful Allah is able to provide that evidence. Reason is my only guide to knowledge. Muhammad's truth-claim must pass the test for logical consistency, as a minimum. Otherwise, the belief in Allah is reduced to personal preference.

Religious truth-claims often come to grief as a result of solid scientific evidence. I just want to follow the evidence whatever it reveals. As we shall see, the hard psychiatric evidence demonstrates that Allah is a myth and the belief in Allah is irrational to the point of absurdity. I have always strenuously supported the right of every man to his opinion, however different that opinion might be to mine. Today, I believe, Muslims will not deny me this right. He who denies to another this right, makes a slave of himself to his present opinion, because he precludes himself the right of changing it.

I know that Muslims will find this hard to believe so I am now going to make many citations and present scientific evidences to prove conclusively that Allah is a delusion. Though this data will be painful for many of our Muslim brethren, it is necessary to face the truth. Facts and facts, and unless you are willing to desert all logic, reason and common sense, and the evidence of your eyes, they must be faced.

About the author
I live in Mumbai, the commercial city of India. Because of the distinctive nature of my job, I travel a lot, mostly abroad. Though I am by nature not a religious person, I am a theist, and respect traditional religious values as well as secular and scientific ones. If a religion promotes unity of mankind, world peace, equality of all the people regardless of their belief and unbelief, reason and understanding, and maintain the deepest values of Human life, I believe in that religion. I long for something that makes life worth living. I also have equal respect for the scientific and tolerant atheism.

The tragic 9/11 incident caused my awakening to the dangers of Islam. After few years of studying Islamic scriptures, I concluded that Islam is a terror campaign in the name of a hateful god. We are all equal in the sight of God. I immensely hate the resound like the drums of war and want to hear the steps of the world march towards interreligious harmony, nonviolence and peaceful coexistence by following the doctrine of universal friendship. According to me world peace is an ideal of freedom, peace, and happiness among and within all nations and people irrespective of their skin color, ethnicity or faith. Though human nature inherently prevents it, world peace is not a theoretical idea of planetary non-violence, we can actually achieve it.

Acknowledgement
This book would not have been possible without the help and excellent advising of many people who had assisted me throughout the process of writing this one. My special thanks go to Ali Sina, Robert Spencer, M. A. Khan, and Abul Kasem – without whom the first line would never have been written. There are many other people whom I owe thanks for various suggestions and constructive criticisms. I am grateful to all of them more than words can tell. I could fill another book of equal size, describing the work of the people who have improved this one.

Introduction

"In what concerns Divine things, belief is not appropriate. Only certainty will do. Anything less than certainty is unworthy of God".

Simone Weil

"By believing passionately in something that still does not exists, we create it. The nonexistent is whatever we have is not sufficiently desired".

Franz Kafka

Allah is at the centre of the Islamic faith. This all-powerful god of Islam is such a clever god that it had managed the amazing feat of being worshipped and invisible at the same time. Muslims use the remotest language possible to explain Allah. They try to make Allah as awe-inspiring as possible in order to discourage people from conducting research on him. But if a Muslim is asked to define Allah, he will just beat about the bush, ascribing attributes to Allah that neither belong to him nor befit him. But is Allah really as mysterious as Muslims would like the world to believe? I seriously doubt.

Allah routinely took time from eternity to reveal the Qur'an to Muhammad but did not reveal himself in his Qur'an. This is especially puzzling because Allah wants us to know his will even more than we want to know it. But he preferred to remain a mystery to the Muslims and non-Muslims alike. In fact, even Prophet Muhammad had no knowledge of Allah.

"No knowledge have I of the Chiefs on high, when they discuss (matters) among themselves. This has been revealed to me: that I am to give warning plainly and publicly". (Q: 38.69, 70)

"Was Muhammad, a warner, an admonisher or the messenger of Allah?" (Tabari: VI.39)

But at the same time this strange god wants the whole humankind to accept his message without question, while the messenger himself was in doubt. This is very puzzling. This mysterious, intangible nature of Allah is the essence of Islam though a god who lives an enigmatic existence does not represent intelligent behavior.

Through Qur'anic revelations, Allah notifies the humankind what he likes and expects from us, and what he forbids. But why he does not do that by showing us what it is like to be god? Allah wants blind obedience, but, then, how do I know that Allah had really appointed Muhammad to act as his Prophet? Also, if Allah cannot be known, how can Allah be known to exist? Caird (1956, p. 60) wrote,

"A God who does not reveal Himself ceases to be God; and religious feeling, craving after a living relation to its object, refuses to be satisfied, with a mere initial and potential revelation of the mind and will of God – with a God who speaks once for all, and then through the whole course of history ceases to reveal Himself."

The whole doctrine of Islam stands or falls with the truth or falsehood of two claims – there is no God but Allah, the Creator of the universe, and Muhammad is his final spokesman who through him passed on the Qur'an to mankind. The first part is a theological claim which is common in many monotheistic religions. But the second part is a rigid truth claim on which we still have unfathomable doubts and no concrete evidence – i.e., Muhammad's claim of having divine communication with God. While revelation is the necessary presupposition of Islam, the idea of revelation is not necessarily exclusive of the activity of reason. It is not necessary to think of revelation as a source of knowledge which is either contrary to reason or above reason – which either revolts human intelligence or reduces it to absolute passivity. The cleft between revelation and reason may be supposed to be absolute, so that what revelation asserts reason denies, and vice versa; in which case, of course, all speculation and philosophy in the province of religion are at an end. When particular understandings become rigidly fixed and uncritically appropriated as absolute truths, well-meaning people can and often become narrow-minded from which they may assume a defensive or even offensive posture. Rigid truth-claim is a warning sign of corrupt religions, particularly in times of conflict these are the basis for demonizing and dehumanizing those who differ.

In Qur'anic revelations the mystery is more in the origin than in the substance of the communication because these revelations are not revelations "of" Allah, but revelations "from" Allah. These revelations had revealed nothing about Allah. Only for this reason, the skeptics find Allah's revelations very difficult to accept, and these revelations drastically upset our logical way of thinking. We have to suppress our rational faculty to believe the genuineness of these revelations. As Lewis (1961, p. 228) argued,

> "How do we know that the words which purport to tell us this are genuinely the words of God? What is the warrant for divine disclosure? What assurance do we have that it is God and not man who is speaking, or if it is in the first place the word of a man, what enables us to say that God speaks to us through him? How does a word become 'the word of God'?"

And to quote from Paine (1974, p. 52)

> "But admitting for the sake of a case, that something has been revealed to a certain person, and not revealed to any other person, it is revelation to that person only. When he tells it to a second person, a second to a third, a third to a fourth, and so on, it ceases to be revelation to all those persons. It is revelation to the first person only, and hearsay to every other, and consequently they are not obliged to believe it.
>
> It is a contradiction in terms and ideas, to call anything a revelation that comes to us at second-hand, either verbally or in writing. Revelation is necessarily limited to the first communication – after this it is only an account of something which that person says was a revelation made to him; and though he may find himself obliged to believe it, it cannot be incumbent on me to believe it in the same manner; for it was not a revelation made to me, and I have only his word for it that it was made to him.

When I am told that the Koran was written in heaven and brought to Mahomet by an angel, the account comes too near the same kind of hearsay evidence and second-hand authority as the former. 1 did not see the angel myself and, therefore, I have a right not to believe it."

For us, this is a crucial problem. If there were a direct disclosure of Allah, and we could see Allah strictly as he is, then there could be no doubt about him and his revelations would carry an absolute guarantee in itself and we knew it was Allah who spoke. If it is Allah's intention to confront us with his presence as personal will and purpose, why has this not been done in an unambiguous manner – by some overwhelming manifestation of divine power and glory? A self-evident truth does not require proof. Lewis (1961, pp. 228, 135-6) concluded,

"If God wants to communicate with us in terms of what we understand as finite beings, if He has to make Himself known within the human situation, how are men able to recognize the ways in which He does this, how does an occasion which is in substance a finite one carry with it some reference or overtone which is more than finite?"

"If the God we are to worship is altogether 'beyond' the sort of experience of things we have, if He is perfect in such a way that none of our conceptions apply to Him, how can He come within our thoughts at all? Must He not remain an unfathomable mystery? But if He is such a mystery can we even say that He exists?"

As Warraq (1995, pp. 130-1) commented,

"It is very odd that when God decides to manifest Himself, He does so to only one individual. Why can He not reveal Himself to the masses in a football stadium during the final of the World Cup, when literally millions of people around the world are watching?"

As Crone (cited Hitchens, 2007, p. 412) observed,

"It is a peculiar habit of God's that when he wishes to reveal himself to mankind, he will communicate only with a single person. The rest of mankind must learn the truth from that person and thus purchase their knowledge of the divine at the cost of subordination to another human being, who is eventually replaced by a human institution, so that the divine remains under other people's control."

Why Allah did not disclose himself? Shaikh (1998a, p. 88) commented,

"The cause of God, would have been served better if He were to show His face to mankind frequently for assuring them that He is there. Since nobody has ever seen Him, He either does not exist or is too great to bother about what people think of Him".

21

If a child refuses to open his clenched fist to show what he has in it, we may, indeed, be sure that it is something wrong – something he ought not to have. Is not the same logic applicable to Allah? No doubt God is a great mystery, but he is not so elusive as to be nothing at all in himself. As Lewis (1961, p. 139) commented,

> *"If we affirm that God is not known as other things are known, if there is no inference to him from the way the world goes, if he stands in no specific relation to other entities and does not admit of being known and characterized in that way, does it make sense that we know him at all? In short, if we say that God is a total mystery we may have well evaded one horn of the attack upon us but only to be firmly impaled on another; we have no longer to provide reasons for believing in God and make these run the gauntlet of criticism".*

Qur'an says,

> *"No vision can grasp Him, but His grasp is over all vision: He is above all comprehension, yet is acquainted with all things". (Q: 6.103)*

> *"It is not fitting for a man that Allah should speak to him except by inspiration, or from behind a veil, or by the sending of a messenger to reveal, with Allah's permission, what Allah wills: for He is Most High, Most Wise." (Q: 42.51)*

If Allah is as incomprehensible to us as religious thought and religious experience and prophesy alike make him out to be, if he is essentially hidden and invisible, how do we come to make many intimate claims (various attributes to Allah) about him as Muslims do in much of their religious life and worship? The answer to this question takes us to the very centre of the philosophy of Islam and Allah. In no other religion does 'the gulf' between man and god receive greater stress than in orthodox Islam. This is one main reason there is so much tension between Islam and other religions.

Throughout the Qur'an there is not a single real philosophical argument for the existence of Allah; it merely assumes. The closest one gets to an argument is perhaps in the Qur'anic notion of "signs", whereby various natural phenomena are seen as signs of Allah's power and bounty. Bell and Watt (1977, p. 122) observed,

> *"The phenomena most frequently cited [in the Qur'an] are: the creation of the heavens and the earth, the creation or generation of man, the various uses and benefits man derives from the animals, the alternation of night and day, the shining of sun, moon and stars, the changing winds, the sending of rain from the sky, the revival of parched ground and the appearance of herbage, crops and fruits, the movement of the ship on the sea and the stability of the mountains. Less frequently cited are: shadows, thunder, lightning, iron, fire, hearing, sight, understanding and wisdom."*

This is a very poor form of a teleological argument. A teleological or design argument is an a posteriori argument for the existence of God based on apparent design and purpose in the universe. This argument has traditionally been considered one of the great proofs of God's existence. But the poor form of this argument that Qur'an represents does not prove the existence of Allah, because all the phenomena adduced by Muhammad in the Qur'an can be explained without assuming the existence of Allah. The apparent order that we all perceive in the universe is the product of an extremely long evolutionary process. Evolution is such a slow process that requires millions of years and thousands of generations to produce any visible changes. Sun, planets, and moon exist and act as they do because during the process of evolution the ceaseless redistribution of matter and motion of those particular masses were conditioned by the surrounding forces and energies to move in such particular orbits and behave in such particular way, and in no other. Evolution does not care what Muslims believe or what Allah says in his Qur'an. There is no hidden cosmic purpose; there is no reason or meaning for such events. They are only accidental and unguided purposeless facts, and absolutely nothing else. We do not need Allah to explain the complexity of living organisms; Darwin did it for us. The theory of evolution by itself gives humans the same status as animals – apart from intellectual capacity. What appears to be the "signs" of Allah is only the projection of an anxious desire to find reason and purpose in the universe in Islamic way. What a Muslim perceives is created in his brain. It is superstition and certainly not a part of the reality.

The idea of revelation is the idea of something which is being shown – more strictly unveiled or unfolded. In Qur'anic revelations Allah gave some instructions to the Muslims. He had also shown what he likes and what he expects from us. But unfortunately, he did not do that by showing us what it is like to be God. He only made himself known through the chosen messenger Muhammad, even though the media he adopted was unusual one. But where is the "divine" verification for "divine" revelations? On this particular point the god of Islam failed miserably. It is not worthy of a true God or a true messenger of God to demand blind trust.

"Put blind faith first, and then study the Qur'an ..." (Sunaan Ibn Majah: 1.61)

"Believe Muhammad blindly and he blesses you seven times ..." (Tirmidhi: 1688, 1689)

History suggests, those who narrowly define ideal temporal structures of the state and determine they are God's agents to establish a theocracy are dangerous. We should be careful of people and groups whose political blueprint is based on a mandate from heaven that depends on human beings to implement. History also suggests that serious trouble lurks just ahead when a god demands blind obedience. Kimball (2002, pp. 29, 72, 99) wrote,

"Religion that requires adherents to disconnect their brain is often a big part of the problem.... Authentic religion engages the intellect as people wrestle with the mystery of existence and the challenges of living in an imperfect world. Conversely, blind obedience is a sure sign of corrupt religion... When individual believers abdicate personal responsibility and yield to the authority of a charismatic leader or become enslaved to particular ideas or teachings, religion can easily become the framework for violence and destruction. ...The

likelihood of religion becoming evil is greatly diminished when there is freedom for individual thinking and when honest inquiry is encouraged."

Why Allah wants us to accept a claim at random? Blind faith can be accepted up to certain extent but somewhere we should draw the line and must seek justification after that. It is for Allah to choose Muhammad as his last Prophet and there could be no question about it, only if we had sufficient evidence to believe in his strange claim. As Clifford (1897, p. 186) commented, *"[In religious belief] it is wrong always, everywhere, and for everyone to believe anything upon insufficient evidence".* When a divine message commands to kill the idolaters wherever they are found, we must give a closer look not only to the message but also to the messenger and his source of inspiration. Kimball (2002, p. 133) commented,

"When people are called upon to do violence to their neighbor in the service of a righteous cause, they should know that something is dreadfully wrong. In the end, human beings remain responsible for their actions."

How can we indentify Allah with any human voice? What are the modes of his manifestation, "the signs of his presence"? In one sense he is everywhere, nothing could be without him. But we are now concerned with the sense in which he is in particular time and places, and speaks to his messenger the particular word. How do we know that this is the word of Allah? The critics of Islam need some external proof. Without evidence, neither Islam nor Muhammad has any stand. It is for Allah to choose the media in which he discloses himself, but an imposter or a deluded person can disclose himself to the men in the same manner also. Therefore, the revelations of a true God cannot be such that it cannot be questioned. That would be like asking, "Why should I believe the truth?" If something is taken to be true then we obviously believe it – but we are often uncertain about what the truth is. When we are not sure about the truth, there is still point in asking what it is for something to be true. There are likewise questions to ask about the Qur'an. There are many to whom it is not clear that Allah had revealed the Qur'an, and even those to whom it is thought that Allah had expressly revealed himself are sometimes in doubt about it themselves. Where is Allah's guarantee for his book, the Qur'an? Can any divine disclosure be beyond any question and criticism as stated in the following verses?

"O ye who believe! Ask not questions about things which, if made plain to you, may cause you trouble. But if ye ask about things when the Qur'an is being revealed, they will be made plain to you, Allah will forgive those: for Allah is Oft-forgiving, Most forbearing". (Q: 5.101).

"Some people before you did ask such questions, and on that account lost their faith". (Q: 5.102)

The sole province of Allah is where reason cannot trade. Hence it is necessary and desirable to suppress free inquiry with the threat of force.

There are two sides of the Qur'anic revelations; it involves the God and as well as his messenger, and I do not see what a revelation could be like that does not involve the use of the faculties with which we are endowed as human beings. If we need to trust Muhammad blindly to accept Allah's revelation, then by applying the same logic, even a stone can be recipient of revelations. Secondly; if Allah's guidance is for the whole mankind, then in what way are our faculties involved in revelation? What certainty does it give, and how is doubt dispelled? If it is God's wish that the human beings should have a superior thinking capability, then certainly that God will not be dealing with us as merely passive recipients of truth, but as creatures with a role of their own to play in attainment of the truth. How can a person believe things in an intellectually irresponsible way and without bringing his God-given faculties in their full and proper exercise to the assimilation of truth given by God? Critics have been asking this question ever since the birth of Islam, but the Muslims are so desperate in their affirmation of Islamic faith that they consider the absurdity of their doctrine to be a merit. A Muslim can live his whole life without considering an alternative view. To remain in the good book of Allah, the Muslims conclude a thing to be true though it seems absurd and to believe it though it seems impossible. They try to silence their doubts by the device of treating reason and revelation as entirely independent authorities. At any cost these Islamic "faith-heads" will not let their faith be shaken. That is why the way of settling of reason and Allah's revelation is an impossible one. What they do not understand is that glorifying an absurdity can hardly serve the cause of a true religion.

"*Revelation is not above reason*", Caird (1956, p. 356) observed, "*Revelation, which is a necessary presupposition of religion, is often understood to fall outside science or philosophy.*" Truth cannot be contrary to truth and reason, and since the study of Philosophy is not merely to find out what others have thought, but what the truth of the matter is, truth cannot be contrary to Philosophy also. So logically, there should be no disagreement between true revelation and Philosophy. It is wrong to say that a proposition is false in Philosophy and true in faith. Does the Qur'anic teaching conform to any other school of philosophical thought throughout the recorded history of humankind? Philosophy recognizes two ways in which humans may come to know whatever there is to be known – one way through experience (stressed by empiricism), and the other is through reasoning (Hick, 1993, p. 68). Aristotle, Socrates and Plato – the three great philosophers of the world did not claim to speak in the name of the revelation but with the authority of reason and their concern with man's happiness. These great teachers did not bring down any revelation from the sky, yet they had contributed much in the growth of the civilization. Allah's guidance and instructions through the Qur'an had contributed nothing positive; human civilization would do much better if there were no Qur'an.

When Muhammad commenced preaching his religion in Mecca, never-ending arguments were going on between the Meccans and Muhammad over his lack of prophetic credentials. In this regard Allah seemed to be very puzzled in the Qur'an,

> "*Is it that their mental faculties of understanding urge them to this, or are they an outrageous folk, transgressing beyond the bounds?*" (Q: 52.32)

The above verse demonstrates Qur'an's lack of divine inspiration. If Allah is the real all-knowing God, he can never ask such a question. Since Allah is timeless, he does not in fact foreknow events; he simply knows all events timelessly, including the actions of the free agents. The entire course of history from creation to kingdom yet to come is and always has been necessarily settled from Allah's epistemic perspective. If Allah is the most perfect being, as the Islamic traditions affirm, then it seems evident that Allah would have the most perfect mode of existence. Intuitively, it also seems that a perfect mode of existence would be timeless rather than temporal. A temporal being, for example, would be moving along with the passage of time and so would not be able to experience all of life at once the way a timeless being would. We wonder, whose inadequacies are reflected in the above verse – Muhammad or his Allah? Qur'an says,

> *"Remember how the unbelievers (Meccans) plotted against you (Muhammad), to keep you in bonds, or slay you, or get you out (of your home). They plotted, and Allah too had arranged a plot; but Allah is the best schemer."* (Q: 8.30).

> *"And they (the disbelievers) schemed, and Allah schemed (against them); and Allah is the best of schemers."* (Q: 3.54)

While revealing these verses, Allah forgot that he was supposed to be the all-powerful and all-knowing. Why Allah needs to arrange a plot if he is all-knowing? It is just an insult to God to say that he is the best plotter or a world-class schemer. It is "impossible" for an omniscient and omnipotent God to experience fear, frustration and despair. In addition, he does not need to be "the best schemer" because he is believed to be in existence forever in time. Moreover, a perfect being who created the world and who has certain divine properties, or attributes, which set him apart from all other beings, does not need to compete with the fallible human beings. Were these Muhammad's own words put in Allah's mouth? Qur'an says,

> *"Man says: 'What! When I am dead, shall I then be raised up alive?' But does not man call to mind that We created him before out of nothing?"* (Q: 19.66-7)

But elsewhere Allah is severely confused about what he had confirmed before in the verse 19.66-7.

> *"Or were they created without there being anything, or are they the creators? Or did they create the heavens and the earth?"* (Q: 52.35, 36).

It means Allah is denying the verses 19.66-7 in the verses 52.35, 36.

All these verses (52.32, 8.30, 3.54, 19.66-7 and 52.35, 36) directly contradict the following verses.

> *"He (Allah) is the Wise, the Knower."* (Q: 43.84)

> *"He hath perfect knowledge."* (Q: 2.29)

Following verse is equally confusing. In fact, it is practically meaningless.

> *"So eat and drink and refresh the eye. Then if you see any mortal, say: Surely I*

have vowed a fast to the Beneficent Allah, so I shall not speak to any man today." (Q: 19.26)

This is Allah's instruction to Mary through an angel. The verse says, Mary can eat and drink but if she meets a person, she should "say" that she has "vowed a fast". Most ridiculous part is – she should "say" that "I shall not speak". Is that similar to – break the law in order to demonstrate that you are not allowed to break the law. How much stupidity is enough?

Such a stupid god is an absolute fake. Allah is not an "all-knowing" God. There is at least one thing which this ignorant god does not know, i.e., "What is real?" Allah is one of the most famous fictional superheroes of all time. Allah did not disclose himself because he lacks one element of perfection – 'existence' and the Qur'anic revelations are actually a parody of Allah for his imperfection.

This is such an Islamic paradox – Muslims have to believe those revelations to keep their faith in Islam, but once they believe those revelations, they are in fact mocking Allah for his deficiencies. Those revelations are actually blasphemous to their god. It is also true other way round. The central theme of Islam is blasphemous to the Islamic religion itself. The plain truth is that every part of Islam contradicts and blasphemes each other if analyzed logically. The god of the Muslims is a severely confused and self-contradictory god. Muslims are so deluded that they come to believe that they are saying meaningful things when in fact they are not saying anything at all but only giving formally correct expression to rubbish or meaningless nonsense. The so-called Islamic scholars often give themselves and others the impression of dealing with profound and significant matters when in fact they only plunged themselves into utter darkness from which only a rationalist is able to deliver them at last. Let us analyze few more verses.

*"So blessed be Allah, **the Best of creators**!"* (Q: 23.14)

*"Will ye cry unto Baal and forsake **the Best of creators**?"* (Q: 37.125)

If Allah is the "Best of creators", then there must be some other gods besides Allah who are also "creators". Therefore, if Qur'an agrees that there are other gods besides Allah, is Islam monotheism or polytheism? Hence, "There is no god but Allah" is a false statement. It should be corrected as – "There are many gods but Allah is the best". However these two verses contradict the following verse.

"Unto Allah belongs whatsoever is in the heavens and the earth. Lo! Allah, He is the Absolute, the Owner of Praise." (Q: 31.26)

If Allah has competitors and there exists other gods who are also creators, then Allah cannot be "the Absolute, the Owner of Praise". Moreover, according to the following verses, it is a sin to associate other gods with Allah.

"Surely Allah does not forgive that anything should be associated with Him, and forgives what is besides that to whomsoever He pleases; and whoever associates anything with Allah, he devises indeed a great sin.". (Q: 4.48)

"Allah forgives not (the sin of) joining other gods with Him" (Q: 4.116)

Now we want to know how the verses 23.14 and 37.125 got included in the Qur'an. These confusing verses prove that either Qur'an has more than one author or Allah changes his mind very frequently.

Qur'an is not only a bundle of contradictions but also a volume of confusion. A true God is neither the author of confusion nor contradictions. These confusions and contradictions coupled with the historic blunders and errors may explain why Muslim scholars resist any serious analysis of their faith.

An academic study of the compilation of the Qur'an text must begin with the character of the book itself as it was handed down by Muhammad to his followers during his lifetime. It was not delivered or, as Muslims believe, revealed all at once. Allah wrote,

> *"This Qur'an is not such as can be produced by other than Allah; on the contrary it is a confirmation of (revelations) that went before it, and a fuller explanation of the Book - wherein there is no doubt - from the Lord of the worlds."* (Q: 10.37)

After composing the Qur'an, Allah kept the original of the document in his possession and sent an earthly version to Muhammad.

> *"And verily, it is in the Mother of the Book, in Our Presence, high (in dignity), full of wisdom."* (Q: 43.4)

This "mother of the book" is so holy that none but the holiest and most exalted of beings, such as the Angel Gabriel, may view this document.

> *"That this is indeed a Qur'an Most Honourable. In Book well-guarded, which none shall touch but those who are clean: A Revelation from the Lord of the Worlds."* (Q: 56.77-80)

The Angel Gabriel then recited the Qur'an to the human Prophet Muhammad by installments.

> *"It is We Who have sent down the Qur'an to thee by stages."* (Q: 76.23)

> *"We have rehearsed it to you in slow, well-arranged stages, gradually."* (Q: 25.32).

Muhammad was illiterate, so he did not write down what Gabriel had recited to him. Instead, Muhammad recited the Qur'an to others, and they either memorized or wrote down what he recited to them. After Muhammad died, the records of his recitals of the Qur'an were gathered together, transcribed, edited, and published as a single document. For reasons best known to themselves, the editors of the Quran's first earthly edition arranged the book so that the longer Surahs were, in general, towards the beginning, and the shorter ones were towards the end, even though this does not represent the order in which he recited the Qur'an to his audiences during the twenty-three years. Therefore, even at this stage, there would have been at least two editions of the Qur'an. The first being the supernatural original of the document, which Allah keeps in his possession, and which no mortal may view. The second one is its first earthly edition. This immediately raises the question – how closely do earthly transcripts of the Qur'an resemble their celestial archetype?

Secondly, there is another very strong and serious problem in the Qur'an. It affirms the scriptures of the Jews and the Christians as authentic and true revelation from God. Allah confirms,

> *"Verily this is a Revelation from the Lord of the Worlds: With it came down the spirit of Faith and Truth upon thy heart, that thou may be (one) of the warners, In the perspicuous Arabic tongue.* (Q: 26.192-5)

> *"And lo! It is in the Scriptures of the men of earlier (Prophets)"*. (Q: 26.196)

The "earlier writings" are the Torah and the Injil for example, written in Hebrew and Greek. For Jews, Arabic was a language of poets and drunkards. How can Arabic Qur'an be contained in books of other languages? Now we have the choice between two different lies in Allah's revelations. Either, because of verse 26.196, the verse "in clear Arabic speech" is contained in the earlier revelations. This is a lie, because they are not in Arabic. Therefore, it cannot be in the earlier revelation. But then verse 26.196 becomes a lie in the Qur'an. In no way we can save the situation. There are more such verses, e.g., the verse 16.103 also claims, *"this is Arabic pure and clear"* which refers to the Qur'an without doubt.

Furthermore, this is causing an infinite loop problem. The verse 29.196 would have to contain this very passage of the Qur'an since the Qur'an is properly contained in them. Hence these earlier writings have to be contained in yet other earlier writings and we are in an infinite loop, which is absurd. The puzzle in the infinite loop problem is like this – How many "earlier writings" were there – finitely many or infinitely many? The verse 26.196 is part of the Qur'an, and hence by its very statement also part of the earlier writings. Let say, it is in earlier writing A. Now, by the very same reason, there has to be an earlier writing B, containing this verse, and earlier writing C containing this verse, and .... without end and we will need infinitely many earlier writings because we otherwise end up in the lie of this verse claiming to be contained in a non-existing earlier writing. The verse 26.196 is a jewel of contradiction just within itself. As infinitely many writings are physically impossible, this verse has to be false. It is very easy to tell a lie, but it is difficult to support the lie after it is told.

Moreover, it raises another serious question – in what language is the one and only true original of the document? Was it written in Arabic, or Latin, or Swahili, or in some language unknown to mankind? The first earthly edition of the Qur'an was published in Arabic, and subsequently it has been translated into other languages. Many Muslims take the view that the Qur'an can exist only in Arabic, and that a translation of the Qur'an into any other language is but a cheap imitation of the real thing, just as a child's drawing of the moon is not itself the moon. But what is the original language of this supposed to be sacred scripture? Nobody on earth, not even the most devout Muslim, knows the answer to this question.

The critics, who doubt that the earthly Qur'an is a transcript of the original supernatural prototype, point out that earthly editions contain many contradictions, inconsistencies, fallacies, errors, and absurdities. From this they conclude that Allah cannot possibly be the ultimate author of any edition of the Qur'an known to mankind. This conclusion has some problem; for example, is it possible to utterly refute the claim that Allah decided to pepper the Qur'an with deliberate mistakes? However, any errors in earthly editions would prove beyond all reasonable doubts that earthly editions are not entirely reliable, and that when, for example, they allege that Allah is their ultimate author, this allegation should be taken with a pinch of salt. The same applies, with some reasonable alterations, for all the other claims in the earthly editions; e.g. that Islam is the only true religion in God's eyes (Q: 3.19), and that whoever rejects Islam is doomed to eternal damnation in hellfire (Q: 3.85).

Islam is an imposing religion. In this religion, man is controlled by a higher power. A Muslim's religious experience is always authoritarian, never blissful. He is slavishly dependent on Allah. For him everything is *"Insha'Allah"* (if Allah wills it – predestination and uncompromising fatalism. Allah's will is the only 'freedom') spoken through Muhammad's tongue.

"Say: 'Nothing will happen to us except what Allah has decreed for us: He is our protector": and on Allah let the Believers put their trust."* (Q: 9.51)

"No misfortune can happen on earth or in your souls but is recorded in a decree before We bring it into existence. That is truly easy for Allah:" (Q: 57.22)

The Arabs write on every letter *Insha'Allah* for only then the letter will arrive (Jung, 1933, p. 131). Hence, whichever way we turn, Allah gets the credit, which, of course, is remarkably convenient for the Muslim clerics. In Allah's world, all exits are covered, contrary evidence is defined out of existence, and the clerics are insulated from attack. This is a clear case of eating one's cake and having it, too. Allah had entered the Muslim lives in such a way that a Muslim can spend his whole life in this Allah-delusion without even thinking once. In this life, everything is *Insha'Allah,* and Muhammad and Allah will take care of the afterlife. Allah is something like a wrathful despot looking down at us from the sky and seeking opportunities to sentence us to unspeakable and eternal torments, specially being disrespectful to him. Qur'an says,

"Indeed, your Lord is ever watchful". (Q: 89.14).

"Who sees you when you stand up? And your turning over and over among those who prostrate themselves before Allah (in worship) ". (Q: 26.218-9).

"Allah warns you to be cautious of Him, the arrival is to Allah". (Q: 3.28).

Allah is entitled to strict obedience, reverence and worship. But the reason for worship, reverence and obedience lies not in the moral qualities of the deity, not in love or justice, but in the fact that the deity has control, i.e., has power over man.

Here comes the question of free will. If a bank clerk was held up at gun-point we could hardly blame him for not stopping the burglars. How can a perfectly good God justifiably damn anyone to hell? How a man can be held responsible if he does not have a free will? This is one version of the problem of hell which has become one of the most widely discussed topics in Islam. How Allah is justified in allowing suffering? Why should a man be sent to hell if Allah alone determines every one of his actions? How could an omnibenevolent being create a hell where countless persons will spend eternity in suffering and agony? There seems to be a conflict here between God's sovereignty and God's goodness. Allah could have created persons who are spiritual saints and thus always choose the good. The *Insha'Allah* theory puts a limitation on Allah's power.

The term *Insha'Allah* is used in the whole Islamic world. By using this term the speaker puts himself into Allah's hands. The fallible humans can use this term, but when Allah puts himself in his wills there is serious problem. Qur'an says,

"*No! Upon Him you will call, and He will remove that for which you call upon Him **if He Wills**, and you will forget that you associate with Him.*" (Q: 6.41)

"*O ye who believe! The idolaters only are unclean. So let them not come near the Inviolable Place of Worship after this their year. If ye fear poverty (from the loss of their merchandise) Allah shall preserve you of His bounty **if He wills**. Lo! Allah is Knower, Wise.*" (Q: 9.28)

"*Blessed is He Who, **if He wills**, will assign thee better than (all) that - Gardens underneath which rivers flow - and will assign thee mansions.*" (Q: 25.10)

"*That Allah may reward the true men for their truth, and punish the hypocrites **if He wills**, or relent toward them.*" (Q: 33.24)

"*Truly did Allah fulfill the vision for His Messenger: ye shall enter the Sacred Mosque, **if Allah wills**, with minds secure, heads shaved, hair cut short, and without fear. For He knew what ye knew not, and He granted, besides this, a speedy victory*". (Q: 48.27)

In these verses "*if Allah wills*" is whose word – Allah or Muhammad? Or, is it Muhammad's word intermingled with the word of Allah? Does Allah not know what his will is? If so, is he uncertain whether his purpose shall come to pass necessitating him to then qualify his statement with the phrase, *Insha'Allah*? Furthermore, if Allah is in fact speaking then whom is he referring to when he says "*if Allah wills*"? Is he addressing himself or someone else? If he is addressing someone else, then how many gods are there besides Allah? Perhaps, Allah has many personalities like schizophrenia patients.

The traditional doctrine of divine immutability is that God has the property of being intrinsically changeless; it is logically impossible for God to change in his intrinsic qualities. One argument for the view is based on God's being absolutely perfect. Whatever is absolutely perfect cannot change, for to change is to become better or worse. Since God is an absolutely perfect being, it is not possible for God to change. Thus God is immutable. Process thinker Charles Hartshorne (1984, p. 7) makes the following point;

"The traditional objection ... to divine change was that if a being were already perfect, meaning that nothing better was possible, then change for the better must be impossible for the being".

But neither Allah is perfect nor his words. Muslims believe that the original copy of the Qur'an (43.3 – "the mother of the book"; 55.77 – "a concealed book"; 85.22 – "a well guarded tablet") is kept in the heaven. To prove that Qur'an is superior to Bible, Muslims say that the Testaments are corrupted and changed. They say, for a holy scripture to be authoritative, it has to be preserved without any changes at all, and point to their Qur'an which claims to have been revealed word by word by Allah. Qur'an claims,

"No change there can be in the words of God". (Q: 10.64)

"There is none that can alter the words (and decrees) of God". (Q: 6.34).

"Perfected is the Word of thy Lord in truth and justice. There is naught that can change His words". (Q: 6.115)

But Qur'an itself confirms that god's word can be changed. This is called the "doctrine of abrogation" by which later revelations can cancel previous ones. One cannot fail to see how time-bound the "eternal" word of Allah is.

"Whatever communications We abrogate or cause to be forgotten, We bring one better than it or like it." (Q: 2.106)

"And when We put a revelation in place of (another) revelation, - and Allah knoweth best what He revealeth" (Q: 16.101)

The word of a perfect and timeless God is unchangeable. Abrogation is an indication of human imperfections and weakness. Al-Suyuti estimates the number of verses abrogated can be as high as five hundred (Warraq, 1995, p. 114). One may wonder, if Allah is really omniscient and omnipotent and his word unchangeable, why he not revealed the right verses to his Prophet from the beginning. Why does he need to issue commands that need revising so often? However, this leads to another question – does God sometimes lose his wisdom and make mistakes? The idea that God would modify truth, which is what progressive revelation really claims, is absurd. Truth does not change; a true God cannot be the author of confusion. Also, if the earthly Qur'an is "updating" one might wonder if the tablets in heaven became updated too automatically.

The doctrine of abrogation puts the Muslims in a very strange situation, where the entire Qur'an is recited as the word of God, yet there are passages that can be considered "false" – in other words, a substantial portion of the Qur'an is accepted conclusively as falsehood. As Warraq (1995, p. 115) concluded,

"The doctrine of abrogation also makes a mockery of the Muslim dogma that the Koran is a faithful and unalterable reproduction of the original scriptures that are preserved in heaven. If God's words are eternal, uncreated, and of universal significance, then how can we talk of God's words being superseded or becoming obsolete? Are some words of God to be preferred to other words of God? Apparently yes. According to Muir, some 200 verses have been canceled by later ones. Thus we have the strange situation where the entire Koran is recited as the word of God, and yet there are passages that can be considered not 'true'; in other words, three percent of the Koran is acknowledged as falsehood."

In the words of Ali Dasti (1985, p. 155),

"On the assumption that the Quran is God's word, there ought to be no trace of human intellectual imperfection in anything that God says. Yet in these two verses the incongruity is obvious. Of course God knows what He sends down. For that very reason the replacement of one verse by another made the protesters suspicious. Evidently even the simple, uneducated Hejazi Arabs could understand that Almighty God, being aware of what is best for His servants, would prescribe the best in the first place and would not have changes of mind in the same way as His imperfect creatures."

However, another verse completely rules out the doctrine of abrogation.

"Say: Whoever is an enemy to Gabriel for he brings down the (revelation) to thy heart by Allah's will, a confirmation of what went before." (Q: 2.97)

It says that the new verses confirm the old verses. This is a clear contradiction. Should we say that the doctrine of abrogation has abrogated even this verse also? Secondly, how does a Muslim know that which verses have been abrogated? Where does the Qur'an explicitly, or even implicitly, state this? Secondly, how does the Muslim know for certain which verses came first? Does the Qur'an give the date these "revelations" were allegedly sent down so that we can know which passage came first? How can one know for certain? This is a serious theological problem.

Finally, *"the Word of thy Lord"* is not yet *"perfected"* though the verse 6.115 claimed so. The Qur'an is not completely revealed and Muhammad left his job unfinished. Qur'an says,

"And if all the trees in the earth were pens, and the sea, with seven more seas to help it, (were ink), the words of Allah could not be exhausted. Lo! Allah is Mighty, Wise". (Q: 31.27)

"If the ocean were ink (wherewith to write out) the words of my Lord, sooner would the ocean be exhausted than would the words of my Lord, even if we added another ocean like it, for its aid". (Q: 18.109)

These verses confirm that a large section of the Qur'an is not yet given to the Muslims. Therefore, Muhammad's claim that he was the last messenger of Allah could not be logically true. However, it contradicts the following verse,

" … This day have I perfected for you your religion …" (Q: 5.3)

Unless the whole Qur'an is revealed, the religion of the Muslims is incomplete. However, the following verse again contradicts all the above verses.

"…Nothing have we omitted from the Book, and they (all) shall be gathered to their Lord in the end." (Q: 6.38)

Often we hear a strange argument from the Muslim apologists – A belief is true when it is good for us to believe it, something like, in science a theory is true if it "works". But this is ambiguous, because in science a theory works if it is in accordance with the facts and explains them. These apologists certainly do not tell us what good things Islam has brought to the society, culture and civilization, but certainly for a logical person, it would seem to be a peculiarly odd view of truth. Some of the oddities of it were well-displayed by Plato in his criticisms of the early and impressive presentation of it by Protagoras (Lewis, 1961, p. 239). The fact that good results follow from adopting some view is very far from proving that the view is a sound one. Good results can be achieved by some delusions, illusions and hallucinations, but they do not make them true. Mistaken beliefs can prompt man to do good, but deep down, these "useful delusions" are "errors"; we simply cannot encourage them. A belief must be known to be true on its own account. Error is itself a gravely bad thing in the long run, and above all once questions and doubts are raised these errors may prove to be more harmful than before. Let alone the critics, even Allah seemed to have not much faith in his Qur'an. Allah says,

*"And indeed He has revealed to you in the Book that **when you hear Allah's communications disbelieved in and mocked at do not sit with them until they enter into some other discourse; surely then you would be like them;** surely Allah will gather together the hypocrites and the unbelievers all in hell". (Q: 4.140)*

Let us analyze another verse.

"To Him belongs every being that is in the heavens and on earth: all are devoutly obedient to Him." (Q: 30.26)

This is absolutely not true. Qur'an itself talks hundreds of times about the disobedient, transgressors, hypocrites and evil-doers, both among men and among jinn. If all the creatures are *"devoutly obedient"* (not that some voluntarily, some reluctantly), why Allah constantly threatens punishment to the disobedient if they only do what Allah wants them to do? What is the necessity of Islamic Jihad? Why he called the nonbelievers by various derogatory names? According to Allah, the nonbelievers are,

Harm-doers: (Q: 2.59; 2.95; 2.145; 2.150; 2.165; 2.193; 2.229; 2.246; 2.254; 2.258; 2.270; 3.57; 3.86; 3.94; 3.128; 3.140; 3.151; 4.74; 5.29; 5.45; 5.107; 6.21; 6.45; 6.58; 6.135; 7.41; 7.47; 7.148; 8.54; 9.23; 11.31, etc.)

Hypocrites: (Q: 4.61; 8.49; 9.64; 9.73; 29.11; 33.1; 48.6; 57.13; 59.11; 63.1; 66.9, etc.)

Liars: (Q: 6.28; 7.66; 9.77; 11.93; 39.3; 40.24, etc.)

Evildoers: (Q: 2.12; 2.26; 2.99; 3.63; 5.47; 5.108; 7.102; 9.24; 10.17; 11.18; 14.22; 17.47; 18.53; 19.86; 24.4; 29.4; 34.42; 37.22; 39.24, etc.)

Indecent language is normally the jargon of low-bred, discourteous people who are lacking in civility and good manners. Is it conceivable that a true God would use such vulgar language to address human beings? The answer is that such vulgar words and obscene language was the cultural heritage of illiterate Muhammad brought up in a desert. People who are evil attack others instead of facing their own failures. A curse uttered by a person who desires to harm another person, but finds himself physically powerless to do so, appeals to a supernatural to inflict such harm.

The simple fact is that Islam is such an absurd religion that it cannot survive criticisms which even the Allah knows. Now we know how miserable the Allah is. This god is so pathetic that Muslims need sword and deception to sell their god. If there were no sword and deception, the law of Allah would not have established. Such a miserable god cannot be the Creator of the universe. Muslims can attribute anything to Allah, but Allah is a dummy, a scarecrow, a clever myth. A god who himself is in such self-doubt cannot be the true God, and the revelations from that god cannot carry its authority expressly in itself. The idea of Allah is literally nonsense. Faith *"is believing something on the authority of another."* (Stanford, 1960, p. 3). But the authority is never a primary source of knowledge, particularly if the supposed authority testifies in its behalf.

If Allah is to be the sort of being we can worship, he must not be limited in any thinkable manner. He must not be dwarfed in thought by still mightier superiorities. He must have an unsurpassable supremacy along all avenues. Also, if Allah is to satisfy the religious claims and needs as mentioned in the Qur'an, then he must be a being in every way inescapable. One does not need a scholastic review of Allah to disprove him; the Qur'an exposes Allah quite nicely. Granted that the Muslims understand what is meant by saying "I believe in oneness of God", "Allah is merciful", "Allah is all-powerful", "Allah will answer my prayers", "Allah has promised us paradise", etc. – how far are these beliefs justified?

All the existing religions acknowledge that God is the Creator of the universe. As Creator of the universe, God must be distinct from the world, and His existence cannot depend on any of His creation. Hence, He is absolutely different from anything else that exists that makes Him totally unknowable. Although God Himself is unknowable, we can, to some degree, understand His relationship to the universe. In this manner, we speak of God through His "attributes of action". Though we cannot know what God is, we can learn much by realizing what He is not. Since God is eternal, there is no creator of God. However, since Allah is not a God but pretending to be God, he has a creator.

All science starts with the tacit presupposition that nature in intelligible, that there is reason or thought in things; and its progress is only the ever-advancing discovery of laws, of rational relations, of a coherent, self-consistent system, in the objects and events of the material world. The history of science is the history of mind or intelligence finding itself in nature. And the same principle applies to the higher investigations which deal with man and the social and moral relations of the spiritual world. After centuries of knowing Allah through faith, we are now ready to understand this supernatural intelligence directly through science, reason and Philosophy. In my 2012 book *Islam Dismantled: The Mental Illness of Prophet Muhammad*, (published by Felibri.com) I had critically examined the claims of Muhammad's prophethood and found them inadequate. In the present book, we will go much further and argue that by this moment in time science has advanced sufficiently to be able to make a definitive statement on the existence or nonexistence of the Allah, the ungodly god of Islam. I condemn not just belief in Allah but respect for the belief in Allah.

In this book, we will re-discover Allah, wrest him out from the hands of the Islamic faith-heads, pull him down from his divine position and put him under the searchlight for everyone to see his true color. We want to find out who had created Allah and how he was created and why he was created. After reading this book if a person wishes to continue believing in Allah, that is his prerogative, but he can no longer excuse his belief in the name of science, reason and moral necessity.

Chapter 1: The god who failed

"Question with boldness even the existence of a God; because if there is one, he must more approve of the homage of reason than that of blindfolded fear".

Thomas Jefferson, 3rd U.S. President

"A God who kept tinkering with the universe was absurd; a God who interfered with human freedom and creativity was tyrant. If God is seen as a self in a world of his own, an ego that relates to a thought, a cause separate from its effect, he becomes a being, not Being itself. An omnipotent, all-knowing tyrant is not so different from earthly dictators who make everything and everybody mere cogs in the machine which they controlled. An atheism that rejects such a God is amply justified."

Karen Armstrong

Throughout the recorded history of humankind, arguments for and against the existence of God have been largely confined to Philosophy and Theology. In the meantime, science has sat on the sidelines and quietly watched this game of words march up and down the field. Today, science has revolutionized every aspect of human life and greatly clarified our understanding of the world. We all agree that science is based on well-tested data; it is based on hard facts which have been verified and which are always verifiable. There is nothing secretive about science – the truths, it reveals, are as clear as day-light. In spite of this, some of us still cherish a belief that science has nothing to say about a Supreme Being that much of the Humanity worships as the source of all reality.

We want to have the experience of God through science. God is invisible, yet performs all miracles. He is the source of every impulse of love. Beauty and truth are both children of this God. When there is an absence of knowing the infinite source of energy and creativity, life's miseries come into being. With a true understanding of God, the fear of death can be healed and we can understand the real purpose and ultimate meaning of life.

But there is an obstacle that stands in our search for the real God of humankind. How to differentiate between the real God and the false god? A false god is an illegitimate god who cannot function in his professed authority or capability. Such a god leads the followers to astray. It is impossible for human beings to have a healthy relationship with such a god.

The real God must have some kind of presence, which means He can be experienced and known through scientific analysis. Also, the real God cannot be personified because He is independent of his creation. False gods are often personified as a convenient way. Such false gods prefer to remain hidden from us while demanding our love and respect. Since we humans are cruel and perverse in nature, the false gods are often ungodly. In spite of this, the false gods are worshipped because they seem more authoritative, practical and insane. That is why they often appear more authentic to many of us. We worship them out of fear, not out of respect. We fear to deny their credentials, obey their imagined instructions, and give them credit where none is due. Ultimately our ethics is reduced to obeying orders. These false gods separate us from the true path of God and Spirituality, yet these false gods are nothing more than projections of our own delusional minds. They are ultimately made up and counterfeit. They are vain imaginings of the mind used to nullify our being. They are satanic and are used to reduce us from human beings to ciphers.

A false god is a prime evil who is operated by a person with subnormal ethical and supernormal violent capacities, often known as a messenger of God or a chosen Prophet, control the lives of millions upon millions of other normal sane people while demanding submission, obedience, and loyalty to the ultimate authority they proclaim for themselves. They are the sinful and false extensions of our own imaginations into bonds of violence that chain us. If we want to remain on the path of spirituality we must utterly destroy such false gods and let no remnant of them remain.

1.1: Allah: The ungodly god

"Faith is often the boast of the man who is too lazy to investigate".
E. M Knowles

"The alleged short-cut to knowledge, which is faith, is only a short-circuit destroying the mind."
Ayn Rand

In the Mosque, the clerics tell us that Allah is almighty, eternal, holy, immortal, immense, immutable, incomprehensible, ineffable, infinite, invisible, just, loving, merciful, most high, most wise, omnipotent, omniscient, omnipresent, patient, perfect, provident, supreme, true etc ... etc – an exaggeration run amuck – but once we read the Qur'an, Tabari's history, and the Hadith collections, the god of Islam does not seem to exert much passionate attraction anymore. Reality is reality; it cannot be distorted. The simple fact is that Allah cannot survive any kind of objective test. The skeptics often wonder how these clerics keep on fooling themselves and others. What these clerics do not understand is that just because Allah is shown to a certain way to us does not mean Allah is that way. Some of them enthusiastically set out to rationally demonstrate the power of Allah, and when pushed into a corner, fall back on an appeal to faith or revelation. In their argument the knowability of their Allah is itself an issue which is unknowable, and no reason can penetrate this supernatural realm. The Doctrine of God and his Divinity are entirely two different things. As Principal Fairbairn commented,

> *"The interpretation of God consists of two distinct yet complementary parts – a Doctrine of God and of the Godhead. God is deity conceived in relation, over against the universe, its cause or ground, its law and end; but the Godhead is deity conceived according to His own nature as He is from within and for Himself".*

In the cartoons a light bulb shows up over somebody's head when he has a bright idea, but it does not happen in real life. For a person who is capable of scientific thinking, the brain is the only concrete way for an idea to enter the mind. The clerics may want us to believe anything about Allah, but it is evident from the very form of Muslim creed that their fundamental conception of Allah is negative. The clerics are well aware of this problem. They understand the danger and impiety of studying or discussing the nature of their god. For this reason they debar any possibility of criticism of Allah and try to keep him shrouded in a mystery. But if there is secrecy, one may suspect there is something wrong.

1.1.1: Allah contradicts himself

Contradicting Himself is impossible with a real God because He cannot deny Himself. Hence, His teachings and decisions cannot change. Muslims consider the Qur'an as the infallible words of Allah, free of any ambiguities, contradictions, errors and irrationalities. For Muslims, the Qur'an is so sacred that no devout Muslim would touch it with his left hand. Guillaume (1978, p. 74) wrote,

"[Qur'an is] the holy of holies. It must never rest beneath other books, but always on top of them. One must never drink or smoke when it is being read aloud. And it must be listened to in silence. It is a talisman against disease and disaster".

The claims are no doubt fascinating, but once we attempt to make an objective study of this book, we can find many "holes" in this supposed to be holy book. Here I wish to demonstrate that far from being perfect, free of ambiguities and errors, the Qur'an is replete with hundreds of contradictory statements that will surprise the critical readers of the Qur'an. It is unbelievable that an all-knowing Allah will have such a demented intellect to construct so many contradictory passages. Here I have documented one hundred major internal contradictions in the Qur'an.

1. Verses 2.21, 3.97, 35.15 and 51.56: God needs man or man needs God? In 2.21, Allah instructs the believers to worship him, but according to 3.97 and 35.15, Allah does not need men and Jinns to worship him because he is self-sufficient. However, in 51.56 Allah needs men and Jinns to worship him.

2. Verses 2.29 and 79.27-30: In 2.29, Allah first created the earth and then he perfected the seven firmaments (heavens). He has the perfect knowledge of all things. But 79.27-30 tell us that Allah created the heavens first, put it into a right good state and then he made dark its night and brought out its light. After that he had spread (created) the earth.

3. Verses 2.34 and 16.49-50: Can angels disobey? In 2.34, all the angels except Iblis, bowed down to Adam. Iblis refused and was haughty. He was one of the angles who rejected faith. But 16.49-50 say that all the creatures fear their Lord (Allah) above them and do what they are commanded. No creature shows pride in front of Allah.

4. Verses 2.35, 2.239 and 42.51: The verse 2.35 says that Allah directly told Adam not to approach the tree of knowledge; otherwise he would run into harm and transgression. However, 42.51 confirms that Allah had never talked directly to any mortal human being. Allah only speaks through a messenger or through a veil. Again in 2.239, Allah speaks directly to an ordinary man whom he caused to sleep for a century, then raised him up – *"He (Allah) said: How long have you tarried? He said: I have tarried a day, or a part of a day. Said He: Nay! you have tarried a hundred years"*

5. Verses 2.47, 3.33-4, and 3.42: In 2.47 Allah blesses the children of Israel more than other believers; He has preferred them above all beings – *"Children of Israel! Call to mind the (special) favor which I bestowed upon you, and that I preferred you to all other (for my message)"*. However, in 3.33-4, Allah preferred Adam, Noah, the house of Abraham, and the house of Imran above all beings – *"Lo! Allah preferred Adam and Noah and the Family of Abraham and the Family of 'Imran above (all His) creatures. They were descendants one of another"*. Again in the verse 3.42, Allah preferred Mary above all women.

6. Verses 2.52, 2.63 and 7.152: In 2.52, Allah forgave the people of Moses – *"Even then we did forgive you; there was a chance for you to be grateful"*. But 2.63 says that Allah raised the Mount Sinai above the Children of Israel and threatened them to submit to him, and the verse 7.152 says Allah punished them.

7. Verses 2.58 and 7.137: The verse 2.58 says that Allah asked the people of Moses to humbly enter a city (Jerusalem or Jericho) through its gate so that they could find all the provisions they needed for their sustenance. But in 7.137 Allah says that he let Moses' people inherit the land east and west, that is, the land of greater Syria.

8. Verses 2.62, 9.17, 3.85, 4.150-1, 5.69 and 5.33: As per 2.62 and 5.69, anyone who believes in Allah and the Last Day and does a righteous deed will get rewards. But 9.17 says, unbelievers will go to hell. In 3.85, Allah says that he only accepts Islam. Again 4.150-1 say, Allah will severely punish those who deny Allah and Muhammad and those who separate Allah from his messengers. In 5.33, Allah commands Muslims to crucify or behead those who criticize Islam and Muhammad or do not convert to the true faith of Islam.

9. Verses 2.63, 4.48, 4.116 and 4.153: In the verses 4.48, Allah says, he does not forgive that anything should be associated with him (he wants to be worshipped alone). But in 4.153, the people of Moses worshipped a calf even after the clear instruction from Allah. In spite of this idolatry Allah forgave them. According to 4.116, Allah may forgive anyone as he likes other than those who join other gods with Allah. But in 2.63, Allah terrorized Moses' people by raising the Mount Sinai above them.

10. Verses 2.97, 2.106 and 16.101: In 2.97, the new revelation confirms the old. But in 2.106 and 16.101, the new revelation substitutes the old verses.

11. Verses 2.97 and 16.102: Who brings down the revelation from Allah to Muhammad? In 2.97, it is Gabriel. But 16.102 says it is the Holy Spirit.

12. Verses 2.107, 13.11, 29.22, 41.31, 50.17-18, 82.10 and 5.55: Protectors or no protectors? The verse 2.107 says that the heavens and the earth belong to Allah; there is no protector besides Him – "*Do you not know that Allah's is the kingdom of the heavens and the earth, and that besides Allah you have no guardian or helper?*" Also 29.22 reads, "*Beside Allah there is for you no friend or helper*". However, in 13.11, 41.31, 50.17-18 and 82.10, Allah says that angels are our protectors and guards. But according to 5.55, Allah, Muhammad and the believing Muslims are the protectors.

13. Verses 2.117, 7.54, 10.3, 11.7, 25.59, 41.9-12 and 50.38: As per 2.117, Allah creates instantly, by decree. He says "be" and it is. "*The Originator of the heavens and the earth! When He decreeth a thing, He saith unto it only: Be! and it is*". But 7.54, 10.3, 11.7, 25.59, 50.38 say that Allah took six days for creation, and the verses 41.9-12 say that Allah took eight days for creation (two days for earth + four days for mountain and two days for seven heavens).

14. Verses 2.122-3, 2.254, 6.51, 20.109, 34.23, 43.86, 53.26 and 82.18-9: The verses 2.122-3, 2.254, 6.51, 82.18-9 say on Judgment Day intercession will not be possible. The verses 20.109, 34.23, 43.86, 53.26 say intercession will be possible. Each position can be further supported by ahadith.

15. Verses 2.139, 9.30, 3.118, 5.51, 3.57, 58.14 and 60.13: The verse 2.139 says that the Islamic, the Jewish and the Christian Allah is the same Allah – "*Say: Do you dispute with us about Allah, and He is our Lord and your Lord, and we shall have our deeds and you shall have your deeds, and we are sincere to Him*". However, the verses 3.118, 5.51, 3.57, 58.14 and 60.13 tell the Muslims not to be friendly with the unbelievers, including Jews and the Christians, and the verse 9.30 says, Allah will destroy them.

16. Verses 2.167, 6.128, 20.101, 32.14 and 78.23: In 2.167, the unbelievers will dwell in the hellfire forever. However, 6.128 says that the punishment will last as long as Allah wishes, not forever. Again as per the verse 78.23, the infidels will remain in hell for a certain period of time – "*They will abide therein for ages.*" But 20.101 says that the punishment will continue till the Day of Resurrection, and 32.14 says that the punishment will last for eternity – "*We too will forget you - taste ye the Penalty of Eternity for your deeds!*"

17. Verses 2.178 and 4.93: The verse 2.178 says, whoever kills deliberately must be killed, or if he is pardoned he must pay the blood money. But according to 4.93, a dreadful penalty (hell, unspecified) is for a Muslim for intentionally killing another Muslim.

18. Verses 2.185, 17.106 and 25.32: The verse 2.185 says that as a guide to mankind, Allah sent the entire Qur'an in the month of Ramadan. But the verses 17.106 and 25.32 say that Allah sent the Qur'an in stages.

19. Verses 2.219, 5.90, 47.15, 76.2 and 83.25: Is wine good or bad? The verses 2.219 and 5.90 say wine is Satan's handiwork – great sin. But 47.15 and 83.25 say, Allah will serve Satan's handiwork, wine, in Islamic paradise – "*They are given to drink of a pure wine, sealed,*" (Q: 83.25) and "*A similitude of the Garden which those who keep their duty (to Allah) are promised ... rivers of wine delicious to the drinkers*" (Q: 47.15). In 76.21, the Satan's handiwork is now sacred – "*... and their Lord will give to them to drink of a Wine Pure and Holy.*"

20. Verses 2.253, 17.55 and 4.152: Allah says in 2.253 that all messengers of Allah are not equal – "*some of them He exalted (above others) in degree*" and in 17.55 – "*We have made some of the prophets to excel others*". But in 4.152, Allah confirms that all his messengers are equal – "*... make no distinction between any of the messengers*".

21. Verses 2.254 and 2.255: In 2.254, there is no intercession for the infidels. But 2.225 says that Allah might appoint intercessor for anyone he wishes, including some unbelievers.

22. Verses 3.20, 38.70 and 8.39: As per 3.20 and 38.70, Muhammad's duty is only to convey the messages of Allah – "*Thy duty is to convey the Message; and in Allah's sight are (all) His servants.*" (Q: 3.20), and "*It is revealed unto me only that I may be a plain warner*" (Q: 38.70). But 8.39 says, Allah commands Muhammad to fight the unbelievers if they do not convert – "*And fight them until persecution is no more, and religion is all for Allah.*"

23. Verses 3.41 and 19.10: In 3.41, the angel (Gabriel) instructed Zachariya to remain silent for three days, communicating only through signs, and offering two prayers in the evening and in the morning. But 19.10 says that Allah commanded Zachariya to remain silent for three nights.

24. Verses 3.42, 3.45 and 19.17: How many angels came to Mary? In 3.42 and 3.45, many angels told Mary that she would give birth to Jesus, but 19.17 confirms that only one angel in the form of a man visited Mary.

25. Verses 3.59, 38.71, 15.26 and 38.75: How Adam was created? The verse 3.59 says that Allah created Adam from dust, and then said to him 'Be' and he was. However, the verse 38.71 says Allah created Adam out of wet clay, verse 15.26 says, Allah created Adam out of sounding (black burnt) clay and mud, and 38.75 says that Allah created Adam with his two hands.

26. Verses 3.124-5 and 8.9: In the battle of Badr, according to the verse 3.124, Muhammad requested Allah to send three thousand angel fighters, but the next verse says that Allah send five thousand angels. The verse 8.9 says that Allah sent only one thousand angels.

27. Verses 3.133 and 57.21: There is a clear discrepancy with reference to the width of the paradise or garden in the Qur'an. The verse 3.133 says that it is all the heavens and the earth combined – "... for a paradise as wide as are the heavens and the earth...". The verse 57.21 says that the width is the (lower?) heaven and the earth combined – "the width whereof is as the width of heaven and earth".

28. Verses 3.45, 3.144, 4.157-8, 5.110, 4.158, 21.98, 23.15 and 39.30: The verse 3.144 says that Muhammad is no more than an apostle; apostles before him had died. But the verses 4.157-8 say that Jesus did not die – "But Allah took him up unto Himself", and "Jesus, Son of Mary; high honored shall he be in this world and the next, near stationed to Allah." (Q: 3.45). Also 5.110 says Jesus taught the people in (up to his) old age. This is wrong because the ministry of Jesus lasted until he was about thirty-three years old. As per 23.15 and 39.30, everyone will die. The verse 21.98 says, all objects worshipped by men besides Allah will be in Islamic hell. It means Jesus will burn in hell because the Christians worship him.

29. Verses 3.157-8, 3.169-7, 9.111, 19.70-1 and 66.8: Are martyrs spared or will all Muslims go to hell? Verses 3.157-8 and 3.169-71 say, those who are slain in Allah's way (in Jihad) do not die; they live in the presence of Allah (in Islamic paradise), and enjoy his provisions. The verse 9.111 is more specific – "And if ye are slain, or die, in the way of Allah, forgiveness and mercy from Allah are far better than all they could amass. And if ye die, or are slain, Lo! it is unto Allah that ye are brought together". But the verses 19.70-1 say that every soul, including that of a Muslim, at least for some time, will be in hell. But 66.8 says that if the disbelievers repent and embrace Islam Allah will send them to Islamic paradise without delay.

30. Verses 3.196-7, 9.55 and 13.31-4: The verses 3.196-7 and 9.55 assert that Allah permits infidels to enjoy happiness in this life so that he can punish them more severely in the next – "Little is it for enjoyment, Their ultimate abode is Hell: what an evil abode." (Q: 3.197). But 13.31-34 state that infidels shall be miserable in this life and the next – "They shall have chastisement in this world's life, and the chastisement of the hereafter is certainly more grievous." (Q: 13.34).

31. Verses 4.5-6 and 65.4: In 4.5-6, Allah instructs the believers to take care of minor orphans and their property unless they have attained maturity or puberty (usually taken as fifteen years of age – marriageable age). But in 65.4, Allah says that the prepubescent girls (minor girls) can be married.

32. Verses 4.15-16 and 24.2: According to 4.15-16, if a woman is found guilty of lewdness four reliable male witnesses are required to testify. If proven guilty the woman should be confined to house until death. If two men are found guilty of lewdness (homosexuality), both should be punished, but if they repent they can be pardoned. According to this verse, the punishment for the men is unspecified. But in 24.22, Allah prescribes one hundred lashes for both men and women in front of other believers who perform lewdness. Apart from the question whether the punishment should be as in 24.2 or 4.15, how come the man and woman are treated equal in 24.2, but seemingly different in 4.15?

33. Verses 4.18 and 10.90: Pharaoh's repentance in the face of death? The verse 4.18 says, those who accept Islam at the moment of dying are not forgiven. For such people Allah has prepared a painful punishment. But in the verse 10.90, Pharaoh submitted to Islam when flood engulfed him.

34. Verses 4.46, 5.13, 5.41, 6.34 and 6.115: According to 4.46 and 5.13, some Jews distort the meaning of the words of their religious book and forgot a portion of it. Hence, Allah cursed them. In 5.41, Allah will not purify the hearts of those Jews who distort the meaning of the Book. But the verses 6.34 and 6.115 say that no one can change the words of Allah.

35. Verses 4.48, 4.116, 4.153, 6.76-8, 2.51-2 and 25.68-71: Does Allah forgive shirk? Shirk is considered the worst of all sins, but the author of the Qur'an seems unable to decide if Allah will ever forgive it or not. In 4.48 and 4.116, the answer is No, but in the verses 4.153 and 25.68-71, the answer is Yes. The verses 6.76-8 assert that Abraham committed the sin of polytheism as he took moon, sun and stars to be his Lord, Yet Muslims believe that all Prophets are without any sin. Also in 2.51-2, Allah forgave the followers of Moses though they had worshipped the calf.

36. Verses 4.75, 9.116, 17.111, 41.31, 42.28 and 5.55: The verse 4.75 says, amongst the believing Muslims Allah will choose someone to protect the oppressed. The verse 41.31 says that the angels are protectors. But the verses 5.55, 9.116, 17.111, 32.4 and 42.28 say, only Allah is the protector.

37. Verses 4.78-9, 16.93, 4.120 and 38.41: Is evil from Satan, ourselves, or Allah? The verse 4.78 says, all things are from Allah, and 4.79 says, evil things are from us. But 4.120 and 38.41 confirm that evil things are from Satan. According to 16.93, Allah misguides those who he wishes.

38. Verses 4.107 and 63.5: Allah does not love the treacherous, sinful person as per 4.107 – "*And do not plead on behalf of those who act unfaithfully to their souls*". But according to 63.5, Allah might forgive the hypocrites if Muhammad sought Allah's forgiveness for them.

39. Verses 4.171 and 4.172: The verse 4.171 says that Jesus was only another apostle of Allah, he was the Word (manifestation) of Allah; Jesus is also a spirit from Allah. But the verse 4.172 says, Allah made Jesus his servant.

40. Verses 5.5, 2.221, 60.10 and 9.30: In 5.5, Allah says, women of the people of the book (Jews and Christian) are lawful for marriage for the Muslims – *"And so are the virtuous women of the believers and the virtuous women of those who received the Scripture before you (lawful for you) when ye give them their marriage portions and live with them in honour"*. But in 2.221 – *"Do not marry unbelieving women (idolaters), until they believe"*, and in 60.10 – *"nor are the (non-Muslims) lawful (husbands) for them"*. But 9.30 says that the Jews and Christians are idolaters.

41. Verses 5.13, 5.54, 5.57, 5.82, 9.5, 9.29, 45.14, 60.13 and 109.6: In 5.13, Allah forgave the Jews though they tampered with their scriptures and broke their covenant with Allah. But in 5.54, Muslims are told to be very harsh and stern towards infidels; and in 9.29, Allah instructs the Muslims to fight the Jews and Christians unless they pay jizya tax or convert to Islam. In 9.5 (the verse of the sword), Allah orders Muslims to kill the infidels unless they convert to Islam. In 109.6, there is no compulsion in religion. The verse 5.82 says, Christians are Muslims' closest friends. In 5.57, the people of the book (Jews and Christians) are not the friends of the Muslims. Verse 45.14 says, Muslims should forgive the unbelievers – *"Tell those who believe, to forgive those who do not look forward to the Days of Allah"*. The verse 60.13 instructs the Muslims not to be friendly with the disbelievers – *"O ye who believe! Be not friendly with a folk with whom Allah is angry, (a folk) who have despaired of the Hereafter as the disbelievers despair of those who are in the graves."*

42. Verses 5.21, 5.26, 7.129 and 7.137: In 5.21, Moses said his people should occupy the holy land (of Palestine, Jerusalem). In 5.26, Allah forbade the Jews to enter the land for forty years. In 7.137, Allah let the Moses' people inherit the land East and West, i.e., the land of greater Syria. In 7.129, Allah destroyed the enemies of Jews and made them inheritors of the earth.

43. Verses 6.12, 14.4, 6.35 and 10.100: The verse 6.12 says, on Resurrection Day people are responsible for their unbelief. The verses 14.4 and 6.35 say, Allah purposely does not guide some people – *"Now Allah leaves straying those whom He pleases and guides whom He pleases"* and *"If Allah willed, He could have brought them all together to the guidance"*. But 10.100 say, *"No soul can believe, except by the will of Allah"*.

44. Verses 6.101, 19.20, 19.21, 19.24, 39.4 and 2.117: Could Allah have a son? The verse 6.101 says, he cannot have a son as he does not have a wife – *"How can He have a son when He hath no consort?"* though he is *"the Creator of all things"* (but he cannot create a son for himself). When Mary said *"How shall I have a son, seeing that no man has touched me, and I am*

not unchaste?" (Q: 19.20), Allah said, *"So (it will be)"* (Q: 19.21), and Mary gave birth of a son (Q: 19.24). The verse 2.117 says – *"when He decrees an affair, He only says to it, Be, so there it is."* But 39.4 says, Allah could have a son (without a wife) – *"If Allah had willed to choose a son, He could have chosen what He would of that which He hath created."* Ironically, when discussing the identity of Jesus, Qur'an says that Allah cannot have a son without a consort, but Mary can have a son without a consort, because all things are easy for Allah.

45. Verses 6.130, 12.109, 22.75, 27.82 and 35.1: Messengers amongst the Jinns, angels and men? Jinns and men are sent as Allah's messengers – *"O ye assembly of Jinns and men! came there not unto you messengers from amongst you"* (Q: 6.130) and *"Allah chooses messengers from angels and from men"* (Q: 22.75) … only men as messengers – *"any but men, whom we did inspire"* (Q: 12.109) … also a beast as messenger – *"we shall produce from the earth a beast to (face) them"* (Q: 27.82) … winged angels as messengers – *"Who made the angels, messengers with wings, - two, or three, or four (pairs)"* (Q: 35.1).

46. Verses 7.20 and 20.120: The verse 7.20 says that Satan whispered evil to both Adam and Eve to transgress Allah's prohibition. But the verse 20.120 says, Satan only whispered to Adam.

47. Verses 7.28, 16.90 and 17.16: Does Allah command to do evil? As per 7.28 and 16.90, the answer is No – *"Allah, verily, enjoined not lewdness."* (Q: 7.28), and, *"He forbids all shameful deeds, and injustice and rebellion"* (Q: 16.90). But as per 17.16, the answer is Yes – *"And when We would destroy a township We send commandment to its folk who live at ease, and afterward they commit abomination therein, and so the Word hath effect for it, and we annihilate it with complete annihilation."* (Q: 17.16)

48. Verses 7.54, 41.9-12, 2.117 and 2.29: The verse 7.54 says, Allah created the heavens (first) and (then) the earth in six days and then he rose over his throne. But according to 41.9-12, Allah created the earth (two days), the mountains (four days) and the heavens (two days) in total of eight days. The verse 2.117 says that Allah creates instantly – *"He only says to it, Be, so there it is."* According to 2.29, Allah created the earth first.

49. Verses 7.77, 26.157, 91.14 and 54.29: The verses 7.77, 26.157 and 91.14 say that some arrogant people killed the she-camel – *"So they slew the she-camel and revolted against their Lord's commandment"*. But 54.29 says, one person (the leader) killed the she-camel – *"But they called their companion, so he took (the sword) and slew (the sea-camel)."*

50. Verses 7.120-3, 7.126 and 10.83-6: Pharaoh's magicians – Muslims or rejecters of faith? The verses 7.120-3 and 7.126 say, *"But the sorcerers fell down prostrate in adoration, saying: 'We believe in the Lord of the Worlds*

- The Lord of Moses and Aaron' ... take our souls unto thee as Muslims (who bow to thy will)!" However, 10.83 says, *"But none believed in Moses except some children of his people, because of the fear of Pharaoh and his chiefs"*. These are two fundamentally different conclusions to the story of Moses' contest with the magicians of the Pharaoh.

51. Verses 7.127 and 28.38: As per 7.127, the chiefs of Pharaoh's people warned Pharaoh that he should not allow Moses to spread mischief and let the people abandon their gods. Pharaoh then decreed to kill sons of Moses' people, but spared their daughters. But 28.38 says, Pharaoh considered only himself the god. It means there was no other god in his kingdom.

52. Verses 7.136, 10.90 and 10.92: Was Pharaoh drowned or saved? In 7.136, Allah drowned Pharaoh and his people in the sea because they rejected Allah's revelations. But 10.92 says that Allah saved Pharaoh, and as per the verse 10.90 Pharaoh converted to Islam.

53. Verses 7.149 and 20.91: The event of worship to the golden calf – as per 7.149, the people repented about worshipping the golden calf before Moses returned – *"When they repented, and saw that they had erred"*. But according to 20.91 they refused to repent but rather continued to worship the calf until Moses came back – *"They had said: 'We will not abandon this cult, but we will devote ourselves to it until Moses returns to us'."*

54. Verses 9.23, 17.23 and 31.15: The verse 9.23 instructs Muslims not to take unbelieving father, brothers as guardians. *"O ye who believe! take not for protectors your fathers and your brothers if they love infidelity above Faith: if any of you do so, they do wrong."* However, the verses 17.23 and 31.15 say, respect parents even if they are unbelievers.

55. Verses 9.30 and 2.139: According to 2.139, the Muslims, Christians and Jews believe the same God – *"Do you dispute with us about Allah, and He is our Lord and your Lord, and we shall have our deeds and you shall have your deeds, and we are sincere to Him"*. However, in 9.30, Allah cursed them because – *"The Jews call 'Uzair a son of Allah, and the Christians call Christ the son of Allah. ... they imitate what the unbelievers of old used to say. ... they are deluded away from the Truth!"*

56. Verses 9.51, 57.22, 41.17 and 18.29: Does man have a free will? 9.51 and 57.22 reply negatively, but 41.17 and 18.29 give man some kind of free-will – *"As to the Thamud, We gave them Guidance, but they preferred blindness (of heart) to Guidance"* (Q: 41.17), and *"The truth is from your Lord': Let him who will believe, and let him who will reject."* (Q: 18.29)

57. Verses 9.116, 3.180, 15.23, 19.40, 19.80, 21.89 and 28.58: In the verse 9.116, Allah is the owner of everything of the heavens and earth – *"Surely Allah's is the kingdom of the heavens and the earth"*. However, the other

verses say that Allah inherits from infidels and other creatures – "*Allah is the heritage of the heavens and the earth.*" (Q: 3.180), "*We are the Inheritor*" (Q: 15.23), "*Surely we inherit the earth and all those who are on it*" (Q: 19.40), "*We will inherit of him*" (Q: 19.80), "*Thou art the best of inheritors*" (Q: 21.89), and "*We are the inheritors*" (Q: 28.58).

58. Verses 10.35, 14.4 and 16.93: The verse 10.35 says that only Allah (not the Gods of other religions) guides to the truth, hence only Allah should be followed – "*Is there any of your associates who guides to the truth? Say: Allah guides to the truth. Is He then who guides to the truth more worthy to be followed, or he who himself does not go aright unless he is guided?*" But the other two verses say, Allah often misguides people – "*Allah makes whom He pleases err and He guides whom He pleases*" (Q: 14.4) and "*He sends whom He will astray and guides whom He will*" (Q: 16.93).

59. Verses 10.47, 16.36, 25.51, 28.46, 32.3, 34.44 and 36.6: Were Messengers sent to all mankind before Muhammad? The verses 10.47, 16.36 and 35.24 say that Allah sent messengers to every group of people – "*To every people (was sent) a messenger ....*" (Q: 10.47), "*For We assuredly sent amongst every People a messenger, (with the Command),*" (Q: 16.36), and "*there never was a people, without a warner having lived among them (in the past)*" (Q: 35.24). But 25.51 says that if Allah willed he could have sent a warner to every town (but he did not). The verses 28.46, 32.3, 34.44 and 36.6 say, Allah had sent no messenger before Muhammad.

60. Verses 11.2 and 12.100: In the verse 11.2, none but Allah is worthy of worship – "*ye should worship none but Allah*". But 12.100 says that Allah allowed Joseph's brethren and his parents to worship Joseph by prostrating before him – "*And he raised his parents upon the throne and they fell down in prostration before him*".

61. Verses 11.38 and 54.9: Was Noah Driven Out? The verse 11.38 says that when Noah began to make the ark the chiefs laughed at him. But 54.9 says, Noah was driven out from the town.

62. Verses 11.42-3 and 21.76: Was Noah's son drowned? Verses 11.42-3 say, Noah's son (Noah's fourth son Yam) was drowned in the flood because he refused to embrace Islam. But the verse 21.76 says, Allah saved Noah's family that included his son.

63. Verses 12.19 and 12.20: The verse 12.19 says that Joseph was rescued by the water drawers of a passing caravan. But the next verse says, Joseph was sold (as a slave) by his brothers for a miserly price.

64. Verses 13.5, 17.98-99, 20.55, 34.7, 75.3-4, 89.27-30 and 31.28: Which enters paradise – soul, body or both? It has been emphasized throughout the Qur'an that after resurrection, it is the body (after reuniting with the

soul?) that enters paradise. But the verses 89.27-30 and 31.28 confirm that soul enters the garden.

65. Verses 14.4, 37.139 and 37.147-8: In the verse 14.4, Allah sends messages only in the Arabic in order to make the message clear to them. But in the verses 37.147-8, Allah sent his messages (in a different language) through Yunus to more than hundred thousand people of Nineveh, in the region of Mosul. Qur'an confirms that Yunus was a messenger of Allah – *"And Yunus was most surely of the messengers."* (Q: 37.139).

66. Verses 16.36, 21.7, 28.46, 29.27, 32.3, 34.44, 36.6: The verse 16.36 says that Allah sent apostles to every people or community or nation. Another verse 29.27 says, Allah gave prophethood only to Abraham's progeny – *"And We bestowed on him Isaac and Jacob, and We established the prophethood and the Scripture among his seed"*. But in the other verse Allah says that He did not send any messenger to the Arabs – *"you may warn a people to whom no warner came before you, that they may be mindful"* (Q: 28.46), *"No warner has come before thee: in order that they may receive guidance."* (Q: 32.3), *"... nor did We send to them before you a warner."* (Q: 34.44), and *"That you may warn a people whose fathers were not warned, so they are heedless."* (Q: 36.6). However, the verse 21.7 says that Allah had sent many messengers before Muhammad – *"Before thee, also, the messengers We sent were but men, to whom We granted inspiration."*

67. Verses 16.103 and 3.7: The verse 16.103 says, though some Arabs accused Muhammad of learning the Qur'an from a foreigner – *"It is a man that teaches him"*, Qur'an is comprehensible Arabic speech – *"this is Arabic, pure and clear"*. But 3.7 reads, *"He it is Who has revealed the Book to you; some of its verses are decisive, they are the basis of the Book, and others are allegorical; then as for those in whose hearts there is perversity they follow the part of it which is allegorical, seeking to mislead and seeking to give it (their own) interpretation. **But none knows its interpretation except Allah**, and those who are firmly rooted in knowledge say: We believe in it, it is all from our Lord; and **none will grasp the Message except men of understanding**"*. In fact, the verse 3.7 contradicts itself. It says that only Allah knows the meaning of these difficult allegorical verses in the Qur'an ... and then it goes on to tell that "men of understanding" can grasp it.

68. Verses 17.15, 16.25, 16.93, 29.13 and 30.9: The verse 17.15 says that Allah guides him who does good deeds and whoever goes astray is due to his detriment. The verses 16.25 and 29.13 say, Allah will doubly punish the arrogant infidels for their unbelief and for misleading others. But according to 16.93, Allah misguides those who he wishes. – *"He leaves straying whom He pleases, and He guides whom He pleases."* The verse 30.9 says, an individual wrongs his own soul, not Allah – *"It was not Allah Who wronged them, but they wronged their own souls."*

69. Verses 17.15, 53.38, 11.109, 16.25, 29.13, 8.28, 2.60-61, 2.63-66, 2.72-73 and 2.92-95: Who suffers the consequence of sins according to the Qur'an? The verses 17.15 and 53.38 state that a person will only be responsible for his actions. Qur'an also states that even people who simply followed the (wrong) customs of their ancestors, i.e. were misled by them into transgressing God's law, cannot pass the burden and punishment to those who led them astray, but will have to bear their punishment in full – *"They worship only as their fathers worshipped aforetime. Lo! we shall pay them their whole due unabated"* (Q: 11.109), i.e. no deduction from the punishment for the reason of having been misled. Yet these statements are contradicted by another two verses – *"Let them bear, on the Day of Judgment, their own burdens in full, and also (something) of the burdens of those without knowledge, whom they misled."* (Q: 16.25), and *"They will bear their own burdens, and (other) burdens along with their own, and on the Day of Judgments they will be called to account for their falsehoods"* (Q: 29.13). Another verse contradicting the principle that "no bearer of burden shall bear the burden of another" is *"And beware of an affliction which will surely not smite exclusively those among you who have done wrong."* (Q: 8.25). Here, even the innocent will suffer the affliction that will smite the wrongdoers. Qur'an also blames the Jews for the sins their ancestors had committed before their time, like making the golden calf in the verses 2.60-61, 2.63-66, 2.72-73 and 2.92-95. These accusations are clearly in contradiction to the "general principle" that nobody shall bear the sins (burdens) of others.

70. Verses 17.23, 15.29 and 16.49: According to the verse 17.23, worship no other God but Allah – *"Thy Lord hath decreed that ye worship none but Him"*. But 15.29 instructs the angels to bow down to Adam – *"do ye fall down, prostrating yourselves unto him (Adam)."* However, 16.49 says that all the creatures including angels prostrate to Allah alone – *"whatever creature that is in the heavens and that is in the earth makes obeisance to Allah (only), and the angels (too)"*.

71. Verses 17.70, 98.6 and 7.179: Preferred for hell? In 17.70, Allah prefers (all) the children of Adam over many of his creatures, but 98.6 declares that the majority of men to be the worst of creatures, and 7.179 says, many of them being even created specifically for hell.

72. Verses 7.179 and 51.56: The verse 51.56 reads, *"I created the jinn and humankind only that they might worship Me"*, and 7.179 reads, *"Many are the Jinns and men we have made for Hell"*. It would be no problem to say that all of them were created to worship Allah, but because some decided to disobey they will be punished in hell. But to state that many were made for hell is an obvious contradictions to the first statement – or else we must conclude that they were created in order to serve Allah in hell, but this would require a serious shift in the understanding of the meaning of hell as well as the issue of justice in who is sent to hell.

73. Verses 17.97 and 19.38: On Judgment Day sinners shall be deaf, dumb, and blind – *"We shall gather, them together, prone on their faces, blind, dumb, and deaf."*(Q: 17.97). But 19.38 says that they shall have especially acute eyesight and hearing – *"How clearly shall they hear and how clearly shall they see on the day when they come to us."* (Q: 19.38).

74. Verses 18.31, 22.23, 35.33, 39.73, 41.30, 57.21, 76.21 78.32, 79.41 and 88.10: The verses 18.31, 22.23, 78.32, and 35.33 say that there are many gardens in the Islamic paradise – *"For them will be Gardens of Eternity"* (Q: 18.31), *"a Garden (of Bliss)"* (Q: 57.21), and *"Gardens enclosed, and grapevines"* (Q: 78.32). But 39.73, 41.30 and 88.10 say, there will be only one garden – *"when they come to it, and its doors shall be opened, and the keepers of it shall say to them '...enter it to abide'"* (Q: 39.73), *"In a high Garden"* (Q: 88.10), *"receive good news of the garden which you were promised."* (Q: 41.30), and *"the Garden will be his home."* (Q: 79.41). Also according to the verse 18.3 Muslims will be given bracelets of gold. But 22.23 and 35.33 say that the bracelets will be of gold and pearls, and 76.21 confirms that the bracelets will be of silver.

75. Verses 19.41-9, 6.74-83 and 21.51-9: Did Abraham smash the idols? In 19.41-9, Abraham shuts up after his father threatens him to stone him for speaking out against the idols. And he seems not only to become silent, but even to leave the area – *"When he had turned away from them and from those whom they worshipped besides Allah"* (Q: 19.49). The verse 21.51-9 assert Abraham smash the idols – *"So he broke them to pieces, (all) but the biggest of them, that they might turn (and address themselves) to it."* (Q: 21.58). But in 6.74-83, Abraham only expressed his detest to his father for his idolatry – *"Ibrahim said to Azar: Do you take idols for gods? Surely I see you and your people in manifest error."* (Q: 6.74)

76. Verses 19.53, 20.29-36, 25.35 and 28.34-5: In 19.53 Allah made Moses' brother, Aaron (Harun) a Prophet. But in 20.29-36 Allah appointed Aaron a minister. Again in 28.34-5 Allah appointed Aaron a helper to Moses.

77. Verses 19.67, 11.61, 16.4, 38.71, 15.26, 21.30, 24.45, 25.54, 30.20, 35.11 and 96.1-2: What was man created from? A blood clot – *"Read: In the name of thy Lord Who created. Created man, out of a (mere) clot of congealed blood"* (Q: 96.1-2), from water – *"we made every living thing of water. Will they not then believe?"* (Q: 21.30), *"Allah hath created every animal of water."* (Q: 24.45) and *"It is He Who has created man from water"* (Q: 25.54), from a thickened fluid – *"He hath created man from a drop of fluid, yet behold! he is an open opponent"* (Q: 16.4) and *"Was he not a drop of fluid which gushed forth?"* (Q: 75.37), from earth – *"It is He Who hath produced you from the earth"* (Q: 11.61), from dust – *"He created you from dust"* (Q: 30.20); from dust and sperm-drop – *"And Allah did create you from dust; then from a sperm-drop"* (Q: 35.11), and from out of nothing – *"We created him before out of nothing"* (Q: 19.67).

However, it contradicts another two verses. According to 38.71 and 15.26, Allah created Adam out of wet clay, black burnt clay and mud.

78. Verses 20.37-9 and 40.25: When Pharaoh ordered the killing of the sons? The verses 20.37-9 say that Allah favored Moses' mother by sending her a message to put Moses inside a wooden chest and to let it float in river. Allah did this to save Moses' life from his enemy. But 40.25 confirms that the Pharaoh ordered the killing of infants after Moses became an adult.

79. Verses 21.30 and 41.11: Have heaven and earth first been of one piece which Allah then parts, or have they first been far apart so that He has to call them together? The verse 21.30 says that in the initial days of creation the heavens and earth were joined together as one solid mass and Allah parted them – *"Do not the Unbelievers see that the heavens and the earth were joined together (as one unit of creation), before we clove them asunder?"*. But the verse 41.11 says that Allah joined the heavens and the earth – *"Then turned He to the heaven when it was smoke, and said unto it and unto the earth: Come both of you, willingly or reluctant. They said: We come, obedient."*

80. Verses 21.98 and 6.108: In 21.98, Allah curses the unbelievers and their idols – *"Surely you and what you worship besides Allah are the firewood of hell; to it you shall come."* However, in 6.108, Allah takes an opposite turn. Muhammad must not disparage the idols of the pagans, lest they disparage Allah. – *"And do not abuse those whom they call upon besides Allah, lest exceeding the limits they should abuse Allah out of ignorance."*

81. Verses 22.47, 32.5 and 70.4: One day of Allah equals how many human years? The verse 22.47 says that it is one thousand human years – *"Verily a Day in the sight of thy Lord is like a thousand years of your reckoning"* and *"… unto Him in a Day, whereof the measure is a thousand years of that ye reckon"* (Q: 32.5). But 70.4 says, it is fifty thousand human years – *"The angels and the spirit ascend unto him in a Day the measure whereof is (as) fifty thousand years."* Perhaps, it originally was "fifty thousand" in both and "fifty" dropped out in one place.

82. Verses 23.101-2, 52.25 and 37.27: On the Day of Judgment there will be no kinship amongst the people – *"there will be no more relationships between them that Day, nor will one ask after another nor will one ask after another"* (Q: 23.101). But 52.25 and 37.27 say that the believers and non-believers will chit-chat and question one another.

83. Verses 24.4-5 and 24.23: Can false accusers be forgiven? Verses 24.4-5 confirm that false accusers (for adultery or fornication) can be forgiven if they repent. However, 24.23 prescribes no forgiveness for them – *"Those who slander chaste women, indiscreet but believing, are cursed in this life and in the Hereafter: for them is a grievous Penalty"*.

84. Verses 26.167, 7.82, 27.56 and 29.29: In the verses 7.82, 26.167 and 27.56, Lot's people threatened to banish him if he does not stop preaching – *"they said, 'Drive them out of your city: these are indeed men who want to be clean and pure!'"* (Q: 7.82); *"They said: If thou cease not, O Lot, thou wilt soon be of the outcast"* (Q: 26.167) and *"they said, 'Drive out the followers of Lot from your city: these are indeed men who want to be clean and pure!'"* (Q: 27.56). But 29.29 says that Lot's people challenged Lot to bring upon them the wrath of Allah – *"they said: Bring on us Allah's punishment, if you are one of the truthful."*

85. Verses 26.170-1 and 7.83: What happened to Lot's wife? In 7.83, Allah saved Lot but not his wife; she was tormented. But 26.170-1 say, Allah saved Lot and all his followers except an old woman. Either this is a contradiction or if indeed Lot's wife is derogatorily called "an old woman" then this does not show much respect for her as a wife of a Prophet.

86. Verses 27.83-4 and 55.39: On Judgment Day sinners shall be questioned about their crimes – *"Allah will ask: Did you reject My communications while you had no comprehensive knowledge of them? Or what was it that you did?"* (Q: 27.84). But 55.39 says, they shall not be questioned – *"On that day neither man nor jinni will be questioned of his sin."*

87. Verses 32.5 and 50.16: How far is Allah from us? As per 32.5, *"He rules (all) affairs from the heavens to the earth: in the end will (all affairs) go up to Him, on a Day, the space whereof will be (as) a thousand years of your reckoning."* But 50.16 says, *"We are nearer to him than His jugular vein."*

88. Verses 32.11, 47.27 and 39.42: who takes the souls at death? The verse 32.11 reads, *"The Angel of Death, put in charge of you, will (duly) take your souls: then shall ye be brought back to your Lord'."* However, 47.27 reads, *"But how (will it be) when the angels take their souls at death, and smite their faces and their backs?"* It means there are more angels. But 39.42 does not speak of angels anymore at all – *"It is Allah that takes the souls (of men) at death; and those that die not (He takes) during their sleep: those on whom He has passed the decree of death."*

89. Verses 33.4-5 and 33.37: In 33.4-5 it is forbidden to adopt sons – *"nor has He made your adopted sons your sons ... Assert their relationship to their fathers; this is more equitable with Allah"*. However, in 33.37, Muslims can marry the divorced wives of their adopted sons – *"... in order that (in the future) there may be no difficulty to the Believers in (the matter of) marriage with the wives of their adopted sons"*.

90. Verses 34.50, 53.2-5, 68.4 and 33.21: Who suffers loss if Muhammad was wrong? The verse 34.50 says, *"Say, 'If I am astray, I only stray to the loss of my own soul: but if I receive guidance, it is because of the inspiration of my Lord to me'."* But the other verses make everything Muhammad does

and says the standard to emulate – *"Your Companion is neither astray nor being misled. Nor does he say (aught) of (his own) desire"* (Q: 53.2-5); *"Certainly you have in the Messenger of Allah an excellent exemplar for him who hopes in Allah and the latter day and remembers Allah much."* (Q: 33.21) and *"thou (standest) on an exalted standard of character"* (Q: 68.4). Based on verses like these, Muhammad is considered the perfect and divinely endorsed role model, and he is followed in the minutest details of life. To claim, therefore, that if he goes astray it will still not result in any harm to those who follow him in everything, is not logical.

91. Verses 37.144-5 and 68.49: Was Jonah cast on the desert shore or was he not? The verses 37.144-5 confirm, Jonah (Yunus) was thrown into the desert from the belly of a fish – *"He would certainly have remained inside the Fish till the Day of Resurrection. But We cast him forth on the naked shore in a state of sickness"*. But 68.49 says, Allah kept Jonah inside the fish's belly to show his mercy – *"Had not Grace from his Lord reached him, he would indeed have been cast off on the naked shore, in disgrace"*.

92. Verses 41.16, 54.19 and 69.6-7: In 41.16, Allah destroyed the A'ad people through a violent wind for several days – *"a furious Wind through days of disaster"*. But 54.19 says they were destroyed in one day – *"For We sent against them a furious wind, on a Day of violent Disaster."* Again 69.6-7 confirm that they were destroyed in seven nights and eight days – *"We sent against them a furious wind... Which He made to prevail against them for seven nights and eight days unremittingly"*.

93. Verses 44.4, 17.13, 20.52 and 57.22: When/how are the fates determined? In 44.4, Allah decides in one night (the night of Laylatul Qadr) – *"In the (Night) is made distinct every affair of wisdom."* Other two verses say – *"The knowledge of that is with my Lord, duly recorded: my Lord never errs, nor forgets"* (Q: 20.52), and *"No evil befalls on the earth nor in your own souls, but it is in a book before We bring it into existence"* (Q: 57.22). But 17.13 says that man alone is responsible for what he does and what happens to him, *"And every man's fate We have fastened to his own neck"*.

94. Verses 56.7, 90.17-19 and 99.6: As per 56.7, on the Day of Judgment Allah will sort out people in three classes. But 90.17-19 say, Allah will sort out people in two distinct groups – the believers are the companions of right hand (paradise) and the unbelievers are companions of the left hand (hell). Again as per 99.6, on that day mankind will be in scattered groups.

95. Verses 58.2, 4.23 and 33.6: How many mothers does a Muslim have? As per 58.2, only one – *"None can be their mothers except those who gave them birth."* Two mothers, as per 4.23, – *"Prohibited to you (for marriage) are your mothers (the real mother and the mother who nursed him)"*. But 33.6 says, all the wives of Muhammad were mothers of Muslims – *"his wives are (as) their mothers"*. (If we discuss modern developments of

surrogate mothers, i.e. implanting fertilized eggs of one woman into the womb of another woman then 58.2 will create another problem. Is the mother only the one who gave birth, even if she is genetically unrelated to the child she delivered?)

96. Verses 66.8, 19.71 and 3.192: Will Allah disgrace the Muslims? 66.8 says, on the Day of Judgment Allah will not humiliate or disgrace the Prophet and those who believe in him. But 3.192 states that whomsoever Allah sends to hell, is disgraced thereby, and 19.71 says, everyone will enter hell.

97. Verses 69.25 and 84.10: Behind their back, or in their left hand? The verse 84.10 says that the lost people are given the record (of their bad deeds) behind their back, but as per 69.25, it is given in their left hand. Some Muslims say that their hands are tied behind their backs and it is given into their left hand, behind their back ... but that's not what the Qur'an says.

98. Verses 73.15-6, 10.75 and 7.103: How many messengers were sent to Pharaoh? The verse 73.15 says only one messenger – "*We have sent to you, (O men) a messenger, to be a witness concerning you, even as we sent a messenger to Pharaoh. But Pharaoh disobeyed the messenger*". As per 10.75 two messengers Moses and Aaron – "*Then after them sent we Moses and Aaron to Pharaoh*". But 7.103 says there was only one messenger, i.e., Moses – "*Then after them We sent Moses with Our signs to Pharaoh.*"

99. Verses 88.12 and 18.31: As per 88.12, there is only one bubbling spring in the paradise. But 18.31 says, there are multiple gardens with rivers flowing underneath.

100. Verses 89.14, 32.5 and 70.4: The verse 89.14 says "*Most surely thy Lord is ever watchful.*" But according to 32.5, "*He regulates the affair from the heaven to the earth; then shall it ascend to Him in a day the measure of which is a thousand years of what you count*". The verse 70.4 reads "*The angels and the spirit ascend unto him in a Day the measure whereof is (as) fifty thousand years*". If an affair takes one thousand years to reach Allah, and the angels and the spirits reach Allah in fifty thousand years certainly he is not ever watchful. Secondly, if Allah is nearer to us than our jugular vein (Q: 50.16), why is there any need for the "affairs"? Why angels and the spirit have to travel at all to reach Allah?

The Qur'an, with its many ambiguous statements, is an ideal scripture to find contradictions. At the same time, its ambiguity provides a good opportunity for the Muslims to find some explanation or the other to negate a contradiction. The internal contradictions prove only one thing for certainty – Allah is not sure and confident of himself. He often hesitates, stumbles and errs like fallible human beings. We might wonder how the creator and the sustainer of all things in the heavens and on earth could construct such a platitude and slovenly written document. When we, the infidels, charge the Muslim clerics that we cannot make sense out of so many internal contradictions, the clerics should reply us that this should not disturb us, because they, by themselves, cannot make sense out of many verses in the Qur'an.

Some very early Muslim scholars openly acknowledged that the arrangements and the syntax of the Qur'an are not miraculous, and work of equal or greater value could be produced by other God-fearing people. Ali Dasti, the noted Iranian scholar of twentieth century, concluded that Qur'an is not the word of God since it contains many instances which confuse the identities of two speakers – Allah and Muhammad. Dasti also noted more than one hundred Qur'anic aberrations from the normal rules (Warraq, 1995, p. 5). A belief must be shown to be sound in itself as well as in some consequences of holding it, as Sina (2008, p. iii) lamented,

"After reading the Qur'an, I was in shock. I was shocked to see the violence, hate, inaccuracies, scientific errors, mathematical mistakes, logical absurdities, grammatical solecisms and dubious ethical pronouncements in the book of God."

As Gibbon (cited Warraq, 1995, p. 10) commented,

"[The Qur'an is an] endless incoherent rhapsody of fable, and precept, and declamation, which seldom excites a sentiment or an idea, which sometimes crawls in the dust, and is sometimes lost in the clouds."

As Carlyle (1973, p. 299) observed,

"[The Qur'an is] a wearisome confused jumble, crude, incondite; endless iterations, long-windedness, entanglement; most crude incondite—insupportable stupidity, in short! Nothing but a sense of duty could carry any European through the Koran."

As Cook and Crone (1977, p. 18) concluded,

"[The Qur'an is] strikingly lacking in overall structure, frequently obscure and inconsequential in both language and content, perfunctory in its linking of disparate materials and given to the repetition of whole passages in variant versions. On this basis it can be plausibly argued that the book is the product of the belated and imperfect editing of materials from a plurality of traditions."

If Allah is the true God why there is so much confusion between Allah's revelation and man's realization? They are supposed to be two aspects of a single process.

1.1.2: Scientific, mathematical, historical and other mistakes in the Qur'an

The historical, scientific, simple mathematics and theological contradictions in the Qur'an are too numerous to list. Could it be that God is wrong? And wrong in so many cases? Or could it be that the one who was wrong here was not God? Maybe Muhammad was a good observer of the world around him, but he was not omniscient. These errors their selves scream out the Qur'an itself is entirely false. Here are just a few.

According to Allah, Abraham and his son Ishmael were the ones who built the Ka'ba in Mecca (Q: 2.127). However, this contradicts all the history books known to man. Guillaume (1956, pp. 61-2) wrote,

> "...there is no historical evidence for the assertion that Abraham or Ishmael was ever in Mecca, and if there had been such a tradition it would have to be explained how all memory of the Old Semitic name Ishmael (which was not in its true Arabian form in Arabian inscriptions and written correctly with an initial consonant Y) came to be lost. The form in the Quran is taken either from Greek or Syriac sources."

Abraham lived in the city of Ur of the Chaldees (South East Iraq), and later he moved west toward Canaan, a land very plentiful in food, not south toward Mecca – an insignificant town in the middle of the desert. Why would Allah promise to give Abraham's posterity a land of abundant resources and then send him into a desert? Voltaire (1971, p. 17) wrote,

> "We are told that [Abraham] was born in Chaldea, and that he was the son of a poor potter who earned his living by making little clay idols. It is scarcely credible that the son of this potter went to Mecca, 300 leagues away in the tropics, by way of impassable deserts. If he was a conqueror he no doubt aimed at the fine country of Assyria; and if he was only a poor man, as he is depicted, he founded no kingdoms in foreign parts."

While some scholars like Muir and Torrey believe that the Abrahamic origin of the Ka'ba was a popular belief long before the time of Muhammad, other scholars, as example, Snouck Hurgronje and Aloys Sprenger opined that the association of Abraham with the Ka'ba was Muhammad's personal invention, and it served as a means to liberate Islam from Judaism. Sprenger (cited Hurgronje, 1951, p. 287) had a harsh conclusion,

> "By this he, . . . Mohammed gave to Islam all that man needs and which differentiates religion from philosophy: a nationality, ceremonies, historical memories, mysteries, an assurance of entering heaven, all the while deceiving his own conscience and those of others".

According to Qur'an, David "received" the Psalms in the way Moses received the Torah; "...and to David We gave the Psalms." (Q: 4.163). But this cannot be historically correct. David probably lived around 1000 BC, and the Psalms were put together much later in the post-exilic period, that is, after 539 BC. According to Howell (1943, p. 75) none of the psalms should be ascribed to David. Several of them, praising some highly idealized monarch, would seem to have been written in honor of one or other of the Hasmonean kings (142-63 BC).

Qur'an says that the calf worshipped by the Israelites at the Mount Horeb was molded by a Samaritan.

"(Allah) said; 'We have tested thy people in thy absence: the Samiri has led them astray'." (Q: 20.85)

"(Moses) said, 'What then is thy case, O Samiri?'" (Q: 20.95)

However, the term "Samari" (Samariton) was not coined until 722 BC, which is several hundred years after the events recorded in the Exodus. The city of Samaria was founded by King Omri in about 870 BC and still to this day in the Middle East there is a small Samaritan community. Thus, they could not have existed Moses, and hence, could not have been responsible for molding the calf; it is historically impossible. There were no Samaritans until seven hundred years after Moses. Muhammad had travelled around in the Middle East and would have known about the Samaritans as well as the contempt of the Jews for the Samaritans. The only thing Muhammad does is trying to explain this contempt of the Jews for the Samaritans but makes the mistake to connect it to the wrong golden calf.

There is a serious historical blunder in the following verse.

"And remember Moses said to his people: 'O my people! Call in remembrance the favour of Allah unto you, when He produced prophets among you, made you kings, and gave you what He had not given to any other among the peoples'." (Q: 5.20)

We can understand the above verse in two different ways, but both lead to serious historical blunders. First; Moses himself could never have said it this way to his people, because Israelis only became distinctive "people" during their time in Egypt and most of this time, they were slaves to the Egyptians. They became a separate nation in their own right in the time of Moses by God's act of liberating them, leading them out of Egypt, and giving them a "constitution" through his covenant with them at Mount Sinai (Exodus: 19-23). Therefore, at the time Moses was standing before the people of Israel there had not yet been any Prophets or Kings from among them that he could call their remembrance to. Muhammad had heard of many Kings and Prophets in Israel, but was not clear about their historical succession, so that his ignorance lead to this historical error in the Qur'an.

Second; there is a possibility that Muhammad reformulated whatever he had heard about Exodus 19 which states,

"Then Moses went up to God, and the Lord called to him from the mountain and said, 'This is what you are to say to the house of Jacob and what you are to tell the people of Israel: 'You yourselves have seen what I did to Egypt, and how I carried you on eagles' wings and brought you to myself. Now if you obey me fully and keep my covenant, then out of all nations you will be my treasured possession. Although the whole earth is mine, you will be for me a kingdom of priests and a holy nation.' These are the words you are to speak to the Israelites." (Exodus: 19.3-6)

If Muhammad referred to this passage, instead of thinking about the whole of Israelite history, then his delusional mind also messed it up considerably, both in content and regarding the time-frame, because in the Torah, it is an futuristic offer (which did not become reality), while in the Qur'an it is a call to remembrance of what Allah has supposedly already given them (however, he never did because of their disobedience). In any case, whatever its exact meaning, this Qur'anic verse is historically wrong. There are historical contradictions in the following verses also.

"... for Pharaoh and Haman and (all) their hosts were men of sin." (Q: 28.8)

"Pharaoh said: 'O Chiefs! no god do I know for you but myself: therefore, O Haman! light me a (kiln to bake bricks) out of clay, and build me a lofty palace, that I may mount up to the god of Moses: but as far as I am concerned, I think (Moses) is a liar!'" (Q: 28.38)

"And Pharaoh said: O Haman! Build for me a tower that haply I may reach the roads. The roads of the heavens, and may look upon the god of Moses, though verily I think him a liar. Thus was the evil that he did made fairseeming unto Pharaoh, and he was debarred from the (right) way. The plot of Pharaoh ended but in ruin." (Q: 40.36-7)

According to the verses 28.8, 38 and 40.36-37, Haman was a minister or official of the Pharaoh who lived in the same time as Moses. But there are enough historical and archeological evidences that Haman served as the minister of Ahasuerus (King of Persia, Xerxes I is his name in Greek). Apart from the error in location, this is placing Pharaoh and Moses, and Haman in the same story even though they lived 1,000 years apart. In addition, in the Qur'an Haman is ordered by Pharaoh to build a tower reaching into heaven (the Tower of Babel) which is a well known story of an event that took place long before Abraham, who lived at least 400 years before Moses. A quote from the Bible,

"They said to each other, "Come, let's make bricks and bake them thoroughly." They used brick instead of stone, and tar for mortar. Then they said, "Come, let us build ourselves a city, with a tower that reaches to the heavens, so that we may make a name for ourselves; otherwise we will be scattered over the face of the whole earth." (Genesis: 11.3-4)

Muhammad's delusional mind had messed up many events considerably, both in content and the time-frame. He had obviously heard some Bible stories, but he seems to have got them confused and mixed up when it came out in his prophetic utterances. Also the command of Pharaoh is a problem for the authenticity and accuracy of the verse 28.38, because at the time of Moses Egyptians did not raise buildings out of burnt clay.

The Qur'an has every mark of fraud and imposition stamped upon the face of it. It says Alexander the Great (Zul-qarnain; means Two-Horned) was a pious Muslim and lived to a ripe old age. "Two-Horned" was a common title of Alexander the Great in the Middle East during the time of Muhammad. This title came from

Alexander's belief that he was the son of the Egyptian God, Ammon, who was represented by a ram with two large horns.

"They ask thee concerning Zul-qarnain. Say, 'I will rehearse to you something of his story'. Verily we established his power on earth, and We gave him the ways and the means to all ends". (Q: 18.83-4)

Authentic historical records however show that Alexander died young at thirty-three (356 - 323 BC), and believed he himself was divine, forcing others to recognize him as such. He was not a monotheist (i.e. he worshipped the Greek Gods). This verse is a clear contradiction of history.

Zul-qarnain travels to a place where a mountain pass separates the lands of an oppressed people from the lands of Gog and Magog. Then he proceeds to build a giant gate made of iron and copper so that the armies of Gog and Magog cannot pass through.

"Until, when he reached (a tract) between two mountains, he found, beneath them, a people who scarcely understood a word. They said: "O Zul-qarnain! the Gog and Magog (People) do great mischief on earth: shall we then render thee tribute in order that thou mightest erect a barrier between us and them?" (Q: 18.93-4)

"He said: "(The power) in which my Lord has established me is better (than tribute): Help me therefore with strength (and labour): I will erect a strong barrier between you and them: "Bring me blocks of iron." At length, when he had filled up the space between the two steep mountain-sides, He said, 'Blow (with your bellows)" Then, when he had made it (red) as fire, he said: "Bring me that I may pour over it, molten lead'." (Q: 18.95-6)

"Thus were they made powerless to scale it or to dig through it. He said: 'This is a mercy from my Lord: But when the promise of my Lord comes to pass, He will make it into dust; and the promise of my Lord is true'." (Q: 18.97-8)

In the verses 21.96-97, Allah will let the armies of Gog and Magog pass through the barrier to ravage the land in the last days. Thus, it is obviously implied that this iron/copper gate still exists somewhere on earth holding back the wicked followers of Gog and Magog.

"Until the Gog and Magog (people) are let through (their barrier), and they swiftly swarm from every hill. Then will the true promise draw nigh (of fulfillment): then behold! The eyes of the Unbelievers will fixedly stare in horror: 'Ah! Woe to us! We were indeed heedless of this; nay, we truly did wrong!'" (Q: 21.96-7)

The problem, however, is that no such gate exists! Satellites have searched every square inch of this planet and have never found some grandiose iron gate that is holding back a giant army just itching to destroy civilization as we know it. We know that the Qur'an meant this story to be taken literally because the Hadiths and

Muslim commentators go at great lengths to prove that such a structure exists or existed but does not any longer. However, the Qur'an predicts that the gate is supposed to stand until the last days. Therefore, either the gate never existed and the Qur'an is historically false, or the gate was destroyed and Allah was powerless to keep his promises. Also, where are the people and armies of Gog and Magog whose nation is supposedly enclosed completely except for a single mountain pass? Either way the Qur'an is completely in error.

Qur'an says that Abraham lived in a land ruled by King Nimrod. He destroyed the idols of his people, and as a result, was thrown into a fire by Nimrod.

"So he broke them to pieces, (all) but the biggest of them, that they might turn (and address themselves) to it. They said, 'Who has done this to our gods? He must indeed be some man of impiety!' They said, 'We heard a youth talk of them: He is called Abraham.'" (Q: 21.58-60)

"They said, 'Burn him and protect your gods, if ye will be doing!' We said, 'O Fire! be thou cool, and (a means of) safety for Abraham!'" (Q: 21.68-9)

However, Nimrod was the great grandson of Noah and the founder of the cities of Babylon and Nineveh (Genesis: 10.8-11), but Abraham was nine generations separated from Noah (Genesis: 11.10-27) and came from Ur of the Chaldees. How could Nimrod (a man who had been dead for many years) throw Abraham (a man who had not even been born yet) into a fire?! This error stems from the fact that Muhammad got this story from a Jewish legend rather than a revelation from God.

Several Qur'anic verses tell the story that Pharaoh's sorcerers believe in the signs and message of Moses, and then Pharaoh threatens to crucify them.

"Surely I shall have your hands and feet cut off upon alternate sides. Then I shall crucify you every one." (Q: 7.124)

"(Pharaoh) said: Ye put your faith in him before I give you leave. Lo! he doubtless is your chief who taught you magic! But verily ye shall come to know. Verily I will cut off your hands and your feet alternately, and verily I will crucify you every one." (Q: 26.49)

In another verse, about four hundred years earlier, we also read of another crucifixion. This is the story of Joseph.

"O my two fellow-prisoners! As for one of you, he will pour out wine for his lord to drink; and as for the other, he will be crucified so that the birds will eat from his head." (Q: 12.41)

There is no historical record that Egyptians used crucifixion as punishment in the time of Moses (around 1450 BC) or even Joseph (around 1880 BC). Crucifixion only becomes a punishment much later in history and then first in another culture before it has been taken over by the Egyptians. Such threats by a Pharaoh at these times are historically inaccurate. As per Encyclopedia Britannica (1993, p. 762),

"Crucifixion, an important method of capital punishment, particularly among the Persians, Seleucids, Jews, Carthaginians, and Romans [was practiced] from about the 6th century BC to the 4th century AD. Constantine the Great, the first Christian emperor, abolished it in the Roman Empire in AD 337, out of veneration for Jesus Christ, the most famous victim of crucifixion. ... [The earliest recording of a crucifixion was] in 519 BC [when] Darius I, king of Persia, crucified 3,000 political opponents in Babylon".

Allah wrote in the Qur'an,

"We verily gave Moses the Scripture and placed with him his brother Aaron as henchman. Then we said, Go together unto the folk who have denied our revelations. Then we destroyed them, a complete destruction". (Q: 25.35-6)

This is plain historical error. Neither Israel nor the people of Egypt were completely destroyed. They have continued to exist from the time of Moses to this day. The Egyptians lost one or more army units which were chasing after the Israelites under the command of Pharaoh. But most of the Egyptians were not touched, nor even most of the leaders of Egypt, since it is unlikely that they all went with the army that chased the Israelites. It seems, Allah got carried away with his doomsday warnings and made this point by far too strong when we look at history and to the people of Israel and the Egyptians. Why Muhammad overlooked the continued existence of the Egyptians when formulating those verses?

While talking to Moses Allah supposedly says,

"Those who follow the messenger, the Prophet who can neither read nor write, whom [the Israelites] will find described in the Torah and the Gospel which are with them." (Q: 7.157)

In this verse, Allah is saying that the Israelites can find predictions of this "Prophet" in the Torah (Old Testament) and the Gospel (New Testament) – *"which are with them"*. The obvious error, here, is that the Israelites of Moses' time did not possess the Gospel! The New Testament would not be written for another fifteen hundred years! Muslims try to reconcile this hopeless passage by saying that this is referring to the Gospel that would come to later Israelites. However, the passage is clearly referring to the Israelites contemporary with Moses because the verbs are in the present tense (i.e. "which are with them"). Secondly, there is no prophecy that predicts the coming of a Prophet who can "neither read nor write" in the Bible.

In several verses Allah confuses Mary the mother of Jesus with Miriam the sister of Aaron and Moses, and daughter of Imran which is about 1400 years off. This is a very prominent error.

*"Then she brought him to her own folk, carrying him. They said: **O Mary**! Thou hast come with an amazing thing. **O sister of Aaron**! Thy father was not a wicked man nor was thy mother a harlot."* (Q: 19.27-8)
*"(Remember) when the **wife of 'Imran** said: My Lord! I have vowed unto Thee that which is in my belly as a consecrated (offering) ... And when she was delivered she said:*

*My Lord! Lo! I am delivered of a female - Allah knew best of what she was delivered - the male is not as the female; and lo! I have named her **Mary**, and ..."* (Q: 3.35-6)

*"And **Mary, daughter of 'Imran**, whose body was chaste, therefore We breathed therein something of Our Spirit. And she put faith in the words of her Lord and His scriptures, and was of the obedient."* (Q: 66.12)

Allah mistakenly thought that the mother of Jesus was the sister of Moses and Aaron. Else, if Allah is correct then Moses was the uncle of Jesus! Undoubtedly this is the biggest historical blunder of the Qur'an.

Qur'an says Pharaoh's wife adopted Moses – *"the wife of Pharaoh said: (Moses will be) a consolation for me and for thee. Kill him not."* (Q: 28.7-9). But the Bible says, when Pharaoh sought to slay all the Hebrew male babies God saved Moses by having Pharaoh's daughter adopt the baby as her own child – *"When the child grew up, she brought him to Pharaoh's daughter, and he became her son. She named him Moses."* (Exodus: 2.1-10), and *"after he had been set outside, Pharaoh's daughter took him away and nurtured him as her own son."*(Acts: 7.21). Since the biblical position is that Moses wrote the first five books of the Hebrew Bible, who better than Moses to know who adopted him? Also the Hebrew Bible was written much closer to the time this event took place. Yet in another logically impossible verse the angel is advising Mary,

"And shake the trunk of the palm-tree toward thee, thou wilt cause ripe dates to fall upon thee." (Q: 19.25)

A pregnant woman cannot be so strong that she can shake the trunk of a palm tree. Also, palm dates come only in the summer (the people of the desert know this very well). Jesus was born in December (or January) and no date fruits during that time. If it was Allah's miracle why the Qur'an did not specifically say so?

Now we can look at the scientific contradictions.

"The Originator of the heavens and the earth! When He decreed a thing, He said unto it only: Be! and it is." (Q: 2.117)

Does this verse not say that Allah creates instantaneous? Does this really leave room for billions of years of development? Other verses say, Allah took six days (Q: 50.37), or eight days (Q: 41.9) for creation. But how could there have been "days" before the creation of the earth and the sun, since a "day" is merely the time the earth takes to make a revolution on its axis? Also, Qur'an tells us that before the creation Allah's throne floated above the "waters". Where did this "water" come from before the creation? Also, how did Allah create existence from the void of nonexistence, or nothingness? "Somehow" is not an intelligent explanation, and "through some incomprehensible means" is a poorer explanation still. A simple "I don't know" would be much more honest. Why is it unreasonable to assume that the materials of the universe always existed? However, the stupidity does not end here.

"We did indeed offer the Trust to the Heavens and the Earth and the Mountains; but they refused to undertake it, being afraid thereof: but man undertook it;- He was indeed unjust and foolish." (Q: 33.72)

Qur'an is a very strange book. What we understand from this verse is that heavens, earth, and the mountains are living creatures. They also have the audacity to disobey Allah! If Qur'an is true then the omnipotent Allah creates the cosmos, and then asks it if it would accept the "trust" or the "faith", and his own creation declines to accept this burden. In addition, the term "heavens" is hopelessly vague; does it mean our solar system, or our galaxy, or the universe? No amount of juggling will make sense of the Qur'anic story of the creation of the "heavens".

Allah created the moon and its phases for man to know the number of the years.

"It is He Who made the sun to be a shining glory and the moon to be a light (of beauty), and measured out stages for her; that ye might know the number of years and the count (of time). Nowise did Allah create this but in truth and righteousness. (Thus) doth He explain His Signs in detail, for those who understand". (Q: 10.5)

But this is a primitive Arabian notion, since all the advanced civilizations of the Hindus, Babylonians, Egyptians, Persians, Chinese, and Greeks used the solar year for the purpose of time reckoning.

According to Qur'an the ants can talk.

"When they came to a (lowly) valley of ants, one of the ants said: 'O ye ants, get into your habitations, lest Solomon and his hosts crush you (under foot) without knowing it'." (Q: 27.18)

"So he (Solomon) smiled, amused at her speech; and he said ... " (Q: 27.19)

This is a scientific contradiction because ants do not talk. Ants do communicate using smells, not modulation of sounds. Solomon could not have heard any talk since ants do not produce any. Ants are nearly deaf to airborne vibrations (except few rare) but extremely sensitive to vibrations carried through the substratum. Of the seventeen "messages" listed fourteen are chemical, two are tactile, and one is "chemical or tactile". In all the intensive studies of ants, "speech" (modulated sound of complex meaning) has never been observed (Holldobler & Wilson, 1990, pp. 228, 257). Only this verse talks about ants in the entire Qur'an, but the information it conveys is wrong. Also, to imagine that the ants communicate such sophisticated information as the Qur'an claims seems rather to belong into the land of fairy tales than science (e.g. an ant being able to distinguish between Solomon and a soldier). After all, who would believe that the ants do think in these terms about humans?

Solomon has an army of birds and an army of jinns (Q: 27.17), but even more "astonishing" is a long conversation with a Hoopoe bird in the verses 27.21-28 which is for sure another fairy tale. How could Solomon keep his sanity if he heard all the voices of all the insects around him? He must have been drowned in constant chatter. Qur'an only shows an understanding on the common level of other fables known from the same time in history.

Qur'an states that nothing holds birds in the air except Allah, as if the air has nothing to do with their flight. The aerodynamic shape of the bird's wings functions as an essential factor for the bird to fly steadily in the air. The wings evolved over millions of years to acquire this feature. But Allah described this ability in the simplest religious way.

> "*Do they not look at the birds, held poised in the midst of (the air and) the sky? Nothing holds them up but (the power of) Allah. Verily in this are signs for those who believe.*" (Q: 16.79)

Allah believes that the bees eat fruit.

> "*Thy Lord taught the Bee to build its cells in hills, on trees, and in habitations. Then eat of all fruits, and follow the ways of thy Lord.*" (Q: 16.68-9)

The scientific fact is that bees do not eat fruit. They feed on nectar and pollen.
The Qur'an's author observed creatures of the desert using their bellies (snake) or two legs (human) or four legs (lizard) to move. However, he failed to include creatures such as Millipedes that have a thousand legs.

> "*And Allah has created every animal from water: of them there are some that creep on their bellies; some that walk on two legs; and some that walk on four.*" (Q: 24.45)

According to Allah, there are only eight types of cattle.

> "*He created you from one being, then from that (being) He made its mate; and He hath provided for you of cattle eight kinds.*" (Q: 39.6)

However, there are more than a dozen kinds of cattle. Allah made this mistake because he had no idea of other types of cattle from the regions outside of Arabia such as reindeer, which are important to people in northern latitudes.
Allah says we can eat all types of seafood.

> "*Lawful to you is the game of the sea and its food, a provision for you and for the travelers.*" (Q: 5.96)

But Allah does not know that a lot of sea creatures are deadly, for example, the puffer fish, poison dart frog, marbled cone snail, blue ringed octopus and stonefish. Some sea-fish are so poisonous that they can kill a person in three minutes,
According to Allah, there is no fault in his creations.

> "*Thou (Muhammad) canst see no fault in the Beneficent One's creation; then look again: Canst thou see any rifts?*" (Q: 67.3)

If this verse is true then what should we say about those disabled animals and humans who have some disability from their birth?
Allah says that the birds can fight elephants.

"Have you not considered how your Lord dealt with the possessors of the elephant? Did He not cause their war to end in confusion, and send down (to prey) upon them birds in flocks, casting against them stones of baked clay." (Q: 105.1-4)

No historian had ever recorded that birds had fought the elephants with stone.

Like the ants and Hoopoe bird which could chatter intelligently, the Qur'an also mentions of the golden calf that could moo like a live cow.

"So Moses returned to his people in a state of indignation and sorrow... They said: We broke not tryst with thee of our own will, but we were laden with burdens of ornaments of the folk, then cast them (in the fire) ... So he brought forth for them a calf, a (mere) body, which had a mooing sound." (Q: 20.86-8)

"And Musa's people made of their ornaments a calf after him, a (mere) body, which gave a mooing sound." (Q: 7.148)

A golden calf that gives a mooing sound is a scientific problem and if we say it was Allah's miracle there is a theological problem. How can Allah give a miracle to this false idol when idolatry is so detested by him?

Qur'an says, the mountains are conscious like humans.

"Surely We offered the trust to the heavens and the earth and the mountains, but they refused to be unfaithful to it and feared from it, and man has turned unfaithful to it; surely he is unjust, ignorant." (Q: 33.72)

How can mountains, being inanimate and senseless objects, be able to "refuse the trust" and "feel fear"? This is a serious scientific blunder.

According to Allah, the mountains prevent earthquake.

"And We have set on the earth mountains standing firm, lest it should shake with them," (Q: 21.31)

"And He hath cast into the earth firm hills that it quake not with you, and streams and roads that ye may find a way." (Q: 16.15)

"He set on the earth mountains standing firm, lest it should shake with you;" (Q: 31.10)

"Verily, they shall soon (come to) know! Have we not made the earth as a wide expanse, and the mountains as pegs?" (Q: 78.5-7)

If Allah is true what Muslims think about the several dozens of earthquakes that happen every year? If the prevention of earthquakes was the purpose for mountains, why are they not preventing them? Why are they not obeying Allah? The simple fact is that the mountains have absolutely no role in quake-prevention. The earth landmass changes continuously and the plate tectonic boundaries usually situated at the mountainous areas are highly unstable. But the Qur'an propagates the idea that mountains are crucial in stabilizing the earth. Also, *"He hath cast into the earth firm hills"* (Q: 16.15) is not true. Mountains are usually formed and produced by the movement of plates. No one had thrown them down like pegs.

Allah thinks that there are mountains in the sky from where the hail is formed.

"Seest thou not that Allah makes the clouds move gently, then joins them together, then makes them into a heap? - then wilt thou see rain issue forth from their midst. And He sends down from the sky mountain masses (of clouds) wherein is hail." (Q: 24.43)

Hail forms in cumulonimbus clouds when supercooled water droplets freeze on contact with condensation nuclei.

According to Allah, the earthquakes are for the non-believers.

"Are they who plan ill-deeds then secure that Allah will not cause the earth to swallow them." (Q: 16.45)

"But they denied him, and the dreadful earthquake took them, and morning found them prostrate in their dwelling place." (Q: 29.37)

Natural disasters do not differentiate between Muslim and non-Muslim nations. Some of the highest death tolls from natural disasters in this millennium were on Muslim lands. But Qur'an regards those natural disasters as violent punishment from God. Allah also says that the violent storms are punishments for non-Muslims.

"What! Do you then feel secure that He will not cause a tract of land to engulf you or send on you a tornado? Then you shall not find a protector for yourselves." (Q: 17.68)

According to Allah, the rainwater is pure. But this is incorrect. Rainwater can be toxic in some industrial areas.

"… and we send down purifying water from the sky." (Q: 25.48)

Yet in two more unscientific verses Allah says,

*"And of **everything** we have created pairs that you may be mindful."* (Q: 51.49)

"And (have we not) created you in pairs," (Q: 78.8)

A bold claim about "everything"! In electricity there is positive and negative charge creating electrical force fields, but there is no counterpart for the gravitation force – it always attracts, never repels. But if Allah meant only living beings, then he is wrong too. There are quite a few examples of organisms which are exclusively parthenogenetic; as examples, *Bdelloid rotifers* are an entire class of animals which, as far as anyone can tell, has been reproducing entirely without any form of genetic

67

exchange for quite some time (perhaps more than fifty million years), with over 350 species identified. Allah's knowledge in bioscience is very poor.

The shooting stars are missiles of Allah to protect paradise from the intruders.

"And we have, (from of old), adorned the lowest heaven with Lamps, and We have made such (Lamps) (as) missiles to drive away the Evil Ones, and have prepared for them the Penalty of the Blazing Fire." (Q: 67.5)

"We have indeed decked the lower heaven with beauty (in) the stars, and for guard against all obstinate rebellious evil spirits, (So) they should not strain their ears in the direction of the Exalted Assembly but be cast away from every side." (Q: 37.6-8)

"He who steals a hearing (of the heaven), so there follows him a visible flame (shooting star)" (Q: 15.18)

"The flames of fire and smoke will be sent on you two (Jinns and men)" (Q: 55.35).

Allah is superstitious about thunder, and regards this natural phenomenon as an angel who glorifies him.

"And the thunder declares His glory with His praise..." (Q: 13.13)

Allah believes that the sun literally sets in a spring.

"Until, when he reached the setting of the sun, he found it set in a spring of murky water: Near it he found a People: We said: 'O Zul-qarnain! (thou hast authority,) either to punish them, or to treat them with kindness'." (Q: 18.86)

"Until, when he came to the rising of the sun, he found it rising on a people for whom We had provided no covering protection against the sun." (Q: 18.90)

What scientific evidence should I present to the Muslims to prove that the sun does not go down in a muddy spring? Secondly, these verses presuppose a flat earth, otherwise how can there be an extreme point in the West or in the East? It does not say, he went as far as possible on land in these directions and then observed sunrise or sunset while standing at this shore. A sunrise there would be basically just the same as at any other place on this earth, at land or sea. It would still look as if it is setting "far away". It does say that he reached "the place" where the sun sets and in his second journey the place where it rises. Let's quote two more absurd verses.

"And the sun runneth on unto a resting-place for him. That is the measuring of the Mighty, the Wise." (Q: 36.38)

"And for the moon We have appointed mansions till she return like an old shriveled palm leaf." (Q: 36.39)

Allah confirms the resting places of sun and moon in these two verses which is furthermore confirmed by Bukhari,

> *"Narrated Abu Dharr: The Prophet asked me at sunset, 'Do you know where the sun goes (at the time of sunset)?' I replied, 'Allah and His Apostle know better.' He said, 'It goes (travels) till it prostrates Itself underneath the Throne and takes the permission to rise again, and it is permitted and then (a time will come when) it will be about to prostrate itself but its prostration will not be accepted, and it will ask permission (from Allah) to go on its course but it will not be permitted, but it will be ordered to return whence it has come and so it will rise in the west. And that is the interpretation of the Statement of Allah (the Qur'anic verse 36.38)'"*. (Bukhari: 4.54.421)

Qur'an supports the concept of a flat earth.

> *"And the earth We have spread out (like a carpet); set thereon mountains firm and immovable ..."* (Q: 15.19)

> *"He Who has, made for you the earth like a carpet spread out ... "* (Q: 20.53)

> *"(Yea, the same that) has made for you the earth (like a carpet) spread out, and has made for you roads (and channels) therein..."* (Q: 43.10)

> *"And the earth- We have spread it out, and set thereon mountains standing firm..."* (Q: 50.7)

> *"And We have spread out the (spacious) earth: How excellently We do spread out!"* (Q: 51.48)

> *"And Allah has made the earth for you as a carpet (spread out),"* (Q: 71.19)

> *"Have We not made the earth as a wide expanse,"* (Q: 78.6)

> *"One Day We shall remove the mountains, and thou wilt see the earth as a level stretch ..."* (Q: 18.47)

> *"And at the Earth, how it is spread out?"* (Q: 88.20)

> *"By the Earth and its (wide) expanse"* (Q: 91.6)

These verses indicate that Allah believed in a flat earth model. The knowledge that the earth is round, in this day and age, would be rather difficult to deny. The fact that the earth is not flat has been known for thousands of years. The Ancient Greeks, e.g., Pythagoras (570 - 495 BC), Aristotle (384 - 322 BC) and Hipparchus (190 - 120 BC) all knew this. The Indian astronomer and mathematician Aryabhata (476 - 550 AD) knew this. Surely if the Qur'an is a letter-by-letter dictation from

Allah, it would also agree with this fact that was known throughout the world before its revelation, and it would surely contradict the flat earth model widely believed in by the seventh century Arab Bedouins. Also, it is interesting to note that Sheik Abdul-Aziz Ibn Baaz, the supreme religious authority of Saudi Arabia, issued a fatwa (religious verdict) in 1993 declaring *"The earth is flat. Whoever claims it is round, is an atheist deserving of punishment"* (Reyes, 2010, p. 564). Previously, in 1966, this cleric wrote another quirky fatwa, *"Sun goes around the earth and earth is motionless"* (Weston, 2008, p. 329). No doubt as devout Muslim, he has good reasons to conclude that the earth is flat, because all these verses clearly state this and not a single verse in the Qur'an hints to a spherical earth.

The sun is also flat like earth.

"When the sun (with its spacious light) is folded up." (Q: 81.1)

If sun is a spherical object, it cannot be folded up. This shows Allah's complete lack of knowledge of astronomy. Qur'an also mentions that the sun and the moon travel in the same orbit around the earth, and the earth is fixed in one place.

"I swear by the sun and its brilliance, And the moon when it follows the sun," (Q: 91.1-2)

"It is not permitted to the Sun to **catch up** *the Moon, nor can the Night outstrip the Day."* (Q: 36.40)

If sun is not permitted to catch up the moon, it means, sun and moon must be following the same orbit, or else, how sun can catch up the moon? Moon tracks across the sky at night, sun at day – as a result, of course they could not "catch up". Muhammad watched the two heavenly bodies racing across the sky, neither one catching the other. But the very idea of catching up shows that, in his seventh century mind, sun and moon were running on the same track. The all-knowing Allah hardly could imagine that all these phenomena are simply due to earth's rotation and not by sun's rotation. The absurd belief of ancient people was reflected in the Qur'an and ahadith. Also, the second part of this verse – *"nor can the Night outstrip the Day"* is not applicable for polar reasons where the longevity of day and night vary during summer and winter.

"And He it is Who created the night and the day, and the sun and the moon. They float, each in an orbit" (Q: 21.33)

There is not a single verse from the Qur'an where it states that the earth is traveling in an orbit. The Qur'an implies that the earth is stationary in relation to the sun and the moon. Science tells us that sun is stationary in relation to the earth, because the earth is stuck to the giant gravitational force of the sun, and the earth also moves along with the sun wherever it goes, just the way we are stuck to the earth's gravitation force and do not feel its movement at all.

"It is God who made for you the earth a fixed place and heaven for an edifice; And He shaped you, and shaped you well, and provided you with the good

things. That then is God, your Lord, so blessed be God, the Lord of all Being." (Q: 40.64)

"It is Allah Who sustains the heavens and the earth, lest they cease (to function): and if they should fail, there is none - not one - can sustain them thereafter." (Q: 35.41)

"Is not He (best) Who made the earth a fixed abode…" (Q: 27.61)

"Have you not considered (the work of) your Lord, how He extends the shade? And if He had pleased He would certainly have made it stationary; then We have made the sun an indication of it". (Q: 25.45)

Allah believes that the shadow (shade) moves because of the sun's movement, not the earth's movement. Like the sun and the moon, stars also rise and set. Stars are small enough to drop on us.

"The stars which rise and set," (Q: 81.16)

"And when the stars fall." (Q: 81.2)

In Allah's cosmology there are only seven planets.

"Allah is He Who created seven Firmaments and of the earth a similar number. Through the midst of them (all) descends His Command." (Q: 65.12)

In Allah's view, moon is located in the middle of the universe farther away than the stars, which are in the lowest part of the universe. The universe consists of seven layers. Once the moon was split into two parts also. Allah does not know that the universe consists of trillions of galaxies with billions of stars each. There is no such thing as seven layers.

"The hour drew nigh and the moon was rent in twain." (Q: 54.1)

"Surely We have adorned the nearest heaven with an adornment, the stars (for beauty)," (Q: 37.6)

"See ye not how Allah has created the seven heavens one above another, 'And made the moon a light in their midst, and made the sun as a (Glorious) Lamp?" (Q: 71.15, 16)

"He it is who made the sun a shining brightness and the moon a light" (Q: 10.5)
In the above verse moon is "Noor". The Arabic word Noor means "a source of light". The terms *"the moon a light in their midst"*, and *"the moon a light"* clearly indicate that in Allah's wisdom, moon is a "source of light" (like a candle), not a reflected light (like mirror). If Allah wanted to have meant reflected light, then the word "in'ikaas" (borrowed light) would have been used.

In Allah's science, the sun and stars are two completely different things and universe was created in six days. Modern science tells differently.

"He created the sun, the moon, and the stars," (Q: 7.54)

"We created the heavens and the earth and all between them in Six Days, and there touched Us not any fatigue." (Q: 50.38)

Qur'an tells us that the sky is a solid object. Allah does not know that the asteroid and meteorites penetrated the atmosphere to hit the earth throughout the course of history; there is no guardian whatsoever to prevent the incidents from happening. The author of the Qur'an thought that the sky is like a ceiling that can fall on someone while the earth can swallow someone too. The sky is made of some kind of rocky material that can crack.

"Who has made the earth your couch, and the heavens your canopy." (Q: 2.22)

"And We have made the heavens as a canopy well guarded." (Q: 21.32)

"See they not what is before them and behind them, of the sky and the earth? If We wished, We could cause the earth to swallow them up, or cause a piece of the sky to fall upon them." (Q: 34.9)

"When the Sky is cleft asunder;" (Q: 82.1)

"Have they not then observed the sky above them, how We have constructed it and beautified it, and how there are no cracks therein?" (Q: 50.6)

This is the height of Allah's knowledge in astronomy! This stupid god does not know that there is no such limitation "The Sky" – a solid "roof" over us. It is only a space with no known boundary at all even if we go billions of light years away in all directions. Qur'an simply reinforces the ancient idea of roof over us which is called sky. If Qur'an is a book of wisdom, then space flight is not possible without the permission of Allah.

"O assembly of the jinn and the men! If you are able to pass through the regions of the heavens and the earth, then pass through; you cannot pass through but with authority." (Q: 55.33)

Space travel was pioneered by the kafir scientists sixty years ago. With current technology, we have already explored the end of the solar system. If space travel is impossible without the consent of Allah, with dozens of atheist astronauts, Muslims should ask why an omniscient Allah made such an erroneous statement.

According to Qur'an, the sun, moon, days and nights are subject to humankind.

"And He hath made subject to you the sun and the moon, both diligently pursuing their courses; and the night and the day hath he (also) made subject to you." (Q: 14.33)

No human being has any influence of them. On the contrary, the humankind is subject to them in various ways. The presence or absence of sunlight (day and night) determines to a great degree what we can or cannot do. The moon heavily influences high tide and low tide of the oceans. People living in coastal areas are subject to it; they cannot change it but have to adjust their lives to it. All life form on earth depends on sun. In spite of our modern technology, sun and moon are still not influenced by us at all. They are not subject to us. It would have been acceptable to say that Allah placed sun and moon in the sky "for our benefit", but to claim "they are subject to us" is simply a scientific blunder. Another unscientific verse is,

"It is Allah that takes the souls (of men) at death; and those that die not (He takes) during their sleep: those on whom He has passed the decree of death." (Q: 39.42)

What Allah does not know is that soul does not leave the body in sleep. No one will believe today that sleep is a kind of death. Allah gave us a fantastic formula to raise the dead. Believers may give it a try.

"When Abraham said: 'Show me, Lord, how You will raise the dead', He replied: 'Have you no faith?' He said, 'Yes, but just to reassure my heart'. Allah said, 'Take four birds, draw them to you, and cut their bodies to pieces. Scatter them over the mountain-tops, then call them back. They will come swiftly to you. Know that Allah is Mighty, Wise'." (Q: 2.260)

According to Allah, humans are created from clay.

"We created man from sounding clay, from mud molded into shape." (Q: 15.26)

Some more unscientific verses are these,

"Then We made the sperm into a clot of congealed blood; then of that clot We made a (fetus) lump; then we made out of that lump bones and clothed the bones with flesh; then we developed out of it another creature." (Q: 23.14)

"Read in the name of your Lord Who created man, out of a (mere) clot of congealed blood." (Q: 96.2-3)

This is not a scientific description of embryonic development. Blood clot cannot grow into anything. Allah ignores to mention the female egg (the second and equally important half) and the process of fertilization when the egg and the sperm unite to form one new cell. Also Qur'an does not mention the invisible sperm that is essential to make a baby. Why Allah does not mention the invisible, that which we know only through modern medicine? This idea came from the Greek. Aristotle erroneously believed that the humans are originated from the action of male semen upon female menstrual blood. Had Allah really wanted to reveal something nobody could know at that time, he would have talked something like the equal contribution of the female through the ovum to form the new person and how the two come together and form one being, etc. Qur'an says that sperm comes from between the spine/backbone and ribs.

"So let man consider from what he is created. He is created from a gushing fluid that issued from between the backbone and ribs." (Q: 86.5-7)

Allah does not know that sperm comes from the testicles, not from between the spine and ribs. Also the opinion *"created from a gushing fluid"* is wrong. Allah did not mention the important role of the female egg in the reproduction of humankind.

"... and He Who (only) knows what is in the wombs ..." (Q: 31.34)

The current technology has enabled observation of the baby's gender through ultrasonic imaging. The ancient Arabs believed that everything was made from four elements – earth, wind, fire and water. However, fire is not a substance, but rather a reactionary chemical process. If Jinn is a living creature, it cannot be created from fire which Allah does not know.

"And He created Jinns from fire free of smoke." (Q: 55.15)

Allah will send some Jinns to hellfire because they did not accept Islam.

"But those (Jinns) who are unjust,- they are (but) fuel for Hell-fire." (Q: 72.15)

Logically, if the Jinns are made of fire they cannot be the fuel of fire. Indeed they will enjoy their heavenly comfort in the hellfire.

According to Allah, all the animals are sinful like human despite the fact that animals are not as self-aware as humans and work on instinct. Therefore, all animals will join the humans in the hereafter to be judged for their sins.

"There is not an animal (that lives) on the earth, nor a being that flies on its wings, but (forms part of) communities like you. Nothing have we omitted from the Book, and they (all) shall be gathered to their Lord in the end." (Q: 6.38)

Allah thought that people use forehead to lie.

"Nay! If he desist not, We would certainly smite his forehead, A lying, sinful forehead." (Q: 96.15-6)

Brain wave technology shows us electrical activity happens in the entire brain when deceitful. Forehead does not tell a lie.

In Allah's wisdom, Milk comes from between excrement and blood, and the milk is readily pure.

"And verily in cattle (too) will ye find an instructive sign. From what is within their bodies between excretions and blood, We produce, for your drink, milk, pure and agreeable to those who drink it." (Q: 16.66)

But the mammary glands where the milk is produced and stored are outside the body, while the excrement is in the intestines which are way inside the body. The two are nowhere near each other. Also, certain cattle milk needs processing, pasteurization, microfilter, creaming and homogenization.

Throughout the Qur'an Allah was grossly mistaken about the beliefs of Jews and Christians. Qur'an erroneously assumes and condemns Christians for believing in three gods consisting of the Father, Mary his wife, and Jesus their offspring.

"... believe therefore in Allah and His apostles, and say not, Three. Desist, it is better for you; Allah is only one God ..." (Q: 4.171)

"In blasphemy indeed are those that say that Allah is Christ the son of Mary. Say: "Who then hath the least power against Allah, if His will were to destroy Christ the son of Mary, his mother, and all every - one that is on the earth?" (Q: 5.17)

"They are unbelievers who say, 'God is the Third of Three'. No god is there but One God." (Q: 5.73)

"And behold! Allah will say: 'O Jesus the son of Mary! Didst thou say unto men, worship me and my mother as gods in derogation of Allah'?"' (Q: 5.116)

Allah mistakenly believes that the Jews say Ezra is the son of Allah. The Jewish people do not believe and have never believed that Ezra is the son of God.

"And the Jews say: Ezra is the son of Allah, and the Christians say: The Messiah is the son of Allah. That is their saying with their mouths. They imitate the saying of those who disbelieved of old." (Q: 9.30)

Allah caused some young men to sleep for three hundred years. It is impossible for a human to sleep for such a long time. Muhammad incorporated this myth from Arabian and Christian folklore of the Seven Sleepers.

"When the young men fled for refuge to the Cave and said: Our Lord! Give us mercy from Thy presence, and shape for us right conduct in our plight. Then We sealed up their hearing in the Cave for a number of years." (Q: 18.10-1)

"And they remained in their cave three hundred years and (some) add (another) nine." (Q: 18.25)
Following verse is equally impossible. It says that Noah lived 950 years.

"And verily we sent Noah (as Our messenger) unto his folk, and he continued with them for a thousand years save fifty years; and the flood engulfed them, for they were wrong-doers." (Q: 29.14)

There has never been recorded in actual history about human with such massive age. Also, science has never attested to this based on the fossil records. Similarly, following verse is a problematic statement.

"... eat and drink until the whiteness of the day becomes distinct from the blackness of the night at dawn, then complete the fast till night..." (Q: 2.187)

How to complete the fast at the Polar Regions? Muhammad was apparently unfamiliar with Polar Regions in which there are six months without sunlight and six months perpetual night during winter and summer. Could it be that Allah is ignorant about the night and day inequality phenomenon in the poles? The Qur'an claims that one should fast from sunrise till sunset. There is similar problem in the following verse. How are those people going to pray sunset prayers all year round?

"Establish regular prayers - at the sun's decline till the darkness of the night, and the morning prayer and reading: for the prayer and reading in the morning carry their testimony." (Q: 17.78)

According to Allah, all animals live in communities.

"There is not an animal in the earth, nor a flying creature flying on two wings, but they are peoples like unto you." (Q: 6.38)

But this is false. Some animals or living beings such as the jaguar or leopard or spiders are well known for being solitary loners; they never live in communities. If one insists that the verses of the Qur'an are literally word of an omnipotent and omniscient God then one is forced to conclude that Allah as a perfect being is even a worse science writer than humans, and if Allah really wanted to communicate scientific facts and principles to his mortal creations, humans, he failed miserably.

In the Qur'an there is no shortage of supernatural tales. Obviously, these are also part of the errors as they are logically impossible. Allah can transform a human into animal. If someone wears silk and wool he can be transformed into apes and swine (Sunaan Abu Dawud: 3.32.4028). Some Jews desecrated the Sabbath, so Allah turned them into apes and swine.

"Ask them (O Muhammad) of the township that was by the sea, how they did break the Sabbath, how their big fish came unto them visibly upon their Sabbath day and on a day when they did not keep Sabbath came they not unto them. Thus did We try them for that they were evil-livers." (Q: 7.163)

"Say: Shall I inform you of (him who is) worse than this in retribution from Allah? (Worse is he) whom Allah has cursed and brought His wrath upon, and of whom He made apes and swine." (Q: 5.60)

"When in their insolence they transgressed (all) prohibitions, We said to them: 'Be ye apes, despised and rejected'." (Q: 7.166)

"And certainly you have known those among you who exceeded the limits of the Sabbath, so We said to them: Be apes, despised and hated." (Q: 2.65)

"Narrated Abu Huraira: Prophet said, 'A group of Israelites were lost. Nobody knows what they did. But I do not see them except that they were cursed and changed into rats, for if you put the milk of a she−camel in front of a rat, it will not drink it, but if the milk of a sheep is put in front of it, it will drink it'." (Bukhari: 4.54.524)

If Allah wishes, food can fall from the sky. It if it really possible, why the poor people from Bangladesh and Sudan cannot see it?

"Jesus, son of Mary, said: O Allah, Lord of us! Send down for us a table spread with food from heaven, that it may be a feast for us... Allah said: Lo! I send it down for you." (Q: 5.114-5)

A stick can miraculously transform into a serpent.

"So he (Moses) threw his rod, then lo! It was a clear serpent." (Q: 7.107)

King Solomon had an army of Jinns and birds.

"And he (Solomon) said: O mankind! Lo! We have been taught the language of birds, and have been given (abundance) of all things. And there were gathered together unto Solomon his armies of the jinn and humankind, and of the birds, and they were set in battle order." (Q: 26.16-7)

Throughout history, kings and emperors had maintained armies. But none was ever recorded to possess armies that entirely consist of birds and Jinns. This is only unique with the Qur'an. Elsewhere in the Qur'an (27.20-5), Solomon wanted to punish a Hoopoe bird because the bird was absent. The Hoopoe bird was in fact busy eavesdropping on a beautiful female ruler, Queen Sheba. King Solomon had the authority to manipulate the wind at his command.

"So We made the wind subservient unto him, setting fair by his command whithersoever he intended." (Q: 38.36)

Jonah performed repentance prayer inside a fish. We do not understand how a human can live inside a fish and perform prayer of repentance in the stomach?

"And the fish swallowed him (Jonah) while he was blameworthy; And had he not been one of those who glorify (Allah) He would have tarried in its belly till the day when they are raised". (Q: 37.142-4).

According to Qur'an, body parts can rebel against the host. Science says, the limbs are controlled by the brain that conveys electrical signal through the nervous system. But Allah believes that the limbs can talk and testify against the host.

"On the Day when their tongues, their hands, and their feet will bear witness against them as to their actions." (Q: 24.24)

Allah brings back a dead man to life so that he can testify against his killer.

"And when you killed a man, then you disagreed with respect to that, and Allah was to bring forth that which you were going to hide." (Q: 2.72)

Scientifically, a man who has died for a few days can never be resurrected. But with the Qur'an, the supernatural overrules the natural world.

Allah will send a beast who will advise human about the truth of Islam. Allah does not tell us how a beast can talk to human.

"And when the word is fulfilled concerning them, We shall bring forth a beast of the earth to speak unto them because mankind had not faith in Our revelations." (Q: 27.82)

Mountains, trees, birds and animals can sing praises to Allah.

"And certainly We gave to Dawood excellence from Us: O mountains! Sing praises (to Allah) with him, and the birds (also); and We made the iron pliant to him," (Q: 34.10)

"To Solomon We inspired the (right) understanding of the matter: to each (of them) We gave Judgment and Knowledge; it was Our power that made the hills and the birds celebrate Our praises, with David: it was We Who did (all these things)". (Q: 21.79)

"And the herbs and the trees - both (alike) prostrate in adoration." (Q: 55.6)

"Do you not see that Allah is He, Whom obeys whoever is in the heavens and whoever is in the earth, and the sun and the moon and the stars, and the mountains and the trees, and the animals ..." (Q: 22.18)

These verses are not simply metaphorical in nature. Ahadith give us a hint that these statements are intended to be taken literally. The author of the Qur'an truly believed that animals, trees etc. could talk in the same way that humans do.

"Narrated Abdullah ibn Mas'ud: the Prophet said: On the night of my Ascent (Mi'raj) I met Abraham and he said to me: Muhammad, convey my salam to your people and tell them that Paradise is a vast plain of pure soil and sweet water and that its trees cry: Holy is Allah, all praise is due to Allah, there is none worthy of worship save Allah, and Allah is Great". (Tirmidhi: 439)

"Narrated Aisha: once when Allah's Messenger was with a number of the emigrants and helpers a camel came and prostrated itself before him. Thereupon his companions said, 'Messenger of Allah, beasts and trees prostrate themselves before you ...'" (Tirmidhi: 963)

From the above sources it is quite evident that the author of the Qur'an believed these things literally. Now we know how much the real science defers from Allah's science. In Islam science can proceed only if the scientist adopts an Islamic worldview. Sagan (1997, pp. 20-1) wrote,

"Science thrives on errors, cutting them away one by one. False conclusions are drawn all the time, but they are drawn tentatively. Hypotheses are framed so they are capable of being disproved. A succession of alternative hypotheses is confronted by experiment and observation. Science gropes and staggers toward improved understanding. Proprietary feelings are of course offended when a scientific hypothesis is disproved, but such disproofs are recognized as central to the scientific enterprise.

Pseudoscience is just the opposite. Hypotheses are often framed precisely so they are invulnerable to any experiment that offers a prospect of disproof, so even in principle they cannot be invalidated. Practitioners are defensive and wary. Skeptical scrutiny is opposed. When the pseudoscientific hypothesis fails to catch fire with scientists conspiracies to suppress it are deduced. "

Muslims like it or not, today the whole world is stuck with science. If we cannot understand Allah's wisdom by reason and science, we do not come closer to understanding it through faith. Faith does not erase contradictions and absurdities; it merely allows one to believe in spite of contradictions and absurdities. Muslims had better make the best of science. When Muslims will finally come in terms with it and fully recognize the power and beauty of science, they will find, in spiritual as well as in practical matters, that they have made a bargain strongly in their favor. The appeal to faith solves nothing and explains nothing; it merely diverts attention from the crucial issue of truth. In the final analysis, not only is the concept of faith irreconcilably opposed to reason, but it is evasive and quite useless as well. If the source of the knowledge is unknown, it must be verified by some scientific means.

In the Qur'an, Allah gives the following rules in regard to dividing of the inheritance,

"Allah (thus) directs you as regards your Children's (Inheritance): to the male, a portion equal to that of two females: if only daughters, two or more, their share is two-thirds of the inheritance; if only one, her share is a half. For parents, a sixth share of the inheritance to each, if the deceased left children; if no children, and the parents are the (only) heirs, the mother has a third; if the deceased Left brothers (or sisters) the mother has a sixth. (The distribution in all cases) after the payment of legacies and debts. Ye know not whether your parents or your children are nearest to you in benefit. These are settled portions ordained by Allah; and Allah is All-knowing, Al-wise." (Q: 4.11)

"In what your wives leave, your share is a half, if they leave no child; but if they leave a child, ye get a fourth; after payment of legacies and debts. In what ye leave, their share is a fourth, if ye leave no child; but if ye leave a child, they get an eighth; after payment of legacies and debts. If the man or woman whose

inheritance is in question, has left neither ascendants nor descendants, but has left a brother or a sister, each one of the two gets a sixth; but if more than two, they share in a third; after payment of legacies and debts; so that no loss is caused (to any one). Thus is it ordained by Allah; and Allah is All-knowing, Most Forbearing." (Q: 4.12)

"Allah directs about those who leave no descendants or ascendants as heirs. If it is a man that dies, leaving a sister but no child, she shall have half the inheritance: If (such a deceased was) a woman, who left no child, Her brother takes her inheritance: If there are two sisters, they shall have two-thirds of the inheritance (between them): if there are brothers and sisters, (they share), the male having twice the share of the female. Thus doth Allah make clear to you (His law), lest ye err. And Allah hath knowledge of all things." (Q: 4.176)

The whole text is not only too difficult to understand and complicated but mathematically impossible also. There are numerous simple cases which are not clear how to deal with them at all, since they are not covered under the instructions given. Let us start with some easy examples.

1. If a Muslim has only one daughter, verse 4.11 says she gets half. But then who will inherit the other half?

2. A son inherits double of what a daughter inherits as per the verse 4.11. Does that mean an only son would get all? Even if there are still parents which should also get a share? Also, it is regulated that one daughter would get half, and more than two daughters will (equally) share in 2/3. Then, how much would two daughters get among them? The average between 1/2 and 2/3?

3. In case of a Muslim widower who has only one daughter, when he dies his one daughter gets half according to verse 4.11. What happens to the rest?

4. Similar is the situation in which he has one daughter and one or more wives – his daughter gets 1/2 (Q: 4.11), wives share 1/8 (Q: 4.12), i.e. 5/8 are distributed. What happens to the other 3/8 of the estate?

5. Suppose a married Muslim woman has no relatives, and she dies without any children. According to 4.12, the husband gets half of her property. But who gets the other half? Only half of the inheritance is regulated according to the Qur'an.

6. In a similar situation with switched roles, the wife would get a quarter, but who gets the other 3/4 of my property?

The situation becomes more difficult if the family includes children. If the Muslim dies leaving his wife and one daughter and no other relatives, which means that his daughter gets 1/2 = 4/8 (verse 4.11) and his wife gets 1/8 (verse 4.12) leaving again 3/8 unaccounted for.

In all these (and several more such) cases the question is – who inherits the rest? This can be taken care of by donating it to charities or the local Mosque (or, spending the money for Allah's Jihad), but the problem is that Allah does not tell us specifically what to do with it. If the rest also to be distributed among the wife and children, it would make their shares different from what has been specified in the above verses. But then what is the point of specifying clear shares and then abandoning the instructions? Qur'an does not say what to do in this and many other cases. The instructions are incomplete.

However, as long as the shares add up to less than total available asset, the things can be settled comparatively easily. The inheritors get at least the share they are supposed to get according to Allah's instruction. But the problem starts when the shares are more than available asset as in the following examples.

1. If the male head of the family dies leaving behind three daughters, both the parents, one wife, then they will receive 2/3 for daughters (2/9 each, verse 4.11), both parents 1/3 (1/6 each verse 4.11) and wife 1/8 (verse 4.12). This adds up to $1 + 1/8$ ($2/3 + 1/3 + 1/8 = 1+1/8$). Where from the extra 1/8 will come from?

2. Similarly, for husband and two sisters – Husband 1/2 (verse 4.12), sisters 2/3 (1/3 each, verse 4.176). It adds up to $1 + 1/6$ ($1/2 + 2/3 = 7/6$).

3. Similarly, for husband, sister and mother – Husband 1/2 (verse 4.12), sisters 1/2 (verse 4.176) and mother 1/3 (verse 4.11). It adds up to $1+ 1/3$.

4. Mother (1/6), brother and sister (2/3 distributed 2:1 to brother : sister) and 1/4 for the wife is more than one.

5. One son and one daughter – the verse 4.11 says that one daughter will get half and a son will get double a daughter's share, which would be everything. 150 percent of the available property is distributed and we have not even looked at the parents and spouse yet.

6. When the Muslim man leaves behind a mother, wife and one sister only – the mother gets 1/3 (because the Muslim has neither children nor a brother, verse 4.11), the wife gets 1/4 (because they have no children, verse 4.12), and the sister gets 1/2 (because he has no children, verse 4.176). Not only do we have again distributed more than there exists (1/12 in overdraft), we also have the very strange result that the direct heirs (people of direct relationship – spouse, children, and parents) get each less than the indirect heir which is his sister. It becomes even worse if he has more than one sister since they then get 2/3 instead of 1/2 and we get even more into overdraft. A logical distribution is not possible by any means.

7. The verse 4.12 says that in case there is no direct heir (parents or children) then "*brother or a sister, to each of the two a sixth*". But the verse 4.176 says that in the same situation that "*they shall receive two-thirds of what he*

leaves". This amount is double of what 4.12 says.

The clerics and Muslim law judges are well aware of the error regarding the inheritance distribution; therefore, they have found other ways to solve their actual inheritance problems in real life. But if we take the information from the Qur'an only, then it does just not work out (Somewhere I read, a Muslim's wonderful response to these contradictions was – "*Anyway, what is important of the above is that we are talking about inheritance not mathematics!!*"). Besides, the instructions on inheritance do contradict the following verses.

"*A Revelation from (Allah), Most Gracious, Most Merciful. A Book, whereof the verses are explained in detail*" (Q: 41.2-3)

If the verses "*are explained in detail*"; why there is no standard of perfection in these laws? None of the proposed solution methods of real life can be derived from the text of the Qur'an. No matter how the clerics try to explain, the Qur'anic contradictions remain. Human rules are necessary to overrule the word that is claimed and believed to be divine. Surely, one logical conclusion is that these verses were not from God, but were Muhammad's own idea.

In the following verses there are semantic / linguistic contradictions.

"*So give them tidings of a painful doom,*" (Q: 84.24)

"*… promise them a painful doom.*" (Q: 3.21)

"*… the tidings that for them there is a painful doom.*" (Q: 4.138)

"*… announce painful punishment to those who disbelieve.*" (Q: 9.3)

"*… announce unto them a most grievous penalty.*" (Q: 9.34)

"*… announce to him a grievous penalty*" (Q: 31.7)

"*… so announce to him a painful punishment.*" (Q: 45.8)

For Allah and Muhammad the painful punishment and torture is cheerful news or glad tidings. The announcement of torture is certainly not good news. It is not cheerful news but a horrible threat. The wrong use in the Qur'an is a semantic contradiction.

I agree that it is not required for all of a Prophet's statements (i.e. statements not intended as revelation) to be in line with modern science, history and logic. Prophets are, after all, human; and as humans they may believe in superstitions and fables. However, when a Prophet proclaims a message from God, it must be accurate. As example, it is natural for a seventh century illiterate Arab to believe that earth is flat and sun revolves around the earth, because it seems that. But the problem begins when Muhammad puts his theory as Allah's word. Similarly, he could see the stars in the sky, but he would also occasionally see a "shooting star".

But what are these stars shooting at? They must be shooting at demons. The problem with Muhammad's position is that he proclaimed it, not as a hypothesis, but as an authoritative revelation from God. In this situation, an honest investigator's only reasonable option is to conclude that Muhammad is not a credible source of divine teachings and the god he claims to represent does not exist.

1.1.3: Conclusion

"Where ignorance is bliss
'Tis [this is] folly to be wise"
                                    Poet Thomas Gray

The Qur'an's authority is wholly invested in the claim that God is its author. If that contention were false, its credibility would vanish like a child's sandcastle before the incoming tide. Just one confirmed self-contradiction in the Qur'an should be enough to refute utterly the allegation that God is its author. The critics have recorded hundreds of contradictions in the Qur'an. Now what should we say about these verses?

"Do they not consider the Qur'an (with care)? Had it been from other Than Allah, they would surely have found therein much discrepancy". (Q: 4.82)

"And Allah is knower of all things." (Q: 2.29)

And this verse where Allah claims there is no confusion in his book?

"This is the Book; in it is guidance sure, without doubt, to those who fear Allah." (Q: 2.2)

Allah claims that his Qur'an is a comprehensive and exact inventory of everything in existence – *"Nothing have we omitted from the Book"* (Q: 6.38), *"... is (inscribed) in a record clear (to those who can read)"* (Q: 6.59), *"... (this) Scripture, fully explained ... revealed from thy Lord in truth"* (Q: 6.114), *"... the path of your Lord, (a) right (path); ... the communications clear for a people who mind."* (Q: 6.126), *"an exposition of that which is decreed for mankind"* (Q: 10.37), *"it is in a clear book"* (Q: 10.61, 34.3), *"not a tale invented ... a detailed exposition of all things, and a guide and a mercy"* (Q: 12.111), *"the Book explaining all things, a Guide, a Mercy,"* (Q: 16.89), *"it should be a guide"* (Q: 16.64), *"it is all in a Record"* (Q: 22.70), and *"all things We have kept in a clear Register."* (Q: 36.12).

Nothing could be further from the truth! The Qur'an fails in every respect. In the words of the late Iranian scholar Ali Dasti (1985, pp. 48-50),

"The Qur'an contains sentences which are incomplete and not fully intelligible without the aid of commentaries; foreign words, unfamiliar Arabic words, and words used with other than the normal meaning; adjectives and verbs inflected without observance of the concords of gender and number; illogically and

83

ungrammatically applied pronouns which sometimes have no referent; and predicates which in rhymed passages are often remote from the subjects. These and other such aberrations in the language have given scope to critics who deny the Qur'an's eloquence. The problem also occupied the minds of devout Moslems. It forced the commentators to search for explanations and was probably one of the causes of disagreement over readings."

To sum up, more than one hundred Qur'anic aberrations from the normal rules and structure of Arabic have been noted. Needless to say, the commentators strove to find explanations and justifications of these irregularities. Among them was the great commentator and philologist Mahmud oz-Zamakhshari (1075-1144), of whom a Moorish author wrote: 'This grammar-obsessed pedant has committed a shocking error. Our task is not to make the readings conform to Arabic grammar, but to take the whole of the Qur'an as it is and make Arabic grammar conform to the Qur'an'."

Often apologists of Islam say that Muslims do not follow the Qur'an alone, but also consult the Hadith collections. But the moment one appeals to the hadiths for clarification of the Qur'anic passages one ends up falsifying the Qur'an. They have to look at the Hadith because Qur'an is incomplete.

The simple fact is that Qur'an is not a book of guidance. This book shows no sign of being a divine book. It is not even logically consistent. Since Allah is self-contradictory, he does not exist. Throughout his career Muhammad had heard only disembodied voices, other than the voice of the direction that we call God.

1.2: The absurdity of Allah's hellfire

"If moral values were constituted wholly by divine commands, so that goodness consisted in conformity to God's will, we could make no sense of the theist's own claims that God is good and that he seeks the good of his creation."

J. L. Mackie

"Religion is based, I think, primarily and mainly upon fear. It is partly the terror of the unknown, and partly ... the wish to feel that you have a kind of elder brother who will stand by you in all your troubles and disputes. Fear is the basis of the whole thing. – fear of the mysterious, fear of defeat, fear of death. Fear is the parent of cruelty, and therefore it is no wonder if cruelty and religion have gone hand-in-hand."

Bertrand Russell

"As children tremble and fear everything in the blind darkness, so we in the light sometimes fear what is no more to be feared than the things children in the dark hold in terror".

Lucretius, On the nature of things (ca. 60 BC)

The Qur'anic ethical system is based entirely on fear. Muhammad used Allah's wrath-to-come as a weapon with which to threaten his opponents, and terrorize his own followers into total obedience to himself. As Gibb (1953, p. 27) wrote,

"That God is the omnipotent master and man his creature who is ever in danger of incurring his wrath – this is the basis of all Muslim theology and ethics."

The notion of an everlasting punishment is incompatible with and unworthy of a benevolent and merciful God. It is even more incompatible when we conjoin it with the Qur'anic doctrine of predestination. Why Allah specially creates creatures to consign to hell? However before commenting the concept of predestination, let us look deep into the description of the Qur'anic hell. The word "Jahannum" appears at least thirty times in the Qur'an (Warraq, 1995, p. 125), and there are 146 references to hell in the Qur'an – out of which ninety-four percent of the reasons for being in hell are for the intellectual sin of disagreeing with Muhammad, an unpardonable crime (Glazov & Warner, 2007). As Gibb (1953, p. 38) commented,

"Man must live in constant fear and awe of [God], and always be on his guard against Him -- such is the idiomatic meaning of the term for 'fearing God' which runs through the Koran from cover to cover".

Several words are used in the Qur'an to evoke the place of torment that Allah seems to take a particular delight in contemplating. Muhammad really let his otherwise limited imagination go wild when describing, in revolting detail, the torments of hell. According to Muhammad, hell is a real place which Allah has created as a torture chamber for the disbelievers. In the hell; nonbelievers will burn forever in hellfire because they are vilest of creatures (Q: 98.5-8), awaits a woeful punishment (Q: 33.8), garments of fire, scalding water will be poured upon their heads, melting skins and which is in their bellies, tortured with hooked iron rods, when they try to escape, they will be dragged, and will be told, "Taste the torment of the Conflagration" (Q: 22.19-22), when the non-believers cry out for help they shall be showered with water as hot as molten brass, which will scald their faces, evil shall be their drink, dismal their resting place (Q: 18.29), punishment will never be lightened, and the non-believers shall be speechless with despair (Q: 43.74-75), seized by their forelocks and their feet (Q: 55.41), chains, fetters and a blazing (fire) (Q: 76.4; 73.12), choking food and a very painful punishment (Q: 73.13), roast the unbeliever in hell (Q: 69.31), neither shade nor shelter from the flames (Q: 77.31), you and your idols shall be the fuel of hell (Q: 21.98), and, food is Zaqqum tree and foul pus (Q: 44.43; 69.36). Chapter after chapter, verse after verse we are told repeatedly about the everlasting hellfire. The psychological impact of the Qur'an is devastating.

"Taste ye then - for ye forgot the Meeting of this Day of yours, and We too will forget you - taste ye the Penalty of Eternity for your (evil) deeds!" (Q: 32.14)

"That is the reward of Allah's enemies: the Fire. Therein is their immortal home, payment forasmuch as they denied Our revelations." (Q: 41.28)

"Allah has promised the hypocritical men and the hypocritical women and the unbelievers the fire of hell to abide therein; it is enough for them; and Allah has cursed them and they shall have lasting punishment." (Q: 9.68)

"And those who followed shall say: Had there been for us a return, then we would renounce them as they have renounced us. Thus will Allah show them their deeds to be intense regret to them, and they shall not come forth from the fire." (Q: 2.167)

As if the above was not clear enough, another verse says that Allah's wrath will never be turned back.

"If they accuse thee of falsehood, say: 'Your Lord is full of mercy all-embracing; but from people in guilt never will His wrath be turned back'" (Q: 6.147)

The hell is not for punishing the Muslim wrong-doers. They will go directly to paradise. Muhammad's recommendation is final and Allah cannot deny it. Hence, all the Muslim terrorists, murderers, rapists, cheats, thugs will go to paradise because they follow Muhammad. All they have to do is to recite the Kalima (incantation) – there is no God but Allah and Muhammad is his Prophet – and they will get free gate-pass to enter paradise.

"Narrated by Abu Huraira; Allah's Apostle said, 'All my followers will enter Paradise except those who refuse." They said, "O Allah's Apostle! Who will refuse?" He said, 'Whoever obeys me will enter Paradise, and whoever disobeys me is the one who refuses (to enter it)'". (Bukhari: 9.92.384)

" ... If you love Allah, and follow me (Muhammad), God will love you, and forgive you your sins." (Q: 3.31)

"We said: 'Get ye down all from here; and if, as is sure, there comes to you Guidance from me, whosoever follows My guidance, on them shall be no fear, nor shall they grieve'." (Q: 2.38)

The "people of the book", idolaters, agnostics and atheists are destined to hell for eternal suffering no matter how pious and God-fearing they may have been. Their good thoughts, good actions or piety are of no value.

"But those who disbelieve and belie Our verses shall be the companions of the Fire, and there they shall live forever". (Q: 2.39)

"As for those who disbelieve and belie Our verses, they shall become the companions of Hell". (Q: 5.10).

What should we understand from such an odd system of values? Allah is obliged to throw a person in hell even if he is sincerely devoted of him but does not believe in Muhammad's prophetic claim. Hence, we can see how helpless the God of the Muslims is. Mill (1874, pp. 113-4) commented,

> "*The recognition, for example, of the object of highest worship, in a being who could make a hell; and who could create countless generations of human beings with the certain foreknowledge that he was creating them for this fate. Is there any moral enormity which might not be justified by imitation of such a Deity? And is it possible to adore such a one without a frightful distortion of the standard of right and wrong?*"

Mill's conception applies to any God of predestination. We cannot properly call such a system an ethical system at all. How disgusting and wicked is the thought that Allah purposefully creates beings to fill hell with, beings who cannot in anyway be held responsible for their actions since Allah chooses to lead them astray. As Warraq (1995, p. 125) commented,

> "*Central to any valid system of ethics is the notion of moral responsibility, of a moral person who can legitimately be held responsible for his actions: a person who is capable of rational thought, who is capable of deliberation, who displays intentionality, who is capable of choosing and is, in some way, free to choose. Under the Koranic system of predestination, 'men' are no more than automata created by a capricious deity who amuses himself by watching his creations burning in hell. We cannot properly assign blame or approbation in the Koranic system; man is not responsible for his acts, thus it seems doubly absurd to punish him in the sadistic manner described in the various suras quoted earlier.*"

If we follow the same line of thinking of Warraq, few questions immediately appear in our minds – Can God be immoral or unethical? Does God stand above morality, defining for us what is moral and what is immoral in accordance with His will? Or, is morality a characteristic that exists independent of what God wills to be moral or immoral? This is a crucial problem for those who think deeply about philosophical and ethical matters concerning religion and God. Regretfully, there has not (at least, not until recently) been any really satisfactory answer from the Muslim clerics to the issues raised by these questions.

Therefore, we can see that at the very core of Islam there is a strong moral argument against Allah. It is unjust for a true God to burn a disbeliever in hell forever. A disbeliever, being a finite being, can only commit a limited amount of sin in his entire life. Eternal torment of hell is an infinite punishment. It is unfair to punish for a finite amount of sin with infinite torment. Also, since such punishment would never end, what constructive purpose will it serve? Can this give any solution to the problem of evil? Why Allah is silent on this issue and did not send a suitable revelation to justify his divine decision? If eternal torment is Allah's will, then on what basis he is "most gracious, most merciful"? Qur'an says,

> "*And if you are slain in the way of Allah or you die, certainly forgiveness from Allah and mercy is better than what they amass. And if indeed you die or you*

are slain, certainly to Allah shall you be gathered together." (Q: 3.157-8)

"Lo! Allah hath bought from the believers their lives and their wealth because the Garden will be theirs: they shall fight in the way of Allah and shall slay and be slain. It is a promise which is binding on Him in the Torah and the Gospel and the Qur'an. Who fulfilleth His covenant better than Allah? Rejoice then in your bargain that ye have made, for that is the supreme triumph." (Q: 9.111)

"And certainly We know best those who are most worthy of being burned therein. Not one of you but will pass over it: this is, with thy Lord, a Decree which must be accomplished". (Q: 19.70-1)

There is a clear contradiction in the above verses. According to the verse 19.71, every Muslim will go to hell (for at least some time), while another passage states that those who die in Jihad will go to paradise immediately. In fact, it is not merely the martyrs in the way of Allah, who have been promised complete immunity from hellfire, but all the believing Muslims have been promised to be kept in protection from the slightest of evil.

"On the Judgment Day wilt thou see those who told lies against Allah;- their faces will be turned black; Is there not in Hell an abode for the Haughty?" (Q: 39.60)

"But Allah will deliver the righteous to their place of salvation: no evil shall touch them, nor shall they grieve." (Q: 39.61)

The believing Muslims shall not only be saved from all evil, but shall be kept so far away from the burning fire that they shall not even hear the horrifying sounds of the growling fires.

"Lo! ye (idolaters) and that which ye worship beside Allah are fuel of hell. Thereunto ye will come. If these had been gods they would not have come thither, but all will abide therein. Therein wailing is their portion, and therein they hear not. Lo! Those unto whom kindness hath gone forth before from Us, they will be far removed from thence. They will not hear the slightest sound thereof, while they abide in that which their souls desire. The Supreme Horror will not grieve them, and the angels will welcome them, (saying): This is your Day which ye were promised." (Q: 21.98-103)

From the above, we understand that all the pious Muslims (*"unto whom kindness hath gone forth before from us"*) shall not be even touched or brought close to the encompassing flames of the hellfire. Thus, it is not merely the martyrs, but all those, who do not deserve to be thrown in the burning fires of hell, shall remain completely immune from even the slightest of pains and tortures of hellfire.

*"Our Lord! Surely whomsoever Thou makes enter the fire, him Thou has indeed **brought to disgrace**, and there shall be no helpers for the unjust."* (Q: 3.192)

The expression *"brought to disgrace"* needs particular attention. Entering the fire is a sign of a person being shamed, humiliated, disgraced by Allah. Since the Qur'an (19.71) confirms that Muslims shall enter hell, this means that Allah has decreed that all Muslims must experience shame, humiliation, and disgrace. Allah obviously delights in humiliating his followers since he has decreed their descent into hell. However, the following verse says exactly opposite.

"O ye who believe! Turn to Allah with sincere repentance: In the hope that your Lord will remove from you your ills and admit you to Gardens beneath which Rivers flow,- the Day that Allah will not permit to be humiliated the Prophet and those who believe with him." (Q: 66.8)

Thus the above two verses introduce an additional problem. Allah says that neither Muhammad nor the believers will be abased, disgraced, humiliated etc., contradicting the verse 19.71 which says that believers shall enter hell and therefore will be disgraced.

Even if we force-believe that all the Muslims will go to paradise and kafirs will enter hell, then also we are not sure which sect of Islam will escape hellfire because every sect of Islam believes that they are following the real Islam. There are hundreds of sects and sub-sects in Islam. Different schools of thought offer different explanations as to what qualifies one as a believer. So who is destined to hellfire?

Orthodox Sunni Muslims strongly believe that they will escape hellfire. Teachers of Sunni law have argued that "Islam" means Sunni Islam only, and sects such as Shiaa, Ahmedi, Sufi etc, will also be sent to hell. In trying to explain why all the other sects are displeasing to Allah, Sunnis offer the following verse.

"Of those who split up their religion and became schismatics, each sect exulting in its tenets." (Q: 30.32)

Sunnis make up nearly ninety percent of all Muslims. Now, if we assume that only Sunnis can escape hellfire we are making a mistake, because it leads to another question. According to Bukhari,

"Narrated Abu Huraira: I heard Allah's Apostle saying, I heard Allah's Apostle saying, 'From my followers there will be a crowd of 70,000 in number who will enter Paradise whose faces will glitter as the moon.'" (Bukhari: 8.76.550)
"Narrated Sahl bin Sa`d: The Prophet said, "Verily! 70,000 of my followers will enter Paradise altogether; so that the first and the last amongst them will enter at the same time, and their faces will be glittering like the bright full moon." (Bukhari: 4.54.470).

"Narrated Ibn `Abbas: Allah's Apostle said, Behold! There was a multitude filling the horizon, it was said to me, 'This is your nation out of whom seventy thousand shall enter Paradise without reckoning.'" (Bukhari: 7.71.606)

Since there is no other place beyond paradise and hell, the billion plus Muslims will burn into hellfire except those lucky 70,000 Muslims. Now, how to identify these 70,000 people? Tabari recorded,

"I asked the Messenger of Allah how many prophets there were. He replied, '124,000'." (Tabari: I.323).

Logically, all the previous Prophets of Allah has first preference to enter paradise. It means, there is no vacancy in paradise, and already 54,000 Prophets had been turned away. Therefore, all the present, past and future Muslims will go to hell along with the kafirs in spite of practicing Islam sincerely. However, there are more confusions. Bukhari wrote,

"Narrated `Ali: Allah's Apostle said, 'Every created soul has his place written for him either in Paradise or in the Hell Fire'" (Bukhari: 6.60.473).

But according to the Qur'an,

"And ye shall be sorted out into three classes" (Q: 56.7)

Therefore, where the third group of people will go? No one knows.

Hell and hellfire were brought into existence by Muhammad's hallucination and weird imagination. He was schizophrenic. When he wanted to lure the Jews and Christians in Islam, he revealed the following verses, according to which the Jews and Christians can also escape hellfire.

"Those who believe (in the Qur'an), those who follow the Jewish (scriptures), and the Sabians and the Christians, – any who believe in Allah and the Last Day, and work righteousness, – on them shall be no fear, nor shall they grieve." (Q: 5.69)

"Those who believe in the Qur'an...and the Christians...shall have their reward with their Lord; on them shall be no fear, nor they shall grieve" (Q: 2.62)

However, the clever Jews and Christians paid little attention to Muhammad realizing that he was an imposter. It made Muhammad frustrated and Allah revealed the following verses, according to which no infidel can escape hellfire.

"And whoever seeks a religion other than Islam, it will never be accepted of him, and in the hereafter he will be one of the losers". (Q: 3.85)

"Those who reject (Truth), among the People of the Book and among the Polytheists, will be in Hell Fire, to dwell therein (for aye). They are the worst of creatures" (Q: 98.6).

"But those who reject Islam and are disbelievers, denying our Signs and Revelations, they shall be the owners of the Hell Fire." (Q: 5.86)

"O Children of Israel! Worship Allah, my Lord and your Lord. Whoever joins other gods with Allah-Allah will forbid him the Paradise and the Fire will be his abode" (Q: 5.72).

The descriptions of hellfire are so vivid that Muslims are mentally paralyzed at the very thought of it. That is why they cannot see the deception of Muhammad. Whenever an analytical discussion is made about Islam, Muslims quickly proclaim scientific miracles in Qur'an, but what they talk is not science but pseudo-science.

"Narrated Abu Jamra Ad−Dabi: I used to sit with Ibn `Abbas in Mecca. Once I had a fever and he said (to me), 'Cool your fever with Zamzam water, for Allah's Apostle said: 'It, (the Fever) is from the heat of the (Hell) Fire; so, cool it with water (or Zamzam water)." (Bukhari: 4.54.483)

"Narrated Rafi` bin Khadij: I heard the Prophet saying, 'Fever is from the heat of the Hell Fire; so cool it with water.'" (Bukhari: 4.54.484)

"Narrated Abu Huraira and `Abdullah bin `Umar: Allah's Apostle said, "If it is very hot, then pray the Zuhr prayer when it becomes (a bit) cooler, as the severity of the heat is from the raging of the Hell−fire." (Bukhari: 1.10.510)

If a person finds science in the above quotes, then he will find enough science in tribal witchcraft also. Some verses are even more ridiculous. Paradise and hell are living creatures and they can argue with each other.

"Narrated Abu Huraira, 'The Prophet explained, 'Paradise and Hell argued.... Allah said to the Hell Fire, 'You are my (means of) punishment by which I torment whoever I wish of my slaves'." (Bukhari: 6.60.373)

"Narrated by Abu Huraira, Allah's Apostle said, 'The Hell Fire complained to its Lord saying, "O my Lord! My different parts are eating each other up." Hence, He allowed it to take two breaths, one in winter and the other in summer. This is the reason for the severe heat and bitter cold you find in weather. "' (Bukhari: 4.54.482)

If hellfire is a living creature, then how different parts of the same body can eat each other? Can a cannibal eat himself? Secondly, how hellfire can be the reason of both 'severe heat' and 'bitter cold'?

"Narrated Abu Huraira: Allah's Apostle said, "Your (ordinary) fire is one of 70 parts of the (Hell) Fire." Someone asked, "O Allah's Apostle This (ordinary) fire would have been sufficient (to torture the unbelievers)," Allah's Apostle said, "The (Hell) Fire has 69 parts more than the ordinary (worldly) fire, each part is as hot as this (worldly) fire." (Bukhari: 4.54.487).

The fire which is sixty-nine times hotter than ordinary fire cannot produce bitter cold. Science does not go along with blind faith but pseudo-science does. Is hellfire already started or is it a futuristic event? Even Allah does not know. According to Bukhari, hellfire is already started.

"The Prophet said: 'I was shown the Hell Fire and the majority of its dwellers were women who are disbelievers or ungrateful.'" (Bukhari: 1.2.28)

But according to Qur'an, it is not yet started.

"When the disastrous calamity comes; and Hell Fire shall be placed in full view for all to see, then for him who rebelled, Hell Fire will be his home." (Q: 79.34)

"When the event befalleth, there is no denying that it will befall, abasing (some), exalting (others)" (Q: 56.1, 2, 3)

"And Hell is brought near that day; on that day man will remember, but how will the remembrance (then avail him)?" (Q: 89.23)

If this is a futuristic event, how Muhammad saw the hellfire? If it is already started, then above verses are false. Whom to believe, Allah or Muhammad? Allah definitely needs tons of fuel to keep the hellfire on. Qur'an says, the stones, Pagan Gods and stubborn unbelievers make the fuel of hell.

"O you who have believed, protect yourselves and your families from a Fire whose fuel is people and stones..." (Q: 66.6)

"...then fear the Fire, whose fuel is men and stones, prepared for the disbelievers." (Q: 2.24)

"Indeed, you (disbelievers) and what you worship other than God are the firewood of Hell. Had these (false deities) been (actual) gods, they would not have come to it, but all are eternal therein." (Q: 21.98-99)

These verses are illogical. The bodies of the disbelievers will only offer a given and finite amount of fuel for fire. Eventually there will be nothing left to burn. This is same for all the deities. Secondly; all leaving creatures will ultimately leave their bodies on the earth at the time of death. It is the "soul" that will either enter hell or paradise, not the body. Since the soul is without body, it is obviously without cells, without neural receptors, and therefore, without pain.

"I will drive him into Hellfire ... it lets nothing remain and leaves nothing (unburned), altering the skins." (Q: 74.26-29)

This verse contradicts itself. It says, the hellfire leaves nothing unburned and at the same time it also says that the hellfire alters the skin. If nothing is left then there is no question of alteration of skin. In some verses Allah's stupidity takes one step further. Now, the souls can have replaceable skin and belly.

"… every time their skins are roasted through We will replace them with other skins so they may taste the punishment." (Q: 4.56)

"… poured upon their heads will be scalding water by which is melted that within their bellies and (their) skins." (Q: 22.19-20)

Muslim scholars have already noticed this inconsistency. They came out with a wonderful logic – hellfire consists of smokeless fire that *"burns, but does not consume"* (Ahmad, 2006, p. 351). But how a fire can burn without fuel? Secondly, if the fire does not consume one's flesh, there is no pain. Pain is caused by neural receptors in the brain alerting the living creature to cells being destroyed. If the fire does not consume one's flesh, no cells are destroyed, and thus there is no pain. Dead bodies do not feel pain because the brain is dead. This is what the real science says.

Eternal flames cannot be a true punishment to be feared. If the fire is never-ending, there is enough time to develop a higher tolerance of pain. It is a fact that humans can reach a mental state where they do not feel pain; example, the Buddhist monks in Vietnam can set themselves on fire without showing any reaction while burning to death (Batchelor, 1994, p. 354). They have nothing to fear from hellfire.

Allah is so revengeful that he has arranged chains, yokes, and fetters in his hell for the disbelievers, who will be tied up with chains and dragged with yokes on their necks (Q: 76.4, 73.12, 34.33, 40.71, 69.32). But these lead to another doubt. Allah says that the hellfire *"lets nothing remain and leaves nothing (unburned)…"* (Q: 74.26-29). If nothing remains, then the chains, yokes, and fetters are of what use?

Next confusion is about the food of the hell. Qur'an says, the kafirs will eat the bitter Zaqqum fruit – *"Is this better as a welcome, or the tree of Zaqqum?"*, and *"Lo! the tree of Zaqqum, the food of the sinner."* (Q: 44.43-4). But the verse 88.6 says, the unbelievers will eat only Dari tree – *"No food for them save bitter thorn-fruit (Dari)"*. Another verse says, the unbelievers will eat only pus and filth – *"Nor hath he any food except the corruption from the washing of wounds"* (Q: 69.36). Yet other verses say, *"This - so let them taste it - is scalding water and (foul) purulence. And other (punishments) of its type (in various) kinds."* (Q: 38.57-58).

Few doubts are immediately raised. The first one obviously is, how Qur'anic verses are contradicting each other. Secondly, how a Zaqqum tree can grow in hell, or boiling water can be available to drink whose fire is sixty-nine times hotter than normal fire? Tree cannot grow in fire, and water will instantly vaporize in such an extreme hot atmosphere. Third; if the hellfire leaves nothing unburned, then how festering pus can ooze out of decaying skin?

Therefore, we can see how absurd the Qur'anic hellfire theory is. It is a sick and disgusting imagination, and tremendous distortion of reality. This contradictory doctrine leaves Muslims with problems; it produces more problems than it does answer. Also, with such confusion and contradiction, can a Muslim really trust what Allah or Muhammad says? More importantly, can Muslims assure non-Muslims that they are safe to believe in Allah and his messenger when the Islamic source material is filled with contradictions and confusion, specifically in relation to significant matters such as the issue of eternal life?

The Islamic doctrine of Judgment Day is equally absurd like the hellfire. The ultimate source of Muhammad's notions of the Last Day was Syriac Christianity which was alien to contemporary Arabian thought (Warraq, 1995, p. 154). Hence, many pagan philosophers mocked this absurd idea. They asked pertinent questions;

> *"How are the dead raised up? And with what body do they come? What was rotten cannot become fresh again, nor scattered limbs be reunited, nor what was consumed be restored. . . . Men swallowed by the sea, men torn and devoured by wild beasts, cannot be given back by the earth"* (Momigliano, 1963, p. 161).

The argument was – what is rotten cannot become fresh again. Qur'an says,

> *"On the Day of Judgment We shall gather, them together, prone on their faces, blind, dumb, and deaf: their abode will be Hell: every time it shows abatement, We shall increase from them the fierceness of the Fire."* (Q: 17.97)

> *"That is their recompense, because they rejected Our signs, and said, "When we are reduced to bones and broken dust, should we really be raised up (to be) a new Creation?"* (Q: 17.98)

By seeing their disbelief, Muhammad declared,

> *"Do they not consider that Allah, Who created the heavens and the earth, **is able to create their like**, and He has appointed for them a doom about which there is no doubt?"* (Q: 17.99)

The statement "... *is able to create their like*" needs to be noted. There is one objection to such an account that Antony Flew (1984, p. 107) has formulated;

> *"Certainly Allah the omnipotent must have "power to create their like". But in making Allah talk in these precise terms of what He might indeed choose to do, the Prophet was speaking truer than he himself appreciated. For thus to produce even the most indistinguishably similar object after the first one has been totally destroyed and disappeared is to produce not the same object again, but a replica. To punish or to reward a replica, reconstituted on Judgment Day, for the sins or virtues of the old Antony Flew dead and cremated in 1984 is as inept and as unfair as it would be to reward or to punish one identical twin for what was in fact done by the other".*

If Muslim apologists say "all is possible for Allah", they are actually admitting the essential irrationality of the Islamic doctrine of reconstitution. As Warraq (1995, p. 155) argues,

> *"The Muslim account is further dogged by contradictions. We are told all mankind will have to face their Maker (and Remaker) on the Judgment Day, and yet sura 2.159 and sura 3.169 tell us that those holy warriors who died fighting in God's cause are alive and in His presence now. God has evidently raised them from the dead before the Last Day. Similarly, without waiting for the Last Day, God will send the enemies of Islam straight to hell. Interesting*

questions arise in this age of organ transplants. If a holy warrior dies fighting for the propagation of Islam, and at the very moment of his death has one of his organs, let us say his heart, transplanted into someone else lying in a hospital waiting for the surgical operation and the organ to save his life, how will the holy warrior be reconstituted. In this case, the same body will not have been refashioned; indeed, it will only be a replica with a different heart."

The psychologists say that the most effective way of securing dominance is by arousing someone's fear. Lovecraft's (1973, p. 51) famously quoted line, *"The oldest and strongest emotion of mankind is fear, and the oldest and strongest kind of fear is fear of the unknown"* is only the beginning of it. Lovecraft continues, *"These facts few psychologists will dispute, and their admitted truth must establish for all time the generousness and dignity of the weirdly horrible tales as a literary form."*

The second one is favor. Whatever man does, he does out of fear or to gain favor. Where we have bribery we usually have blackmail. These two factors severely influence judgment. Muhammad had very skillfully exploited man's psychological mechanism, which consists of fear and favor. In the hellfire doctrine the fear factor works and offsets the scale of common sense of the people. Though Allah gave horrible description of hell; neither Allah nor Muhammad could provide a single evidence of the existence of hell and its fire. They contradicted each other on many points. It means either Allah or Muhammad, or both of them were damn liars. In spite of this, Muslims are always one step ahead of their opponents to give a special explanation why hellfire is real. But the clarifications only raise further questions. If they apply a little logic and common sense, they will be able to realize that hellfire theory is pure absurd; it relies upon ignorance and thrives in it. The deeper one digs, the more obvious the deception becomes. But regretfully; skepticism and rational enquiry are practically nonexistent in Islam.

1.3: The embarrassment of the satanic verses

Traditional Islamic sources admit that Muhammad was at one time inspired by Satan to put some verses into the Qur'an. When Muhammad first began preaching in Mecca, he thought that the native Arabs would accept his religion. But the Arabs were not receptive to him which made him angry, and he started taunting them for years by insulting their religion and Gods. They refused all dealings with him and his group. Eventually to appease them, Muhammad recited some Qur'anic verses,

"Have you then considered the al-Lat and al-Uzza and Manat, the third, the last ... these are the exalted Gharaniq (a high flying bird) **whose intercession is approved"**. (Q: 53.19-20)

Al-Lat, al-Uzza and Manat were some of the local idols worshipped in Mecca. Previously Muhammad had spoken against them in his monotheist preaching but now he recited that their "intercession is approved". This made the Arabs very pleased and the boycott was lifted shortly. Bukhari confirms that after Muhammad recited Surah fifty-three the Quraysh Arabs accepted him and prayed with him.

"Narrated Ibn Abbas: The Prophet ... prostrated while reciting An-Najm (Sura

95

53) and with him prostrated the Muslims, the pagans (the Quraysh), the jinns, and all human beings". (Bukhari: 2.19.177)

Soon Muhammad realized that by acknowledging the local idols he had made a terrible blunder. He had undermined his own position that of the sole intermediary between Allah and the people, and by doing so he made his new religion indistinguishable from pagan beliefs and hence redundant. So he retracted and said that the two verses acknowledging pagan idols were satanic verses, i.e., the verses inspired by Lucifer, the Biblical Satan. This was his most embarrassing moment.

"Then Gabriel came to the apostle and said, 'What have you done, Muhammad? You have read to these people something I did not bring you from God and you have said what He did not say to you'." (Ishaq: 166)

Islam crumbled in the wake of the Prophet's satanic indulgence. He desperately tried to make amends for the satanic verses and recited the following verse.

"Allah forgiveth not (The sin of) joining other gods with Him; but He forgiveth whom He pleaseth other sins than this: one who joins other gods with Allah, Hath strayed far, far away (from the right)." (Q: 4.116)

Subsequently, the relevant verses were also modified with the final form what is now in the modern Qur'an.

"Have ye thought upon Al-Lat and Al-'Uzza. And another, the third (goddess), Manat? What! for you the male sex, and for Him, the female? Behold, such would be indeed a division most unfair!" (Q: 53.19-22)

Many of his followers left him on this account realizing that Muhammad was either making up the Qur'an, or he was delusional (Sina, 2008, p. 16). The shame of defeat was so much that Muhammad and Abu Bakr had to flee through window to run away from Mecca. On their way out of town, both hid in a cave for fear the Meccans would find them (Winn, 2004, p. 587). Muhammad just hammered a nail into his own prophetic coffin.

"When the Messenger decided upon departure, he went to Bakr and the two of them left by a window in the back of Abu's house and went to a cave in Thawr, a mountain below Mecca". (Ishaq: 223)

"The Messenger came back to Mecca and found that its people were more determined to oppose him and to abandon his religion, except for a few weak people who believed in him". (Tabari: VI.118)

However, after this blunder Muhammad was more careful not to make the mistake again. Muslims are very uncomfortable with the satanic verses episode, and this had been the subject of endless and bitter controversy (Walker, 2002, p. 111). But there is no reason to reject this incident. It was recorded by devout Muslims;

like, al-Wikidi, al-Baydawi, al-Zamakshari, Tabari, Ibn Ishaq, Ibn Hisham, Ibn Sa'd and Bukhari. It is most unlikely that such a story would have been fabricated by all of them. Ahmed (1999, p. i; 1998, p. 70) wrote,

> *"The Satanic verses incident constituted a standard element in the historical memory of the Muslim community in the first 150 years of Islam, and was recorded by almost all prominent scholars working in the fields of tafsir and sirah-Maghazi".*

> *"The Satanic verses incident is narrated in numerous reports (between 18 and 25, depending on how one reckons an independent riwayah) scattered in the sirah nabawiyyah and tafsir literature originating in the first two centuries of Islam. The indications are that the incident formed a fairly standard element in the historical memory of the early Muslim community regarding the life of its founder".*

While this event is well documented in Islamic sources, current day Islamic leaders rarely tell Muslims or the general public about it. They do so because they believe a Prophet could not sin this way. However, this is to edit history to make it fit their view of Muhammad; we must not do this. Our view of Muhammad should come from history, and not from what we would like him to be.

We can make three logical conclusions from this satanic verses incident. First; a verse can be modified or deleted at a later date. Second; it casts a shadow over the veracity on Muhammad's entire claim to be a Prophet, and finally; Satan proved that Qur'an is not a miracle. Qur'an challenges, *"produce a Surah of the like thereof, and call your witness beside Allah if ye are truthful"* (Q: 2.23); Satan took the challenge and did it. Did Muhammad carefully planned a ploy to win the hearts of the Meccans, or was it his subconscious mind that had suggested to him a sure formula which provided a practical road to unanimity? In context of the satanic verses, Tabari and Ibn Sa'd recorded these disgraceful words of Muhammad,

> *"I have fabricated things against God and have imputed to Him words which He has not spoken".* (Tabari: VI.111).

> *"I ascribed to Allah, what He had not said".* (Ibn Sa'd, Kitab Al-Tabaqat Al-Kabir, vol. 1)

This single confession of Muhammad is enough to disqualify him of his prophetic claim. Muhammad said that he was deceived by Satan and a revelation from Allah confirmed it. But how can we be sure that the second revelation was also not from Satan? The guaranty of "genuineness" of one revelation cannot be another revelation. If Muhammad could be deceived by Satan once, how could he know on all the other occasions that he had not been deceived? How can we ignore the possibility that Gabriel was actually the Satan himself in disguise, and hence, the whole Qur'an is satanic? Allah made some big challenges in the Qur'an,

> *"Say: 'Then bring ye a Book from Allah, which is a better guide than either of them, that I may follow it! (do), if ye are truthful!'"* (Q: 28.49)

"And if you are in doubt as to that which We have revealed to Our servant, then produce a chapter like it and call on your witnesses besides Allah if you are truthful". (Q: 2.23)

"Or they say: He hath invented it. Say: Then bring ten surahs, the like thereof, invented, and call on everyone ye can beside Allah, if ye are truthful!" (Q: 11.13)

"Say: Verily, though mankind and the jinn should assemble to produce the like of this Qur'an, they could not produce the like thereof though they were helpers one of another." (Q: 17.88)

"Or say they: He hath invented it? Nay, but they will not believe! Let them then produce a recital like unto it,- If (it be) they speak the truth!" (Q: 52.33-4)

"Or do they say: He has forged it? Say: Then bring a Surah like this and invite whom you can besides Allah, if you are truthful." (Q: 10.38)

Satan took Allah's challenge and easily produced "a Surah like this". Muslims believe that Qur'an is miraculous in beauty, and no one can make anything to compare to it because it is divine. Satan produced the verses, and Muhammad spoke those words from Satan, but everyone including Muhammad himself thought that those verses were part of the Qur'an. Surely those satanic verses sound exactly like those of the Qur'an. If not, then surely Muhammad, his followers and the Quraysh would never have accepted them. The second point is related to Qur'anic verses 15.39-40. According to these two verses, Satan can deceive and mislead only those who are not sincere to Allah. Therefore, if Satan were able to deceive Muhammad and distort the revelations of Allah, it follows that Muhammad could not have been a sincere slave of Allah.

There is another way of looking at this divine mystification. Qur'an says,

"Perfected is the Word of thy Lord in truth and justice. There is naught that can change His words. He is the Hearer, the Knower". (Q: 6.115).

Qur'an also confirms that the Bible, or in the Islamic language, Taurat, Zabur and Anjeel are the words of God. Thus, they cannot be tampered with, and one can rely upon the truthfulness of the stories that have been narrated therein. Therefore, based on the Qur'anic sanction, we can rely upon the truthfulness of the Bible. Bible says, *"But the Prophet who speaks a word presumptuously in My [God] name which I have not commanded him to speak . . . that Prophet shall die"*. (Deuteronomy: 18.20).

From the above statement we can conclude that either Muhammad was a false Prophet, or Qur'an was false. In any case the loser is Muhammad. The satanic verses incident confirms that Qur'an was corrupted. But then Qur'an (6.115) also says that no one can change God's words. Therefore, Qur'an itself confirms that Qur'an is falsified. There is another important point to note. Muhammad really had a very painful death. He died as a result of eating poison-mixed food that he did not know about (Bukhari: 5.59.713, 719, 731) – *"O `Aisha! I still feel the pain caused by the food I ate at Khaibar, and at this time, I feel as if my aorta is being cut from that poison."* (Bukhari: 5.59.713). If he were a real Prophet, Allah would have warned him in advance by a timely revelation.

1.4: Allah approves treachery and lying

The value and importance of truth is proclaimed in every religion. Bible does not condone or allow for deceit of any kind (Revelation: 22.15). Believers are commanded to keep their oaths even to their own detriment (Joshua: 9; Psalm: 15.4). Bible describes Jesus as Truth (John: 14.6) and instructs that the believers should be holy as God is Holy (Leviticus: 19.2; Peter: 1.16), you will know the truth, and the truth will set you free. (John: 8.32). In Hinduism; the guiding principles of the Vedas are truthfulness and nonviolence. Muslim apologists repeatedly tell us that telling lies is an unpardonable sin in Islam. Since Qur'an is a cheap copy of the Bible, it tries to condemn falsehood in few verses.

"When you speak, be just, even if it affects your own kinsmen. Fulfill the covenant of Allah". (Q: 6.152).

"And cover not Truth with falsehood, nor conceal the Truth when ye know (what it is)." (Q: 2.42)

"Say: It is Allah Who gives guidance towards truth, is then He Who gives guidance to truth more worthy to be followed, or he who finds not guidance (himself) unless he is guided?" (Q: 10.35)

Now, based on the above verses, we should never expect Muhammad to tell lies, or to fervently incite other Muslims to gleefully resort to lies and deception, but No! The statement – lying is the greatest sin in Islam – itself is the greatest lie ever told; lying is a core part of the religion of Islam. Both Muhammad and Allah were habitual liars. Muhammad even taught his followers how to lie and deceive because deception is an authorized Islamic strategy. In Islam lying is not only permitted, but actually fostered and sometimes even commanded. Though Muhammad did his best to pretend that he was chosen by the same God who gave missions to Moses and Jesus, but with regard to lying and deceit he stuck to his tribal culture. Allah claims at least thirty times in the Qur'an that he misleads people astray, and that he is the best deceiver (Wallahu khairul Makirin) (Q: 3.54; 4.88, 143; 6.39, 126; 7.178, 186; 8.30; 13.27, 31; 14.4; 16.93; 17.97; 30.29; 35.8; 36.8-10; 39.23; 40.33, 34, 74; 42.44, 46; 74.31). Even the first rightly guided Caliph Abu Bakr said (cited Khalid, 2005 p. 99), *"I swear to Allah that I do not feel safe from Allah's cunning even if one of my feet is already inside Paradise...."*. As for Islam's alleged concern with truth, Islamic faith is to free inquiry what the Mafia is to free enterprise.

God playing with men's souls is an embarrassing thing in a religion. How are Muslims to differentiate between Allah and Satan? How a "khairul Makirin" can be trusted? Satan does all he can to keep an unsaved person deceived and in darkness.

For Muslims, Muhammad was the "perfect example" to be followed by all. This "perfect example" Muhammad believed that lying was acceptable and even taught his followers how to lie and how to expiate (make amends for) an oath. Bukhari recorded Muhammad's disgraceful words,

> "*Narrated by Zahdam; Once we were in the house of Abu Musa ... by Allah, Allah willing, if ever I take an oath to do something, and later on I find that it is more beneficial to do something different, I will do the thing which is better, and give expiation for my oath*". (Bukhari: 4.53.361).

If we translate the above Hadith in common English, it means – "By the will of Allah, I am a liar; you should not trust me. You are forewarned". Now, let us read the above Hadith in conjunction with following Hadith. These two quotes if joined together speak volumes.

> "*Abu Musa reported the Apostle of Allah as saying: Make intercession to me, you will be rewarded, for Allah decrees what He wishes by the tongue of His Prophet*" (Sunnan Abu Dawud: 3.5112).

Therefore, the conclusion is, Allah speaks through a liar's mouth. Nobody had seen or heard Allah, and Qur'an was revealed through a habitual liar. Then, where is the trustworthiness of the Qur'an? The above two ahadith are enough to destroy the entire religious credential of the Qur'an. How can a real God speak through an immoral and untrustworthy person? Lying and deception had found a place in the Sharia law. It permits a Muslim to tell lies if and when necessary for the benefit of Islam. The Qur'anic word "Sharia" means path of spiritual salvation (Shienbaum & Hasan, 2006, p. 200). This word was used to legitimize political governance; therefore, it is possible to achieve "spiritual" salvation by telling lies. As Keller (1999, p. 745) commented, "*When it is possible to achieve such an aim (the victory of Islam) by lying but not by telling the truth, it is permissible to lie if attaining the goal is permissible.*" Imam Jafar Sadiq (cited Richardson, 2006, p. 170) advised,

> "*One, who exposes something from our religion, is like one who intentionally kills us.... You belong to a religion that whosoever conceals it, Allah will honor him and whosoever reveals it, Allah will disgrace and humiliate him*".

This is called al-taqiyya (legal deception) in Islam which allows the Muslims to literally deny any aspect of their faith, and defined as, "*Taqiyya is merely uttering of the tongue, while the heart is comfortable with faith.*" (Richardson, 2006, p. 172). The ultimate purpose of taqiyya is to confuse and split the enemy so that they can be defeated easily. Taqiyya was originally a Shiaa practice. The Shiaas used to protect their faith from Sunnis by practicing taqiyya (Miller, 1997, p. 433; Lewis, 2003, p. 25). The sixth Shiaa imam made taqiyya obligatory for the Shiaas to make sure the faith would survive (Nasr, 2007, p. 54). However, now the whole Muslim world practices it. Deception for the cause of Islam was one main reason Islam spread in Malaysia and Indonesia. Muhammad saw nothing wrong in practicing duplicity. According to Allah, treaties are not binding (Q: 47.35; 2.224, 225; 66.1, 2; 16.91, 94) and used to provide time to regroup and rearm. Muhammad's common practice was to say one thing and do exactly the opposite if something appealed to him otherwise. He sent men to kill people unaware in their homes and also gave them permission to tell lies in order to deceive the people being killed.

If a god needs to lie to propagate his faith, there is a problem. Fortunately for Islam, a suicide bomber cannot return to demand a refund. The dishonest god of Islam is not worthy of a religion, devotion, sacrifice, or martyrdom. Islam is nothing more than a wicked plan of a vulgar imposter for making profit. The deception is at the very core of Islam. I cannot find any difference between Muhammad and a con man on the street.

Islam is the most hateful and violent fraud ever perpetrated on humankind. Both Allah and Qur'an were created from the sick mind of a criminally insane pervert and moral monster. Every established religion has produced some spiritual books which they claim to be holy. The trustworthiness of these books is often doubted by the rivalries. But Qur'an is a book which is proven to be the most untrustworthy and most hateful amongst all. The author of the Qur'an is a deceiving god and his spokesman is a confirmed liar by his own conviction. Though Qur'an claims to be a divine guidance, in reality it revealed the path to damnation.

I agree that to accuse someone of being a liar is quite an insult. But lying is practiced so much by common Muslims and the scholars alike that it became an integral part of their religion. So if I do not call them liars and put them on the same line with non-Muslims, it would be an insult to the rest of the humanity. Muhammad started it and it is continued throughout the history of Islam, and now the most respected scholars allow lying as a means to propagate Islam.

According to Ibn Kathir's Tafsir – the Qur'anic verse 3.28 (cited Richardson, 2006, p. 173),

"Abu Ad-Darda said, 'We smile in the face of some people although our hearts curse them'."

Sunnis often say that the doctrine of taqiyya is a Shiaa practice, but according to Ibn Kathir's Tafsir, taqiyya is indeed a doctrine for all Muslims and it is allowed until the Day of Resurrection. Taqiyya holds a central place in Islam. Since the god is not trustworthy, the holy book is not trustworthy and the Prophet was not trustworthy, how the followers can be trustworthy? A poisonous tree produces only poisonous fruits – the evidence screams out from the pages of the Qur'an.

1.5: Allah is greedy

"Ministers say that they teach charity. This is natural. All beggars teach that others should give."

Robert Ingersoll

The God, who made the world and everything in it, being Lord of heaven and earth, does not need anything, since He himself gives to all mankind life and breath and everything. He is sufficient, or all-sufficient, and therefore needs not anything from without Himself to support Himself, or to make Himself happy. He is the "first" of Beings, the first and the last; therefore His existence is not owing to any; nor has He received any assistance or support from any; being self-existent, He must be self-subsistent; as He existed of Himself. Such a God can receive nothing from His creatures. But in Islam, Allah borrows money from Muslims to wage jihad against the non-Muslims. More precisely, Allah uses Muslims' money (hard cash) to buy war implements to fight the non-Muslims.

"Ye will not attain unto piety until ye spend of that which ye love. And whatsoever ye spend, Allah is Aware thereof." (Q: 3.92).

"Who is it that will lend unto Allah a goodly loan, so that He may give it increase manifold?" (Q: 2.245)

"The likeness of those who spend their wealth in Allah's way is as the likeness of a grain which groweth seven ears, in every ear a hundred grains. Allah giveth increase manifold to whom He will." (Q: 2.261).

"All that you spend in the Way of Allah shall be repaid to you. You shall not be wronged." (Q: 8.60).

"If ye loan to Allah, a beautiful loan, He will double it to your (credit), and He will grant you Forgiveness: for Allah is most ready to appreciate (service), Most Forbearing". (Q: 64.17).

"And whatsoever ye spend (for good) He replaceth it. And He is the Best of Providers". (Q: 34.39)

"Those who lend a good loan to Allah, shall be repaid in multiples. They shall receive a generous wage". (Q: 57.18).

When Muhammad demanded money from the wealthy Banu Qaynuqa Jews, they laughed at him by saying that his Allah was a poor god. This made Allah angry and the following verse was revealed.

"Allah has certainly heard the saying of those who said: Surely Allah is poor and we are rich. I will record what they say, and their killing the prophets unjustly, and I will say: Taste the chastisement of burning." (Q: 3.181).

These verses prove that Allah is not self-sufficient. He is a dependent god. He cannot sustain himself; it is man who sustains him. Also, if the man refuses to sustain him, he becomes angry. If Allah is really the lord of creation in no way he would be limited by it. A true God cannot be part of finite reality.

"And know that whatever ye take as spoils of war, lo! a fifth thereof is for Allah, and for the messenger..." (Q: 8.41)

"It has been narrated on the authority of Abdullah b. 'Umar that the Messenger

of Allah used to give (from the spoils of war) to small troops seat on expeditions .... and Khums (one-fifth of the total spoils) was to be reserved (for Allah and His Apostle) in all cases." (Muslim: 19.4337)

"Allah divided the booty stolen from the first caravan after he made spoils permissible. He gave four-fifths to those He had allowed to take it and one-fifth to His Apostle." (Ishaq: 288)

Now, according to Qur'an (Q: 3.180, 15.23, 19.40, 19.80, 21.89, 28.58), Allah is the inheritor of the heavens and earth. He will also inherit from the infidels and other creatures on the earth. Qur'an also says (Q: 2.116, 3.189, 20.6, 21.19, 57.2), Allah is supposed to be the ultimate owner of all things. Another two verses say,

"Surely Allah's is the kingdom of the heavens and the earth." (Q: 9.116)

*"To Allah belong all things in heaven and earth: verily **Allah is free of all wants**, worthy of all praise."* (Q: 31.26)

If Allah is free of all wants why in other verses he is asking for a loan?

By plundering in the name of Allah Muhammad gathered a vast wealth for himself and at the time of his death he was one richest man in Arabia. When he became *de facto* ruler of Arabia, many Muslim noblemen would visit him for advice. Muhammad found a good opportunity to make a profit. Allah, through a timely revelation, prescribed certain amount of money to be paid to the Prophet by anyone who wanted to meet and talk to him and the payment should be made before the consultation.

"O you who believe! When you consult the Messenger, then offer something in charity before your consultation; that is better for you and purer; but if you do not find, then surely Allah is Forgiving, Merciful." (Q: 58.12)

By seeing the greed of Muhammad, the visitors preferred to stay away from him. This frustrated Muhammad and the next verse was revealed.

"Is it that ye are afraid of spending sums in charity before your private consultation (with him)? If, then, ye do not so, and Allah forgives you, then (at least) establish regular prayer; practice regular charity; and obey Allah and His Messenger. And Allah is well-acquainted with all that ye do." (Q: 58.13)

In another verse Allah addresses his messenger directly and orders him to take alms from the wealthy Muslims, in order to purify and pardon them.

"Take alms out of their property, you would cleanse them and purify them thereby, and pray for them; surely your prayer is a relief to them." (Q: 9.103)

Such a God, who is the owner of everything, cannot be greedy. The real God is necessarily omnipotent – all powerful. But what does it mean to be all powerful? It means that there are no limits to God's power, to what He is capable of doing or achieving, and that there is absolutely nothing that can stop Him from achieving His desire (including that which it is necessarily impossible to do). He should have unlimited potential and unlimited possibilities. He can turn necessary impossibilities into possibilities. But the god of Islam is not unlimited in any sense (except it be for his greed, perhaps). Muslims can choose to believe whatever they want about Allah's abilities, but in reality Allah falls terribly short of omnipotence in any sense whatsoever, and he can provide no evidence of his unlimited potential. All that he has in the Qur'an are empty words inflated with human-like pride. A god who is injured by pride has not the courage and the strength to exist.

1.6: Satanic attributes to Allah

"Satan's successes are the greatest when he appears with the name of God on his lips."

Mahatma Gandhi

If we look at the ninety-nine names of Allah (Geisler & Saleeb, 1993, pp. 24-7), we will find many abusive names in that list. The plain truth is that the god of the Muslims is untrustworthy, cruel, angry, and proud – qualities not to be admired.

1. khairul makirin (the best deceiver):

    "And (the unbelievers) plotted and planned, and Allah too planned, and the best of planners is Allah." (Q: 3.54)

    "Verily, the hypocrites seek to deceive Allah, but it is He Who deceives them..." (Q: 4.142)

    "They plot and plan, and Allah too plans; but the best of planners is Allah." (Q: 8.30)

    "Those before them did (also) devise plots; but in all things the master-planning is Allah's." (Q: 13.42)

    "And when We make people taste of mercy after an affliction touches them, lo ! they devise plans against Our communication. Say: Allah is quicker to plan; surely Our messengers write down what you plan." (Q: 10.21)
    "And those before them did indeed scheme (makara), but all scheming (al-makru) is Allah's ..." (Q: 27.50)

The Qur'an itself testifies that Allah is the greatest of all "makirin". The term for scheme in Arabic is makara which denotes one who is a deceiver, one who is conniving, a schemer. It is always used in a negative sense. Allah is thus seen as the best of deceivers, the premiere schemer and conniving one. Why should anyone believe and follow a deceiving god? If anyone still have a doubt, he should consider Abu Bakr's testimony to the deceptive character of Allah (aforementioned), *"I swear to Allah that I do not feel safe from Allah's cunning even if one of my feet is already inside Paradise...."*. The testimony of Abu Bakr is consistent with the Qur'an which tells Muslims that they should not feel secure against the Makr or deception of Allah.

"Did they then feel secure against the plan of Allah?- but no one can feel secure from the Plan of Allah, except those (doomed) to ruin!" (Q: 7.99)

Abu Bakr being a true Muslim could not feel safe from Allah's deception even though he was promised paradise by Allah and Muhammad. If Allah is the greatest of all deceivers what hope do we have that the rest of the Qur'an can be trusted? Why should a deceiving god be followed?

Even Satan accused Allah of misleading him. When Allah commanded all the angels to worship Adam, Satan did not obey. Allah asked, *"O Iblis! what is your reason for not being among those who prostrated themselves?"* (Q: 15.32). Satan replied, *"O my Lord! Because you misled me, I shall indeed adorn the path of error for them (mankind) on the earth, and I shall mislead them all."* (Q: 15.39)

2. al mutakabbir (the proud one, the haughty one):

"He is Allah, than Whom there is no other Allah, the Sovereign Lord, the Holy One, Peace, the Keeper of Faith, the Guardian, the Majestic, the Compeller, the Superb. Glorified be Allah from all that they ascribe as partner (unto Him)." (Q: 59.23)

The name al-mutakabbir implies that Allah is haughty or arrogant. Allah being the most proud helps us to understand why Jinns and humans were created to worship him, apparently in order to feed his ego – *"I created the jinn and humankind only that they might worship Me."* (Q: 51.56). The ahadith expressly say that Allah loves nothing more than to be praised!

"Abdullah reported Allah's Messenger as saying: None is more self-respecting than Allah and it is because of this that He has prohibited abominable acts-both visible and invisible-and none loves His praise more than Allah Himself". (Muslim: 37.6646)
"Narrated Abu Wail: 'Abdullah (bin Mas'ud) said, 'None has more sense of ghaira than Allah... and none loves to be praised more than Allah does, and for this reason he praises himself". (Bukhari: 6.60.158, 6.60.161)

"Abdullah b. Mas'ud reported that Allah's Messenger said: None is more self-respecting than Allah ... and nothing is loved by Allah more than the praise of his oneself and it is because of this that He has praised Himself". (Muslim: 37.6647)

"Abdullah b. Mas'ud reported that Allah's Messenger said: None loves one's own praise more than Allah, the Exalted and Glorious, does. It is because of this that He has praised Himself, and none is more self-respecting than Allah ..." (Muslim: 37.6648)

Surprisingly, this is the one quality which Allah hates and condemns people to hell for.

"I shall turn away from My revelations those who magnify themselves wrongfully in the earth ..." (Q: 7.146)

"... so certainly evil is the dwelling place of the proud." (Q: 16.29)

"... is there not in hell an abode for the proud?" (Q: 39.60)

"Thus does Allah set a seal over the heart of every proud, haughty one." (Q: 40.35)

In other words, Allah is the most proud of them all (in 59.23, Allah calls himself holy), and yet condemns and hates this very quality when others have it despite the fact that he himself possesses it in all its fullness.

3.   al jabbar (the compeller, the oppressor, the tyrant):

"He is Allah, than Whom there is no other Allah, the Sovereign Lord, the Holy One, Peace, the Keeper of Faith, the Guardian, the Majestic, the Compeller, the Superb. Glorified be Allah from all that they ascribe as partner (unto Him)." (Q: 59.23)

Nothing can prevent Allah from compelling his creation upon what he wants. According to some scholars, the name means – He is the one who forces his creation upon what he commands and upon what he has forbidden. In other words, whatever Allah wills, his will is executed.

4.   al qahhar (the subduer):

Al qahhar is the one whose vengeance nobody can withstand. He humiliates oppressors, splits the spine of kings and emperors. He is the one besides whose might all creation is powerless, without whose power all beings are helpless. It means the overtaking of something or someone with the intention to humiliate him.

"One day the earth will be changed to a different earth, and so will be the heavens, and (men) will be marshaled forth, before Allah, the One, the Irresistible." (Q: 14.48)

"Say: Allah is the Creator of all things, and He is the One, the Supreme." (Q: 13.16).

"Say: 'Truly am I a Warner: no god is there but the one Allah, Supreme and Irresistible - The Lord of the heavens and the earth, and all between,- Exalted in Might, able to enforce His Will, forgiving again and again." (Q: 38.65-6)

"Be He Glorified! He is Allah, the One, the Absolute." (Q: 39.4)

"... That of Allah, the One the Irresistible!" (Q: 40.16)

5. al khafid (the abaser):

    Al khafid is the one who has lowered the status of those who do not believe in him (meaning abasing the unbelievers who occupy the lowest ranks of hell while exalting the believers to the highest ranks of paradise). Allah abases at will. Al khafid is the one, who lowers through humiliation,

    "Abasing (some), exalting (others);" (Q: 56.3)

    "Then do We abase him (to be) the lowest of the low," (Q: 95.5)

6. al mudhill (the humiliator):

    "Go ye, then, for four months, backwards and forwards, (as ye will), throughout the land, but know ye that ye cannot frustrate Allah (by your falsehood) but that Allah will cover with shame those who reject Him.." (Q: 9.2)

    "O Allah! Lord of Power (And Rule), Thou givest power to whom Thou pleasest, and Thou strippest off power from whom Thou pleasest: Thou enduest with honour whom Thou pleasest, and Thou bringest low whom Thou pleasest: In Thy hand is all good. Verily, over all things Thou hast power." (Q: 3.26)

    As per Qur'an Allah degrades whomever he dislikes. In classical Arabic definitions, Mudhill is an intensive epithet which denotes exceeding lowness or baseness. Mudhill (dishonorer) is similar to, but much more intensive and unpleasant than Khafid (humbler).

7. al mumit (the death giver):

    "O ye who believe! ... It is Allah that gives Life and Death, and Allah sees well all that ye do." (Q: 3.156)

"He brings to life and causes to die therefore believe in Allah and His messenger." (Q: 7.158)

"And verily, it is We Who give life, and Who give death." (Q: 15.23)

"It is He Who gives life and death," (Q: 23.80)

"It is He Who gives Life and Death; and He has Power over all things." (Q: 57.2)

8. al muntaqim (the avenger):

    "And who is more unjust than he who is reminded of the communications of his Lord, then he turns away from them? Surely We will give punishment to the guilty." (Q: 32.22)

    "And if We take thee away, We surely shall take vengeance on them." (Q: 43.41)

    "On the day when We shall seize them with the greater seizure, (then) in truth We shall punish." (44.16)

9. al mua'khkhir (the delayer, the backward):

    "He will forgive you some of your faults and grant you a delay to an appointed term; surely the term of Allah when it comes is not postponed; did you but know!" (Q: 71.4)

10. ad-darr (the harmer the afflicter):

    "If Allah touch thee with affliction, there is none that can relieve therefrom save Him, and if He touch thee with good fortune (there is none that can impair it); for He is Able to do all things." (Q: 6.17)

These are satanic attributes. One does not need an academic review of Allah to disprove him. The Qur'an alone is enough to expose him – a real God cannot be the best deceiver, oppressor, tyrant, proud, avenger, harm-doer, etc. and worst of all, world conquest by way of sword and deception. No wonder, this satanic god is capable of taking personal responsibility for terrorism, rape, enslaving women and children, pedophilia, assassination, deception, and thievery – all in the name of "spiritual guidance". Ibn Ishaq recorded Muhammad's words put in Allah's mouth,

"I am the best of plotters. I deceived them with My guile so that I delivered you from them." (Ishaq: 323).

In Islam, the word "guile" is used in the same way the Bible defines Satan – *"insidious and cunning, a crafty or artful deception, duplicity"* (Winn, 2004, p.

361). The guile of Islam is extremely evil. Let us analyze two verses.

"Now Allah leaves straying those whom He pleases and guides whom He pleases: and He is Exalted in power, full of Wisdom." (Q: 14.4)

"He punishes whom He pleases, and He grants mercy to whom He pleases." (Q: 29.21)

But how do we know in which of Allah's categories of pleasure we fall? How sure can a Muslim be that he is one of those guided right and not one of those led astray? In addition to this, the doctrine of abrogation leaves us with the difficulty of having a god who does not remain consistent and often changes his revealed purpose. This being the case, how is one to know that the promises of such a being in regard to eternal security can be trusted? Just as he changes his mind in relation to the revelation, he can also decide to change his mind in regard to the believer's ultimate destiny without anything stopping him from doing so. As Ayoub (1992, pp. 165-6) brings up the question, *"How the word makr (scheming or plotting), which implies deceitfulness or dishonesty, could be attributed to God?"* After listing several Muslim sources Ayoub quotes ar-Razi as arguing that *"scheming (makr) is actually an act of deception aiming at causing evil. It is not possible to attribute deception to God"*. For the Muslims this is a crucial problem.

Indeed how do we know that all of Islam is not the "leading astray" category and rest all the faiths are true path to God? Also, where is the surety that Allah does not "take pleasure" in punishing people and leading them astray? No matter how we try to justify those verses, Allah's actions seem very arbitrary and it is his will or pleasure to lead some astray and punish them and nothing can be done on our side to counter this decision. Therefore, the ultimate question is – Who is responsible for my life and is punishing me for something God has "forced" me to do still possible to be called "justice"?

1.7: Conclusion

"A lie is a lie even if everyone believes it. The truth is the truth even if nobody believes it."

David Stevens

"The invisible and the non-existent look very much alike."

Delos B. McKown

Muslim clerics often tell us that Allah is epistemologically transcendent; i.e., he falls beyond the scope of man's intellectual comprehension. The full nature of Allah is not merely unknown; it is unknowable. Man's rational capacity does not allow him to understand the true nature of Allah, and any knowledge that man does possess concerning Allah is necessarily inadequate in some respect. Thus, Allah, by definition, is that which Muslims cannot understand. What then shall we say about Allah? What Muslims had been able to understand is not Allah but something else instead of Allah. It leads to confusion – What identifiable characteristics does Allah possess? In other words, how will we recognize Allah if we run across him? To state that Allah is supernatural and unknowable does not provide us with an answer. If clerics are to talk intelligibly about Allah, they must presuppose that Allah has characteristics by which he can be identified. But once the idea of supernatural existence is introduced, an existence apart from the limitations of natural law, they exclude the possibility of assigning any definite characteristics to Allah – because by so doing they bring their Allah within the realm of limitations and hence within the realm of natural law. The standard defense of the clerics is actually flawed. It is foolishness to introduce the "unknowable" as a supposed characteristic of the concept itself. If Allah is completely unknowable, the concept of Allah is totally devoid of content, and the word Allah becomes a meaningless sound.

Also, if Allah must remain forever outside the context of man's knowledge, a "supernatural explanation" is a contradiction in terms. Nowhere in the Darwinian theory of evolution did I have find "divine intervention" of Allah. Indeed, to explain everything in terms of Allah is precisely not to explain anything – it is to cut all inquiry dead, to stifle any intellectual curiosity, to kill any scientific progress. To explain the wonderful and awesome variety and complexity of living organisms as "miracles" is not to give a very helpful, least of all a scientific explanation. One cannot explain the unknown with reference to the unknowable.

The adaptation of Occam's razor to this controversy consists in demonstrating that Allah is a redundant identity in the pantheon of Gods. This god cannot be shown to be necessary for any explanatory purposes, and unless science and reason are vigorously attacked and hard scientific truth is distorted, this failed god cannot gain a foothold. When the door is wide-opened for science and reason, the subject of faith in Allah does not arise in the first place since it is much simpler to assume that the world is logical and scientific where the moral and ethical values are approved by God, and therefore these qualities always have higher priority. A true God, if he exists, cannot be immoral. It is much easier to believe that Muhammad was the actual author of the Qur'an, and an ungodly god – a god of intolerance, violence, treachery, lying and, above all stupidity and confusion – does not exist. The hypothesis of Allah as a creator explains nothing; it merely asserts the futility of explanation. It simply pushes the problem one floor upstairs! It is futile and redundant.

Chapter 2: Allah under investigation

"… we are confronted with the task of finding out how those who have faith in a Divine Being could have acquired it, and whence this belief derives the enormous power that enables it to overwhelm reason and science."

Sigmund Freud (1939, p. 183)

There is a fundamental view of religious faith in our modern age that is seriously in error. Religious claims are accepted blindly, and thus are excluded from the arena of knowledge, believing that such claims cannot be tested to evaluate whether or not they correspond to reality; i.e. their truthfulness. Most people think of faith as a blind leap into the supernatural or the non-provable, rather than a reasoned judgment in reality. Even in this scientific age we live in, it is believed that because we cannot evaluate religion in a test-tube that there is no way to evaluate religion at all, so religion must be relegated to the realm of blind faith. Science has come to be viewed as the only avenue to truth. If something cannot be "proven" scientifically, then it is not worthy of belief.

Scientific minds do not simply believe because they choose to, but rather because the evidence compels them to believe. The difference between the truth-claims of religion and the truth-claims of other academic topics lies in the penalty for getting it wrong. A student or a teacher who comes up with the wrong answer to a crucial question in Science or Mathematics might get a bad grade or, at the worst, fail to be promoted. These are real risks, but in a religion – at least a stubborn religion like Islam – if we fail to identify the "one true God" and the appropriate ways to worship him like a slave adorns his master we will fall behind in the rat-race for salvation, and even get condemned to an eternity in hell. It is something more than life and death problem because our mistakes in this life will control our after-life. Therefore, we must put Allah under a serious investigation and place the religious truth-claim of Islam back into the arena of knowledge.

2.1: Allah is only a "truth-claim" of Muhammad

"We can only pursue the truth by cultivating the truth."

Nicholas Rescher (1985, p. 170)

"The most formidable weapon against errors of every kind is reason. I have never used any other, and I trust I never shall".

Thomas Paine, The Age of Reason

Any religious statement, if it is to be significant at all, must make some truth-claim. The primary truth-claim in religious statements is a proposal that something is "more important than anything else in the universe". In Islam, this truth-claim is in the recitation of Kalima (the declaration of faith) – there is no God but Allah and Muhammad is his Prophet. This rigid truth claim of Islam is not incidental to its identity; it is "the" identity.

Though for a true believing Muslim this is the "ultimate concern", we need to establish a criterion of judgment by making a useful criticism of paradox, myth and superstition, insofar as they purport to convey some allegedly trans-rational truth. Though such devices have their proper function, they become a source of obscurantism when used as substitutes for argument. Kalima, the religious statement of Islam, like any other, must satisfy the requirements of logical consistency; it must be capable of some factual corroboration (or disproof); and it must be subject to principles of judgment. The question whether Allah is the "only" god is not an important issue. By keeping in mind the divisive and hurtful teachings of Allah, we need to go far deeper; today we want to know – How much truth is there in Muhammad's truth-claim? If we put the Qur'an in chronological order and correlate it with the context of Muhammad's life as was reported in Sira, Sunna and Hadith; we find Allah mirrored Muhammad's character. Allah was too dumb to be God and too immoral to be divine.

There is something unique within the very nature of Allah itself that complicates its subjection to academic study. When we wish to understand the concept of Allah – not by its borders, but by its roots – we can see a clear warning sign in Muhammad's own means of epistemological justification – Jihad in the name of Allah, the declaration of holy war against infidels (The exact phrase is "*al-jihad fi sabil Allah*" – striving in the cause of Allah; Arimbi, 2006, p. 88; Willis, 1967, p. 396). At the heart of every major religious tradition we find abiding truths and principles that provide the first antidote to violence and extremism. Therefore, in depicting the wars as holy causes, Muhammad continued to compound the errors of the past and distort the very concept of the god he claimed to be defending. Declaring war 'holy' is a sure sign of corrupt religion. In fact, at the center of an authentic religion one always finds the promise of peace, both an inner peace for the adherent and a requirement to seek peaceful coexistence with the rest of creation. How could a merciful God also have the capacity to legitimize the wars and killings of the nonbelievers and justify slavery?

We have to account for the truth. Today, when the researchers are unearthing the roots of religious feeling in the neural disorder that accompanies the spiritual epiphanies of the Patriarchs, Prophets, Saviors and other people of faith, Muhammad's experience of intense union with Allah cannot be accepted on blind faith. Muhammad's belief on Allah was just an opinion, not judgment. Justification requires some rational support. Religious people often make such truth-claims based on their strange experiences. If Allah really exists, the knowledge of "the truth" about Allah should not be beyond the human grasp.

2.1.1: Delusional truth-claims of various Prophets from the History

"Humans see what they want to see."

Rick Riordan

Muhammad was not the first person who claimed to have received messages from God. Throughout the recorded history, there are literally thousands of people who declared themselves as a spokesman of God. Even today, in the mental hospitals and in the cult scene, we can find many mentally disordered and strange people who, likewise, believe to be regular recipients of messages from some unknown divine sources despite intensive studies conducted by parapsychologists, to date there is no scientific evidence on the existence of psychic abilities.

Such truth claimants often declare with all seriousness that he alone is the truth and other opinions are false. They are "honest" in their claim and "sincere" in their declaration. Some make a living or earn celebrity on such grounds, making it at times hard to distinguish between failed good intentions and purposeful dishonesty. Often those strange people come with well-packaged gimmickry and manage to make others believe in their claims too. Many of them set themselves up as cult leaders, revered by a group of followers as their direct "telephone line" to God or the spirit world, example; the strange Mahdi claimants in Islam. The Mahdi is a Messianic figure who, it is believed, will appear on earth before the Day of Judgment and, will rid the world of wrongdoing, injustice and tyranny.

Throughout Islamic history, several significant Mahdi claimants have arisen all across the Muslim world and gathered a significant following. Salih ibn Tarif, the second king of the Berghouata, proclaimed himself Prophet of a new religion in the eighth century. He claimed receiving new revelations from Allah called a new Qur'an, written in the Berber language with eighty chapters. He established laws for his people which called him Salih al-Mu'minin (Restorer of the Believers) and the final Mahdi. Several tenets of his teaching contrast with orthodox Islam, such as capital punishment for theft, unlimited marriages and divorces, fasting of the month of Rajab instead of Ramadan, and ten obligatory daily prayers instead of five.

Another contemporary Mahdi claimant was Abdallah ibn Muawiya. Though he was defeated by a strong military action by the Caliph, his followers did not believe his death and said that he went to occultation and he would return as Mahdi (Halm, 2004, p. 22). Muhammad ibn Hasan ibn Ali, also called Muhammad al-Mahdi, is the twelfth imam of Twelver Shiaa Islam. He is believed to be the ultimate savior of humankind and the final Imam of the Twelve Imams. According to Shiaa belief he did not die, rather was hidden by God (referred to as the Occultation), and will later emerge in order to fulfill his mission of bringing peace and justice to the world.

In tenth century one such Mahdi claimant, Ubayd Allah al-Mahdi Billah, even successfully established a state. He was the first Caliph of Fatimid state, established in 909. In the twelfth century, Muhammad ibn Abdallah ibn Tumart, a Moroccan, declared himself Mahdi, imam and masum (innocent or free of sin). He made a council of ten of his oldest disciples and later added an assembly of fifty tribal leaders. Later in fifteenth century, Muhammad Jaunpuri, born in northeastern India, claimed to be the Mahdi on three occasions – first in Mecca, and later twice in India, attracting a large following, and opposition from the Ulema. Jaunpuri died in 1505, aged sixty-three, but his followers, known as Mahdavis, continue to exist and are centered around the Indian city of Hyderabad. In seventeenth century, Ahmed ibn Abi Mahalli, a Moroccan religious scholar proclaimed himself Mahdi and led a revolution against the reigning Saadi dynasty.

The nineteenth century provided several Mahdi claimants, some of whose followers and teachings survive to the present day. As example; Prince Diponegoro, the Prince of Yogyakarta, Java, saw himself as a Javanese Mahdi. Ali Muhammad

Shirazi, claimed to be Mahdi in 1844, took the name Bab and founded the religion of Babism. He was later executed by firing squad. He is the Prophet of the Bahai Faith and forerunner of Baha'u'llah (means glory of God). The declaration by the Bab to be Mahdi is the beginning of the Bahai calendar (Smith, 1999, pp. 55-9). In June 1881, Muhammad Ahmad, a Sudanese Sufi sheikh, declared himself Mahdi and went on to lead a successful military campaign against the Turko-Egyptian government of Sudan. In British India, Mirza Ghulam Ahmad claimed to be both the Mahdi and the second coming of Jesus in the late nineteenth century. He founded the Ahmadiyya religious movement in 1889 to revive Islam, which, although considered by its followers to be Islam in its pure form, is not recognized as such by the majority of mainstream Muslims. This community, since Ahmad's death, has been led by his successors and has grown considerably.

In twentieth century, another Mahdi claimant Muhammad bin abd Allah al-Qahtani led over two hundred militants to seize the Grand Mosque in Mecca on 20 November 1979. The uprising was defeated after a two-week siege in which at least three hundred people were killed. Another Mahdi claimant, Riaz Ahmed Gohar Shahi, founded the spiritual movements *Messiah Foundation International* and *Anjuman Serfaroshan-e-Islam*. He is declared Mahdi, Messiah, and Kalki Avatar by his followers. They claim that his face became prominent on the moon, sun, nebula star and the black stone in Mecca, and these appearances were sure signs from Allah. Shahi had also supported this claim. Shahi's death has not been confirmed but some say, he is serving a lifetime prison in Pakistan. Another Mahdi claimant, Ariffin Mohammed, also known as "Ayah Pin", the leader and founder of the banned Sky Kingdom, claimed to be the incarnation of Jesus, Muhammad, Shiva, and Buddha. Devotees consider him the supreme object of devotion, and believe that one day, Ayah Pin will return as the Mahdi. Therefore, Muhammad was not the only truth-claimant of Islam. When Islam was successfully established as a profitable religion, many imposters tried to follow Muhammad's footstep. Some of them were more or less successful.

We can find such strange truth-claimants in every religion. Many people in recent times have claimed to be *Maitreya* (successor of Gautama Buddha). Some had used the Buddha incarnation claim to form a new Buddhist sect or a new religious movement or cult, as example; Ram Bahadur Bomjon (nineteen years old Nepalese ascetic whom many have hailed as a new Buddha. Some say, a "very clear and white" light "different from sunlight" emanated from his head), Ron Spencer (a former truck driver who claims to be an incarnation of *Maitreya*. His organization is called The Tibetan Foundation), Li Hongzhi (the founder of Falun Gong who proclaimed himself a Buddha; many of his pictures show him posing like Buddha), Ching Hai (a meditation master who professes to be an incarnation of Buddha), Lu Sheng-yen (he calls himself "Living Buddha Lian Sheng", and claims to have reached enlightenment while training under a formless teacher), Claude Vorilhon (claims that in 1973 he was visited by extraterrestrials who informed him that he was to found a new Buddhist movement to bring a new enlightenment to the world), L. Ron Hubbard (founder of Scientology, claimed in his book *Hymn of Asia* he was an incarnation of Buddha), Ruth Norman (claims that he had fifty-five past lives, some included were reincarnations of the Buddha, Socrates, King Arthur, Confucius and a king of Atlantis) and many others.

In Hinduism, there are many such truth-claimants who are considered by others to be *Avatars* of the Supreme Being or of a more limited expansion of *Ishvara* or other expression of divinity, as example; Meher Baba (claims, "*I am the Avatar of this Age! I say on my authority that I am the Avatar, You know that you are a human being, and I know that I am the Avatar. It is my whole life*"; Iyer, 2009, p. 202), and Mother Meera (claims to be an avatar of the Mother Goddess). Similarly, in Jewish and Christian faith there is no shortage of messiah (messiah originally meant a divinely appointed king, such as David, Cyrus the Great or Alexander the Great) claimants. Sometimes they predict dates for apocalyptic events such as the Rapture, Last Judgment, or any other event that would result in the end of mankind.

Then there are many human beings who claimed divinity or were worshipped as deities during their lifetimes, example; Egyptian Pharaohs (considered by their culture to be gods), Chinese Emperors (deified as "Son of Heaven"), Roman Emperors (many of them called themselves "Son of the Divine One"), Dalai Lamas (considered reincarnations of Buddha in Tibetan Buddhism), Japanese Emperors (claimed to be divine descendants of the Goddess Amaterasu) and many others.

What we understand from the above account is that every religious truth-claim should be doubted because man is a fallible being; he is capable of making mistakes. Little is known about the clinical features associated with religious delusion and how religious delusion may differ across various diagnostic groups. Despite the frequency and importance of delusions, a relatively small amount of research has been conducted in this field. Several atheists including Dawkins, Hitchens and Wright have argued recently against the existence of God; however, they have failed to consider the possibly huge influence of people's psychology upon their religious beliefs. The "sincerity" of these truth-claimants is not a proof. Some people may sincerely believe in the existence of ghosts, whereas others may sincerely disbelieve in it, but whose sincerity is authentic? If Muhammad is justified in appealing to a supernatural authority without proof, then each of the above delusional truth-claimants are similarly justified.

The human mindset is strange. These delusional truth-claimants genuinely believe that they have real encounters with God(s) or demons, or real contact with supernatural realities. They assert they are always right and all the misfortunes that had befallen them in their life were always someone else's fault and never their own. They often get very angry and threatening when someone disagrees with them. Their strange belief does not fit in with the norm of everyday activities and life experiences, and its connection is with the individual's perception of the divine.

The spiritual quest may be as old as humankind itself, but now there is a new place to look – inside our heads. Using tools of modern neuroscience, researchers are attempting to pin down what happens in the brain when people experience mystical awakenings during prayer and meditation or during spontaneous utterances inspired by religious fervor. Probably there is a God spot in the brain. Studying religious experience objectively is a difficult task, as it is entirely a subjective phenomenon. But, commonalities and differences between religious experiences have enabled scholars to categorize them for academic study.

2.1.2: Muhammad's strange prophetic claim

Early in the seventh century of the Christian era the old Arabian paganism was in a process of slow disintegration, and Judaism and Christianity were gaining wide popularity. Several self-proclaimed Prophets had arisen with various degrees of success in convincing people. In the beginning Muhammad was such a self-proclaimed Prophet, but with time he successfully synchronized certain basic elements of Judaism and Christianity with the pagan practices and added some nationalistic Arab pride and it has become a world religion today.

From the authentic Islamic sources it appears that Muhammad thought of himself as in the succession of the Old Testament men of faith who was sent on a divine mission by the one true God, Allah. Throughout the Qur'an he pretended that his mission was the sequel of the previous Semitic Prophets. Like Noah, Jonah, and Elijah, he preached a religious message in the name of this Supreme Lord; like Moses he issued legislation in His name; and like Abraham, he was not only a maintainer of righteousness but also the founder of a community of the righteous. But unlike Christianity, his religious endeavor was an utter failure unless he was able to draw the sword and use it successfully to impose his religion on others.

Muhammad's first confrontation with Gabriel in the cave Hira was sudden and dramatic. Around the age of forty it had been his custom to retire to a cave on Mount Hira outside Mecca for solitary contemplation of the meaning of life and the pagan practices of his kinsmen. Muslim traditions confirm that the call from Allah was sudden; but it was known that Muhammad had occupied himself with religious questions for some time previously (Gatje, 1996, p. 5). Bukhari (1.1.3) recorded that his first meeting was less heavenly and more demonic.

> *"Narrated Aisha: The truth descended upon him while he was in the cave of Hira. The angel came to him and asked him to read. The Prophet replied, "I do not know how to read. The Prophet added, "The angel caught me (forcefully) and pressed me so hard that I could not bear it any more. He then released me and again asked me to read and I replied, 'I do not know how to read.' Thereupon he caught me again and pressed me a second time till I could not bear it any more. He then released me and again asked me to read but again I replied, 'I do not know how to read (or what shall I read)?' Thereupon he caught me for the third time and pressed me, and then released me and said, 'Read in the name of your Lord, who has created (all that exists) has created man from a clot. Read! And your Lord is the Most Generous." (Q: 96.1, 96.2, 96.3). Then Allah's Apostle returned with the Inspiration and with his heart beating severely"*.

Now the most distressing questions are;

1. The angel did not introduce himself as Gabriel. Then how did Muhammad know that it was really Gabriel?
2. Why the Gabriel did not know that Muhammad was illiterate? Why Allah did not tell him? Did Allah forget; is it possible for a God to forget?
3. How Gabriel could be aggressive towards Muhammad repeatedly, the

dearest messenger of Allah? It is recorded in the Qur'an (33.56) that Muhammad was so close to Allah that, even Allah showered praises on Muhammad and the angels saluted him.

None had witnessed the above incident. Later on several times Gabriel visited Muhammad, but nobody else had ever seen this supernatural creature. Muhammad too could not give a single proof of the existence Gabriel. If Gabriel existed, at least someone would have seen him or heard him. A real experience can be shared by others, not a hallucinatory experience. But luck favored him; at least some people around him could not see the fallacy of his story. This is how Muhammad started his divine business of Islam.

The fact that Allah's messages started descending upon Muhammad in a violent way is entirely sufficient for a rational person to have doubt on the truthfulness of the Qur'anic revelations. Surprisingly, Muhammad himself was the first person to doubt the genuineness of the revelations. Bewildered and terrorized, he hurried back to his wife; "*What's wrong with me?*" he asks his wife. Just as kids hide under the covers when they are afraid of monsters in the dark, Muhammad told his wife to wrap him in a blanket. He did not want to see the cause of terror again, and thought that he was either going mad or possessed by an evil spirit. This openly-expressed doubt about the source of the revelations strengthens the suggestion that he was sincere in his claim. If he had been a charlatan, he would probably have regularly embellished and increased his visionary claims as he went along.

After this first revelation, Allah was silent for about three years. Muhammad was so sad that he wanted to commit suicide. Several times he intended to throw himself from the top of high mountains but every time he went up the top in order to throw himself down, Gabriel would appear before him and said, "*O Muhammad! You are indeed Allah's Apostle in truth*". This is how Muhammad began to believe that he was a messenger of God – a messenger of such a demonic god whose influence caused him to attempt suicide. How many Muslims are aware of his suicide attempts? Few Islamic leaders will teach this to their fellow Muslims as it casts a stain upon Muhammad; it brings doubt to his trustworthiness and the credibility of his assumed "heavenly" experience. Some Muslims deny the sources of the story while others, knowledgeable about the sources, respond by saying that the shock of the experience caused him to attempt suicide.

Allah confirms (Q: 33.40), Muhammad was the seal of the Prophets. According to Islamic sources (Muslim: 30.5790; Sunnan Abu Dawud: 32.4071; Bukhari: 1.4.189), Muhammad had a big mole as big as a pigeon's egg on his back between the shoulders which he claimed as the proof of his prophethood. There is no religious scripture which confirms that a mole between the shoulders is a sign of prophethood. What he showed as a proof of Allah's seal was a physical defect which anyone can have. There is no divinity in this. It is simply beyond the capacity of a logical thinker how this is supposed to be one of the proofs that can convince people of Muhammad's prophethood!

Muhammad gave no concrete proof of his heavenly appointment. Did he lie shamelessly to fool the Arab pagans? Was he under delusion? The validity of Islam depends absolutely on the reliability of Muhammad. If there is no solid reason to conclude that he was the true messenger of God, we may reasonably suppose that Islam is false. If we can prove that he was untrustworthy, Islam self-destructs. The scholars, who are most familiar with Arabic sources and have clear understanding of the life and time of Muhammad, e.g., Margoliouth, Hurgronje, Lammens, Arthur Jeffery, Clair-Tisdall, Andrew Rippin, Ibn Warraq, and Caetani, are the most decisive against Muhammad's prophetic claim. The more we read their valuable research works, the more we find it difficult to disagree with them. Muhammad declared that lying is acceptable if it is used to propagate the cause of Islam. This particular statement should make us wonder how often Muhammad took advantage of this principle while claiming his title of a Prophet and preaching his message.

If we take Qur'an as the primary foundation of Muhammad's prophethood, the doubt is still not dispelled at all. We need to ascertain how firm ground does it provide. There are serious doubts about the trustworthiness of Qur'an also. Like his prophetic claim, Qur'an itself is self-declarative – there is no external proof. This book describes itself by various generic terms, comments, explains, distinguishes, puts itself in contrast with other religious books and claims to be holy. The Qur'anic claims are great, but what is miserable is that, this supposed to be holy book fails to prove either Muhammad's prophethood or its divine origin. Ultimately, it becomes a circular reasoning. Qur'an is God's word because Muhammad said so, and Muhammad was God's Prophet because Qur'an says so.

2.1.3: A critical analysis of Muhammad's prophetic claim

"Nothing is so difficult as not deceiving oneself."

Ludwig Wittgenstein

Circular reasoning is not a proof; it is a logical fallacy, so further argumentation is required. Muhammad's first meeting with Gabriel was a religious delusion, a classic case of psychosis induced by spiritual practice. In this disorder the patient holds unproven beliefs with high and ruthless conviction tenaciously even when there are irrefutable proofs which contradict these unproven beliefs and show them to be false. Many patients who have this disorder appear to be normal people unless they begin to act according to their beliefs. Most of them have distorted views that can lead them to do stupid and even criminal things. Such experiences make up the volume of many religious books. Just because one hears voices, sees lights and visions, does not mean that these experiences have a spiritual nature. The fact that many seriously mentally ill people also have such visions and voices proves that such experiences are as much of a warning sign as a sign that one is being visited by heaven. These experiences can take place in the same part of the brain that can be called for the lay person, the "dream hemisphere" where the unconscious attains visual imagery and auditory sensation.

Many who have visions, voices and the other types of experiences do not easily seek psychiatric help. For many of them, this phenomenon falls under the heading of being spiritual. For them their delusion is a genuine material. When Muhammad claimed prophethood and started preaching in Mecca, the early Arab intellectuals turned away from him knowing that he was delusional. We cannot blame them; they had seen many imposters like Muhammad. During those days, prophetic business was a thriving profitable industry in Arabia. Therefore, they ignored Muhammad as they ignored any other madman. Qur'an says,

> "*The Hypocrites and those in whose hearts is a disease said: 'Allah and His Messenger promised us nothing but delusion; they have promised only to deceive us'*". (Q: 33.11).

> "*Then they had turned away from him and said: One taught by others, a madman!*" (Q: 44.14).

> "*They said: 'Are we going to abandon our gods for the sake of a mad poet?'*" (Q: 37.36)

> "*And when they see you, they treat you only as a mockery*". (Q: 25.41).

> "*And those who disbelieve say: Shall we point out to you a man who informs you that when you are scattered the utmost scattering you shall then be most surely (raised) in (to) a new creation? He has forged a lie against Allah or there is madness in him. Nay! Those who do not believe in the hereafter are in torment and in great error.*" (Q: 34.7-8)

However, they were kind to Muhammad and left him alone in his fantasy world and allowed him to believe in whatever fables he wanted. They were even ready to pay for medical advice to cure his mental illness. Utbah ibn Rabi'ah, a distinguished leader of Arabia, convinced the Quraysh at one of their community meetings to delegate him to approach Muhammad. Hence, on behalf of the Quraysh he came to Muhammad to assist him with different alternatives. The Egyptian Muslim scholar and historian, Haykal (1976, chapter 5) recorded Utbah's words,

> "*If you are unable to cure yourself of the visions that you have been seeing, we shall be happy to seek for you at our expense all the medical service possible until your health is perfectly restored*".

But instead of listening to them, Muhammad put up resistance in the interest of his illness and against those people who wanted to help him. People who have religious-based delusions can spend many years under them. Some never try to get help for them, for they do not believe in the model of psychiatry. Compared with patients with other types of delusions, these patients hold the delusions with greater conviction making them more challenging to treat (Siddle et al., 2002, pp. 130-8; Appelbaumm et al, 1999, pp. 1938-43). Some may believe that seeking medical care is proof of weak faith, whereas others may feel that psychiatric treatment is forbidden or incompatible with their beliefs (Mohr et al., 2010, pp. 158-72).

For an ordinary person hearing voices is a stigma, but for Muhammad it is confessed as a virtue. A patient under religious delusion simply concludes that since he is having an extrasensory experience, it must be supernatural and hence divine. He does not see his condition as a mental illness, so it is a diagnosis in which it is hard to do therapy because the person does not admit that he is sick. In these cases, the hallucinations are often solacing to the person. The delusion may give him esteem or be an extension of the type of experience of having imaginary companions in childhood. They simply cannot have the insight that visions and voices often have no objective external reality. Allah revealed,

> *"When the Unbelievers see thee, they treat thee not except with ridicule. "Is this, (they say), the one who talks of your gods?" and they blaspheme at the mention of (Allah) Most Gracious!"* (Q: 21.36)

In sum, Muhammad had suffered a complete intellectual defeat and the most embarrassing social humiliation. Arabs were particularly incensed by the Qur'an description of the Last Judgment, which they dismissed as primitive and irrational. Arabs did not believe in the afterlife and should give no credence to such "fairy tales". They called Muhammad, *"charlatan, who only pretended to be a Prophet"* (Armstrong, 2001, p. 10). Such critics were not merely the dead voices of the past. They were asking the same questions about his heavenly mission that we still ask in our time without getting any answers from the Muslim scholars. These questions are as old as Islam. As his lies were exposed, Islam was destined to vanish in its infancy. To console him, Allah assured him by sending down new revelations,

> *"By the Favor of Allah, you are neither a soothsayer, nor mad"*. (Q: 52.29).

> *"Allah shall pay them back their mockery, and He leaves them alone in their inordinacy, blindly wandering on"*. (Q: 2.15)

> *"By the grace of your Lord you are not mad. And most surely you shall have a reward never to be cut off."* (Q: 68.2, 3)

> *"And your companion is not gone mad."* (Q: 81.22)

> *"Do they not reflect that their companion has not unsoundness in mind; he is only a plain warner."* (Q: 7.184)

The patients subconsciously act the parts of the voices that they hear. They do not even notice that they are actually playing the roles of the voices and causing these roles to exist. Muhammad needed Allah to support him. Those revelations were actually coming from his diseased mind. One might call it "finding the inner voice". Though Qur'an is believed to be the uncreated and eternal Word of Allah, it has many passages where deliberate guidance is given for particular events in Muhammad's life and comments are made on battles, etc. which had just taken place. Also we cannot help but see how expediently Muhammad produced revelations to help him get over awkward situations whenever these arose. It justified his actions which could not be excused in any other way.

Muhammad's first meeting was strangely very similar to the experience of one of his close friends, Hassan Bin Thabit. Hassan was a poet of Medina, who later became Muhammad's personal Poet Laureate. Hassan came to write poetry under the influence of a female Jinni. Macdonald (cited Zwemer, 2011, pp. 126-7) wrote,

> *"She [the female Jinni] met him [Hassan] in one of the streets of Medina, leapt*

upon him, pressed him down and compelled him to utter three verses of poetry. Thereafter he was a poet, and his verses came to him ... from the direct inspiration of the Jinn. He refers himself to his 'brothers of the Jinn' who weave for him artistic words, and tells how weighty lines have been sent down to him from heaven".

There is an extraordinary parallel between the terms used in the story of Hassan's encounter with the female Jinni and the accounts of Muhammad's first confrontation with Gabriel. The expressions Hassan used are exactly those used of the sending down, i.e., revelations of the Qur'an. Did Muhammad's sick mind play a trick on him, recapture Hassan's story and subconsciously pass it off as his own?

This vision in the cave Hira is interpreted differently by various critics. Some believe, it was Satan himself who visited Muhammad in the guise of Gabriel. But leaving aside a superstition-based argument, it might be a command that originated from Muhammad's own subconscious, as Walker (2002, p. 97) brought forward his argument – possibly, his subconscious commanded him to read and study the books of Jews and Christians, whose scribes were given pens to write down the truth of God's dispensation in their scriptures, which the Arabs lacked. The first revelation which he received in the cave was a representation of an ancient Semitic tradition of revelation (Shaikh, 1995, p. 6). Moses mediated between God and man and narrated the story of a burning bush which though burnt suffered no consumption at all (Exodus: 3.2). It was the genius of Moses who realized that it was God of Abraham, Isaac and Jacob under whose glory such a mysterious event was taking place. Moses did not forget to tell his people that he did not want to be their leader but was acting under duress. Moses told God that he was not willing to be the divine viceroy owing to his stammer and lack of eloquence (Exodus: 4.10). However, he agreed to carry the yoke of authority because his attitude angered the Lord. Thus Moses had no choice but to become God's viceroy and announced that God had sent him to his people. This way first he found a God for the people, and then appointed himself as God's messenger to enforce certain commands in the name of his God.

Now let us re-examine Muhammad's mystic experience and summarize all the facts. In all probability; a command originated from his subconscious mind "to read and study", which mixed up with the amazing story of Hassan and took the model of the Semitic tradition of revelation of Moses. These impressions interacted and commingled with one another, took a strange shape, and surfaced in its manifest form as a vivid hallucination. This resultant impression was so strong that even Muhammad himself could not recognize it. He thought that it was generated from an external supernatural source, Allah.

2.1.4: Psychosis induced by excessive spiritual practice

"The human brain is a complex organ with the wonderful power of enabling man to find reasons for continuing to believe whatever it is that he wants to believe."

François-MarieArouet (Voltaire)

Excessive spiritual practice is a major cause of psychosis. Though spirituality is difficult to study from a neuropsychological perspective in normal populations, the researchers have reported that normal individuals who hold above-average beliefs in spiritual and psychic phenomena are more prone to paranormal or transcendental experiences (Brugger & Graves, 1997, pp. 251-72; Persinger & Makarec, 1987, pp. 179-95). Also delusional and schizoid thinking has been shown to occur more frequently in members of religious cults (Peters et al., 1999, pp. 83-96; Spencer, 1975, pp. 556-9). The Japanese researcher Morita described psychosis induced by spiritual practice for the first time in 1915. For an over-religious patient auditory hallucinations, excitement, confusion, or self-hypnotic mannerisms arise during relatively short periods. Often it lasts for few days and then disappears without any residual syndrome. After the first psychotic episode in the cave, Allah was silent for about three years. Muhammad was so depressed that he wanted to commit suicide.

According to Morita (1915, pp. 286-7), this type of psychosis tends to occur in superstitious people with low educational levels. Later, various other researchers (Andoh et al., 1994, pp. 313-20; Miyamoto & Oda, 1965, pp. 133-218; Nakayama, 2008, pp. 157-68; Nawata & Nishimura, 2005, pp. 362-8; Nozaki et al., 1992, pp. 1691-6; Sakurai, 1938, pp. 932-9; Yasuda et al., 2008, pp. 11-17) had developed the original theory of Morita. Slowly, a new era of the psychological study of religious experiences, beliefs, and activities began and a new term coined – neurotheology (also, spiritual neuroscience, biotheology). A detailed study on this subject is outside the scope of this book. However, in this section, I intend to provide an overview of the neurological basis for religious and spiritual experiences with suitable case studies that will help us to understand Allah in a better way.

In 1997, while addressing the general meeting for the *Society of Neuroscience,* Ramachandran, a renowned neuroscientist at University of California, made his radical statement that catapulted the science of neurotheology well into the public eye. "*There is a neural basis for religious experience,*" Ramachandran commented. And the aim of the neurotheology is to question and "*explore theology from a neurological perspective...helping us to understand the human urge for religion and religious myth*" (Newberg et. al, 2001, p. 177). Muhammad's mysticism or divine mission or enlightenment, whatever the Muslims want to call it, was just a psychotic state that was induced by extreme religious indulgence. Muslim scholars agree that Muhammad was avidly religious from his pre-prophetic days.

"*According to the Muslim tradition, the calling occurred suddenly; however it is known that Muhammad had occupied himself with religious questions for some time previously, either consciously or unconsciously*". (Gatje, 1996, p. 5)

"*Muhammad was now approaching his fortieth year. Always pensive he had of late become even more thoughtful and retiring. Contemplation and reflection engaged his mind, and the moral debasement of his people pressed heavily on him. His soul was perplexed with uncertainty as to what was the right path to follow. Thus burdened, he frequently retired to seek relief in meditation amongst the solitary valleys and rocks near Mecca*". (Khan, 1980, p. 23)

Right from the beginning one discovers much that is subjective in the development of his conviction that he was called to be the messenger of Allah. It is probable that the incident at the Ka'ba a few years earlier, when he was singled out to replace the sacred black stone in the house of Allah, had a profound effect on him and initiated the belief that he was marked out as the leader to guide his people into the true worship of one God, the Allah. According to the traditions, Muhammad was a Prophet when the body and soul of Adam were still in the making. Allah very generously declared, "*Were it not for you, I would not have created the universe.*" (Tabaqat, Volume - 1). Apart from thinking that he was the "*seal of the Prophets*" (Q: 33.40); this megalomaniac psychotic regarded himself as "*Khayru-l-Khalq*" (the best of creation), an "*excellent example*" (Q: 33.21), and suggested that he was "*exalted above other Prophets in degrees*" (Q: 2.253). He also claimed to be "*the preferred one*" (Q: 17.55), sent as a "*Mercy to the Worlds*" (Q: 21.107), and will be "*raised to a praised estate*" (Q: 17.79). In ahadith, he made many strange claims – I am from Allah and believers are from me, the very first thing Allah ever created was my soul, first of all things the Lord created my mind, Allah created me noble and gave me noble character (Adil, 2002, p. 29). Incidentally, when Muhammad had all the stone idols in the Ka'ba destroyed after the city had surrendered to him many years later, the black stone was spared and retained its ancient sanctity.

Nakaya and Ohmori (2010, pp. 161-3), two world-renowned professionals from Japan, presented a case study which is worth mentioning here because of its similarity with Muhammad. Mr. Takumi (name changed to protect identity), a Buddhist by faith and a thirty year old married man was a car dealer. According to his wife, he was very sensitive to his reputation and took great pride in himself. However, he faced a hard time in his work because of his lack of leadership qualities, and as a result his sense of self-worth diminished. During this period of inner conflict, he experienced insomnia and loss of appetite, and began to rely on Buddhism, chanting the sutras for a few hours every day.

One day he chanted the sutras in front of a Buddhist altar for two hours and suddenly saw five small men with ancient clothes walk out of the Buddhist altar and another great man sit down there. These visions lasted several seconds, and he considered this vision suggesting the greatness of Buddhism. Three days later, when he looked at his wife during his chant, her face swelled and many worms came out of her face. The worms disappeared after few seconds, and her face returned to normal. He was confused and this confusion led him to visit a psychiatrist.

He described both his inner conflict about a job as well as his visions during his chants. Results of physical and mental examinations were normal and no drugs had been administered. Still facing a financial hardship due to unemployment, Mr. Takumi became more absorbed in chanting the sutra, but no abnormal change was found in his behaviors. At this time, he reported that he felt a lack of emotional exchange between himself and his wife and a gap was created between them.

After two weeks of consulting the psychiatrist, he visited the grave of his family with his mother. He chanted the sutra in front of the grave and noticed a circle figure on the surface of the grave. This led him to believe that his ancestors were imprisoned in the grave and that if he gave his power to the circle figure, through his chant, the life power in the cosmos would be released. Continuing the chant, he felt himself incorporated into the stream of life in the cosmos, which went around in his abdomen. At the same time, he heard voices saying that they were healing his soul and body. He considered himself the center of the world and felt that everything moved according to his will but that as a result, the world might be ruined. When he became afraid of ruining of the world, he came to himself, and stood up beside his mother. His mother noted no abnormality.

After this vision, he got a job of much lower status and low income. According to him, just after the vision, his judgment of values had changed. Before the vision he had considered that the value of a man was determined by his job. The loss of status led him to experience a loss of self-value. However, after the episode, he no longer believed that a man's job determined his value. He stated that jobs were mere means of life, and that life itself was important. At the same time, he began to experience emotional exchanges between his wife and himself. After this realization, he visited the psychiatrist only once in three months. He has continued to work over three years without any problems and chants the sutra everyday for only a few minutes without any prophetic vision anymore.

This case was diagnosed as brief psychotic disorder according to American Psychiatric Association. It has strange similarity with the case of Muhammad. Like Mr. Takumi, the Prophet of Islam did not get a meaningful employment during his early adult days and remained unmarried till twenty-five. He was poor and coward. Before his marriage to Khadija, Muhammad used to attend sheep with a miserly small payment. For the Arabs, this was an unmanly profession mostly reserved for girls. Muhammad took this unmanly job for two reasons – first, he was unsuitable for any better job. Secondly, he had a low self-esteem, and as a result he used to avoid interaction with others. Though in the early days he was not much religious, during his forties he would seclude himself in the cave to engage in the Tahannuth (pagan religious rites performed in Ramadan that included fasting) worship for a number of nights before returning to Khadija and getting provisions for a like period (Tabari: VI.67). His this kind of behavior was not normal. He had a rich wife; he could get the desired ritualistic seclusion in his home. If Allah is everywhere, then why the privacy of a cave was essential? In all probability, he felt a lack of emotional exchange between himself and his wife Khadija.

Cave Hira is the size of a small toilet – about 3.5 meters by 1.5 meters (Sina, 2008, p. 154). Since he liked loneliness, it is obvious that he used to close the small entrance of the cave. Days and nights of pointless thinking (fantasy daydreaming), psychological stress, deprivation of food or water or sleep, lack of oxygen inside the cave, mental fatigue – most likely, this entire thing caused a hallucination and his psychological problems started, similar to the absorption of Mr. Takumi in chanting the sutras that directly led to those brief psychotic episodes. The mother and wife of Mr. Takumi did not notice any abnormality in his behavior. Though Muhammad was in severe self-doubt about the genuineness of his first revelations, his wife Khadija mistook his hallucinations as spiritual experiences, and his prophethood was confirmed by Waraqa Bin Naufal, a cousin of Khadija who converted from Judaism to Christianity (Bukhari: 9.87.111). Chanting of the sutras in front of a Buddha altar and heavy engagement in practice of pagan religious rites and fasting inside the seclusion of a cave caused both of them to be absorbed in a delusion. These were the only factors in these two psychotic episodes.

This absorption was provoked by their poor financial status, which made them feel worthless. In a state of heavy religious self-indoctrination both of them felt an emotional detachment with their respective wives. Their pre-morbid conflicts

124

consisted of the discrepancy between their demands for a job with high status, or social recognition and real pathetic poor condition. Mr. Takumi believed that his ancestors were imprisoned in a circle figure of the grave and tried to release the life power in the cosmos through his chant. He had delusional experiences of the inflow of life in the cosmos into himself and had auditory hallucinations that involved healing his soul and body. Muhammad believed that he was the Apostle of Allah, who was on a mission to conquer the world for Allah. This is the power of religious delusion. It profoundly changes the judgment of values of the person.

2.1.5: Muhammad's al-Miraj delusion

"Fool yourself into happiness, while pretending not to do so."
Christopher Hitchens

Muhammad's famous night journey (al-Isra and al-Mi'raj) with Gabriel to Jerusalem and then to heavens was a religious delusion. Buraq, a white animal, half mule, half donkey, with a human head and with wings (some enthusiastic Muslim sources even add the tail of a peacock) carried Muhammad on her back. Muhammad and Gabriel went their way until they arrived at the temple at Jerusalem where he found Abraham, Moses, and Jesus, along with a company of Prophets and acted as their imam in prayer. After prayer, Buraq took him to each of the heavens till the seventh heaven, and he received royal treatment in each of the heavens.

Muslims go out of their way to give some credibility to this stupid story. The stupidest part of the story is that when Muhammad allegedly visited the temple in Jerusalem, there was no temple in Jerusalem. About six centuries before al-Buraq took flight, the Romans had already destroyed it. By 70 AD not a single stone was left on another. According to Bible, the Temple of Solomon was built around tenth century BC. The Dome of the Rock was raised on the foundations of the Roman Temple of Jupiter in 691 and the al-Aqsa mosque was constructed over a Roman basilica on the southern end of the Temple Mount in 710 by the Umayyads (Sina, 2008, p. 120). If there was no temple then which temple did he visit, unless we conclude that the whole incident was a hallucinatory experience?

And then, what about the divine animal Buraq – the half mule, half donkey white animal with a human head? This divine transportation system of Allah had wings on its sides with which it propelled its feet, putting down each forefoot at the limit of its sight. Muhammad had seen angels in the seven heavens.

"The first heaven was of pure silver and the stars suspended from its vault by chains of gold; in each one an angel lay awake to prevent the demons from climbing into the holy dwelling places and the spirits from listening indiscreetly to celestial secrets." (Haykal, 1976, Chapter 8)

"After the completion of my business in Jerusalem, a ladder was brought to me [Muhammad] finer than any I have ever seen. An angel was in charge of it and under his command were 12,000 angels each of them having 12,000 angels under his command." (Ishaq: 184)

It is difficult to imagine that 144,000,000 angels were holding a single ladder. *"There [in the first heaven] Muhammad greeted Adam. And in the six other heavens the Prophet met Noah, Aaron, Moses, Abraham, David, Solomon, Idris (Enoch), Yahya (John the Baptist) and Jesus".*

"He saw the Angel of Death, Azrail, so huge that his eyes were separated by 70,000 marching days. He commanded 100,000 battalions and passed his time in writing in an immense book the names of those dying or being born".

"He saw the Angel of Tears, who wept for the sins of the world; the Angel of Vengeance with brazened face, covered with warts, who presides over the elements of fire and sits on a throne of flames; and another immense angel made up half of snow and half of fire surrounded by a heavenly choir continually crying: `O God, Thou hast united snow and fire, united all Thy servants in obedience to Thy Laws'." (Haykal, 1976, Chapter 8)

The stupidity of al Mi'raj is again at its peak. Is it possible to imagine a creature made up half of snow and half of fire? Such distorted thoughts lead to stress to a healthy mind. The Angel of Death, Angel of Tears and Angel of Vengeance were the products of Muhammad's hallucination. In the seventh heaven, Muhammad saw such a strange creature which cannot be even envisioned. Haykal continues,

"In the seventh heaven where the souls of the just resided was an angel larger than the entire world, with 70,000 heads; each head had 70,000 mouths, each mouth had 70,000 tongues and each tongue spoke in 70,000 different idioms singing endlessly the praises of the Most High."

It is not only difficult but also stressful to visualize a creature like this. How did he know that the angel was larger than the world? How did he count the creature's number of heads, mouths, tongues, etc., when he was believed to be illiterate? Why Allah created such a horrible beast? Why Allah allowed the beast to enter paradise, while it was supposed to be in hell? After seeing the absurdities of Muhammad's night journey, many of his followers left Islam. To save Muhammad from further humiliation, Allah revealed,

"Behold! We told thee that thy Lord doth encompass mankind round about: We granted the vision which We showed thee, but as a trial for men ... We put terror (and warning) into them, but it only increases their inordinate transgression!" (Q: 17.60).

This verse is too silly. Muhammad claimed to have visited a temple which was destroyed long before him and claimed to have seen angels, gibberish creatures at heaven but could not produce any proof, but Allah wanted the Muslims to believe him without question because it was a test to them – *"but as a trial for men"*, and if men refuse to believe him then, *"We put terror (and warning) into them"* – nice argument indeed for an all-powerful Allah. However, the Arabs refused to accept his gigantic claims and ridiculed him saying that his night journey was either a dream, or a fabricated story. Qur'an says,

"Nay, say they, (these are but) muddled dreams; nay, he hath but invented it; nay, he is but a poet. Let him bring us a portent even as those of old (who were Allah's messengers) were sent (with portents)." (Q: 21.5)

Helpless Muhammad took Allah as witness.

"He said: My Lord knows what is spoken in the heaven and the earth, and He is the Hearing, the Knowing". (Q: 21.4).

The al-Mi'raj had an extraordinary parallel with another account *The Secrets of Enoch*, which, composed by an unknown Jewish sectarian group, predates Muhammad by four centuries. Enoch, a three hundred and sixty-five years old man, was taken by two angels and made to pass through the seven heavens, one by one. According to folklore (Charles, 1999, pp. 4-11, 13-24, 37-39), while Enoch was fast asleep, two angels came to him, called him by his name and said, *"Have courage, Enoch, do not fear; The Eternal God sent us to thee. Thou shalt today ascend with us into heaven"*. They took him on their wings and bore him up to the first heaven and placed him on the clouds. In various layers of the heaven, Enoch saw two hundred angels who fly with the wings (some of them had six wings) and rule the stars, angels guard the treasure houses, seven bands of very bright and very glorious angels in sixth heaven singing loudly all sweet songs of praise, etc. Possibly, the al-Mi'raj dream-hallucination was a subconscious representation of this ancient story of Enoch which Muhammad might have heard somewhere. However, a quote from Ishaq will put an end to all the arguments.

"Umm, Abu Talib's daughter, said: "He [Muhammad] slept in my home that night after he prayed the final night prayer. A little before dawn he woke us, saying, 'O Umm, I went to Jerusalem.' He got up to go out, and I grabbed hold of his robe and laid bare his belly. I pleaded, 'O Muhammad, don't tell the people about this for they will know you are lying and will mock you.' He said, 'By Allah, I will tell them.' I told a Negress [female Negro] slave of mine, 'Follow him and listen'." (Ishaq: 184)

Therefore, Umm, the daughter of Abu Talib, confirmed that Muhammad's famous night journey actually happened in his dream which Muhammad mistook as a real experience. It means, the incident was actually a dream-hallucination. Many of the Meccans also believed the same. Qur'an confirms it.

"He said: My Lord knows what is spoken in the heaven and the earth, and He is the Hearing, the Knowing. Nay! say they: medleys of dreams; nay! he has forged it; nay! he is a poet; so let him bring to us a sign as the former (prophets) were sent (with)." (Q: 21.4, 5).

To say that Allah had spoken to Muhammad in a dream, is no more than to say Muhammad dreamed of having a dealing with divine. Dream itself is a controlled hallucination which everyone passes through. Hence, this is not a sufficiently strong logic to win belief from any man. The dreamer may err, or may lie.

2.1.6: A critical analysis of al-Miraj delusion

"I cannot sleep for I am asleep as it were with my eyes open and I feel chills and cold come over me and a sort of nightmare ..."

Poet Clare (quoted Claridge et. al, 1990, p. 132)

It is not always clear when a patient is hallucinating. Some people confuse realistic, "vivid" dreams, with hallucinations. A psychotic patient will discuss things that he dreamed about the previous night as if they actually occurred. This is a very common source of confusion.

Dream is a mild hallucination. It transforms the thoughts into sensory images, mostly of a visual sort. Freud calls it "hallucinatory satisfaction" and "hallucinated fulfillment of wish". Jung's (1933, p. 2) analysis is that dreams are direct expression of unconscious psychic activity, and unconscious plays a causal part in neurosis. Though there are some minor differences between Freud and Jung's analysis, both agreed that interpreting a dream can be justified entirely from a scientific standpoint. Since the subconscious mind plays an important part in neurosis, the practicability of dream-analysis is beyond any question.

A healthy mind can very easily distinguish between dream and reality; but the psychotics who cannot identify dreams and take it as a real experience need serious medical attention. For them, the dream is a genuine material, not a distorted substitute for something else. A dream does not simply give them expression to a thought but represent the wish-fulfillment as a hallucinatory experience often with a distortion. Muhammad could not differentiate dream from reality. Bukhari wrote,

"Narrated Ibn 'Abbas' ... Allah's Apostle actually saw with his own eyes the vision of all the things, which were shown to him on the Night Journey to Jerusalem. It was not a dream." (Bukhari: 8.77.610)

While dreaming, the psychotics often do not understand that they are asleep. In proper psychological term, this is called "Type 2 false awakening" (A false awakening is a vivid and convincing dream about awakening from sleep, while the dreamer in reality continues to sleep. Type 2 is more severe which usually occurs with a psychotic patient). Often these dream-hallucinations are highly complex, colorful and with a "movie-like" continuation (Bassetti et al, 2005, p. 403). Type 2 false awakening afflict the patient with a sense of anxiety and insecurity. Green (1968, p. 121) characterizes this experience as this,

"In this type of false awakening the subject appears to wake up in a realistic manner, but to an atmosphere of suspense. These experiences vary in respect of the length of time which elapses before the subject becomes aware that something unusual is happening. His surroundings may appear normal, and he may gradually become aware of something uncanny in the atmosphere, and perhaps of unwonted sounds and movements. Or he may 'awake' immediately to a 'stressed' and 'stormy' atmosphere. In either case, the end result would appear to be characterized by feelings of suspense, excitement or

apprehension".

This false awakening is a sure sign of Muhammad's psychosis. Psychotics in fact oscillate, even in daylight hours, between true waking and the dreaming state.

According to Freud, dream has a sense and it can give meaningful clues if it is translated "backwards" and the distortion is undone. If we analyze this dream-hallucination of Muhammad, we can uncover many facts and create a mental map of this seventh century mental patient.

In 1900, Freud published a major work on the interpretation of dreams where he concluded that the study of dreams is not only the best preparation for the study of the neurosis but dreams are themselves a neurotic system. He used two terms for dream-interpretation, namely, **Manifest dream-content** (what the dream apparently tells us) and **Latent dream-thoughts** (the unconscious thoughts that occur to the dreamer), and concluded (Strachey & Gay, 1966, p. 139), "*Dream as a whole is the distorted substitute for something else, something unconscious, and that of the task of interpreting a dream is to discover this unconscious material.*" Muhammad's dream-hallucination has both the above distinctive characteristics.

Manifest dream-content: Buraq; Muhammad met Abraham, Moses, and Jesus, along with a company of Prophets, and acted as their imam in prayer; visiting a non-existent temple; silver and gold in Allah's paradise; various angels, etc.

Latent dream-thoughts: wish-fulfillment, ambition fulfillment, erotic wishes, anger, self-glorification, frustration.

When Muhammad's prophetic claim was under serious doubt after the satanic verses incident, he had a strong desire to reinforce it. As Freud (Strachey & Gay, 1966, p. 264) wrote, "*Dream-work consists essentially in the transformation of thoughts into a hallucinatory experience. How this can happen is sufficiently mysterious*". Muhammad wanted to replace the Ka'ba with a more credible shrine, desperately needed a new Qibla (direction of prayer) and a new object to exploit. He simply dreamed off the satisfaction of his secret needs. Allah had at his power to have taken Muhammad from his bed (or Umm's bed) straight up to the heavens, but to impress the importance of Jerusalem upon Muslims, Muhammad was first taken to Jerusalem. In doing so, Allah made the al-Aqsa mosque of Jerusalem "a new object to exploit". Once the religious importance of al-Aqsa mosque was established, Muslims turned their Qibla towards Jerusalem. However, after 16 /17 months, Allah commanded in his wisdom for the Muslims to face Ka'ba again.

The second troubling question is; why suddenly Allah decided to invite Muhammad to his garden in the seventh sky? The reason was that Muhammad desperately needed a miracle and the al-Mi'raj served that purpose. All he wanted was to elevate himself at the cost of Allah. He had an insatiable craving for praise; his secret desires were projected as a hallucination. Allah was just speaking out Muhammad's thoughts loudly. Qur'an says,

"Glorified be He Who carried His servant by night from the Inviolable Place of Worship to the Far distant place of worship the neighborhood whereof We have blessed, that We might show him of Our tokens! Lo! He, only He, is the Hearer,

the Seer." (Q: 17.1)

The first few words of this verse need to be read between the lines. "Glorified be He" – it is absurd to think that God wanted to glorify Himself. Rather, it was Muhammad who was elevating himself in the name of God. If God is glorified by allowing Muhammad to enter paradise, undoubtedly, Muhammad was overvalued. The ego satisfaction comes from comparing ourselves to our opponent and feeling that we are better in some way. Muhammad used Allah for an ego boost. Freud (Strachey & Gay, 1966, p. 175) wrote, "*... the dreamer's own ego appears in every dream and plays the chief part in it.*"

Another latent dream thought was ambition. Muhammad wanted to rise above all other Biblical Prophets. All of them had routinely made exacting and detailed predictions to demonstrate their divine authority. But Muhammad was not capable of producing a single miracle, and he knew this inadequacy very well. Hence, in his hallucination, he was greeted by all the Prophets; e.g., Adam, Noah, Aaron, Moses, Abraham, David, Solomon and Jesus. By doing so, this ambitious neurotic patient joined the rank of a Prophet without having a single miracle in his account. Then he led all the Prophets in prayer. It proved his superiority over other Prophets; he was glorified amongst all. Of course Muhammad was superior to all Prophets, otherwise why Allah sent Buraq – a special transport system for him? Ishaq shows, what an important person Muhammad was!

> "*When I came up to mount him (Buraq), he shied. Gabriel placed his hand on its mane and said, 'Are you not ashamed, O Buraq, to behave in this way? By Allah, none more honorable before Allah than Muhammad has ever ridden you before. The animal was so ashamed that he broke out into a sweat, and stood so that I could mount him*". (Ishaq: 182).

Now, we will talk about his erotic wishes – another latent dream-thought.

> "*He took me into Paradise, and there I saw a damsel with dark red lips. I asked her to whom she belonged, for she pleased me much when I saw her. She said, Zaid (Muhammad's adopted son). The Apostle gave Zaid the good news about her*". (Ishaq: 186)

This damsel with ruby lips was Zaynab, the wife of his adopted son, Zayd, whom Muhammad married later by trickery. In Muhammad's hallucination, Zaynab traveled from earth to paradise and then back to the land of her future husband. Nobody knows how she could be present in paradise before her death and without being tried by Allah on the Day of Judgment, which, according to Muslim belief, is yet to come.

In his dream, Muhammad saw the Angel of Death and the Angel of Tears. The latent dream-thoughts are revenge, anger, frustration and unhappiness (caused by frustration). Anger because he was ridiculed by the opponents, and frustration because his newfound religion was not shaping well. Hence, in spite of Allah being all-merciful, he did not see the Angels of Smile, Happiness, Love, Mercy, Kindness, Optimism and Humanity. All these angels did not come to Muhammad because he was a creature of hate and revenge. His dreams were censored in his subconscious.

Another point demonstrates the fallacy of his al-Mi'raj. Though Muhammad took a visionary travel to the paradise, nowhere can we find any statement that he was awestruck neither by the previous Prophets whom he bragged to have visited in different skies nor by facing Allah himself. Were the demonic creatures, angels and Buraq more awe-inspiring than visiting legendary Prophets in the grandeur of the seven heavens and talking with Allah? The reason is, the "picture" was already there in his subconscious mind. He just dreamed off the pre-fabricated picture according to his need.

All dreams are obstructed by dream-distortions which make the dream seems strange and unintelligible to us. For the children, there is hardly any distortion; for adults, the distortion is less; while for the neurotic patients, obviously it is much more. Often there are omissions, modifications, fresh groupings of the material; which are the activities of dream-censorship and instruments of dream-distortion. These two factors give the dream the strangeness on account of which the dreamer himself is not inclined to recognize it as his own production and makes "surprising discoveries" which confuse others.

The al-Mi'raj fascinates the Muslims so much that they try to redecorate the various dream-distortions of their Prophet to give some credibility to it. The unique physical appearance of Buraq – the half mule, half donkey with a human head – tells us that it was a dream-distortion. Why Buraq did not resemble to an elephant? It is because Muhammad did not know how an elephant looks like. During those days there was no elephant in Arabia. Elephants are entirely vegetarian and most of Saudi Arabia is covered in desert with hardly any vegetation for these huge animals to survive. Muhammad loved donkey-riding and the name of his legendary donkey was Yafur (Warraq, 2000, p. 241). Hence, Buraq was at least half donkey. Why a human head? It was because a creature with a human head is more intelligent than a creature with an animal head. Allah's divine creature has to be smart. I am not sure why the other half looked like a mule, or more scientifically, what was the unknown content for this "distorted substitute", i.e., the half mule. Allah knows best!

According to Muhammad, the first heaven was of pure silver and the stars were suspended by chains of gold. Angels lay awake to guard it and to prevent the spirits from listening indiscreetly to celestial secrets. If heaven is an absolute spiritual place, why it was decorated with pure silver and gold – the earthly things which need to be guarded? Let me undo the distortion and remove the censorship. It is not unusual for a beggar to dream of a grand feast, or a cobbler to become a king, or a political novice to become the President of his state, or a greedy person like Muhammad to dream pure silver and chains of gold, etc. When a person is unhappy in real life, his secret wishes are often censored and rise up in his dream.

The distortion is greater when the wishes that are to be satisfied by hallucination worsen. Much stringent examination is needed to undo the distortion of other manifested elements; e.g., the angel larger than the world with seventy thousand mouths. We often hear of fabulous beasts in ancient mythology and folklore, which were no doubt "creative" imaginations. Though we call this as creative, actually this type of imagination is quite incapable of "inventing" anything. It only combines components that are strange to one another and makes a composite figure (Strachey & Gay, 1966, p. 211); as example; A is dressed like B, acts like C, thinks like D, and looks like E etc. This is what we call a composite structure. Buraq itself was a composite structure of a mule, donkey and a human. When the final product "condenses", it takes totally a new shape which presents an alien appearance to the dreamer himself and much more so to anyone who is unacquainted with him personally.

2.1.7: Conclusion

"Objective evidence, not faith, is the ultimate criterion of truth in the order of natural knowledge."

Celestine N. Bittle (1936, p. 315)

"Men are very prone to believe what they do not understand."

Ibn Warraq (2011, p. 193)

The presence of an idea or belief in one's consciousness does not constitute knowledge; one can have false ideas and false beliefs. If man is to acquire knowledge, he must have a method of distinguishing truth from falsity – beliefs which correspond to reality from beliefs which do not. To qualify as knowledge (i.e., as a correct identification of reality), a belief must be justified; it must warrant acceptance by rational standards. If a belief meets the requirements of these standards, it is a rational belief. If a belief cannot meet the requirements – but is adopted nonetheless – it is an irrational belief, or simply a truth-claim.

Scientists and theologians alike make truth-claims based on extraordinary experiences that may be accessed by only a select group of highly trained individuals, yet they maintain these truths are universal, throughout space and time and for all possible subjects. The difference between scientific and religious claims is that the former can be verified by third-person criteria, whereas the latter cannot. Often religious claims are overactive imaginations, or personal experiences. When it comes to scientific and mathematical assertions about the nature of reality, a certain degree of consensus has been established as to how to evaluate such claims. But there is no such consensus regarding the alleged discoveries of contemplatives of different religious traditions.

The theologians use the metaphor of shell and the kernel (it means, if you can crack the hard shell you can reach the soft kernel) to make the point. The religious ceremonies, fable, folk-lore, traditional belief, religious holidays and pilgrimages — these are merely the outward signs of "something" that is believed to be informing them and giving them significance. That "something" is the religion's truth-claims. In Islam, this "something" is the Allah. Muhammad's truth-claim and religious assertions were purely dogmatic in nature; they are not based on logical reasoning. If we take away the outward signs of Allah, whatever remains is something like an ancient Arabic video game of a superhero created by Muhammad. This superhero is even more exciting than the Marvel comics' heroes.

2.2: Muhammad's delusionary confusions

Islam had spread by sword and deception. Muhammad had to be ruthless in imposing adherence to his belief in his own divine mission because his belief could not stand on its own, based as it was on a delusion. He had shown all the symptoms of his lunacy. He had a total loss of insight, i.e. there was a loss of awareness that his beliefs were not shared by others and were results of being unwell. He clearly had a different version of reality than the rest of us.

2.2.1: Muhammad was deluded about his Allah

"He who would distinguish the true from the false must have an adequate idea of what is true and false."

Benedict Spinoza (1632-1677)

During those days when Muhammad began preaching Islam in Mecca there was much idolatry in practice with hundreds of deities around. This made him utterly confused. When he received the first revelation, overnight he changed his rank from a merchant-man to a Prophet without even knowing from whom he received the divine instruction. The "voice" he had heard in the cave did not tell him about the identity of his god. In spite of that, he started warning the Meccans with dire consequences if they did not accept him as a Prophet while he himself was in such a delusion. Thereafter he had experimented with various brands of Allah, but the Meccans disappointed him, and hence he changed his mind several times.

Surprisingly, the real Allah did not come forward to remove his confusion. Later on he realized that all the pagans, despite their numerous idols, were wholly devoted to their Moon God, Allah, because they believed that Allah had the ability to inflict punishment as well as rewards. This is the only reason Muhammad choose the pagan Allah as his God. Therefore, those who try to single out Allah and glorify him above the other Meccan idols should remember that Muhammad could just as easily have picked Manaf, al-Lat, al-Uzza, or any of the others. Allah did not find Muhammad but it was Muhammad who looked for a suitable "Allah" to preach in his name. Every time, as situation demanded, Muhammad made some necessary changes to his version of Allah. Finally he designed his own Allah to go well with his requirement and hence Allah had the likes and dislikes similar to him. Qur'an says, Muhammad and the pagans did not worship the same God.

"Say: O disbelievers! I worship not that which ye worship; Nor worship ye that which I worship. And I shall not worship that which ye worship. Nor will ye worship that which I worship. Unto you your religion, and unto me my religion." (Q: 109.1-6)

The above verses pose a basis problem. Allah is referring to exactly whom? Are they people of the book (Christians, Jews and Sabians)? Are they Meccan idolaters? Are they every non-Muslim? Allah did not specify whom Muhammad was supposed to address this way. This is a crucial problem, because the above verses contradict many other verses of the Qur'an. As example,

*"Surely those who believe, and those who are Jews, and the Christians, and the Sabians, **whoever believes in Allah and the Last day** and does good, they shall have their reward from their Lord, and there is no fear for them, nor shall they grieve."* (Q: 2.62)

*"Say: Do you dispute with us about Allah, and **He is our Lord and your Lord,** and we shall have our deeds and you shall have your deeds, and **we are sincere to Him**."* (Q: 2.139)

*"And argue not with the People of the Scripture unless it be in (a way) that is better, save with such of them as do wrong; and say: We believe in that which hath been revealed unto us and revealed unto you; **our Allah and your Allah is One, and unto Him we surrender.**"* (Q: 29.46)

*"Say: O followers of the Book! **Come to an equitable proposition between us and you that we shall not serve any but Allah** and (that) we shall not associate aught with Him, and some of us shall not take others for lords besides Allah; but if they turn back, then say: **Bear witness that we are Muslims**."* (Q: 3.64)

This confirms that Allah was the same God of the people of the book. But the following verses say that the Pagan Meccans also believed the same God.

"And if you ask them, Who created the heavens and the earth and made the sun and the moon subservient, they will certainly say, Allah. Whence are they then turned away? ... surely Allah is Cognizant of all things. And if you ask them Who is it that sends down water from the clouds, then gives life to the earth with it after its death, they will certainly say, Allah. Say: All praise is due to Allah. Nay, most of them do not understand." (Q: 29.61-3)

"And the idolaters say: Had Allah willed, we had not worshipped aught beside Him, we and our fathers, nor had we forbidden aught without (command from) Him. Even so did those before them." (Q: 16.35)

"Had Allah willed, they had not been idolatrous. We have not set thee as a keeper over them, nor art thou responsible for them." (Q: 6.107)

*"**Surely pure religion is for Allah only**. And those who choose protecting friends beside Him (say): **We worship them only that they may bring us near unto Allah.** Lo! Allah will judge between them concerning that wherein they differ. Lo! Allah guides not him who is a liar, an ingrate."* (Q: 39.3)

These verses confirm that the Pagans main direction of worship was Allah, and other Gods were only intermediaries/intercessors for the purpose of bringing them near to Allah. It means Allah was not just one of their many Gods, but the main and highest one of all their Gods. Hence, this indirectly indicates that Allah is not the

134

only God. Another verse confirms that the pagans knew and believed in Allah.

"If thou ask them, who it is that created the heavens and the earth. They will certainly say, "Allah". Say: "Praise be to Allah!" But most of them understand not." (Q: 31.25)

If these verses are true that why the verses 109.1-6 claim that the unbelievers were not worshipping that which Muhammad worshipped? How can we call the Qur'an a holy book when the Allah himself is severely confused about himself and his worshippers? Let us analyze one more verse.

"Say: O people! if you are in doubt as to my religion, then (know that) I do not serve those whom you serve besides Allah but I do serve Allah, **Who will cause you to die**, *and I am commanded that I should be of the believers."* (Q: 10.104)

In this verse Allah will cause the unbelievers to die because of their unbelieving status. But the verse 16.35 says *"Had Allah willed, we had not worshipped aught beside Him"*. If their unbelieving status is also the will of Allah why Allah should cause them to die? However, this is not the end of the confusion. Qur'an says,

"To Him belongs every being that is in the heavens and on earth: all are devoutly obedient to Him." (Q: 30.26)

If all the creatures are *"devoutly obedient"* to Allah, then when Muhammad conquered Mecca why there was a necessity that nearly all the citizens were converted to Islam by force with the consequence that Allah was then no longer just one of their gods but their one and only object of worship? Similar to this there are many questions which need to be answered. God cannot be deluded; it was the imposter who claimed to be a Prophet was deluded. Now what should we say about the following verses?

"But what is the mission of messengers but to preach the Clear Message?" (Q: 16.35)

"This is the Book; in it is guidance sure, without doubt, to those who fear Allah." (Q: 2.2)

According to traditions Muhammad was a megalomaniac. In Islam only belief in Allah is not enough to enter paradise and Muslims must believe the prophethood of Muhammad also. If Muhammad was only a spokesman of God, why Muslims have to praise him in their daily prayers? Though in Islam Allah is portrayed as all-powerful, this is in theory only. In practice, Muhammad is the central figure in Islam and Allah is just a piece of decoration. Allah is obliged to throw a person in hell even if he is sincerely devoted to him but does not believe in Muhammad. Now we know how helpless the God of Islam is. Traditional sources confirm that Muhammad was a denier of reality. He re-interpreted reality to fit his fantasies.

"Allah's Apostle said, 'Whoever obeys me, obeys Allah, and whoever disobeys me, disobeys Allah, and whoever obeys the ruler I appoint, obeys me, and whoever disobeys him, disobeys me'." (Bukhari: 9.89.251)

"Allah's Apostle said, 'Whoever obeys me will enter Paradise, and whoever disobeys me will not enter it'." (Bukhari: 9.92.384)

"Allah's Apostle; the Lord of the Muslims, Leader of the Allah Fearing, Messenger of the Lord of Worlds, the Peerless and Unequalled". (Ishaq: 233)

"Allah addressed the believers and said, 'In Allah's Apostle you have a fine example for anyone who hopes to be in the place where Allah is'." (Ishaq: 467)

"I heard Allah's Apostle saying, 'He who obeys me, obeys Allah, and he who disobeys me, disobeys Allah'." (Bukhari: 4.52.203)

"Those who speak negatively of Allah and His Apostle shall be cursed". (Q: 33.57)

Though Muhammad placed himself as a humble servant of Allah, we cannot see any humbleness in these words, and surprisingly, his Allah tolerated his arrogance. And after a certain period elapsed, Allah became less important than Muhammad and Muhammad emerged as "the living God". With this appearance, the person of Muhammad stood out above all in front rank and Allah was given a secondary position in his capacity as the auxiliary of the Prophet. Allah is no longer the Supreme Being and now he is inferior to Muhammad. Qur'an says,

"Lo! Allah and His angels pray peace to Prophet (Muhammad).O ye who believe also shower praises on him and salute him with a worthy salutation." (Q: 33.56)

*"... and when they (nonbelievers) come to thee, **they salute thee, not as Allah salutes thee**, (but in crooked ways) ... Enough for them is Hell: In it will they burn, and evil is that destination!"* (Q: 58.8)

The above two verses are enough to prove that the Allah was a myth and Muhammad was a rude imposter. He not only ridiculed and belittled his god, but at the same time also represented the entire divine system as a big joke. Throughout Qur'an, Allah has no authority alone and he is so pitifully helpless without his messenger that if we completely erase the name of Allah from hundreds of verses throughout the Qur'an, and Muslims are asked to believe in, to submit to, and to obey Allah and his Apostle, practically nothing would change.

2.2.2: Muhammad was deluded about his religion

"No matter how you look at Islam it turns out to be a foolish religion."
Ali Sina (Ghamidi et. al, 2007, p. 211)

Muhammad was not only deluded about his god, but also about the religion he was supposed to propagate. Qur'an says,

"*And strive in His cause as ye ought to strive, (with sincerity and under discipline). He has chosen you, and has imposed no difficulties on you in religion; it is the cult of your father Abraham.* **It is He Who has named you Muslims, both before and in this (Revelation)**." (Q: 22.78)

It means, there were Muslims before Muhammad received the Qur'an, but there is some ambiguity about who named them Muslims. Though most interpreters believe it is Allah and this is probably the intended meaning, there are some scholars who think the pronoun "he" refers to Abraham, the nearest antecedent to the pronoun, i.e. "*it is the cult of your father Abraham. It is he (Abraham) who has named...*" Allah is probably the intended subject in the naming process, but the Qur'an is ambiguous. Had the Qur'an said "We named you Muslims ..." or "Allah named you" instead of "he named you", the confusion could have been avoided.

The second issue with the statement, "*It is He Who has named you Muslims, both before and in this*", is this – Whom exactly does the pronoun "you" refers to? There is no doubt that the Qur'an gives the name "Muslims" to those who believe in it and obey its message. It certainly includes the companions of Muhammad and all believers in his message from then on. Does it also include polytheist believers (Qur'an confirms that Alexander the Great was a Muslim and history confirms that he was a polytheist) before Muhammad's time? No doubt there is much ambiguity in the formulation of the statement. Some verses say Abraham was the first Muslim.

"*And when Abraham and Ishmael were raising the foundations of the House, (Abraham prayed): Our Lord! Accept from us (this duty). Lo! Thou, only Thou, art the Hearer, the Knower. Our Lord! Make of us Muslims, bowing to Thy (Will), and of our progeny a people Muslim, bowing to Thy (will).*" (Q: 2.127-8)

"*When his Lord said to him (Abraham), Be a Muslim, he said: I submit myself to the Lord of the worlds.*" (Q: 2.131)

"*Abraham was not a Jew nor a Christian but he was (an) upright (man), a Muslim, and he was not one of the polytheists.*" (Q: 3.67)

The statements, "*Our Lord, make of us Muslims*" and "*Lord said to him, be a Muslim*" confirm that Allah named Abraham Muslim. Now, if Abraham was the original messenger of Islam, a verse that says Adam was the first Muslim is wrong.

"*Then Adam received from his Lord words (of revelation), and He relented toward him.*" (Q: 2.37)

Adam being the first human predates Abraham. If Islam is as old as Abraham then Adam cannot be a Muslim. Another verse says that Jesus and his followers were first Muslims.

"*When Jesus found Unbelief on their part He said: "Who will be My helpers to*

(the work of) Allah?" Said the disciples: "We are Allah's helpers: We believe in Allah, and do thou bear witness that we are Muslims." (Q: 3.52)
Yet two other verses say Moses was the first Muslim.

"We gave Moses the Book and followed him up with a succession of messengers;" (Q: 2.87)

"... Moses fell down in a swoon. When he recovered his senses he said: 'Glory be to Thee! to Thee I turn in repentance, I am the first to believe.'" (Q: 7.143)

Another verse says that some magicians of Pharaoh were the first Muslims.

"They said: Only, our desire is that our Lord will forgive us our faults, that we may become foremost among the believers!" (Q: 26.51)

But some other verses confirm that Muhammad was the first Muslim.

"Nay! but I am commanded to be the first of those who bow to Allah (in Islam), and be not thou of the company of those who join gods with Allah'." (Q: 6.14)

"No partner hath He: this am I commanded, and I am the first of those who bow to His will." (Q: 6.163)

"And I (Muhammad) am commanded to be the first of those who bow to Allah in Islam." (Q: 39.12)

The name Muslim is found only in the Qur'an. There is no other scripture that predates Qur'an mention the Muslims. But if various ambiguous verses claim that Moses, Jesus, Adam, Abraham and Egyptians were also Muslims, why do not we find the name "Muslim" in other scriptures? When we examine the Bible, we see that it never uses the term Muslim, neither the Arabic word nor its Hebrew or Greek equivalent. When the Qur'an considers earlier Prophets to be Muslims by actually making several statements to that effect, how to verify such a claim unless we find some references in the earlier scriptures? This is a quite serious historical error in the Qur'an because the statement *"He named you Muslims before and in this"* (Q: 22.78) contains a historical claim. It is not a matter of faith but a question of history, and it is either true or false based on objective reality. This claim is, thus, subject to historical evaluation that can be checked against the known historical facts.

Muhammad, the actual author of the Qur'an, exerted great efforts to connect Islam with Abraham, Adam, Moses and Jesus and pretended that his mission was the sequel of the previous Semitic Prophets. The second part of the verse 22.78 claims exactly that – *"it is the cult of your father Abraham"*.

One verse brings more confusion in this discussion. It says that all the Prophets who were given the Torah were Muslims.

"Lo! We did reveal the Torah, wherein is guidance and a light, by which the prophets who surrendered (unto Allah) judged the Jews, and the rabbis and the

priests (judged) by such of Allah's Scripture as they were bidden to observe, and thereunto were they witnesses." (Q: 5.44)

This verse confirms all the Biblical Prophets before Muhammad were Muslims though they knew nothing of the Qur'an.

"We gave him Isaac and Jacob: all (three) guided: and before him, We guided Noah, and among his progeny, David, Solomon, Job, Joseph, Moses, and Aaron: thus do We reward those who do good. And Isma'il and Elisha, and Jonas, and Lot: and to all We gave favor above the nations." (Q: 6.84-6)

Now we can realize that there is a very serious ambiguity at the very basic belief system of Islam. Literally "Muslim" simply means "one who submits" and it is at times used in a very generic sense. The concept of "submitting to God" is nothing that is distinctive of Islam. It is an essential part in nearly every religion. Somebody in submission to the old Egyptian Gods Isis and Osiris, to the Greek Gods Zeus and Poseidon, to the Hindu Gods Vishnu or Shiva, or to any other God that is clearly not the Allah of Islam, could or should not be called "a Muslim". If Christ and Moses were also Muslims, then should the Christians and Jews call themselves Muslims? If so, why the Jews and Christians are the prime target of Muslim hatred and terrorism? A Hadith from Bukhari compounds the problem.

*"Narrated Abu Huraira: Allah's Apostle said, '**Every child is born with a true faith of Islam** (i.e. to worship none but Allah Alone) but his parents convert him to Judaism, Christianity or Paganism, as an animal delivers a perfect baby animal. Do you find it mutilated?'"* (Bukhari: 2.23.441)

But following verse indicates something else.

"This day have those who disbelieve despaired of your religion, so fear them not, and fear Me. This day have I perfected for you your religion and completed My favor on you and chosen for you Islam as a religion". (Q: 5.3)

If Allah has perfected the faith only during the time of Muhammad, then how every person who lived before Muhammad was already a Muslim? Needless to say, if we consider the Qur'an to be an eternal word of a true God, the question itself does not arise when Islam started or who was the first Muslim. But we have already seen how time-bound the eternal word of Allah is. Now what should we say about the following verse?

"It is those who believe and confuse not their beliefs with wrong - that are (truly) in security, for they are on (right) guidance." (Q: 6.82)

Islam is indeed a very confusing religion, because the Prophet of Islam was utterly confused. Muhammad did not have a clear idea about God and spirituality. Any attempt to talk about the unknowable Allah would eventually lead to strange and paradoxical assertions. The simple fact is that every Qur'anic contradiction on this subject leads to another contradiction if we logically read them. A sincere reader finds himself immersed in hopeless absurdities. Undoubtedly, Muslims have a lot of problems that they must deal with.

2.2.3: Muhammad's false prophecy

"Most religions prophecy the end of the world and then consistently work together to ensure that these prophecies come true."

Anonymous

The word "Prophet" originally means one who foretells future events. False Prophets are those who falsely claim the gift of prophecy. Often Muslim clerics argue that Qur'an contains accurate prophecies which provide great evidence of a supernatural influence. Let us examine few predictions made by Muhammad in the Qur'an and Islamic traditions to see if he passes the test. Muhammad's most important and oft repeated prophecy is the Day of Doom. About this calamitous event Qur'an says,

"There is no denying that it will befall - abasing (some), exalting (others); when the earth is shaken with a shock and the hills are ground to powder so that they become a scattered dust. " (Q: 56.2-6)

But when is it going to occur? When Muhammad's prophecy will come true?

"The Prophet said, 'I was sent immediately before the coming of the Day of Doom. I preceded it like this one preceding that one'-- referring to his index and middle finger." (Tabari: I.181)

"A'isha reported that when the desert Arabs came to Allah's Messenger they asked about the Last Hour as to when that would come. And he looked towards the youngest amongst them and said: If he lives he may not grow very old till (he would see) the Last Hour coming to you". (Muslim: 41.7050)

"Anas b. Malik reported that a person asked Allah's Apostle: When would the Last Hour come? Thereupon Allah's Messenger kept quiet for a while, then looked at a young boy in his presence belonging to the tribe of Azd Shanilwa and he said: If this boy lives he would not grow very old till the Last Hour would come to you. Anas said that this young boy was of our age during those days." (Muslim: 41.7052)

Muhammad believed that the world was about to end shortly after his advent.

"Anas reported Allah's Messenger as saying: I and the Last Hour have been sent like this and (he while doing it) joined the forefinger with the middle finger". (Muslim: 41.7049)

About fourteen centuries have passed after Muhammad had shared his divine insight in the seventh century. But we did not notice anything – neither the earth was shaken, nor the hills were ground to powder to become a scattered dust.

Muhammad was not the only Prophet who failed in his prediction of the end of the world prophecy. In the words of Robert L. Snow (2003, p. 109),

"Practically everyone has seen the cartoon with a character wearing the sandwich sign that proclaims, "The end is near". While this meant as a joke, throughout history, a large number of people have proclaimed with all seriousness that they have unique knowledge that the end of the world is coming. Through this proclamation, many Prophets of doom have attracted large group of followers who believe that these doom forecasters have some type of special insight, special vision or special relationship with God that gives them inside knowledge about the impending end of the world. Once this belief system is established, the doomsday forecasters then have tremendous control over the lives of the people who believe in them."

Muhammad did not perform any better. This lunatic had no unique knowledge about unseen and unknown. According to Bukhari, Muhammad announced that everyone would be dead within a hundred years.

"Narrated 'Abdullah bin 'Umar: Once the Prophet led us in the 'Isha' prayer during the last days of his life and after finishing it (the prayer) (with Taslim) he said: "Do you realize (the importance of) this night? Nobody present on the surface of the earth tonight will be living after the completion of one hundred years from this night'." (Bukhari: 1.3.116)

"Narrated Abdullah: "One night Allah's Apostle led us in the 'Isha' prayer and that is the one called Al-'Atma by the people. After the completion of the prayer, he faced us and said, 'Do you know the importance of this night? Nobody present on the surface of the earth tonight will be living after one hundred years from this night.'" (Bukhari: 1.10.539)

Nearly fourteen centuries have gone by but the Human race is still not extinct. These particular ahadith (plural of hadith) were so troubling that another narration tries to explain it away by arguing that Muhammad really meant that none of his generation would be alive in a hundred years.

*"Narrated 'Abdullah bin 'Umar: The Prophet prayed one of the 'Isha' prayer in his last days and after finishing it with Taslim, he stood up and said, "Do you realize (the importance of) this night? Nobody present on the surface of the earth tonight would be living after the completion of one hundred years from this night.' **The people made a mistake in grasping the meaning of this statement of Allah's Apostle and they indulged in those things which are said about these narrators** (i.e. some said that the Day of Resurrection will be established after 100 years etc.) But the Prophet said, "Nobody present on the surface of earth tonight would be living after the completion of 100 years from this night"; he meant, 'When that century (people of that century) would pass away'."* (Bukhari: 1.10.575)

The statement *"The people made a mistake in grasping the meaning of this statement of Allah's Apostle"* needs to be noted. The honest admission of the narrator that Muslims understood from Muhammad's words that the world was going to end in a hundred years provides supporting evidence that the plain meaning of Muhammad's so-called prophecy was that the last day would occur within a hundred years. Moreover, if we are really expected to believe that what Muhammad meant was that no one of his generation would be alive within a hundred years when there is nothing amazing about such a claim. To say that one's generation would all be dead within a hundred years does not require supernatural knowledge. The only thing required to make such a claim is a common observation since life expectancy was low in those days.

Even if we give him the benefit of doubt, still it is false. Muhammad said *"on the surface of the earth"* – that is a large place. Although centenarians are rare, they certainly existed at all times. Even during Muhammad there was at least one such person. Abu Afak is reported to have lived to the age of 120. Muhammad got him murdered because he criticized him in his poetry. In another false prophecy Muhammad said,

> *"He said: 'Allah will not make this nation [of Islam] incapable of lasting half a day - a day being a thousand years.'"* (Tabari: I.182)

This means that the earth should have been annihilated 500 years after Muhammad shared his divine insight in seventh century. The twelfth century came and went without incident. The only mystery is – why we still see Islam around us?

On the appearance of the antichrist, Muhammad predicted that the antichrist (called the Dajjal) would appear after the Muslim conquest of Constantinople.

> *"Narrated Mu'adh ibn Jabal: Prophet said: The flourishing state of Jerusalem will be when Yathrib is in ruins, the ruined state of Yathrib will be when the great war comes, the outbreak of the great war will be at the conquest of Constantinople and the conquest of Constantinople when the Dajjal comes forth... This is as true as you are here or as you (Mu'adh ibn Jabal) are sitting."* (Sunnan Abu Dawud: 37.4281)

> *"Narrated Mu'adh ibn Jabal: Prophet said: The greatest war, the conquest of Constantinople and the coming forth of the Dajjal (Antichrist) will take place within a period of seven months."* (Sunnan Abu Dawud: 37.4282)

> *"Narrated Abdullah ibn Busr: Prophet said: The time between the great war and the conquest of the city (Constantinople) will be six years, and the Dajjal (Antichrist) will come forth in the seventh."* (Sunnan Abu Dawud: 37.4283)

Muslims conquered Jerusalem in 636 AD and Constantinople in May 1453 AD. Yet the prophecy regarding Yathrib (Medina) being in ruins and Antichrist's advent to take place seven months after the conquest of Constantinople did not materialize. Based on the preceding traditions Antichrist was to appear in November 1453. Muhammad's predictions failed to materialize.

This verse talks about Allah's prediction on the Roman conquest of Persia.

"The Roman Empire has been defeated - in a land close by: But they, (even) after defeat of theirs, will soon be victorious – within ten years." (Q: 30.2-4)

There is a fundamental problem with this alleged prophecy. According to the authentic historical records the victory did not come until nearly fourteen years later. The Persians defeated the Byzantines and captured Jerusalem at about 614-5 AD. The Byzantine counter-offensive did not begin until 622 AD and the victory was not complete until 628 AD, making it a period between thirteen to fourteen years, not "within ten years". A prophecy from a true God would specify the exact time of the victory. When God specifies a time frame as an important part of a prophecy we would expect that it be precise, not a mere guess. Otherwise, what would be the point of such an announcement? Elsewhere, Muhammad predicted,

"Narrated 'Abdullah bin 'Umar: Prophet said, "On the Day of Resurrection, the Sun will come near (to, the people) to such an extent that the sweat will reach up to the middle of the ears, so, when all the people are in that state, they will ask Adam for help, and then Moses, and then Muhammad". (Bukhari: 2.24.553)

This is absolutely ridiculous. The sun coming down to scorch people and they sweat so much to get drowned in their own sweat is surly an art work of imaginative power of a lunatic.

In view of the above, we can safely conclude that Muhammad's failed the test since none of his prophecies were fulfilled, and his prophetic credential is much under question. For Allah to guess the future as opposed to specifying the exact year is inconsistent with the belief in an omniscient, omnipotent Being.

2.2.4: The anthropomorphic descriptions of Allah

"Men have ascribed to God imperfections that they would deplore in themselves".

W. Somerset Maugham

"People fashion their God after their own understanding. They make their God first and worship him afterwards."

Oscar Wilde

In the initial days of Islam, it was too difficult for Muhammad to explain to the illiterate and superstitious Bedouin folks his twisted concept of Allah. The desert people always associated their concept of God(s) to a physical entity. Therefore, when Muhammad introduced his new Allah to them they were very confused. They suspected Muhammad and questioned his sanity. Hence he associated his Allah with some living creatures. At first, he associated the appearance of Allah with the first and the original human being, i.e., Adam.

"Narrated Abu Huraira: Prophet said, 'Allah created Adam in his complete shape and form (directly), sixty cubits (about 30 meters) in height'. Prophet added 'So whoever will enter Paradise, will be of the shape and form of Adam. Since then the creation of Adam's (offspring) (i.e. stature of human beings is being diminished continuously) to the present time." (Bukhari: 8.74.246)

"...on the authority of Ibn Hatim, Allah's Apostle is reported to have said: When any one of you fights with his brother, he should avoid his face for Allah created Adam in His own image". (Muslim: 32.6325)

Contrary to popular Muslim belief, Allah is not shapeless. He has a physical form, and he can be seen and heard. Qur'an says,

"And when Musa came at Our appointed time and his Lord spoke to him, he said: My Lord! show me (Thyself), so that I may look upon Thee. He said: You cannot (bear to) see Me but look at the mountain, if it remains firm in its place, then will you see Me". (Q: 7.143)

Since Allah looks like a human being, it is logical to believe that Allah must have all the physical features of a human being.

"He is the One that hears and sees (all things)." (Q: 42.11).

"(Allah says) But construct an Ark under Our eyes and Our inspiration, and address Me no (further) on behalf of those who are in sin: for they are about to be overwhelmed (in the Flood)" (Q: 11.37)

"(Allah) said: O Iblis! What prevents thee from prostrating thyself to one whom I have created with my hands?" (Q: 38.75)

"Surely those who swear allegiance to you do but swear allegiance to Allah; the hand of Allah is above their hands." (Q: 48.10)

"Allah has indeed heard (and accepted) the statement of the woman who pleads with thee concerning her husband and carries her complaint (in prayer) to Allah: and Allah (always) hears the arguments between both sides among you: for Allah hears and sees (all things)." (Q: 58.1)

The above verses confirm that Allah has eyes, ears and hands. A hadith from Muslim confirms that Allah is not deaf; he can talk and listen and he is really a physical entity just like a human being.

"Abu Musa reported that he and his other companions were climbing upon the hillock along with Allah's Messenger and when any person climbed up, he pronounced (loudly), 'There is no god but Allah, Allah is the Greatest'. Thereupon Allah's Apostle said: Verily, you are not supplicating One Who is deaf or absent." (Muslim: 35.6528)

Allah's hands are huge. With his huge arms Allah can shake hands with the believers. Also his two physical hands are outstretched.

"Narrated Abu Huraira: I heard Allah's Apostle saying, 'Allah will hold the whole earth, and roll all the heavens up in His Right Hand, and then He will say, 'I am the King; where are the kings of the earth?'" (Bukhari: 6.60.336)

"Ubayy b. Ka'b reported that Allah's Messenger said, "The first person with whom Allah will shake hands (on the Day of Judgment), will be 'Umar and he will be the first man to whom Allah will pay salutation (say: Assalamu 'alaika) and he will be the first man whom he will hold with his Hand and make him enter the Paradise." (Sunaan ibn Majah: 1.104)

"The Jews say: 'Allah's hand is tied up'. Be their hands tied up and be they accursed for the (blasphemy) they utter. Nay, both His hands are widely outstretched: He gives and spends (of His bounty) as He pleases." (Q: 5.6)

On the Judgment Day Allah will use his two outstretched hands to fold up the heavens (universe), like folding a piece of rug. After folding up the heavens with his two outstretched hands, he will then hold them (the universe) in his right hand. In other hand he will hold the balance of justice.

"No just estimate have they made of Allah, such as is due to Him: On the Day of Judgment the whole of the earth will be but His handful, and the heavens will be rolled up in His right hand: Glory to Him! High is He above the Partners they attribute to Him!" (Q: 39.67)

"Narrated Abu Huraira: Allah's Apostle said, 'Allah said, 'Spend (O man), and I shall spend on you'. He also said, 'Allah's Hand is full, and (its fullness) is not affected by the continuous spending night and day'. He also said, 'Do you see what He has spent since He created the Heavens and the Earth? Nevertheless, what is in His Hand is not decreased, and His Throne was over the water; and in His Hand there is the balance (of justice) whereby He raises and lowers (people)'." (Bukhari: 6.60.206)

"Narrated Abu Huraira: The Prophet said, 'The right hand of Allah is full, and its fullness is not affected by the continuous spending night and day. Do you see what He has spent since He created the Heavens and the Earth? Yet all that has not decreased what is in his right hand. His Throne is over the water and in His other hand is the bounty or the power to bring about death, and He raises some people and brings others down." (Bukhari: 9.93.515)

Allah also has huge feet so that he can put his foot on hellfire.

"Narrated Anas: The Prophet said, 'The people will be thrown into the (Hell) Fire and it will say: 'Are there any more (to come)?' (Q: 50.30) till Allah puts His Foot over it and it will say, 'Qati! Qati! (Enough Enough!)'" (Bukhari: 6.60.371)

"Narrated Abu Huraira: The Prophet said: As for the Fire (Hell), it will not be filled till Allah puts His Foot over it whereupon it will say, 'Qati! Qati! (Enough Enough!)'" (Bukhari: 6.60.373)

"Anas b. Malik reported that Allah's Apostle said that the Hell would continue to say: Is there anything more, until Allah, the Exalted and High, would place His foot therein and that would say: Enough, enough." (Muslim: 40.6823)

"Abd al-Wahhab b. Ata reported: We would say to Hell on the Day of Resurrection: Have you been completely filled up? And it would say: Is there anything more? And he stated on the authority of Anas b. Malik that Allah's Apostle said: (The sinners) would be thrown therein and it would continue to say: Is there anything more, until Allah, the Exalted and Glorious, would keep His foot therein and..." (Muslim: 40.6823).

This confirms the physical nature of Allah's foot. Muslim scholars try to twist the meaning of those ahadith and contain that the mentions of the physical attributes of Allah are metaphorical. But in doing so they actually deny this verse,

"Lo! Allah graspeth the heavens and the earth that they deviate not, and if they were to deviate there is not one that could grasp them after Him. Lo! He is ever Clement, Forgiving." (Q: 35.41)

Unless Allah has huge physical hands, how can he hold the earth and heavens in one place? Because the earth is physical, not metaphorical, it can only be hold in one place by physical force. Therefore to deny that Allah's hands are symbolic is same as denying the verse 35.41. Muhammad really wanted us to believe that Allah has huge physical hands. Similarly Allah's hearing and seeing capabilities are also not symbolic. This hadith confirms that Allah really has the organs of hearing and seeing, i.e. ears and eyes.

"Abu Yunus Sulaim b. Jubair said: I heard Abu Hurairah recite this verse (Q: 4.58): "Allah doth command you to render back your trusts to those to whom they are due ... for Allah is He who heareth and seeth all things. He said: I saw the Apostle of Allah putting his thumb on his ear and finger on his eye. Abu Huraira said: I saw the Apostle of Allah reciting this verse and putting his fingers. Ibn Yunus said that al-Muqri said: "Allah hears and sees" means that Allah has the power to hearing and seeing." (Sunaan Abu Dawud: 3.4710)

Muhammad even compared the limbs of the idols of the Arab Pagans to those of Allah. Ridiculing the idols of the Arab polytheists, he told them that their idols' limbs were useless, whereas Allah's hands, eyes, and feet are real and workable. It proves that Allah is superior to the Pagan Gods.

"Have they feet with which they walk, or have they hands with which they hold, or have they eyes with which they see, or have they ears with which they hear?

146

Say: Call your associates, then make a struggle (to prevail) against me and give me no respite." (Q: 7.195)

Since Muhammad wanted to show that his Allah was real, he attributed Allah with physical organs like human beings. Allah even has shin which will be shown on the Judgment day.

"*The Day that the shin shall be laid bare, and they shall be summoned to bow in adoration, but they shall not be able.*" (Q: 68.42)

This hadith says quite unmistakably that on the Judgment Day there will be no problem in seeing Allah in his physical form; he will be recognized by his shin.

"*Narrated Abu Sa'id Al-Khudri: Then the Almighty will come to them in a shape other than the one which they saw the first time, and He will say, 'I am your Lord', and they will say, 'You are not our Lord'. And none will speak to Him then but the Prophets, and then it will be said to them, 'Do you know any sign by which you can recognize Him?' They will say. 'The Shin', and so Allah will then uncover His Shin whereupon every believer will prostrate before Him and there will remain those who used to prostrate before Him just for showing off and for gaining good reputation. These people will try to prostrate but their backs will be rigid like one piece of a wood*" (Bukhari: 9.93.532)

While giving Allah the human attributes, Muhammad suddenly realized that the Arab polytheists may compare Allah with the Dajjal (anti-Christ). Therefore, just to separate the Dajjal from Allah, he declared that Dajjal is one-eyed, but Allah is not.

"*Narrated Ibn Umar: Once Allah's Apostle stood amongst the people, glorified and praised Allah as He deserved and then mentioned the Dajjal saying, 'I warn you against him (Dajjal) and there was no prophet but warned his nation against him. No doubt, Noah warned his nation against him but I tell you about him something of which no prophet told his nation before me. You should know that he is one-eyed, and Allah is not one-eyed.'*" (Bukhari: 4.55.553)

In the Qur'an Allah says that he has a very handsome face.

"*But will abide (for ever) the Face of thy Lord - full of Majesty, Bounty and Honour.*" (Q: 55.27)

Muhammad's Allah speaks like a human. He spoke to Moses – "*O Moses! Verily, I am Allah, the exalted in might, the wise! Now do thou throw thy stick*". (Q: 27.9-10). When the stick turned into a snake, Moses was frightened and turned back, but Allah called him back – "*O Moses!, fear not: truly, in My presence, those called as messengers have no fear* (Q: 29.10), and, "*O Moses!, draw near, and fear not: for thou art of those who are secure.*" (Q: 28.31). Another verse says, Allah talked from a tree – "*But when he came to the (fire), a voice was heard from the right bank of the valley, from a tree in hallowed ground: 'O Moses! Verily I am Allah, the Lord of the Worlds....'*" (Q: 28.30). Yet on another occasion Allah called

Moses in the sacred valley of Tuwa – *"Behold, thy Lord did call to him in the sacred valley of Tuwa: Go thou to Pharaoh for he has indeed transgressed all bounds and say to him, 'Wouldst thou that thou shouldst be purified (from sin)? And that I guide thee to thy Lord, so thou shouldst fear Him?'"* (Q: 79.16-9). How was it possible for Moses to hear and understand Allah's voice if Allah did not use the same language as a human would to communicate verbally with Moses?

Not only Allah looks and talks like a human being but his thinking capability is often like imperfect human beings also. Muslims often overlook the fact that many of the Qur'anic references are simply anthropomorphic descriptions of Allah. These verses describe Allah's activities in a human manner to such an extent that Allah often comes down to the level of fallible man.

*"… they should answer My call and believe in Me that **they may walk** in the right way."* (Q: 2.186)

*"**Do you think** that you will enter the garden while **Allah has not yet known** those who strive hard from among you, and **(He has not) known** the patient."* (Q: 3.142)

*" … on the day when the two armies met, was by permission of Allah; that **He might know the true believers**, And that **He might know the hypocrites** …"* (Q: 3.166-7)

*"… that **Allah might know** who fears Him in secret."* (Q: 5.94)

*"And warn with it those who fear that they shall be gathered to their Lord-- there is no guardian for them, nor any intercessor besides Him-- that **they may guard** (against evil)."* (Q: 6.51)

*"See how We explain the signs by various (symbols); that **they may understand**."* (Q: 6.65)

*"The righteous are not responsible for the utterances of those people, but **it may help** to remind them, **perhaps they may be saved**."* (Q: 6.69)

*"… **it may be that** you will give up part of what is revealed to you."* (Q: 11.12)

*"Yet **it may be**, if they believe not in this statement, that thou (Muhammad) wilt torment thy soul with grief over their footsteps."* (Q: 18.6)

*"And speak to him mildly, **perhaps he may accept** admonition or fear Allah."* (Q: 20.44)

*"**Perhaps** you will kill yourself with grief because they do not believe"* (Q: 26.3)

*"**Allah will certainly know** those who are true from those who are false."* (Q: 29.3)

" ... *most certainly We will try you **until We have known** those among you who exert themselves hard, and the patient, and made your case manifest.*" (Q: 47.31)

"*Who created death and life that **He may try you** ...*" (Q: 67.2)

"*That **he may know** that they have indeed conveyed the messages .*" (Q: 72.28)

"*What could inform thee but that **He might grow** (in grace) or take heed and so the reminder might avail Him?*" (Q: 80.3-4)

"***Allah may know** those who believe and take witnesses from among you*" (Q: 3.140)

All the above (and many more) verses prove that Qur'an actually teaches that Allah does not know all things, and even has to guess at times. Even many Muslim scholars agreed to it, as example; Ayoub (1992, p. 330) lists Ar-Razi's response to the verse 3.140 and commented;

"*Razi is interested in the theological problems raised by the phrase 'in order that God may know.' He argues that 'the literal sense of God's saying, "in order that God may know" **would suggest that God alternated [the days] in order to acquire knowledge.** Obviously, this is impossible of God.' Razi cites verse 143, and a number of other verses where this phrase, or one like it, occurs. He alleges that **Hisham b. al-Hakkam, a well-known disciple of the Sixth Imam Ja'far al-Sadiq, used such verses to argue that God does not know incidents until they occur.** 'The answer of the theologians to this argument," Razi says, "is that rational proofs have conclusively established that no change ever occurs in God's knowledge. The linguistic usage of calling something that is known with the metaphor "knowledge", or something that is subject to power with the metaphor "power" is well known. Thus any Qur'anic verse the literal sense of which indicates acquisition of knowledge [by God] actually means the occurrence of a known.*"

The author of the Qur'an must have thought that Allah was actually uncertain about the future and could only hope that it would unfold according to his desires. It means Allah could only hope and wish like fallible human beings that things turned out his way. It also implies that the author of the Qur'an didn't think that Allah really knows everything or that he has total control over the affairs of his creation. A perfect God knows all things. He does not need to guess anything like imperfect creatures. No Muslim will ever dare to ask, why the Qur'an speaks of Allah in the same manner that it does of imperfect creatures.

2.2.5: The hidden atheist arguments in Allah's 'omni' attributes

What we understand from the Qur'an is that Allah is necessarily omniscient (all knowing), necessarily omnipotent (all powerful) and necessarily omnibenevolent (all merciful). But what the Muslims do not understand is that there is a serious conflict in these "omni" attributes of their Allah. If Allah is necessarily omnipotent, i.e., he has unlimited power then certainly he cannot be omniscient because such necessary omnipotence precludes him from having the experiences that are needed to acquire certain concepts. For example, it is impossible for an omnipotent Allah to comprehend fully certain concepts, such as fear, frustration, despair and greed that an omniscient being needs to possess. Here lies the hidden antitheist argument which the brainwashed Muslims cannot see. If Allah is omniscient then he has to understand all concepts fully. And one's full understanding of such concepts as fear, frustration, and despair requires one to experience fear, frustration and despair, respectively. But Allah cannot have those experiences because, by definition, he is necessarily omnipotent and so could not fall prey to the weakness entailed by the having of such experiences. Therefore, the argument concludes that the god of the Muslims does not exist.

Now, Muslims can argue that even if Allah himself cannot experience fear, frustration and despair there is no reason to conclude that he cannot possess concepts of them. Allah can possess such concepts by directly perceiving the "contents of human consciousness". For instance, someone – say, in a prayer – reflects vividly on his fear, then Allah will be able to perceive this person's feeling and to come to understand fully what fear is. But still there are difficulties with this reply. First of all, the omniscient Allah cannot depend on insignificant human beings to perceive the contents of human consciousness, simply because he is omniscient. Also, a timeless Allah cannot perceive human feelings, in particular, human sufferings. Allah, who transcends space and time, is not in a position to share human feelings. This is the doctrine of divine impassibility.

Moreover, the omnipotent God cannot be jealous. He cannot crave for praise and remembrance. But Allah is jealous and his mind is full of hatred for the mortal human beings.

> "*Jabir b. 'Atik reported that Prophet as saying: There is jealousy which Allah loves and jealousy which Allah hates. That which Allah loves is jealousy regarding a matter of doubt and that which Allah hates is jealousy regarding something which is not doubtful. There is pride which Allah hates and pride which Allah loves. That which Allah loves is a man's pride when fighting and when giving sadaqah and that which Allah hates is pride shown by oppression. The narrator Musa said: 'by boasting'.*" (Sunaan Abu Dawud: 2.2563)

Allah even promises to forgive all the sins if a believer praises him one hundred times after every prayer.

> "*Abu Huraira reported Allah's Messenger as saying: If anyone extols Allah after every prayer thirty-three times, and praises Allah thirty-three times, and declares His Greatness thirty-three times, ninety-nine times in all, and says to*

complete a hundred: 'There is no god but Allah, having no partner with Him, to Him belongs sovereignty and to Him is praise due, and He is Potent over everything', his sins will be forgiven even ff these are as abundant as the foam of the sea." (Muslim: 4.1243)

Qur'an repeatedly says that Allah is omnibenevolent. If Allah is all-powerful and perfectly good, why is there evil in the world? If Allah is omnipotent, then every occurrence, including every human action, every human thought, and every human feeling and aspiration is also his work. How is it possible to think of holding men responsible for their deeds and thoughts before such an almighty Allah? In giving out punishment and rewards Allah would to a certain extent be passing judgment on himself. How can this be combined with the goodness and righteousness ascribed to him? Secondly, Allah cannot know what it is like to have an evil desire, because he, who is necessarily omnibenevolent, cannot have an evil desire. But the history of Islam is an ongoing record of human pain arising from people' inhumanity. Qur'an itself confirms that Allah created evils.

"Say: I seek refuge in the Lord of the dawn, from the evil of what He has created." (Q: 113.1-2)

"No misfortune can happen on earth or in your souls but is recorded in a decree before We bring it into existence: That is truly easy for Allah." (Q: 57.22)

If Allah is a perfectly loving God, he must wish to abolish all evil, and if Allah is all-powerful he must be able to abolish all evil. If we have to believe the verse 2.117 that Allah creates instantly, by decree; he says "be" and it is, then within the same logic Allah could say "no evil" and evil would disappear in a second. But evil exists; hence Allah is neither omnipotent nor omnibenevolent.

Though there is problem of evil in the philosophy of every religion, in Islam, the problem is at the root. Here the god itself is evil, and hence, his judgment is also evil. He is more prone to punish than to reward, to inflict pain than to bestow pleasure, to ruin than to build. It is Allah's singular satisfaction to let created beings continually feel that they are nothing else than his slaves, his tools to propagate his religion. His slaves have no other choice; jihad is obligatory to them. Such a god can be anything but omnibenevolent. Muslim apologists have noted this discrepancy and they come out with an explanation that there are greater goods that justify the evil's presence in the world. But this logic is flawed, because without knowledge of what the greater goods could be, one cannot have a successful theodicy. In fact, the problem of evil does not need to be encountered in Islam because Allah is neither omniscient nor omnipotent; hence the existence of evil is explicable.

In addition, there is a moral constraint. If an evil is necessary because it secures a greater good, then it appears we humans have no duty to prevent it, for in doing so we would also prevent the greater good for which the evil is required. Even worse, it seems that any action can be rationalized, as if one can actually perform it, then it must be permitted by Allah for the sake of the greater good. From this line of thought one may conclude that, as these conclusions violate our basic moral intuitions, no greater good theodicy is true, and Allah does not exist.

The righteousness and justice of God is the aspect of God's holiness that is seen in his treatment of his creatures. Warraq (1995, pp. 127-8) argues,

> *"We are told that God is omnipotent, omniscient, and benevolent; yet He behaves like a petulant tyrant, unable to control his recalcitrant subjects. He is angry, He is proud, He is jealous: all moral deficiencies surprising in a perfect Being. If He is self-sufficient, why does He need mankind? If He is All-powerful, why does He ask the help of humans? Above all, why does He pick an obscure Arabian merchant in some cultural backwater to be His last messenger on earth? Is it consistent with a supremely moral being that He should demand praise and absolute worship from creatures He Himself has created? What can we say of the rather curious psychology of a Being who creates humans—or rather automata-some of whom are preprogrammed to grovel in the dirt five times a day in homage to Himself? This obsessive desire for praise is hardly a moral virtue and is certainly not worthy of a morally supreme Being."*

The omnipotent, omniscient Allah who is supposed to have total knowledge of everything and total control of the universe cannot even reach the man's knowledge and understanding. If we read the Qur'an with a logical mind we will find that any attributes to Allah is dependent largely on the experience of humans. Since no human is perfect, all these attributes have much deficiency in them, as I have shown before that Allah has all the human strengths and weaknesses of a mortal human being. He is not at all supernatural or having any godly qualities.

Secondly, the concept that we have about a thing does not include its existence in the meaning. When I say that the existence of a thing is not included in the meaning of a concept, it means that concepts cannot cause their meaning to exist. No Muslim cleric can cause the existence of Allah by defining his concept. If he imagines a perfect being, and then adds all the things that make it perfect, it is still in his imagination. Muslim clerics cannot prove an existence by making a sum of its properties; they also need to prove the relationship between their concepts and the world. Simply speaking; you cannot prove that the creature of your fantasy is real with your description alone, or giving it one hundred "omni" attributes. It is nothing more than to say that some unknowable being possesses some unknown qualities in an unknowable way. Something unknowable is useless as qualities. Who can rescue such a god from the oblivion of nonexistence? If I claim that a triangle can have four sides, but if there is no such triangle anywhere within sight, then the concept is only in my mind. A triangle can only have four sides if it exists. Allah can only have attributes if he exists. So clerics first need to prove that Allah exists before they can describe his nature. Otherwise this is an argument to ignorance.

Since there is no evidence of Allah, his existence is equivalent to nothing. If the existence of Allah is equivalent to nothing, then the only thing that remains about the concept of Allah is the belief that the Allah exists. Consequently, Allah exists only in the imagination of the believer. A god that exists only in the imagination of the believer is a delusion. The Allah simply collapses into atheism (and from there into irrationalism) under scrutiny.

The real God necessarily has to be entirely self-sufficient, not dependent upon anything or anyone outside of himself. He exists in His own right as an independent being. Allah's knowledge of fear, frustration and despair relies on the contents of human consciousness is inconsistent with this doctrine of divine independence. By fitting some "omni" attributes to a fantasy hero does not make it realistic. It actually strengthens the atheist argument.

2.2.6: Conclusion

"I do not feel obliged to believe that the same God who has endowed us with sense, reason, and intellect has intended us to forgo their use".

Galileo Galilee

"Getting rid of a delusion makes us wiser than getting hold of a truth".

Ludwig Borne

The Qur'anic revelations do not carry any internal evidence of divinity with it. On the contrary, Qur'an contains much – far too much – that is totally unworthy of a deity. This book is an insult to the intellect. Muhammad was his own and his only witness, and for authentication he pointed to the words he himself spoke on behalf of his Allah. Whether they are made to look like coming from Allah, or not, they are the words coming to us from Muhammad, and there is no outside confirmation of his prophethood. Even if there were prophecies, as Muslim scholars claim, about an unlettered Prophet in Torah and Gospel, any illiterate person could claim them as referring to himself. On which basis should we accept such a claim?

Allah is a grand delusion. It is the blind faith of the Muslims that makes Allah seem authentic to us, and then it seems insane to deny Allah's credentials where none is due. It is this delusion that sends Muslims to the deaths that they crave. The very meaning of "Islam" – "submission" – notifies the Muslims of their proper role in Allah's religion. When Muslims fear this Allah delusion they are bound to obey Allah's imagined instructions. Yet Allah is nothing more than the projection of Muhammad's own mind that is ultimately made up and counterfeit. As Warraq (1995, p. 159) commented,

> *"The effects of the teachings of the Koran have been a disaster for human reason and social, intellectual, and moral progress. Far from being the word of God, it contains many barbaric principles unworthy of a merciful God. Enough evidence has been provided to show that the Koran bears the fingerprints of Muhammad, whose moral values were imbued with the seventh-century world view, a view that can no longer be accepted as valid."*

Muhammad, the false Prophet and the prime evil of Islam, and his companions used Allah to reduce the common believers from human beings to ciphers, and today the false priests of Islam are doing the same thing. They control the lives of millions upon millions of other normal people while demanding submission, obedience, and loyalty to the ultimate authority they proclaim for themselves.

When the voice of reason comes to conclusions which are openly contradictory to the ones gigantic claim, either there is trickery or self-delusion. A critical study of

Muhammad's divine experience and his idea of prophethood consistently produce the impression that a large section of the Qur'anic text is a reflection of his own personality. His image is so stamped on the whole unfolding development of the revelation that we must conclude that, while he believed the book was made known to him from above, it really is an expression of his own experiences, perception and fluctuating thoughts.

2.3: The origin of Allah and Islam

"One person's theology is another's belly laugh."
Robert Heinlein

"A myth is a religion in which no one any longer believes."
James Feibleman

For past several thousand years, there had been two main religious groups predominant in much of the civilized world – the sun-worshippers and the moon-worshippers. The main solar religions thriving today are Hinduism, Christianity and Buddhism (Buddhists follow largely lunar calendar but the main characteristic and many important doctrines and traditions are solar); whereas lunar religions are Islam and Judaism. Hitti (2002, p. 97) writes that the moon-worshiping is principally a pastoral society and the sun-worshiping is mainly an agricultural society.

Allah has quite an interesting history. In ancient Arabia, much before Muhammad, the desert Bedouins used to worship a deity by the name Allah. The name Allah is of Christian Syriac origin (Woodberry, 1996, p. 173). Syriac-speaking Christians have always believed this, and scholars like Jeffery (1938, p. 66) have noted this as well. Wellhausen also cites pre-lslamic literature where Allah is mentioned as a great deity (Warraq, 1995, p. 42). Those half-starved anarchic desert Bedouin tribes had a nomadic life as they were incapable of sustaining an agricultural society (Rodinson, 1980, p. 17). Daytime travel was nearly impossible due to the unbearable heat of the sun. Most journeys were undertaken at night, on moonlight and beneath a sky bedecked with glittering stars. Those indigent Bedouin Arabs were so intimately connected with the moon and its phases that their lives were literally governed by the moon. To them, the moon was their life-sustainer; an absolute holy entity to be worshipped and revered with utmost zeal.

After Muhammad forced Islam on these desert Arab indigents; these neo-Muslim Bedouins still continued with the practice of their age-old belief. Therefore, they associated Allah with the moon – *Allah Taalaa*, the Supreme God. Islam is intimately connected with the moon. All its rituals are based on the sighting of the moon or on the moon calendar. Every religious act and ritual, Jihad and Islamic bloodshed, attack on non-Muslims and every Islamic law is designed for only one purpose – to please Allah.

Although Muslim historians emphasize the paganism and depravity of pre-Islamic Arabia, this is actually a deliberate overstatement. It serves to exaggerate the religious transformation effected by Islam on Arab culture. A more accurate description is that Judaism had been in Arabia from ancient times, long before Christ was born, with several tribes having converted, and this had been followed by a wave of conversions that made Christianity the dominant religion in most of Arabia. The Christian Church quickly grew and there is suggestive evidence that at least parts of the Old Testament had been translated into Nabataean Arabic by third century, presumably using Nabataean script, although it is possible that it was a translation into Nabataean Aramaic (Beeston et al, 1983, p. 22). The indigenization of Christianity among Arabian tribes proceeded rapidly from the late fourth and early fifth centuries. In the Ka'ba itself in 630 AD when Muhammad captured the city, paintings of the Virgin Mary and Jesus occupied positions on the pillars along with Abraham and the Prophets (Langfeldt, 1994, p. 53). When the Ka'ba was being demolished and rebuilt in 605 AD, five years prior to the birth of Islam, an Aramaic-Syriac inscription was found on the foundation cornerstone of the Ka'ba. A literate Jew read it to them as follows;

> "*I am Allah the Lord of Bakka [an earlier name for Mecca]. I created it on the day that I created heaven and earth and formed the sun and moon, and I surrounded it with seven pious angels...*".

In 570 AD one of the stones of the Ka'ba was found to have writing on it, and the words he quoted were clearly taken from Matthew: 7.16 (Guillaume, 2002, pp. 86-7). Shahid (1989, p. 528-foot-note) concludes that some of the pre-Islamic Arab churches had developed an Arabic-language liturgy and lectionary in the fourth or fifth century. Consequently Christian Arabic poetry developed, and Cragg (1991) and Trimingham (1979) list five of the poets by name – the poetry that survives, from Nabigha al-Dhubyani (died 604 AD), shows that he used the term Allah. The logical conclusion is that pre-Islamic Jews and Christians referred to God as Allah.

The hardest pre-Islamic evidence comes in the form of stone inscriptions that bear theophoric Arab names, i.e., Arabic names that incorporate a word for deity, as example; 'wahab-allah' (gift of Allah). Later, one does find the name 'abd al-'ilah (Abdullah – servant of Allah). Though Qur'an is believed to be eternal word of Allah, the Arabic script was not developed until the fifth or sixth century.

This archaeological evidence is supported by historical sources as well. For example, a leader of the Christians who was martyred in Najran in 523 AD is said to have been "Abdullah". Not only does he bear a theophoric name that means "servant of Allah", he is also said to have worn a ring that said "Allah is my Lord". Similarly, when four of the leading pre-Islamic men of Mecca pledged to renounce idolatry, worship God alone, and seek the true religion, it was Allah whom they acknowledged, and three of them found him in Christianity (Guillaume, 2002, pp. 18, 99, 100). The name of Muhammad's father, for instance, was Abdullah. There is no reason to think that the one who named him, his father Abdul Muttalib, was a monotheist rather than a polytheist.

Later on when Muhammad faced increasing resistance and disputation from the Christians, a number of Qur'anic verses cited these disputes. Some of these verses quote statements made by the Christians, and it might be noted that the Christians are quoted as using the term Allah.

> "*In blasphemy indeed are those (Christians) that say that Allah is Christ the son of Mary.*" (Q: 5.17)

"(Both) the Jews and the Christians say: "We are sons of Allah, and his beloved." Say: "Why then doth He punish you for your sins? Nay, ye are but men,- of the men he hath created:" (Q: 5.18)

"The Jews call 'Uzair a son of Allah, and the Christians call Christ the son of Allah." (Q: 9.30)

Nowhere in the Qur'an is there any indication that Arab Christians and Jews referred to God by a name different from those used in the Qur'an. All of the disputation passages reflect situations in which the same God was in view. This fact answers the questions – Why Allah was never defined in the Qur'an? Why did Muhammad assume that the pagan Arabs already knew who Allah was? Noldeke (cited Warraq, 1995, p. 42) commented,

"In any case it is an extremely important fact that Muhammad did not find it necessary to introduce an altogether novel deity, but contented himself with ridding the heathen Allah of his companions subjecting him to a kind of dogmatic purification. . . . Had he not been accustomed from his youth to the idea of Allah as the Supreme God, in particular of Mecca, it may well be doubted whether he would ever have come forward as the preacher of Monotheism".

Many Qur'anic verses confirm that Pagans were ever cognizant about Allah.

"Has he made the gods (all) into one Allah? Truly this is a wonderful thing!" (Q: 38.5)

"Say: "To whom belong the earth and all beings therein? (say) if ye know. They will say, 'To Allah!' say: 'Yet will ye not receive admonition?'" (Q: 23.84-5)

"Say: 'Who is it in whose hands is the governance of all things,- who protects (all), but is not protected (of any)? (Say) if ye know'. They will say, '(It belongs) to Allah'. Say: 'Then how are ye deluded?'" (Q: 23.88-9)

"And if indeed thou ask them who it is that sends down rain from the sky, and gives life therewith to the earth after its death, they will certainly reply, 'Allah!' 'Say, Praise be to Allah!' But most of them understand not." (Q: 29.63)

"And should you ask them, Who created the heavens and the earth? They would most certainly say: Allah." (Q: 39.38)

"And they say: If the Beneficent Allah had pleased, we should never have worshipped them. They have no knowledge of this; they only lie." (Q: 43.20)

The term Allah is derived from Syriac word for God "Alaha". Syriac was the form of Aramaic commonly used in literature and scripture in the Middle East from fourth to ninth centuries. Thomas (2006, p. 171), Winnett (1938, p. 247) and Jeffery (1938, p. 66) support this view. Syriac-speaking Christians, most of whom speak

Arabic as well, have had the same opinion that the Arabic term Allah is a loanword from Syriac. Shehadeh (2004, pp. 14-26), director of an Arab Christian seminary, has supported the argument from the perspective of an Arab Christian scholar.

Most of the common-era pre-Islamic inscriptions found in Arabia are written in varieties of Aramaic, although there are also inscriptions in Greek and Arabic. The Qur'an also contains a great many Aramaic and Syriac words indicating extensive borrowing of ideas – words such as Sawt (scourge), Madina, Masjid (a place of worship), Sultan (king), Sullam (a ladder), Nabi (a Prophet) etc (Warraq, 1995, p. 51). To quote from Warraq (1995, p. 108),

> "*Although al-Suyuti enumerates 107 foreign words, Arthur Jeffery in his classic work finds about 275 words in the Koran that can be considered foreign: words from Aramaic, Hebrew, Syriac, Ethiopic, Persian, and Greek. The word 'Koran' itself comes from the Syriac, and Muhammad evidently got it from Christian sources.*"

The crescent, the emblem of Islam, was originally the symbol of sovereignty in the city of Byzantium. Arabic script, which was developed at a late date, may well have been invented by Christian missionaries and ultimately derived from the Phoenician alphabet, via Nabatean and Aramaic (Warraq, 1995, p. 194). Now what should we say about the following verse?

> "*We have sent it down **as an Arabic Qur'an**, in order that ye may learn wisdom.*" (Q: 12.2)

In Aramaic, God is called "alah-a", where the final "-a" is removable. It is the same word that Christ would have used when speaking Aramaic. Woodberry (1996, pp. 173-4) cites a number of key religious terms that were borrowed into Islam from Christian usage, and the work of Jeffery (1938) is well known. Given the prevalence of Judaism and Christianity in Arabia, no other explanation seems possible except that the Syriac word "alah-a" was borrowed into Arabic as Allah by dropping the final "-a" vowel. It is quite normal for words to undergo some alteration when they are borrowed into another language. As Shehadeh (2004, pp. 19–20) pointed out, when the name Alexander was arabicized, it was reinterpreted as al-iskander. Also the strict monotheism is not something new in Islam. It was already accepted in Pagan Arabia much before the advent of Islam. Warraq (1995, p. 51) described that the uncompromising monotheism of Judaism profoundly impressed Muhammad, and he adopted it from them.

Muslim clerics aggressively reject the concept that Allah was actually a loanword from Syriac. The reason is not hard to find; the Islamic doctrine of the primordial composition of the Qur'an in heaven (written in the past in Classical Arabic – the language of God) would be falsified if it were admitted that the Qur'an contained contemporary loanwords, especially if the main term for God himself was a loanword.

2.4: Qur'an originated in Pagan legends and mythology

"Nothing has sprung from nothing."
Democritus

There is much truth in this dictum of ancient Greek philosopher Democritus, and Islam, as it would be shown now, is certainly no exception to this. In Allah's religion there is hardly anything that is not plagiarized from other systems.
Allah says that Qur'an is full of new wisdom.

"Even as We have sent among you a Messenger from among you who recites to you Our communications and purifies you and teaches you the Book and the wisdom and teaches you that which you did not know." (Q: 2.151)

However, the Qur'an itself also confirms that there were Arab skeptics in Mecca who did not accept the "fables" recounted by Muhammad.

"And they say: 'Tales of the ancients, which he has caused to be written: and they are dictated before him morning and evening'." (Q: 25.5)

Allah's response to this is to deny it completely and call it a lie.

"Those who disbelieve say: This is naught but a lie that he hath invented, and other folk have helped him with it, so that they have produced a slander and a lie." (Q: 25.4)

But this is not true. Those non-believing Arabs were right. The stories in the Qur'an are almost the exact same narratives that are found in the Jewish, Christian, Hindu, Arabic, and Persian apocryphal fables, legends, fairy-tales and other fictional narratives except for the names of the characters in some cases. Whatever good exists in Islam was mostly plagiarized from earlier scriptures. As Gibbon (cited Warraq, 1995, p. 10) wrote,

"[The Qur'an is an] endless incoherent rhapsody of fable, and precept, and declamation, which seldom excites a sentiment or an idea, which sometimes crawls in the dust, and is sometimes lost in the clouds."

If we remove all the unscientific, illogical, and violent verses from the Qur'an, we will be left with an odd collection of plagiarized and twisted Bible stories and meaningless gibberish of a mentally deranged person. As Voltaire (cited Walker, 2002, p. 313) concluded, *"There is nothing new in the religion of Islam except the claim that Muhammad is the Prophet of Allah. All else is borrowed".* He also retained many customs from the Pagan Arabs, e.g., polygamy, slavery, easy divorce, and social laws like, circumcision, and ceremonial cleanliness.
Often Allah speaks of a created race of beings called Jinn. The Westerners commonly call them genies – the same shadowy beings from Aladdin and the Magic Lamp, etc. These jinn, spirit beings who lived in the caves, ground, trees, and

other natural places, were a popular superstition in Arabia before Islam. The she-camel story told in the Qur'an about the Prophet, the rock that "gave birth" to a she-camel (Q: 7.73-79), and the story about Moses striking a rock with his staff and twelve springs of water for each of the twelve tribes coming forth (Q: 2.60) were Jewish and Arab legends that was around well before Islam.

The narrative about Abraham mocking the people for their idols and being saved by God from Nimrod's fire (Q: 21.51-71) is taken from the Hebrew collection of writings *Midrash Rabbah*. The story about a raven covering up Abel's body after Cain killed him (Q: 5.27-32) was taken from the tradition preserved by *Pirke Rabbi Eleazar* and the Jewish *Mishnah*. The tale about God lifting up Mount Sinai over the Israelites as a threat if they did not follow the law (Q: 7.171) comes from the second century AD Jewish fable, *Abodah Sarah*. The narrative in which the golden calf-idol that the rebellious Israelites forge actually moos (Q: 20.85-88) is from a Jewish legend that was recorded by *Pirke Rabbi Eleazar*. The story that Pharaoh was saved by God from the enclosing Red Sea that Moses and the Israelites journeyed through (Q: 10.90-92) is from *Pirke Rabbi Eleazar* and *Midrash Yalkut*. The fable about Solomon, the Hoopoe bird, and the Queen of Sheba (Q: 27.17-44) came straight out of the Jewish *II Targum of Esther*.

According to the verses 42.17 and 101.6-11, Allah will send the mankind either to heaven or hell based on the weight of good and bad deeds being placed in a balance. This belief is plagiarized from the Jewish Testament of Abraham (Warraq, 1995, p. 45) – on Last Day, two angels will stand on the bridge between heaven and hell, examining every person as he passes. One angel, representing divine mercy, will hold a balance in his hand to weigh the actions of all men; if good deeds preponderate the persons will be permitted to pass into heaven; otherwise the second angel, representing God's justice, will throw them into hell.

The story about a man that died for a hundred years and woke up perfectly fine (Q: 2.259) was an apocryphal Jewish fable about *Ezra*. The verses 2.56-57 say, Moses was killed by lightning and resurrected. This story came from the Jewish Talmud and in Tract *Sanhedrin* (Part 5). The tale where a Jewish village was turned into apes and swine because they broke the Sabbath (Q: 2.65, 5.60) was an old Jewish fable. The belief that the Qur'an was written by Allah on preserved tablets in heaven (Q: 85.21-22) came from a legend that arose amongst the Jews that the whole of the Old Testament and the Talmud were written on stone tablets in heaven. In fact, this legend included the belief that the two stone tablets that Moses had written the Law on were duplicate copies of those written by God.

In the Qur'an Muhammad told us that Allah's throne is above the waters – "*And His Throne was upon the water…*" (Q: 11.9). This is plagiarized from Genesis 1.2 – "*The glorious throne stood in the heavens and moved over the face of the waters*". In the verse 43.77, "*They will cry: 'O Malik! would that thy Lord put an end to us!'*", there is a reference to Malik as the keeper of hell who presides over the tortures of the damned; similarly the Jews talk of the Prince of Hell. Malik is obviously a corruption of the Fire God of the Ammonites, Molech, mentioned in Leviticus, I Kings, and Jeremiah (Waraq, 1995, p. 52). From these examples we understand that Jewish impact on Islam was profound, and can be traced at the deepest roots of that faith. As Zwemer (2011, p. 17) commented, "*Islam is nothing more nor less than Judaism plus the apostle-ship of Mohammad*".

In the beginning Muhammad respected the Jews, and he borrowed heavily from the Jewish scriptures to attract them into his creed. Torrey (cited Warraq, 1995, p. 50) commented,

> *"On almost every page are encountered either episodes of Hebrew history, or familiar Jewish legends, or details of rabbinical law or usage, or arguments which say in effect that Islam is the faith of Abraham and Moses."*

Many Muslim historians had confirmed that the Jews played an important part in the social and commercial life in Medina that had influenced Islam. Tabari wrote,

> *"In this year, the Prophet commanded Zayd bin Thabit to study the Book of the Jews, saying, 'I fear that they may change my Book'"*. (Tabari: VII.167)

The Jews distanced themselves from Muhammad when he became critical of their not recognizing him as a Prophet. Once it was clear that the Jews would not accept him, Muhammad began to minimize or eliminate the Jewish influence on his beliefs and turned to the Christian scriptures and folklore, and new revelations started coming down from Allah confirming Biblical stories.

Christianity was widely diffused throughout Arabia before Islam, but it was probably of the Syrian kind. Muhammad himself had personal contact with the Christians of the Syrian Church. Thus, there is no shortage of Qur'anic borrowings from Syrian Christianity. The story that baby Jesus spoke from the cradle (Q: 19.29-30) was copied from the apocryphal Christian legend, *The First Gospel of the Infancy of Jesus Christ*. Also, the story where Jesus took clay and turned it into living birds (Q: 3.49) is undoubtedly from *Thomas' Gospel of the Infancy of Jesus Christ*. The tale of "Zul-qarnain" (Q: 18.83-97) is clearly from the sixth century Christian legend, *The Romance of Alexander*. The fable of Imran, his wife, and Mary (Q: 3.35-7) is stolen from an apocryphal Christian fable *The Protevangelion's of James the Lesser*. Muhammad's account of the creation is clearly based on that found in Exodus 20.11 (Warraq, 1995, p. 52). In spite of heavy borrowing from Christianity, Muhammad never understood the Doctrine of Trinity.

Many stories are the exact same narratives that are found in the fables of the ancient Arabs, Persians, Jews, and Christians. Only difference that one may find is that the characters have slightly different names. As example, Warraq (1995, p. 54) had listed many Old Testament characters those are mentioned in the Qur'an.

Aaron - Harun; Abel - Habil; Abraham - Ibrahim; Adam - Adam; Cain - Qabil; David - Daud; Elias - Ilyas; Elijah - Alyasa; Enoch - Idris; Ezra - Uzair; Gabriel -Jibril; Gog - Yajuj; Goliath - Jalut; Isaac - Ishaq; Ishmael - Ismail; Jacob - Yacub; Job - Aiyub; Jonah - Yunus; Joshua - Yusha; Joseph - Yusuf; Korah - Qarun; Lot - Lut; Magog - Majuj; Michael - Mikail; Moses - Musa; Noah - Nuh; Pharaoh - Firaun; Saul - Talut; Solomon - Sulaiman; Terah - Azar.

As Goldziher (1981, pp. 4-5) commented,

> *"The most important stages in [Islam's] history were characterised by the assimilation of foreign influences.... . Its founder, Muhammad, did not proclaim*

new ideas. He did not enrich earlier conceptions of man's relation to the transcendental and infinite. . . . The Arab Prophet's message was an eclectic composite of religious ideas and regulations. The ideas were suggested to him by contacts, which had stirred him deeply, with Jewish, Christian, and other elements."

In many verses Qur'an refers to the seven heavens – *"The seven heavens and the earth ...."* (Q: 17.44); *"We made above you seven heavens ..."* (Q: 23.17); *"Say: Who is the Lord of the seven heavens ...?"* (Q: 23.86); *"So He ordained them seven heavens ...."* (Q: 41.12); *"Allah is He who created seven heavens ..."* (Q: 65.12) etc. These seven heavens idea was stolen from old Hindu Mythology. Also, the Qur'anic description of celestial virgins in Allah's paradise resembles the Hindu stories of the Apsarasas, described as, *"seductive celestial nymphs who dwell in Indra's paradise"* (Stutley, 1977, p. 16). These nymphs are the dancers of God. Muhammad must have heard the stories of Hindu Mythology from the Hindus settled in Mecca during his days and included them in his Qur'an. Even in plagiarizing from other sources, he had shown little creativity. As Torrey (1933, p. 108) puts it,

"His characters are all alike, and they utter the same platitudes. He is fond of dramatic dialogue, but has very little sense of dramatic scene or action. The logical connection between successive episodes is often loose, sometimes wanting; and points of importance, necessary for the clear understanding of the story, are likely to be left out. There is also the inveterate habit of repetition, and a very defective sense of humor. . . . In sura 11.27-51 is given a lengthy account of Noah's experiences. . . . It contains very little incident, but consists chiefly of the same religious harangues which are repeated scores of time throughout the Koran, uninspired and uniformly wearisome. We have the feeling that one of Noah's contemporaries who was confronted with the prospect of forty days and forty nights in the ark would prefer to take his chances with the deluge."

The early Arab skeptics accused Muhammad of plagiarizing the pagan Arab poets. Some verses were attributed to al-Qays (Imra'ul Qays) a famous pre-Islamic Arabian poet (Warraq, 2003, p. 41). Muhammad stole several poems of this poet and added them to his Qur'an. It was the custom of the orators and the poets to hang up the composition of their literary work upon the Ka'ba. One day, Fatima, the daughter of Muhammad was repeating two passages from Sabaa Mu'allaqat. Suddenly, she met the daughter of Imra'ul Qays who cried out (Warraq, 1998, pp. 235-6), *"O that's what your father had taken from one of my father's poems and calls it something that has come down to him out of heaven"*. Even today this story is told amongst the Arabs. Allah's plagiarism is so prominent that Muslims cannot deny this. But how can they explain this incident? Did the poems of al-Qays were also divinely inspired like Qur'an? Ali Dasti (cited Warraq, 1995, p. 5) points out,

"The Koran contains nothing new in the sense of ideas not already expressed by others. All the moral precepts of the Koran are self-evident and generally acknowledged. The stories in it are taken in identical or slightly modified forms

from the lore of the Jews and Christians, whose rabbis and monks Muhammad had met and consulted on his journeys to Syria, and from memories conserved by the descendants of the peoples of 'Ad and Thamud'. . . . In the field of moral teachings, however, the Koran cannot be considered miraculous. Muhammad reiterated principles which mankind had already conceived in earlier centuries and many places. Confucius, Buddha, Zoroaster, Socrates, Moses, and Jesus had said similar things.... Many of the duties and rites of Islam are continuations of practices which the pagan Arabs had adopted from the Jews."

A real God does not need to plagiarize. He would know history and science and thus would not have made such a fool of Himself. There was nothing genuine in Muhammad's doctrine because he was not an original thinker. Islam is pagan beliefs plus the prophethood of Muhammad. Muhammad's intention was to borrow from other scriptures everything that seemed capable of strengthening his doctrine and attracting followers. Whatever good exists in Islam was all shamelessly stolen from Judaism and Christianity. The plagiarists seldom credit the true originators of ideas. For them, objective truth does not exist. The only "truth" is whatever will best achieve the outcome that meets their needs. This "ignorance" and "spiritual bankruptcy" of Islamic doctrine and pre-Islamic rituals continued well in the first Islamic century. Indeed Islam could not be properly said to have existed in the sense of a fixed dogma until later (Warraq, 2003, p. 42). The "indoctrination" of Islam continued taking shape when Islam had to confront Christianity, a much more advanced rival religion. Zwemer (2011, p. 24) commented,

"[Islam] is not an invention, but a concoction; there is nothing novel about it except the genius of Mohammad in mixing old ingredients into a new panacea for human ills and forcing it down by means of the sword".

As Sina (2008, p. 67) concluded,

"It is a mistake to think of Islam as a religion. The religious/spiritual aspect of Islam was created later by Muslim philosophers and mystics who gave esoteric interpretations to Muhammad's asinine words. His followers molded the religion according to their penchant, and with the passage of time, those interpretations inherited the seal of antiquity and thus credibility".

Muhammad simply did not know how to have a logical and organized thinking. Bits and pieces he had learnt here and there about Christianity and Judaism, and based on this, his handicapped brain worked overtime and produced those hallucinations. But, once Allah stamped them in the Qur'an, the hallucinations became heavenly. Allah's authority is so strong that no Muslim is capable of questioning them ever since the birth of Islam. For them the belief comes before the understanding. As Dasti (cited Warraq, 1995, p. 4) lamented, *"Belief can blunt human reason and common sense".* All they have to do is to believe. Logic and understanding have no value at all. It never occurred to their brains that the voice of Allah might have been the voice of Muhammad's own disturbed mind.

Chapter 3: Allah: The psychotic delusion of Muhammad

"You talk to God, you're religious. God talks to you, you're psychotic".
Doris Egan (1955 –)

Psychotic disorders are a group of serious illnesses that severely affect the mind. These illnesses alter a person's ability to think clearly, make good judgments, respond emotionally, communicate effectively, understand reality and behave appropriately. When symptoms are severe, people with psychotic disorders have difficulty staying in touch with reality. Today, even the most severe psychotic disorders usually are treatable by medication or various types of psychotherapy.

There are various types of psychotic disorder, and delusional disorder is very common of them. Here the patient suffers from persistent and organized false beliefs, and that do not go away after receiving logical or accurate information. The major symptoms are hallucinations and delusions. Most of the religious experiences (delusions) are generally rated as positive (Nielsen, 2000, pp. 308-10), may even be associated with happiness and excitement (Runions, 1979, pp. 147-51), but some, e.g., evil presences, disturbance of the self-concept and depersonalization can be terrifying (Persinger, 1993, pp. 915-30; Persinger, 1994, pp. 1059-70; Roberts & Owen, 1988, pp. 607-17). In recent years, the researchers have extensively studied religious beliefs, paranormal beliefs and delusions – as well as changes thereof, as in religious conversions and repeatedly tell us, with brain imaging evidence, that religious activity is dependent on particular brain systems and religious delusion is specifically associated with Temporal Lobe Epilepsy (TLE) and Schizophrenia. Even though some other forms of epilepsy have been linked to religion as well, TLE has been linked to religion most often (Ogata & Miyakawa, 1998, pp. 321-25; Devinsky & Lai, 2008, pp. 636-43). Additionally, TLE is the only form of epilepsy in which hyper-religiosity (extreme form of religiosity) has been reported as a fairly common symptom. Many early writers, including Echeverria, Clouston, Howden, and Kraeplin have described this (cited Trimble & Freeman, 2006, pp. 407-14). This personality disorder is also known as the Gastaut-Geschwind syndrome, named after the two researchers who first discovered this cluster of symptoms, and it is suggested that the prevalence of this disorder is seven percent in TLE patients (Devinsky & Lai, 2008, pp. 636-43). Geschwind (1979, pp. 217-9) describes this personality disorder in details and states that this disorder has a higher prevalence in TLE compared to other forms of epilepsy. Paranoid Schizophrenia and TLE exhibit a very high co-morbidity. Slater et al (1963, pp. 95-150) first proposed the term "schizophrenia-like psychosis of epilepsy" and demonstrated that all of the symptoms of classic schizophrenia are seen in patients with psychosis and epilepsy.

3.1: Introduction

We can find detailed records of Muhammad's mystical experiences in the traditional Islamic sources. People around him called him a liar, hence Muhammad made his Allah describe what he saw. When they asked Muhammad how he received the divine revelations, Muhammad replied,

*"Sometimes it is like the **ringing of a bell**, this form of Inspiration is the hardest of all and then this state passes off after I have grasped what is inspired. Sometimes the Angel comes in the form of a man and talks to me and I grasp whatever he says.' 'Aisha added: Verily I saw the Prophet being inspired divinely on **a very cold day and noticed the sweat dropping from his forehead** (as the Inspiration was over)."* (Bukhari: 1.1.2)

Elsewhere we find,

*"At the moment of inspiration, **anxiety pressed upon the Prophet**, and his countenance was troubled. ... **for some hours he used to become drowsy like a sleepy person.**"* (Ibn Sa'd Tabaqat: Volume 1)

*"A'isha reported 'The first (form) with which was started the revelation to the Messenger of Allah was the true vision in sleep. And he did not see any vision but **it came like the bright gleam of dawn'.**"*(Muslim: 1.301)

*"The Prophet said, 'I had been standing, but **fell to my knees; and crawled away, my shoulders trembling.**'"* (Tabari: VI.67)

*"Then Allah's Apostle returned with the inspiration, **his neck muscles twitching with terror** till he entered upon Khadijah and said, 'Cover me! Cover me!'"* (Bukhari: 9.87.111)

*"Revelation came to the Apostle of Allah and he was covered with a cloth, and Ya'la said: Would that I see revelation coming to the Apostle of Allah. He (Omar) said: Would it please you to see the Apostle of Allah receiving the revelations? Omar lifted a corner of the cloth and I looked at him and **he was emitting a sound of snorting**. He (the narrator) said: **I thought it was the sound of a camel.**"* (Muslim: 7.2654)

All these are symptoms of temporal lobe dysfunction. TLE is the form of a chronic neurological condition characterized by recurrent seizures. The features of the seizures can be extremely varied, but certain patterns are common. There is a mixture of different feelings, emotions, thoughts, and experiences, which may be familiar or completely foreign. Often, a series of old memories resurfaces. In others, the person may feel as if everything – including home and family – appears strange. Experiences during seizures vary; sometimes the seizures are so mild that the person barely notices. Otherwise, the person may be consumed with fright, intellectual fascination, or even extreme pleasure. Muhammad had epileptic seizures from his childhood. Halima, Muhammad's wet nurse, reported to have said,

"His [Halima's own son] father said to me, 'I am afraid that this child [Muhammad] has had a stroke, so take him back to his family [to his mother, Amina] before the result appears.'... She [Amina] asked me what happened and gave me no peace until I told her. When she asked if I feared a demon had possessed him, I replied that I did." (Ishaq: 72)

In Arab traditions, epileptic fits has consistently been seen as an infliction or possession by a supernatural demonic power (Magiorkinis et al., 2010, pp. 103-8). Interesting descriptions of epileptic seizures can be found in the texts of Rhazes (Temkin, 1942, pp. 102-17), and those of Abulcasis (Spanish Muslim Philosopher, 936 - 1013 AD) who also refers to cases of epilepsy due to demonic possession (Foyaca-Sibat, 2011, p. 136). Those ignorant Arab doctors did not have the wit to understand the theories of Hippocrates. Constantinus the African (1020–1087 AD), a translator of Islamic texts, advised the parents of epileptics to take the patient to church to expel the demons (Temkin, 1971, p. 105). There is no wonder Halima mistook Muhammad's epileptic seizures as demon possession.

Hallucinations are prominent component of TLE seizures (Roberts et. al., 1990, pp. 127-43). Currie et al (1971, pp. 173-90) found that seventeen percent of 514 patients with TLE had auditory hallucinations as a component of their seizures. It consists of a buzzing sound, voice(s), or muffling of ambient sounds. Hallucinations of music, people, smells, or tastes may occur which is called "auras" or "warnings." These may last for just a few seconds, or may continue as long as a minute or two. Distortions of shape, size, and distance of objects are often reported. There may be intense emotions and sensory experience including vibrancy of colors. Things may appear shrunken or larger than usual and visual images of a face, ghosts, UFO or even God are seen. TLE often occurs unexpectedly and without any prior notice to the patient. If the seizures have occurred for more than five years, the patient may suffer from memory loss. Neurotheologians suggest that the individuals with TLE have a natural tendency to experience states of consciousness such as euphoria or *Samadhi* and they have functioned in human history as religious figures or mystics.

3.2: The psychiatric aspects of Muhammad's divine experience

"Our greatest blessings come to us by way of madness, provided the madness is given us by divine gift."

Socrates (cited Dodds, 1951, p. 64)

"Man think epilepsy divine, merely because they don't understand it. But everything if they called divine which they don't understand, why, there would be no end of divine things."

Hippocrates (fourth century BC)

The "religiosity" of the epileptic has been recognized scientifically since the mid-1800s. There are cases when a person has converted after experiencing an epileptic fit. Howden reported as early as 1872 (cited Dewhursta & Beard, 1970, pp. 497-8), the patient believed that he was in heaven. He would appear to have been depersonalized, as it took three days for his body to be reunited with his soul. He maintained that God had sent it to him as a means of conversion and he was now a new man, and had never before known what true peace was. He became a religious man and was convinced that he would have no more fits. One patient, who, after many years of depression, attempted suicide and appeared to die, after visiting hell and heaven, he cast off his depression, and acquired a state of religious ecstasy accompanied by visual and auditory hallucinations. Another scientist, Boven (1919, pp. 153-69) reported of a fourteen-year-old boy who after a seizure *"saw the good God and the angels, and heard a celestial fanfare of music"*. Muhammad's divine experience is very similar to what those patients had experienced.

> *"Narrated Anas bin Malik: The Prophet said, 'Nobody who dies and finds Paradise would wish to come back to this life even if he were given the whole world and whatever is in it.'* (Bukhari: 4.52.53)

> *"Narrated Ibn `Abbas: The Prophet once came to us and said, "All the nations were displayed in front of me, and I saw a large multitude of people covering the horizon"*. (Bukhari: 4.55.622).

> *"Glorified be He Who carried His servant by night from the Inviolable Place of Worship to the Far distant place of worship the neighborhood whereof We have blessed, that We might show him of Our tokens! Lo! He, only He, is the Hearer, the Seer"*. (Q: 17.1)

> *"Blessed is He in Whose hand is the Sovereignty, and, He is Able to do all things"*. (Q: 67.1)

Today we can explain Muhammad's religiosity as being the result of his mental disability, social isolation and his enhanced need for the consolation of religion. The intensified piety of the epileptic Prophet of Islam was due to experiences acquired in the course of an epileptic aura and in the subsequent confusional state. Finally he became preoccupied with a cure which he believed depends entirely on God, and this belief was the basis of his euphoria. Qur'an says,

> *"The eye did not turn aside, nor did it exceed the limit. Certainly he saw of the greatest signs of his Lord"*. (Q: 53.17-8).

> *"Or do they say: He has forged it? Nay! it is the truth from your Lord that you may warn a people to whom no warner has come before you, that they may follow the right direction"*. (Q: 32.3).

> *"And your companion is not gone mad. And of a truth he saw himself on the clear horizon"*. (Q: 81.22-3)

In 1899, H. Mabille discussed religious hallucinations associated with epilepsy, and presented four case-studies with hallucinations of a religious theme. One of these cases is interesting. After the seizure, the patient declared that God had given him a mission to reform the world by force. He also heard the voices of God and the

Virgin Mary who commanded him not to eat until his project was finished (cited Dewhursta & Beard, 1970, pp. 497-8). Muhammad was convinced that he was sent on a divine mission by the one and only God, Allah. When his belief could not stand on its own, he had to be ruthless in imposing adherence to his belief. It is this illusive "truth" that gave him such a strong willpower. Qur'an says,

"*Do not rise up against Allah, I come to you with clear authority*". (Q: 44.19).

"*Those who swear allegiance to you (Muhammad) indeed swear allegiance to Allah*". (Q: 48.10).

In a research paper, Karagulla and Robertson (1955, pp. 748–52) discussed four temporal lobe epileptics with visual hallucinations. One of them, a thirty-two years old female had a seizure pattern which included a vision of "*Christ coming down from the sky*". However, they did not state whether the vision had enhanced the patient's religiosity. Muhammad had a similar hallucination, except in the place of Christ, he saw the Gabriel. Sedman (1966, pp. 1-16) mentions that in the state of ecstasy the patient sees the heaven open, hears God speaking, and feels himself transfigured and even believes that he is God. Glaser (1964, pp. 271-8), in reviewing the incidence of psychosis arising from TLE, mentioned the frequent occurrence of religious preoccupations. Several patients, when carrying out a series of tests, tended to associate themes of religiosity with each problem. In a study of the schizophrenia-like psychosis of epilepsy, Slater and Beard (1963, pp. 5-129, 143-50) found that mystical delusional experiences were "*remarkably common*" and the patients were convinced of the reality and validity of their religious experiences.

Beard (1963, pp. 113-29) found that twenty-six patients out of sixty-nine showed symptoms of religiosity, associated with egotism, stubbornness, fearful utterance, strong determination, impaired memory, impaired thought, lack of spontaneity and retardation. Only eight patients had religious interests before the onset of their illness. Now, out of these twenty-six cases, I will discuss six cases that are most suitable to understand the phenomenon of Muhammad. All these cases show, as several researchers (Bayley, 1996, pp. 727-9; Davidson & Strauss, 1992, pp. 131-45; Shaner & Eth, 1989, pp. 588-97) propose, hallucinatory and delusional disturbances can shatter the patient's experience of themselves, the world, and others. To protect their identity I have changed their names.

3.2.1: Case 1 (Richard, aged 55, Maudsley Hospital, London)

At the age of three months Richard was an orphan. By his own account; he was a shy and timid child of only average ability. At thirteen he started working as a messenger boy. Afterwards he became a bus driver and then a bus conductor.

He had a happy marriage. He was quiet and reserved, with few friends; somewhat meticulous in his habits and high in his moral standards; teetotal; attended church and Sunday School regularly up to the age of eighteen. He had suffered from periodic depression and suspiciousness. In later life he attended church intermittently although his interest in religion never waned. He continued to regard himself as a Christian and insisted on his children attending church.

The seizures began at the age of thirty-seven. The major seizures were at first occurred on average every third night. The frequency gradually declined to one a month. There were no personality or mood changes prior to these fits. An attack was ushered in with a scream and rolling of the eyes that lasted about two minutes.

Following the first psychiatric episode Richard was free from major attacks but minor seizures for nearly two years. In these, his expression became blank and he stared straight ahead, sucking his lips. Sometimes he mumbled incoherently or counted. These seizures usually lasted about three minutes. He also had periods of automatism. At night he would get up, go downstairs, and if questioned appear to be confused. He had no memory of these episodes next morning. At the age of forty-five, while driving his bus, he seems to have had an attack of this type. He drove off the main road and round some back streets, eventually regaining his proper route after a period of about twenty minutes. Later he had no recollection of this event, which led to a period of sick leave and his demotion to bus conductor.

His first religious experience occurred at the age of fifty-one at the end of a week in which he was unusually depressed. In the middle of collecting fares, he was suddenly overcome with a feeling of bliss. He felt he was literally in heaven. He collected the fares correctly, telling his passengers at the same time how pleased he was to be in heaven. When he returned home he appeared not to recognize his wife, but she did get from him a somewhat incoherent account of his celestial experience.

On admission to the hospital observation unit, he was constantly laughing to himself. He said that he had seen God and that his wife and family would soon join him in heaven; his mood was elated, his thought disjointed and he readily admitted to hearing music and voices: *"I wish they would tell me I could go to earth. Look at you cooped up here. I could give you a game of tennis"*. He remained in this state of exaltation, hearing divine and angelic voices, for two days. Afterwards, he was able to recall these experiences and he continued to believe in their validity. He was discharged from hospital after ten days.

During the next two years, there was no change in his personality; he did not express any peculiar notions but remained religious. In September 1958, following three seizures on three successive days, he became elated again. He stated that his mind had *"cleared"* (A letter to his wife, in which he attempted to express his religious ideas, was in fact unintelligible). During this episode he lost his faith – *"I used to believe in Heaven and Hell, but after this experience I do not believe there is a hereafter"*. He also lost his belief in the divinity of Christ – *"he had been born, had a father and mother, and therefore could not be the son of God"*.

This sudden conversion was marked by an elevation of mood and a general sense of well-being and clarity of mind. He considered that this second episode also had the nature of a revelation. Thereafter, he retained belief in the validity of his second experience and continued in an attitude of agnosticism.

3.2.2: Case 2 (David, aged 35, Maudsley Hospital, London)

David had an uneventful early life. At the age of two he had four grand mal seizures (a type of generalized seizure that affects the entire brain). There were no further fits until he was twenty-three. He then started to have an occasional minor seizure. A year later he had a major seizure with an aura of derealization.

When he was a child his father, who was very concerned that his son should live a religious life, took him to church. At the age of nine David decided to become a minister. He would get up at six A.M to sing hymns. But his interest in religion ebbed as the years passed and had become minimal by the time he was twenty-one.

David had his first major seizure at twenty-three. He was then serving military and living a simple and isolated life. A fortnight after the seizure, while walking alone, he suddenly felt God's reality and his own insignificance. As a result of this revelation, he recovered his faith and determined to live in a Christian manner. However, this religious experience gradually lost its impact and he once again ceased concerning himself with religion. Then at the age of thirty-four he had two of his rare grand mal attacks in one day. Within twenty-four hours of the second seizure he had another religious experience as part of a florid religious psychosis that lasted a week. He had a sudden dream-like feeling, saw a flash of light, and exclaimed, "*I have seen the light*". He suddenly knew that God was behind the sun and that this knowledge meant power; he could have power from God if he would only ask for it. He had a series of visions in which he felt that his past life was being judged; a book appeared before him, a world atlas with a torn page; a pendulum was swinging and when it stopped the world would end.

Some elements in this experience had a paranoid trend. David knew that his thoughts were being recorded. He saw people looking down at him from heaven and heard one of them laugh and say, "*David is going to commit suicide*". Later, in the hospital, he heard heavenly voices abusing him, felt rays were being flashed on him to punish him (they caused a sensation of burning), and said he had been twisted round until his bones were nearly broken. He attempted suicide by breaking a window and trying to cut his throat.

With these experiences, his religiosity intensified and five months later he was so involved in his psychotic experience that he had no interest in other topics. He completely believed in the validity of everything he had seen and heard during the acute phase, and specifically rejected the idea that the experience could have been the product of a disordered mind. He considered that he had received a message from God to mend his ways and help others, and the fact that he had been singled out in this way meant that he was God's chosen instrument. After one year there were no new psychotic experiences to record, but his religious beliefs remained strong and he was attending church regularly. But he had since remained fit-free.

3.2.3: Case 3 (Doran, aged 37, Maudsley Hospital, London)

Doran belonged to middle class Jewish parents. He had an average school career, then a long series of unsatisfactory jobs. He was brought up strictly in the Jewish orthodox faith and remained devout until seventeen. He had seizures with an average frequency of two or three a week from the age of four. The attacks lasted between seven and ten seconds and were followed by drowsiness and headache.

His first religious experience occurred when he had a vision in which he was in the cockpit of an aircraft flying over a mountainous region of France. The aircraft gained altitude and brought him to a different land, a land of absolute peace – no cares and no burdens. He felt that the power of God was upon him and was changing him for the better. Afterwards, *"people seemed changed somehow"*. When asked if this was a religious experience, he said, *"I prefer the words change of heart; I became intensely interested in following the teachings of Jesus Christ"*. As soon as he came out of the hospital he went to a Billy Graham meeting where *"he gave his heart to the Lord and his name to the Counselor"*. One night a year later he had a very vivid dream of the Crucifixion. About two months after this he had a day-time visual hallucination in which he saw angels with their harps, praying and worshipping. He was able to continue working in a desultory way throughout this purely visual experience. He believed that he was able to pick up other's thoughts.

He was hospitalized and after two and half years the fits were less frequent and less severe. He would go blank for a few seconds only, and never fell. The frequency was one or two a week. However, there was little diminution in his preoccupation with religion. He soon brought any conversation round to a religious topic and frequently said that we must all believe in the Christ. He even walked on the streets carrying a banner with the legend "Be prepared to meet thy God", and showed no ability to modify his conversation. He continued to believe that a religious meaning underlay every ordinary events.

3.2.4: Case 4 (Michael, aged 33, National Hospital, London)

Michael was timid and inclined to worry. He was never particularly religious. At the age of eighteen he had his first recorded seizure. Later, he began to have classical grand mal seizures that lasted for about two minutes. At the age of thirty-three, he became severely confused and forgetful. At this stage he suddenly realized that he was the Son of God; he possessed special powers of healing and could abolish cancer from the world. He had visions, and believed that he could understand other people's thoughts. In an interview he mentioned a "holy smell" and gave the following account of his conversion.

> *"It was a beautiful morning and God was with me and I was thanking God, I was talking to God; I was entering Aldwych, entering the Strand, between Kingsway and the Strand, going down some steps . . . I was not thanking God, I was with God. God isn't something hard looking down on us, God is trees and flowers and beauty and love. God was telling me to carry on and help the doctors here, and I was telling Him back, not aloud, I wasn't talking to myself, they would call you crackers if they heard that; God was telling me, at last you have found someone who can help you, and He was talking about you, doctor, He was talking about you ...."*

At the age of thirty-six Michael showed hardly any change. His talk was rambling, his thoughts disordered, his manner inconsequential and his mood childish and joyful. He was still attending as an outpatient to a psychiatric hospital. After some time he had a feeling that his dead father was trying to get in touch with him, and also had a marked passivity experience. *"God or a power – electrical power – was making me do things"*. At the same time he saw a light going round the room which stopped just over his head. He considered that God had put these ideas into his head in order to convert him to the true way of life. Five years later Michael showed considerable improvement. He was brighter and quicker in manner and the fits had been rare, and he would talk about God in an indirect way only.

3.2.5: Case 5 (Judith, aged 60, National Hospital, London)

Judith, the youngest of nine children, had a happy childhood. But she had to leave school at the age of eleven because of a nervous breakdown. This occurred when her brother caught a moth and put it down her dress. As a result, she went into hysterics, and then had a nightmare in which she saw her brother as a ghost, and finally became unconscious for two days. The doctor advised that "*her brain should be kept calm*" and she stayed at home for the next four years. Judith began to have petit mal attacks in her teens and the frequency rapidly built up to eight or ten a day.

Judith was always religious, but her feelings suddenly intensified at the age of fifty-seven when she was having trouble with her landlord and her fellow tenants. In despair, she buried her head in a towel and pleaded, "*I beseech you Lord to come to me. I plead with you God to help me!*" Then she said the Lord's Prayer. About three hours later she heard a soft and tender voice say, "*A human life is like a tree or a shrub. It either grows straight up or bends and goes right over. As long as it is upright it has the hand of God*". It was difficult to decide whether it was the voice of a man or woman. Later, on the same day, she heard a church bell ring in her right ear, and the voice said; "*Thy Father hath made thee whole. Go in peace!*"

Soon, she was admitted to hospital, where she expressed many paranoid ideas about her landlord and other tenants. She accused them of breaking up her furniture, exploding her radio and whitewashing all her ornaments. She also said she had trouble with "bogus policemen and policewomen" who were in league with her persecutors. She had various new hallucinations in the hospital. She saw an arm with lights coming out of the fingers, eight-sided rockets – "*the new weapon*", a woman in a black dress and people in her bedroom. She also admitted to hearing the Almighty's voice again on several occasions. She had a mildly grandiose attitude towards her visions and ideas, and was garrulous and cheerful in disposition.

3.2.6: Case 6 (Harry, aged 50, Maudsley Hospital, London)

Harry had an uneventful school career. He was unreligious and never attended Church. At the age of forty-eight he had a major seizure in which his wife found him rigid and foaming at the mouth. These seizures recurred at yearly intervals thereafter. After his first seizure, Harry woke up feeling better than before, and said,

> "*I felt completely relaxed. I felt that I had now found my situation in life and that this had been specially selected by God. I was fanatical, terrified that I would not be able to carry out my belief that the greatest power is the love of God. Somehow I had to find a way to prove it because the Russians had found another. I had to find some way to prove that the Bible was true*".

171

Harry was admitted to a psychiatric hospital. But after a while his mood shifted to depression; he felt lonely, spent the nights moaning and groaning, and became paranoid, believing that he was being poisoned and refusing to take his medicine.

At the age of fifty he was again admitted to hospital. During this time his speech was slow, ponderous, diffuse and circumstantial. He still retained his religious beliefs, "*We have got to achieve a high standard before God will do anything for us. This needs an open mind and I have got it. Truth comes into my head when the atmosphere is clean*". When asked the reason for his admission to hospital, he replied, "*I feel I have been chosen as a suitable person to be tested for this new amount of power*". When asked what sort of power, he replied, "*It's splitting the acorn of true love and watching its behavior*". The special power within him was to be used to search for the truth about God and also to prevent the Russians from dominating the world. He was trying to get into "*the orbit of the love of God*". This love could deflect rockets and provide a new elemental power.

After six months he had a succession of fits and the nature of his delusions changed. Now he experienced "*an animal feeling, as though there were dogs and cats about. My salivary glands behaved as though I wanted to dribble. My brain was an open feeling in my mind. I could no longer get hold of the higher truths I used to get hold of*". Two years later there was no fundamental change in his mood.

3.2.7: Conclusion

There is clear evidence of hyper-religiosity in varying degrees in these clinical disorders reviewed here. There is not a single reported case of individuals without a psychiatric or neurological disorder that suffer from hyper-religiosity (Bouman, 2011, p. 4). The question therefore remains if hyper-religiosity is an extreme form of normal religiosity, or, it is to be considered as an expression of psychopathology that has nothing to do with regular expressions of religion. Similar to these cases, the hyper-religious Prophet of Islam had vivid hallucinations that he interpreted as mystical and divine indication. When he claimed that he heard voices, saw angels and other ghostly entities and met Allah, he was not lying consciously; he just could not distinguish reality from fantasy. Traditional Islamic sources repeatedly tell us that Muhammad was delusional. Allah had a "mystic" presence like a light.

"*...indeed, **there has come to you light** and a clear Book from Allah.*" (Q: 5.15)

"***Allah is the light of the heavens and the earth***; *a likeness of His light is as a niche in which **is a lamp, the lamp is in a glass**, (and) the glass is **as it were a brightly shining star**, lit from a blessed olive-tree ... the oil whereof almost gives **light though fire touch it not – light upon light**.*" (Q: 24.35)

"*That He is the Lord of Sirius (the Mighty Star).*" (Q: 53.49)

[The magnificent star Sirius is the brightest star in the firmament in the early part of the solar year, say from January to April, and its bluish light causes wonder and terror in Pagan minds (Ali, 1983, p. 1450, foot-note 5119). No

Arab historian ever recorded that Meccans were scared of the appearance of the star Sirius. They honored Sirius as a Goddess similar to moon as God Allah. In this verse Muhammad twisted their long-held belief.]

*"Their intention is **to extinguish Allah's Light** (by blowing) with their mouths: But Allah will complete (the revelation of) His Light, even though the Unbelievers may detest (it)."* (Q: 61.8)

*"Verily, **from the Light of their Lord**, that Day, will they be veiled."* (Q: 83.15)

*"And the earth shall **beam with the light of its Lord**."* (Q: 39.69)
*"On that day you will see the faithful men and the faithful women -- **their light running before them** and ..."* (Q: 57.12)

*"Jabir b. 'Abdullah reported that Allah's Messenger said, "When the inmates of Paradise will (enter) into their blessings, **a light will suddenly shine upon them**. Upon this, they will raise their heads (and see) that their Lord is glancing them from above ... **His Light and His Blessings** will last on them in their houses."* (Sunaan ibn Majah: 1.184)

*"Narrated Aisha: The beginning of divine inspiration to Allah's Messenger was in the form of dreams **that came true like a bright light**."* (Bukhari: 1.1.3)

Allah's one name is the Light (an-Nur). Seeing God like a source of light is a very common feature among the epileptics. These visions often are simple, brief, stereotyped, and fragmentary and often consist of small, brightly colored spots or shapes that flash (Panayiotopoulos, 1999, pp. 536-40). Henri (1954, pp. 532-3) underlines the following phenomenological characteristics of epileptic visions,

"What most frequently occurs are visions colored red, very bright and mobile: visions of flames, of dazzling wakes, balls of fire, bundles of sparks, flashes repeatedly coming on and going off, points of light whirling about ... . All writers agree on the generally simple character of these hallucinations and on the great asthenia and the criticism to which the patient subjects them."

The famous Christian mystic Hildegard of Bingen (1098-1179) was epileptic. In her hallucination she had seen the light that is *"not physical, but infinitely clearer than the shining of the sun"* (Buber, 1995, p. 64). In another epileptic episode, she saw *"a burning light coming from heaven ... a flame which does not burn but rather enkindles ... just as the sun warms something with its rays"* (Alvarez, 1998, p. 48). Another epileptic mystic John Tauler (1300-61) saw two angels and then he was *"completely surrounded by so much light that it cannot be described in words"* (Tauler, 1990, p. 43). Tauler speaks of suffering alternating suddenly, and for no apparent reason with experiences of bliss and joy.

Ellen G. White, a Christian mystic and the founder of *Seventh-day Adventist Church* had many visionary experiences. She often smelled a fragrance around her, saw light, and frequently heard a very soft voice spoke to her directly (White, 1981, pp. 23, 53, 143). In an interview she said that often a strange light filled her room by circling around the room. Once she saw a silvery light and her pain disappeared (Stewart, 1907, p. 53). Elsewhere she reported to hear the angels singing as well as the voice of Jesus, *"Fear not; I am your Savior. Holy angels are all about you"*. But none of the family saw the light or smelled or heard voices. The doctors who had investigated her case concluded that she was an obvious case of TLE and complex partial seizures. The contents of her visions were paranoid. David (case 2) exclaimed, *"I have seen the light"*; Michael (case 4) saw a light going round the room which stopped just over his head, which according to him was the God, and Judith (case 5) saw an mystical arm with lights coming out of the fingers and Muhammad interpreted the light he had seen in his hallucination as Allah.

*"O Khadija, **I see light and hear sounds and I fear I am mad.**"* (Kitab al-Tabaqat al-Kabir by Ibn Sa'd: 225)

*"Hammad ibn Salama said that the Prophet said, '**I hear a voice and see a light and I fear that there is some madness in me.**'..."* (Ash Shifa: 284)

*"It is narrated on the authority of Abu Dharr: I asked the Messenger of Allah: Did you see thy Lord? He said: **He is a Light**; how could I see Him?"* (Muslim: 1.341)

*"Abdullah b. Shaqiq reported: Abu Dharr said: What is that thing that you wanted to inquire of him (Muhammad)? He said: I wanted to ask him whether he had seen his Lord. Abu Dharr said: I, in fact, inquired of him, and **he replied: I saw Light.**"* (Muslim: 1.342)

*"Abu Musa reported: The Messenger of Allah was standing amongst us and he told us five things. He said: Verily the Exalted and Mighty God does not sleep, and it does not befit Him to sleep. He lowers the scale and lifts it. The deeds in the night are taken up to Him before the deeds of the day and the deeds of the day before the deeds of the night. **His veil is the light.**"* (Muslim: 1.343)

*"Narrated Jarir bin `Abdullah: We were in the company of the Prophet on a fourteenth night (of the lunar month), and he looked at the (full) moon and said, '**You will see your Lord as you see this moon**, and you will have no trouble in looking at Him."* (Bukhari: 6.60.374)

*"With your Lord there is neither night nor day. **The light of the heavens comes from the light of His face.**"* (Tabari: I.230)

*"Gabriel brings to the sun a garment of luminosity **from the light of Allah's Throne** according to the measure of the hours of the day."* (Tabari: I.232)

*"When the Messenger was asked, he replied, 'When Allah was done with His creation He created two suns **from the light of His Throne**."* (Tabari: I.233)

"Allah thus sent Gabriel to drag his wing three times over the face of the moon,

*which at the time was a sun. **He effaced its luminosity and left the light in it**.*" (Tabari: I.234)

"*It has been narrated on the authority of Abdullah b. Umar that the Messenger of Allah said: Behold! The Dispensers of justice will be seated **on the pulpits of light** beside God ...*" (Muslim: 20.4493)

"*Jabir b. 'Abdullah reported that Allah's Messenger said, "When the inmates of Paradise will (enter) into their blessings, **a light will suddenly shine upon them. Upon this, they will raise their heads (and see) that their Lord (Allah) is glancing them from above**. He will say, "Assalamu 'alaikum, O the inmates of the Paradise!" He will look towards them and they will look towards Him and will not pay any attention to anything of the Divine favors as long as they will keep looking towards Him till He will hide (Himself) from them and **His Light and His Blessings will last on them in their houses**".* (Sunaan ibn Majah: 1.184)

"*Allah then created for the sun a chariot with 360 handholds **from the luminosity of the light of the Throne** ...*" (Tabari: I.244)

Joan of Arc, who led the French army against the English and eventually crowned the Dauphin, making him King of France, had suffered from TLE. At the age of thirteen, Joan heard a voice that she attributed to God which urged her to raise the siege of Orleans. She continued to hear these voices with varying frequencies and for differing lengths of time until her death. Sometimes she had heard the voices three times a day, and she seldom heard the voices without a light – "*generally there was a great light*" (Barrett, 1932, p. 156). The voices sometimes commanded her to do things that she did not want to do. Although Joan revered her voices and loved their presence, she did occasionally protest their commands on the grounds of her inability. When the voices first ordered her to begin her mission, she tried to refuse it, saying, "*that she was a poor maid, knowing nothing of riding or fighting*" (Barrett, 1932, pp. 32-43). Joan was an orthodox Christian and most probably the Church bells, a meaningful part of Joan's life and a common sound across France, have triggered seizures in which Joan had "*visions from God and saw the light*" (Foote-Smith and Bayne, 1991, p. 811). Lippincott (2010, p. 2) suggested that the external triggers for the seizures include stimuli such as flashing lights and sounds, and the internal triggers can include psychological or physical stress, sleep deprivation, or hormonal changes. Although many of these issues pertain to recent times and problems, the underlying themes would still be valid for someone in Joan's position and could still cause social issues.

Since Allah is a source of light, he has the power to change the sign of the day and night. Qur'an confirms,

"*And We have made the night and the day two signs, then We have made the sign of the night to pass away and We have made the sign of the day manifest, so that you may seek grace from your Lord.*" (Q: 17.12)

This is how Muhammad had interpreted the light he saw in his epileptic fit. His superstitious mind transformed it into a theological code. Another curious story, strongly suggestive of TLE, concerns the sudden conversion of Joseph Smith. In 1820 Smith was seized with some strange power which rendered him speechless. Darkness gathered round him, and he was greatly afraid. "*Just at this moment of great alarm*", he writes (Dewhursta & Beard, 1970, p. 503), "*I saw a pillar of light exactly over my head, above the brightness of the sun, which descended gradually until it fell upon me. It no sooner appeared than I found myself delivered ....*". As per Cheng et. al, (2001, p. 98), the experience of seeing flashes of light suggested a seizure arising from the occipital lobe which has been confirmed by EEG reports.

Langfitt (1995, p. 101) suggests that epilepsy is "*associated with a poor quality of life*", that includes social embarrassment, anger, anxiety, depression, low self-esteem, social isolation and withdrawal, familial maladjustment and unemployment. Patients with advanced TLE typically have severe deficits in memory function – both visual and verbal (Hermann et al. 1997, pp. 369-76). The seizures damage the brain affecting the memory – more severe seizures bear a greater risk of damage than less severe seizures (Drane, 2012, abstract). Richard (case 1) had seizures in his workplace, and after coming back home he appeared not to recognize his wife. Muhammad suffered from impaired memory function. Muslim (26.5428) and Bukhari (6.60.658; 7.71.661) recorded, a Jew had worked magic on Muhammad and he was so bewitched that he began to imagine doing things which in fact, he had not done. Bukhari (7.71.660) confirms, Muhammad was so much bewitched that he mistakenly thought he had sexual relations with his wives. His companions concluded that it must be the hardest kind of magic because it had such an effect. After a temporal lobe seizure, visual memory impairment may last for hours despite otherwise complete recovery (Helmstaedter et al. 1994, pp. 1073-8). None had worked magic on Muhammad. Possibly, he had a seizure causing a severe memory loss which his superstitious companions understood as some kind of magic. The number of TLE patients displaying memory deficits is very high. Many Qur'anic verses were lost because Muhammad forgot them.

"*Revelations... We abrogate or cause to be forgotten*". (Q: 2.106)

"*The Prophet said, 'It is a bad thing that some of you say, 'I have forgotten such-and-such verse of the Qur'an'. For truly, I have been caused by Allah to forget it. So you must keep on reciting the Qur'an because **it escapes faster than a runaway camel'**.*" (Bukhari: 6.61.550).

If Qur'an is the eternal word of God, why "*it escapes faster than a runaway camel*"? What should we think about a God who causes his word to be forgotten? In the context of a true God, this is utterly senseless. One of the reasons many verses were abrogated simply because the epileptic Prophet forgot what he revealed before. Memory establishes continuity in a steadily changing world but since his memory was characteristically impaired, many revelations were "readjusted" (abrogated) causing a severe discontinuation in the process of revelation.

The Temporal lobe dysfunction contributes in large part to the production of very sexual as well as bizarre, unusual and fearful mental phenomenon including feelings of depersonalization, and hallucinogenic and dreamlike recollections involving threatening men, naked women, sexual intercourse, religion, experience of god, as well as demons and ghosts and animals walking upright dressed as people. One patient even reported to have met the Stone Age Flintstones. TLE also makes it possible to experience not just spiritual and religious awe, but all the terror and dread of the unknown that can generate feelings of hellish, nightmarish fear. The sensory filters are removed and the patient thinks that something which was divinely concealed is now revealed to him and it leaves him in an overwhelming confusing majesty (Joseph, 2002, p. 411). In this particular moment the patients have reported communing with spirits or receiving profound knowledge from the extraterrestrials or Gods. Some have reported hearing even the singing of angels and the voice of "God". Richard (case 1) had a sudden feeling of bliss and heard heavenly music and angelic voices. David (case 2) had a sudden dream-like feeling and he "knew" that God was behind the sun and that this knowledge meant power. He also "knew" that he had received a message from God to mend his ways and help others, and the fact that he had been singled out in this way meant that he was God's chosen instrument. Such was the case with Muhammad. His inner voice confirmed him of his divine mission.

The voices that the TLE patients hear are often abusive. David (case 2) heard heavenly voices abusing him, and saw ghostly people from the heaven laughing at him. Michael's (case 4) God was like an electrical power that forcefully made him do things. He believed that God had deliberately put ideas into his head in order to convert him to the true way of life. Muhammad's Allah was equally abusive.

"In that case, We would have made you taste a double portion (of punishment) in this life and a double portion (of punishment) after death. And then you would have found none to help you against us". (Q: 17.75)

"Truly I fear, if I should rebel against my Lord, the chastisement of a dreadful day". (Q: 10.15)

"And set not up with Allah any other god, lest thou be cast into hell, reproved, abandoned". (Q: 17.39)

"If you join others in worship with Allah, (then) surely (all) your deeds will be in vain, and you will certainly be among the losers". (Q: 39.65)

"And if he (Muhammad) had forged a false saying concerning Us (Allah), We surely should have seized him by his right hand (or with power and might), And then certainly should have cut off his life artery (Aorta), And none of you could withhold Us from (punishing) him". (Q: 69.44-46)

If Muhammad cannot perform well in propagating Allah's religion, Allah threatens him to send a beast as the final messenger of humankind.

"And when the Word falls on them, We will bring out from the earth a beast that shall speak to them: 'Indeed the people were not certain of Our verses'." (Q: 27.82)

Allah is the God of destruction, punishment and revenge – not love. Next, I will discuss on Muhammad's schizophrenia. Epilepsy is not a single illness, but a variety of disorders that reflect underlying brain dysfunction of differing etiologies (Fisher et al., 2005, pp. 470-2). Dodrill (1992, pp. 383-94) described the epilepsies as "*a basket of related disorders*" with their own related features. Epileptics are at increased risk of having psychotic symptoms that resemble those of schizophrenia, because these two disorders have a high degree of genetic, epidemiological, and behavioral linkage (Bearden et. al,, 2001, pp. 106-50; Sachdev, 1998, pp. 325-36). Schizophrenia is also one of the main psychiatric diagnoses associated with violent behavior (Coid, 1996, pp. 965-6; Modestin & Ammann, 1996, pp. 69-82; Stueve & Link, 1997, pp. 327-42; Swanson et al., 1990, pp. 761-70). Hence it is an undeniable phenomenon which requires special attention due to its negative impact on the lives of people with such conditions. The positive symptoms of schizophrenia are distorted perceptions of reality, hallucinations, delusions, disordered thinking and severe reduction in emotional expressiveness. People with schizophrenia may have perceptions of reality that are strikingly different from the reality seen and shared by others around them.

3.3: Muhammad's schizophrenia

In the traditional Islamic sources there are clear evidences that Muhammad was suffering from paranoid schizophrenia. Bouman (2011, p. 18) reported, the activity of the temporal lobes is increased in schizophrenia. There are multiple periods in TLE in which symptoms of schizophrenia may occur – during a seizure (ictal), after a seizure (postital) and in between two seizures (interictal) (Devinsky & Lai, 2008, pp. 636-43). Paranoid schizophrenia bears the closest relationship to TLE, occurring in up to ten percent of postical or interictal periods, with the seizures and psychotic symptoms frequently alternating (Hyde & Weinberger, 1997, pp. 611-22; McAllister, 1998, pp. 211-23; Sachdev, 1998, pp. 325-6; Sherwin, 1984, pp. 92-103). Interictal psychosis can occur at any time between seizures but is considered to be less episodic. The patient usually has a clear sensorium (Kanner, 2004, pp. 22-7). Both disorders involve physical damage and/or heightened electrical activity in the medial-basal temporal lobe, although these are greater in the case of TLE (Hyde & Weinberger, 1997, pp. 611-22). Changes in personality are also linked to the dysfunctioning of the temporal lobes.

Gearing et. al. (2011, pp. 150-63) reviewed seventy case-studies that connect religion to schizophrenia and found forty-three percent of the patients had religious delusions and hallucinations. Thirty studies focused on delusions and ninety percent of those found religious delusions in the patients. Thirteen studies also included hallucinations and 84.6% of these studies reported religious hallucinations to be a symptom. Delusions are more common than hallucinations as a religious symptom in schizophrenia. Cannon and Kramer (2012, pp. 323-27) investigated the content of delusions in schizophrenic patients across a 100-year time span. They found that religious delusions were the second most common delusion content with thirty-eight percent of the delusions having a religious content.

Living in a world distorted by hallucinations and delusions, individuals with schizophrenia may feel frightened, anxious and confused. Although hallucinations can occur in any sensory form – auditory (sound), visual (sight), somatic/tactile (perception of a physical experience), gustatory (taste), and olfactory (smell) – hearing voices that other people do not hear is the most common type (Chen & Berrios, 1996, pp. 54-63). A feeling of déjà vu is also very common with these patients along with hallucinations. Wouldn't it be great if God just told us out loud what he wanted us to know and to do? Voices may describe the patient's activities, carry on a conversation, warn of impending dangers, or even issue orders to the individual. Muhammad's hallucinations were visual, somatic and auditory.

"The apostle, at the time when Allah willed to bestow His grace upon him and endow him with prophethood, would go forth for his affair and travel far afield, until he reached the glens of Mecca and the beds of its valleys, where no house was in sight, and not a stone or tree that he passed by, but would say, 'Peace unto thee, O apostle of Allah.' And the apostle would turn to his right and left and look behind him, and he would see only trees and stones." (Ishaq: 105)

More specifically what are auditory hallucinations? According to Stinson et. al, (2010, pp. 179-84), these are *"internal mental events, such as cognitions, which are perceived by the individual to be of a non-self origin"*. Some researchers view auditory hallucinations as equivalent to "dreaming awake" (Kingdon & Turkington, 1993, p. 77). About seventy-five percent patients suffer from auditory hallucinations (Nayani & David, 1996, pp. 177-89). The main and most notable area that is associated with auditory hallucinations is the temporal lobe (Loo et. al, 2010, pp. 541-6). This is not the only place in the brain that deals with auditory hallucinations, but it is most prominent. Ali Dasti (cited Islam-Watch, 2007) mentioned, while wandering around the lonely spots near Mecca, Muhammad used to hear voices.

"In the days before the appointment, whenever Mohammad walked beyond the houses of Mecca to relieve nature's demands, and as soon as the houses disappeared behind the bends in the path, a voice saying 'Peace upon you, O Apostle of God!' rang out from every rock and tree that he passed. But when the Apostle looked to one side or the other, he did not see anybody. There were only rocks and trees around him."

There are other areas that showed activation during an auditory hallucination. These areas are mainly in the language areas of the brain, left superior temporal lobe (Diederen et. al., 2010, pp. 427-35). Saks (2007, p. 27) reported of a patient who had shown first-rank symptoms of schizophrenia. He had a hallucination which is strikingly similar to Muhammad.

*"As I walked along, I began to notice that the colors and shapes of everything around me were becoming very intense. And at some point, I began to realize that the houses I was passing were sending messages to me: Look closely. You are special. You are especially bad. Look closely and ye shall find. There are many things you must see. See. See...the houses were talking and I was hearing them. ... the words just came into my head – **they were ideas I was having. Yet**

I instinctively knew they were not my ideas. They belonged to the houses, and the houses had put them in my head."

What an extraordinary parallel to the divine experience of Muhammad! He attributed his alien ideas to the rocks and trees, and the patient, with first-rank symptom of schizophrenia, attributed his ideas to the near-by houses. Basically both are same. The delusions of a schizophrenic depend on at least two components. In proper scientific term, this is called the two-factor model. The two-factor model has been developed in a series of papers by many researchers (Pickard, 2010, p. 56; Davies & Coltheart, 2000, pp. 1-46; Davies et al, 2001, pp. 133-58; Broome and Bortolotti, 2009, pp. 285-323). The basic idea is simple – the schizophrenic's delusions depend on at least two factors. On the one hand, there is an aberrant or unusual experience that is the ground for the delusional belief. On the other hand, there are the various belief formation and retention processes that cause the wayward experience to be taken as grounds for belief in the first place, and the belief to be retained, even in the face of strong counter-evidence. Applying this two-factor model to alien thoughts of Muhammad is helpful, because it allows us to isolate what the basic content of his aberrant or unusual experience is likely to be, as against the more cognitive processes likely to be involved in his delusion.

But how is it possible to have a mental event that one experiences as not one's own? Our minds wander idly; we daydream and fantasize. Having a thought enter our mind unbidden, unexpected, and even unwelcome, is a perfectly ordinary part of mental life. But this is what the schizophrenics do not understand. They not only disown their own thoughts; they also disown the "mental state" with the impulses and feelings – "*they were ideas I was having. Yet I instinctively knew they were not my ideas*" – the sense of ownership of thoughts, emotions and impulses. Mellor (1970, p. 17) described the experience of one patient,

"I cry, tears roll down my cheeks and I look unhappy, but I have a cold anger because they're using me in this way, and it's not me who's unhappy, but they're projecting unhappiness onto my brain. They project upon me laughter, for no reason, and you have no idea how terrible it is to laugh and look happy and know it's not you, but their emotions."

Spencer (2003, p. 127) concluded that reading the Qur'an is often like walking in on a conversation between two people with whom one is only slightly acquainted. Frequently they make reference to people and events without bothering to explain what is going on. Noldeke (cited Warraq, 1995, p. 111) commented,

"[The Qur'an] is by no means a first rate performance. . . . Many sentences begin with a 'when' or 'on the day when' which seems to hover in the air, so that commentators are driven to supply a 'think of this' or some such ellipsis. Again, there is no great literary skill evinced in the frequent and needless harping on the same words and phrases; in xviii, for example 'till that' occurs no fewer than eight times. Mahomet in short, is not in any sense a master of style."

The process of Allah's revelation to Muhammad was a classic case of paranoid delusion. Schizophrenia, especially of the paranoid variety, is most clearly linked to hyper-religiosity and there exist fundamental similarities between the mystical, meditative, and schizophrenic states (Buckley, 1981, pp. 516-21; Castillo, 2003, pp. 9-21). The paranoia can be either external (e.g. the world is a dangerous place, people are dangerous), or internal (e.g. a threat to one's view of oneself as a capable/acceptable person who will be able to achieve life's important goals). Brewerton (1994, pp. 302-4), and Kroll and Sheehan (1989, pp. 67-72) found, schizophrenics have stronger religious beliefs and more religious experiences than normal people. Many other researchers have also found a high percentage of schizophrenics with religious delusions (Cothran & Harvey, 1986, pp. 191-9), a positive correlation between religious delusions, psychoticism and religiosity in schizophrenics (Feldman & Rust, 1989, pp. 587-93; Getz et al., 2001, pp. 87-91), or a larger number of schizophrenics in cult religions (Peters et al., 1999, pp. 83-96; Spencer, 1975, pp. 556-9). But the correlation between psychosis and religiosity in the general population has consistently been shown to be negative (Francis & Wilcox, 1996, pp. 1265-6; Maltby, 1997, pp. 827-31; Roman & Lester, 1999, p. 1088). Schizophrenia is the best-studied disorder and a voluminous literature exists concerning its neuroanatomical, neurochemical, and behavioral profiles.

A large section of the Qur'an seems to be twisted rant. The pronouns jump back and forth – sometimes Allah refers to himself in third person singular (He), then shifts to first person plural (We) and sometimes to first person singular (I and Me). If Qur'an is the word of a single God, then God cannot allude to himself in third person. If we read the Qur'an thoroughly, we will find this error in the entire Qur'an. Also, these shifting of pronouns are without any prior indication. Haleem (1992, pp. 407-32) commented, the most common type of shifting is from third to first person (over one hundred and forty instances), then first to third person is the second largest (nearly one hundred instances), third to second person (nearly sixty instances) and second to third person (about thirty instances). For example, I have chosen some verses where there is a sudden shift in the pronoun of the speaker or the person spoken about.

"Call on your Lord with humility and in private: for Allah loveth not those who trespass beyond bounds". (Q: 7.55)

"Do you not see that Allah sends down water from the cloud, then We bring forth therewith fruits of various colors ..." (Q: 35.27)

"And He it is Who sends down water from the cloud, then We bring forth with it buds of all (plants), then We bring forth ..." (Q: 6.99)

"But when He delivers them, lo! they are unjustly rebellious in the earth. O men! your rebellion is against your own souls -- provision (only) of this world's life-- then to Us shall be your return, so We will inform you of what you did." (Q: 10.23)

"And Noah called upon his Lord, and said: "O my Lord! Surely my son is of my family! And Thy promise is true, and Thou art the justest of Judges!" He said: "O Noah! He is not of thy family: For his conduct is unrighteous. So ask not of Me that of which thou hast no knowledge! I give thee counsel, lest thou act like the ignorant!" Noah said: "O my Lord! I do seek refuge with Thee, lest I ask Thee for that of which I have no knowledge. And unless thou forgive me and have Mercy on me, I should indeed be lost!" (Q: 11.45-47)

Did Muhammad keep on forgetting that he should represent the Qur'an as word of Allah and hence Allah should not allude to himself in third person? Muslim scholars have noticed this discrepancy too, but they have a readymade answer for this. They say that Qur'an is a masterpiece of Arabic literature. It is not just a bland piece prose in Arabic that was revealed to hand down some instructions to Muhammad. The unusual use of pronouns is actually a style of presentation. A reader who is not fully conversant with literary writings may consider this as an error of the author (in this case Allah). For this reason, the Qur'anic style of presentation should not be critically examined from the point of view of ordinary logic. In a brief, these apologists want to say that in Allah's language, wrong uses of pronouns add beauty to the language. But the fact is, switching from one pronoun to another without notice only creates confusion and it does not transform a prosaic writing into a masterpiece of literature. In the cold-eyed view of the trained psychiatrist, this is a first-rank symptom of schizophrenia. Linguistic beauty is pure nonsense. The Qur'an, believed to be the Allah's eternal speech, is far from being the standard of Arabic eloquence; it even fails to effectively communicate its intended meaning in a clear enough manner. It makes much more sense to recognize this as being a very human error of the person who composed the Qur'an.

Schizophrenia affects a person's ability to "think straight". The schizophrenic universe is like a vast jigsaw puzzle, where none of the pieces fit together. Thoughts come and go rapidly; he is not able to concentrate on one thought for very long and easily distracted, unable to focus attention. He cannot sort out what is relevant and what is not relevant to a situation, because he is simply unable to connect thoughts into logical sequences. Hence, the thoughts become disorganized and fragmented. This lack of logical continuity of thought, termed "thought disorder," can make the conversation very difficult. Muhammad suffered from thought disorder.

"Allah has said: Take not (for worship) two gods: for He is just One Allah: then fear Me (and Me alone)". (Q: 16.51)

Who is the speaker of the words "Allah has said"? No way could Allah have expressed himself in those words, and even if he did so, it proves that he was crazy. The later part of the sentence *"then fear Me"* indicates whom? It is definitely not Allah, because he already said before *"He is just One Allah"*. Therefore, this "Me" should be someone else and he is also the speaker of the same verse.

*"And **We have not taught him** (Muhammad) poetry, nor is it meet for him. This is naught else than a Reminder and a Lecture making plain".* (Q: 36.69).

*"Lo! **We inspire thee** as We inspired Noah and the prophets after him, as We inspired Abraham and Ishmael and Isaac and Jacob and the tribes, and Jesus and Job and Jonah and Aaron and Solomon, and ..."* (Q: 4.163)

The doubt is who used to teach and inspire Muhammad besides Allah? In the following verse, the use of the words like "He said", "your Lord says", "easy to me" in one sentence are not only confusing but also self-contradictory. The author of this verse is utterly confused.

"He said: So shall it be, your Lord says: It is easy to Me, and indeed I created you before, when you were nothing". (Q: 19.9).
In the following verse, both Allah and Muhammad speak together.

"Glorified be He Who carried His servant by night from the Inviolable Place of Worship to the Far distant place of worship the neighborhood whereof We have blessed, that We might show him of Our tokens! Lo! He, only He, is the Hearer, the Seer." (Q: 17.1)

A merciful, compassionate and all-wise God cannot praise Himself. The first sentence of the above verse is Muhammad's thanksgiving to Allah for his favor. In the second sentence Allah is speaking. The third sentence is clearly Muhammad's word. All these verses lead to one conclusion – Muhammad was the actual author of this book. Allah was just saying Muhammad's *"own thoughts out aloud"*. According to Schneider (1957, pp. 487-90) this is a sure sign of schizophrenia. In another verse, Allah is almost "begging" to the skeptics to obey Muhammad.

"And know that among you is Allah's Messenger; should he obey you in many a matter, you would surely fall into distress, but Allah has endeared the faith to you and has made it seemly in your hearts, and He has made hateful to you unbelief and transgression and disobedience; these it is that are the followers of a right way." (Q: 49.7)

The voices that a schizophrenic hears have a very significant repercussion on the life of that person (they repeatedly make him feel fear, anxiety, stress, etc). Chadwick and Birchwood (1994, pp. 190-201) have demonstrated that beliefs about voices are meaningfully related to their emotional and behavioral consequences. That's the reason such delusional beliefs once formed is strongly maintained, as they are *"firmly sustained despite what almost everyone else believes and despite what constitutes incontrovertible and obvious proof or evidence to the contrary"* (DSM-IV-TR, 2000, p. 821). Bukhari (9.93.532) wrote,

*"The Prophet added, 'Then the prophets and Angels and the believers will intercede, and (last of all) the Almighty (Allah) will say, '**Now remains My Intercession.**' He will then hold a handful of the Fire from which He will take out some people whose bodies have been burnt, and they will be thrown into a river at the entrance of Paradise, called the water of life ..."*

"Now remains My Intercession" – this exact statement needs particular attention. Here the voice Muhammad heard is interceding himself! This is what a psychiatrist would call schizophrenic duplicity. God cannot have duplicity; the problem is with Muhammad's schizophrenia. Allah jumps from singular to plural very frequently, and "I", "we", "me" and "our" are routinely used in the same verse. The reason of the frequent jumping from singular to plural is that the schizophrenics sometimes hear more than one voice either sequentially or simultaneously. Two or more voices may conduct a conversation between themselves. A voice or voices may speak to the patient or about the patient. They may comment on his thoughts or actions, or on some futuristic events either in this world or thereafter. As example, Allah says in the Qur'an;

> *"Children of Adam, whenever messengers come from amongst you, rehearsing My [singular] signs and revelations to you, act rightly so that you have no fear, nor reason to grieve. But those who reject Our [plural] signs and scorn them with arrogance, they are inmates of the Fire forever."* (Q: 7.35)

> *"Verily We [plural] take upon Ourselves [plural] (to show) the way, and verily unto Us [plural] (belong) the last and the first. Therefore do I [singular] warn you of a Fire blazing fiercely..."* (Q: 92.12)

> *"Not a messenger did We [plural] send before you but We revealed to him: La ilaha illa Ana (No gods but I), so worship Me [singular]."* (Q: 21.25)

How swiftly Allah changed from *"My signs"* to *"Our signs"* in the verse 7.35. This god cannot even keep himself together, talking in first person singular and plural in the same verse. This confusion is there throughout the Qur'an. As Bell and Watt (1977, p. 66) concluded,

> *"The assumption that God is himself the speaker in every passage, however leads to difficulties. Frequently God is referred to in the third person. It is no doubt allowable for a speaker to refer to himself in the third person occasionally, but the extent to which we find the Prophet apparently being addressed and told about God as a third person, is unusual. It has, in fact, been made a matter of ridicule that in the Quran God is made to swear by himself. That he uses oaths in some of the passages beginning, "I swear (not) . . ." can hardly be denied [e.g., 75.1, 2; 90.1]. . . . "By thy Lord," however, is difficult in the mouth of God. . . . Now there is one passage which everyone acknowledges to be spoken by angels, namely 19.64: "We come not down but by command of thy Lord; to him belongs what is before us and what is behind us and what is between that; nor is thy Lord forgetful, Lord of the heavens and the earth and what is between them; so serve him, and endure patiently in his service; knowest thou to him a namesake?"*

> *In 37.161-166 it is almost equally clear that angels are the speakers. This, once admitted, may be extended to passages in which it is not so clear. In fact, difficulties in many passages are removed by interpreting the 'we' of angels rather than of God himself speaking in the plural of majesty. It is not always*

easy to distinguish between the two, and nice questions sometimes arise in places where there is a sudden change from God being spoken of in the third person to 'we' claiming to do things usually ascribed to God, e.g., 6.99; 25.45."

Qur'an has other literary difficulties also. Subjects, verbs, and objects are routinely omitted from Allah's sentences. Rippin (cited Winn, 2004, p. xxiv) noted,

"*The subject matter within surahs jumps from one topic to the next, with duplications and inconsistencies in grammar, law, and theology, the language is semi-poetical, while its grammar, due to omission, is so elliptical as to be obscure and ambiguous. There is grammatical discord such as the use of plural verbs with singular subjects, and variations in the treatment of the gender nouns. Many times sentences leave verbs out. The Qur'an is replete with dangling modifiers. It has few explanations. Consequently the Qur'an is difficult to read and impossible to comprehend*".

The voices that the schizophrenics hear rarely speak in complete meaningful sentences – they usually say only a few disjointed words in brief utterances. While the content of auditory hallucinations may have immediate meaning for the patient, frequently it does not. Using brain imaging techniques, researchers have shown that when a person with psychosis speaks to himself internally or repeats conversations in his head he experiences some fractions of his internal conversations with apparently meaningless words as voices from outside. Many Surahs of the Qur'an start off with specific Arabic letters which it nowhere explains, as example, Alif Lam Ra (Surah: 10, 11, 12, 14, 15), Alif Lam Mim (Surah: 2, 3, 29, 30, 31, 32), Alif Lam Mim Ra (Surah: 13), Alif Lam Mim Sad (Surah: 7), Ha Mim (Surah: 40, 41, 43, 44, 45, 46), Ha Mim 'Ain Sin Qaf (Surah: 42), Sad (Surah: 38), Ta Sin (Surah: 27),Ta Sin Mim (Surah: 26, 28), Ta Ha (Surah: 20), Qaf (Surah: 50), Ka Ha Ya 'Ain Sad (Surah: 19), Nun (Surah: 68), and Ya Sin (Surah: 36).

Do these Arabic letters mean anything at all? Muslim scholars admit that there are no reports from either Muhammad himself or his companions where Muhammad commented or explained the meaning and purpose of these mysterious letters. Asad (1993, p. 992) candidly acknowledged,

"*About one-quarter of the Qur'anic suras are preceded by mysterious letter-symbols called muqatta'at ('disjointed letters') or, occasionally, fawatih ('openings') because they appear at the beginning of the relevant suras. Out of the twenty-eight letters of the Arabic alphabet, exactly one-half - that is, fourteen - occur in this position, either singly or in varying combinations of two, three, four, or five letters. They are always pronounced singly, by their designations and not as mere sounds - thus: alif lam mim, or ha mim, etc.*

The significance of these letter-symbols has perplexed the commentators from the earliest times. There is no evidence of the Prophet's having ever referred to them in any of his recorded utterances, nor any of his Companions having ever asked him for an explanation. None the less, it is *established beyond any possibility of doubt that all the Companions - obviously following the example of the Prophet - regarded the muqatta'at as integral parts of the suras to which they are prefixed, and used to recite them accordingly: a fact which disposes effectively of **the suggestion advanced by some Western orientalists that these letters may be no more than the initials of the scribes who wrote down the individual revelations at the Prophet's dictation, or of the Companions who recorded them** at the time of the final codification of the Qur'an during the reign of the first three Caliphs.*

*Some of the Companions as well as some of their immediate successors and later Qur'anic commentators were convinced that these letters are abbreviations of certain words or even phrases relating to God and His attributes, **and tried to 'reconstruct' them with much ingenuity; but since the possible combinations are practically unlimited, all such interpretations are highly arbitrary and, therefore, devoid of any real usefulness ...'"***

After summarizing several different interpretations, Asad honestly admitted,

*"... and so, in the last resort, we must content ourselves with the finding that a solution of this problem **still remains beyond our grasp. This was apparently the view of the four Right-Guided Caliphs**, summarized in these words of Abu Bakr: 'In every divine writ (kitab) there is [an element of] mystery - and **the mystery of the Qur'an is [indicated] in the openings of [some of] the suras**.'"*

For Abu Bakr, these mysterious words prove divinity of the Qur'an, but for an experienced psychiatrist, these disjointed words are the fractions of Muhammad's internal conversations with as voices from Allah. There is no wisdom in them; these are clinical manifestation of abnormal language in schizophrenia. Now what should we say about this verse?

"Alif Lam Ra (This is) a Book, whose verses are made decisive, then are they made plain, from the Wise, All-aware" (Q: 11.1)

This verse is ironic since these unintelligible letters appear right before the assertion that the Muslim scripture is a clear book. Allah's disorganized speech and thoughts points out that, the schizophrenic Prophet often had difficulty forming a logical sequence of thoughts reflected in his delusional conversation. At times, his speech and thinking were so disorganized that he clearly appeared to be incoherent. This is what we can make out from the above verse 11.1. The meaning of a sentence, known as its propositional content, is determined by the way the meanings of words combine in syntactic structures. Muhammad simply lost control over the choice of vocabulary elements in his speech (i.e., the Qur'anic revelations). He was also not able to make predictability judgments on normal speech.

The use of unclear and ambiguous verbal references appears to be a stable trait of schizophrenia (Docherty et. al., 1988, pp. 437-42) In addition; schizophrenic utterance is rich in metaphor. Although metaphor is an indispensable tool of thought and expression – a characteristic of all human communication, even of that of the scientist, we use only the labeled metaphors. The peculiarity of the schizophrenic is not that he uses metaphors, but that he uses unlabeled metaphors (Bateson et al, 1956, pp. 251-4). Hence, though he hears fragmented sentences and disorganized words he immediately knows the meaning.

Often the schizophrenic complains about "thought insertion". This term implies the idea that another thinks through the mind of the patient. The patient is unable to distinguish between his own thoughts and those inserted into his minds. Frith (1992, p. 80) puts the point succinctly.

"Thought insertion, in particular, is a phenomenon that is difficult to understand. Patients say that thoughts that are not their own are coming into their head. This experience implies that we have some way of recognizing our own thoughts. It is as if each thought has a label on it saying 'mine'. If this labeling process goes wrong, then the thought would be perceived as alien."

Qur'an confirmed that Allah's revelations found expression in Muhammad's consciousness rather than in his ears. Contrary to popular Muslim belief, the revelations were inspirational, something like "suggested" rather direct verbal revelation rote in the ears of Muhammad.

"It is no less than inspiration sent down to him". (Q: 53.4)

This is a clear case of "thought insertion", or "forced thinking". The automatic occurrence of ideas with great force pervading the awareness of the patient is a typical psychic manifestation of partial seizures. Despite being the most frequent cognitive manifestation, it has not yet received the attention that it deserves (Mendez et al., 1996, p. 79). The patient suddenly finds himself invaded by ideas that are so intense that they pervade his awareness as if they were true, and it becomes totally impossible for him to concentrate on anything else. Alvarez (1998, pp. 35-6) explains,

"[Thought insertion] is a psychical phenomenon that suddenly invades the consciousness, imposing itself on it in a completely passive way and with great intensity so that it takes it over completely. ... it is accompanied by such a strength of experience that it imposes itself furthermore to such a degree of passivity on the part of the individual that there is nothing that can be done voluntarily to keep it up or reject it, and one can only stand by like a bewildered onlooker as the unheard-of experience unfolds in one's consciousness. The whole experience is so intense, with such vivid affective and intellective contents, that they are strange and ineffable, like bearers of a new meaning that is impossible to explain".

Henri (1954, p. 542) observed that during the intellectual aura, *"Clear and rational thought is replaced by an incoercible and irrational idea that the patient obeys"*. Despite this lack of rationality, the idea imposes itself on the awareness with such force that it seems to have a new and significant value. Henri continues; *"It is precisely because of this irrepressibility with which the subjective illusion of clarity of thought seems to be bound up"*.

187

Forced thinking, conceived thus, i.e., as a vague idea content that nevertheless pervades the awareness with an extreme force of conviction, is highly similar to what in mysticism is known as intellectual visions, where the religious patient is convinced of having acquired new knowledge with vast intensity and yet it is impossible for him to analyze its idea content. When Muhammad was believed to be receiving revelations from Allah, in fact, forced thinking was imposing itself automatically and paroxystically on the awareness during his epileptic discharge. Rahman (1979, p. 33) wrote,

> "*The Qur'an is thus pure Divine Word, but, of course, it is equally intimately related to the inmost personality of the Prophet Muhammad whose relationship to it cannot be mechanically conceived like that of a record. **The Divine Word flowed through the Prophet's heart.**"*

Thus, though the Muslim dogmatists claimed that a mechanical dictation of the Qur'an was made to Muhammad, the truth is that Qur'an is very much the product of the experience Muhammad himself had of his developing prophetic career and that the passages are codifications in his own words of the striking perceptions he experienced which he believed were being directly suggested to him from external sources. As one patient reported (Frith, 1992a, p. 66) – "*Thoughts are put into my mind. It's just like my mind working, but it isn't. They come from this chap, Chris [Chris is the patient's friend in delusion, like Allah to Muhammad]. They're his thoughts*". Muhammad undoubtedly spoke the real truth when he stated that he had never dared to dream that revelations would come to him. Qur'an says,

> "*And you did not expect that the Book would be inspired to you, but it is a mercy from your Lord, therefore be not a backer-up of the unbelievers.*" (Q: 28.86)

Schizophrenia is basically a semiotic disorder, a disorder of the recognition and use of sign relations (word-to-object, thought-to object, and object-to-object) (Covington et al., 2005, pp. 85-98). Hall et al (1978, pp. 1315-20) confirms, forty-six percent of these cases, the patient is unaware of the presence of a medical condition. What is so striking about the phenomenon of thought insertion in schizophrenics is that it involves an error of identification. A patient who supposes that someone else has inserted thoughts into his mind is right about which thoughts they are, but wrong about whose thoughts they are. The voices may come from anybody. Muhammad was so convinced that the "suggestions" he was constantly receiving were from Allah that he openly claimed that, although he could perform no signs and wonders as other Prophets had done, the Qur'an itself was a miracle, a true *mu'jizah*. It shows how much his mind was impressed on the book.

It is well known that chronic schizophrenia patients suffer from a variety of movement disorders. They make mistakes about the agency of various bodily movements. They may make peculiar involuntary movements, grimaces, with lips and mouth (Frith, 1992; Owens et al., 1982, pp. 452-61; Crow et al., 1982, pp. 336-40). McGuigan (1966, pp. 73-80) found a significant increase in oral muscle activity just before a patient indicated hearing a voice. Gould (1948, pp. 367-72) observed a hallucinating patient making frequent sounds from her nose and mouth, interpreted as originating from alien sources. Many researchers had also observed the same in other patients. These patients are suffering from delusion of control and feel that movements are made or caused by someone or something else. This is such a pathetic situation in which no matter what the patient does, he "cannot win". The following narration of Bukhari (6.60.451) needs to be understood carefully.

*"Narrated Musa bin Abi Aisha; When Gabriel revealed the divine Inspiration in Allah's Apostle, **he moved his tongue and lips**, and **that state used to be very hard for him**, and **that movement indicated that revelation was taking place**."*

The involuntary tongue and lips movement (i.e., oral muscle activity) of Muhammad – *"that state used to be very hard for him"* – indicates a minor seizure (similar to Richard – case 1), and the revelation that followed was an occurrence of a schizophrenic voice hallucination in postical or interical periods – *"that movement indicated that revelation was taking place"*.

Frith (1992a, p. 66) gave an example of a schizophrenic who complained, *"The force moved my lips. I began to speak. The words were made for me"*. I do not suggest that Muhammad was consciously staging a drama by artificially producing those acts. It was in fact his own motor action. He genuinely believed that he was receiving messages from his Allah in that involuntary movement of tongue and lips, but he made an error of identification concerning who produced this motion. The sense of agency, rather than the sense of ownership, is disrupted. The schizophrenic knows that it is his lips and that he speaks, but his lips were moved and the words were made by someone else. An example provided by Mellor (cited Spence, 1996, p. 82) makes this clear – A shorthand typist described her actions as *"When I reach my hand for the comb it is my hand and arm which move, and my fingers pick up the pen, but I don't control them"*.

The revelations "inserted" into Muhammad's mind were indeed in some senses his, just because it had been successfully inserted into his mind; it has some special relation to him and he has some specifically direct knowledge of it. The words Muhammad used as Allah's revelation and the meaning he was trying to express often satisfied his selfish needs. For this reason often Allah seems to be very anxious to fulfill Muhammad's will ... as Aisha observed on some occasions.

"Narrated Aisha: ... I said (to the Prophet),' I feel that your Lord hastens in fulfilling your wishes and desires". (Bukhari: 6.60.311).

Qur'an confirms that Muhammad was privileged above other Muslims.

*"O Prophet! Lo! We have made lawful unto thee thy wives unto whom thou hast paid their dowries, and those whom thy right hand possesseth of those whom Allah hath given thee as spoils of war, and the daughters of thine uncle on the father's side and the daughters of thine aunts on the father's side, and the daughters of thine uncle on the mother's side and the daughters of thine aunts on the mother's side who emigrated with thee, and a believing woman if she give herself unto the Prophet and the Prophet desire to ask her in marriage - **a privilege for thee only, not for the (rest of) believers**."* (Q: 33.50)

This latter self-ordained "permission" by Muhammad is the most suspect – "*a privilege for thee only, not for the (rest of) believers*". God's "revelations" that sexually or financially benefit a founder or leader of a religious movement always raise concern for objective outsiders, as it should for those within the group, unless someone has the imbecilic belief that the human founder has achieved "sinless perfection" and can do no wrong. Even so, the sexual sin in itself automatically cancels out that same supposed sinless perfection. Lings (1975, p. 33) commented,

> "*On one occasion after the death of Muhammad when his favorite wife Aisha was asked what he was like, she replied; 'His nature was as the Qur'an'. This must be taken to mean that from her intense and intimate experience of the Prophet she formed the impression that he was an incarnation of the revealed Book.*"

Much of the Qur'anic text was a reflection of Muhammad's own personality. Tisdall (cited Trifkovic, 2002, p. 75) concluded,

> "*The Qur'an is a faithful mirror of the life and character of its author. It breathes the air of the desert, it enables us to hear the battle-cries of the Prophet's followers as they rushed to the onset, it reveals the working of Muhammad's own mind, and shows the gradual declension of his character as he passed from the earnest and sincere though visionary enthusiast into the conscious imposter and open sensualist. All this is clear to every unprejudiced reader of the book*".

Since a schizophrenic often cannot tell the difference between what is real and imagined he often contradicts. He is experiencing something related to one of his senses, but the experience is not caused by anything that is actually there. It is, essentially, in his mind but not part of reality. Thus, there are urgent needs for rapid correction of errors. In Islam this is what we call the doctrine of abrogation.

Schizophrenics often ignore their hygiene and go around looking quite unkempt. Often they are seen with dirty cloths, overgrown nails and unbearable body stench. Muhammad and the early converts maintained poor hygiene.

> "*Narrated AbuMusa al-Ash'ari: Abu Burdah said: My father said to me: My son, if you had seen us while we were with the Apostle of Allah and the rain had fallen on us, you would have thought that our smell was the smell of the sheep.*" (Sunaan Abu Dawud: 32.4022)

What others see as disorderly, unhygienic and completely messy, the schizophrenics see as normal. For this reason often other diseases result from their unhygienic way of life. Their mind is in a place where they just cannot do any better, no matter how much people complain, criticize, point or laugh. Muhammad lived so filthy that he had developed lice on his head! Bukhari wrote,

> "*Narrated Anas bin Malik: Allah's Apostle used to visit Um Haram bint Milhan, who would offer him meals. Um-Haram was the wife of Ubada bin As-*

Samit. Allah's Apostle, once visited her and she provided him with food and started looking for lice in his head." (Bukhari: 4.52.47)

"*Narrated Anas bin Malik: Allah's Apostle used to visit Um Haram bint Milhan she was the wife of 'Ubada bin As−Samit. One day the Prophet visited her and she provided him with food and started looking for lice in his head.*" (Bukhari: 9.87.130)

What we understand from this is that Muhammad lived in filthiness, took infrequent bath, so much so that lice found a fertile breeding spot on his head. Now what should we say about this verse where Allah says that he likes cleanliness?

"*... truly Allah loves those who turn unto Him, and loves those who have a care for cleanness.*" (Q: 2.222)

3.4: Conclusion

It is no wonder that Muhammad's companions took Muhammad's epileptic fits as a sure sign of his divine approval; it was the parlance of the day. Though the recorded history of religious faith is as old as that of mankind, an elevated level of religiosity has been noted in clinical populations dating back to antiquity. For example, the original meaning of the Hebrew word "Nabi" was "insanity" (Goldwert, 1993, pp. 331-5). In South America the epileptic seizures initially attributed to voodoo spirit possession (Carrazana et al., 1999, pp. 1041-6). Also, the ancient Greeks viewed epilepsy as a "sacred disease" brought about by a visitation from the Gods or demons (Saver & Rabin, 1997, pp. 498-510). Behind the name "sacred illness" there lie hidden the beliefs of the day, not only those of a popular nature, but those of the more erudite, concerning the divine origin of the illness, considered to be sent by a God, the patient therefore being possessed by a divine force during an attack. Men regard its nature and cause as divine from ignorance and wonder, because it is not at all like to other diseases, and a "god of the gaps" is assigned responsibility. The notion of its divinity is kept up by their inability to comprehend it, and the simplicity of the mode by which it is cured, for men are freed from it by purifications and incantations. In Rome, people believed that the power taking over an epileptic was of supernatural origin, as is borne out by the Roman practice of suspending the comitia (assembly for electing magistrates and passing laws) whenever one of those present had a seizure, for it was thought to be a bad omen (an epileptic attack tended to spoil the day of the comitia, the assembly of the people – Foyaca-Sibat, 2011, p. 133). This custom gave rise to the name *morbus comitialis*, the English equivalent comitial sickness.

The Hippocratic Treatises (1983, pp. 387-421) give no less than a whole volume over to epilepsy, entitled Sacred Disease, in which its definition, etiology, clinical manifestations and treatment are dealt with. Hippocrates (1989, p. 364) disputed the divine origin of epilepsy by saying;

"*This disease is in my opinion no more divine than any other; it has the same nature as other diseases, and the cause that gives rise to individual diseases. It is also curable, no less than other illnesses, unless by long lapse of time it be so ingrained as to be more powerful than the remedies that are applied".*

However, Hippocrates attempt to dissociate epilepsy and religion had failed. Subsequent religious figures were asked to heal people with epilepsy. In Indian medicine, Atreya (sixth century BC) attributed epilepsy to a brain dysfunction and not to divine intervention. In the *Caraka Samhita Sutra*, he defines epilepsy as; *"paroxysmal loss of consciousness due to disturbance of memory and [of] understanding of mind attended with convulsive seizures"* (Pirkner, 1929, pp. 453-80). Today with the development of medical science we know to a great extent the cause and nature of this disease. Muhammad's bizarre belief in his prophetic mission, Allah's revelation, demon possession – all these have their base in Muhammad's psychotic delusions. The researchers have proved psychosis is rarely a consequence of epilepsy originating outside of the temporal lobe (McAllister, 1998, pp. 211-23; Sherwin, 1984, pp. 92-103). If Muhammad were living today, he would be treated for temporal lobe epilepsy and schizophrenia for his supposed visions. Neither God nor the devil had anything to do with the religion he preached.

3.5: Traditional Islamic sources on Muhammad's hallucination

"If a delusion is not to be got rid of by reference to reality, no doubt it did not originate from reality either".

Sigmund Freud

Hallucinations may occur in any sensory modality, are involuntary, and tend to be transient in nature with simple content. These are of two types – when falling asleep (hypnagogic) and on waking (hypnopompic) (Adler, 1997, p. 28). Traditional Islamic sources show us that Muhammad regularly hallucinated – both hypnagogic and hypnopompic. Most of his hallucinations were accompanied with symptoms suggestive of a complex partial seizure.

1. Once during the childhood of Muhammad two men in white clothes came to him with a golden basin full of snow. They took him and split open his body, took his heart and split it open and took out from it a black clot which they threw away. Then they washed his heart and his body with that snow until they made them pure (Ishaq: 72).

2. Magic was worked on Muhammad by a Jew and he was bewitched so that he began to imagine doing things which in fact, he had not done. (Bukhari: 7.71.661, 6.60.658; Muslim: 26.5428).

3. Magic was worked on Muhammad so that he used to think that he had sexual relations with his wives while he actually had not. That is the hardest kind of magic as it has such an effect. (Bukhari: 7.71.660).

4. Omar asked Muhammad, *"Tell me; what is the most amazing saying which your familiar spirit communicated to you?"* Muhammad replied, *"He came to me a month before Islam and said: Have you considered the Jinn and the hopelessness and despair of their religion?"* (Ishaq: 93).

5. One day two persons came to Muhammad in his dream. One of them asked the other, *"What is the ailment of this man?"* *"He has been bewitched. He is under the spell of magic."* *"Who cast the magic spell?"* *"A Jew."* *"What material did he use?"* *"A comb, the hair knotted on it, and the outer skin of the pollen of the male date-palm."* (Bukhari: 4.54.490, 7.71.658).

6. The stem of a date-palm tree used to cry like a pregnant she-camel, when a pulpit was placed upon it for Muhammad to give a sermon till the time he got down from the pulpit and placed his hand over it (Bukhari: 2.13.41).

7. When Muhammad used to eat, he had seen the foods glorifying Allah (Bukhari: 4.56.779).

8. Muhammad saw Gabriel with six hundred wings. Gabriel can also take the form of a human being (Bukhari: 6.60.380, 4.56.827).

9. Once a tree informed Muhammad that the Jinns heard the Qur'an (Bukhari: 5.58.199).

10. When Muhammad was in Mecca, the roof of his house was opened and Gabriel descended, opened his chest, and washed it with zamzam water. Then he brought a golden tray full of wisdom and faith and having poured its contents into his chest he closed it (Bukhari: 1.8.345).

11. Once when Muhammad was offering prayer, Satan came in front of him and tried to interrupt his prayer, but Allah gave Muhammad an upper hand; he choked him. Muhammad thought of tying the Satan to one of the pillars of the mosque until Muslims get up in the morning and see the Satan. But Allah made the Satan return with his head down (humiliated). (Bukhari: 2.22.301).

12. Muhammad had even seen the future. On the Day of Resurrection, the sun will come near (to the people) to such an extent that the sweat will reach up to the middle of the ears, so, when all the people are in that state, they will ask Adam for help, and then Moses, and when everyone is failed, they will come to Muhammad. (Bukhari: 2.24.553).

13. Dead bodies could listen to Muhammad's words, but they could not answer (Ishaq: 306; Bukhari: 5.59.314-7).

14. Muhammad heard the sound of torture of the Jews in their graves. (Muslim: 40.6861)

15. Muhammad could hear the voices of the dead persons in their grave. Once he went through the graveyards of Medina and heard the voices of two humans who were being tortured in their graves. By hearing the conversation between two dead people he said, "They are being punished, but they are not being punished because of a major sin, yet their sins are great. One of them used not to save himself from (being soiled with) the urine, and the other used to go about with calumnies". Then he asked for a green palm tree leaf and split it into two pieces and placed one piece on each grave, saying, "I hope that their punishment may be abated as long as these pieces of the leaf are not dried". (Bukhari: 8.73.81).

16. Muhammad saw the signs of Allah in a green screen covering the horizon. (Bukhari: 6.60.381).

17. Muhammad saw the display of paradise and hell on the wall of a mosque facing the Ka'ba. (Bukhari: 1.12.716).

18. Muhammad could see in front and behind of him. (Muslim: 4.853-6).

19. Once Gabriel brought a kettle from which Muhammad ate and gained the power of sexual intercourse equal to forty men (Ibn Sa'd: Volume 1).

20. Muhammad heard Bilal's footsteps in paradise in front of him (Bukhari: 2.21.250).

21. Muhammad saw a man dragging his intestine in hell. (Muslim: 40.6838)

The list is never-ending, but I stop here. The "schizophrenia-like psychosis of epilepsy" is more than simply hallucinating or creating divine stories – it has long-lasting effects on the psyche of the person experiencing the illness that is often hard to overcome. All his bad dreams, trances, visions, delusions and hallucinations, which led to the religion of Islam, were so troubling for him that at times he sought escape by suicide. He feared that he was going mad, and surely he was correct in this assertion. Even though Khadija did not personally partake of these dreams and visions, and did not see the Angel Gabriel herself, she definitely did see the advantage of having a husband revered as a "messenger (or, secretary) of Allah" and a "gatekeeper to Allah's erotic brothel".

3.6: The psychiatric foundation of Muhammad's hyper-religiosity

"... delusions are always more alluring than facts."
Clarence Darrow

Religious delusions caused by epilepsy and schizophrenia were described in different cultures and in different times. Wrobel (1990, p. 104) pointed out that the first symptom of schizophrenia is often a sense that everything in one's environment is filled with special meaning. This proceeds to delusions of reference and a breakdown of communication. That's the reason they say strange things at strange times, and ultimately fall into the trap of hyper-religiosity. Many historical figures, from Socrates and Caesar to Descartes and Joan of Arc, have been reported to "hear voices" (Johnson, 1978, pp. 1-40). The existence of different phenomenological forms of religious delusions is clinically evident. Always hyper-religiosity includes a direct reference to organized religious themes (e.g., prayer, sin, possession), or religious figures (e.g., God, Jesus, devil). These were categorized as supernatural if they included more general mystic references (e.g., black magic, spirits, demons, being bewitched, mythical forces, ghosts, sorcery, voodoo). Examples of religion based delusions include, "I have committed a sin under the control of Satan", and "I will die a martyr" (Tateyama et al., 1998, pp. 59-68). Whereas, the religious content in hallucinations was primarily auditory (e.g., hearing voices from God), or visual (e.g., identifying biblical figures), the supernatural based nature of delusions centered on evil spirits, voodoo curses, paranormal experiences with spiritual forces, ghosts, black magic, and being bewitched.

The affinity schizophrenia to religion was recognized and was a topic for intense research already in the nineteenth century (Stompe et. al, 1999, pp. 225-34). Also, the hyper-religiosity in patients with TLE motivated early researchers linking religiosity with limbic and temporal areas (Geschwind, 1983, pp. 23-30; Devinsky, 2003, pp. 76-7). Male patients most often considered themselves as God, while female patients most often considered themselves as Saints. One thing is certain, the theme of religious delusions always correspond with the themes of myths in ancient cultures. Studies of religious delusions and hallucinations with religious content are of prime interest because these symptoms may lead to violent behavior as we have seen in Muhammad and his creed.

Freud, Wernicke, Bleuler, Kraepelin and many others who dedicated their lives to the suffering of the mentally ill were convinced that psychosis is a brain disease, though they admitted that it was not possible for them to demonstrate the fact with the available methods. Even though some people consider religion and hyper-religiosity as supernatural and thus unapproachable by science, today these phenomena can be explained by psychiatry. Here I will discuss Muhammad's hyper-religiosity from the perspective of psychiatry.

Muhammad had an insufficiently developed personality. Though he was a historical figure, it is really surprising how little the psychiatrists have explored his religiosity. Over the past three decades, there was a marked increase in the investigation on the relationship of religion and schizophrenia, specifically focusing on hallucinations and delusions.

The schizophrenics create fantastic worlds, full of symbols and new meanings which in some cases become striking apocalyptic visions. But for a trained psychologist these are only symptoms, that is to say, signals of an underlying pathology whose significance the psychiatrist is unable to explain. A schizophrenic is a failed "genius" in a rude society that does not accept his "revealed wisdom" and needs the involvement of psychiatrists to silence him. Schizophrenics have highly disparate relationships with the voices – fear, reassurance, engagement, resistance. All the patients view their voices as omnipotent and omniscient (i.e. commenting accurately on the patient's present thoughts and past history, and predicting his future) and extraordinarily powerful (Chadwick & Birchwood, 1994, pp.190-1). In the Qur'an Muhammad repeatedly told us that the voice he heard was omnipotent and omniscient.

> "... that you may know that Allah has power over all things and that Allah indeed encompasses all things in (His) knowledge." (Q: 65.12)

> "He surely is Able to do all things" (Q: 46.33)
> "... and it is He Who is Able to do all things." (Q: 22.6)

> "... and He is Able to do all things." (Q: 57.1; 64.1; 67.1)

For the schizophrenic these voices are personal. Some people experience them as immensely distressing and frightening whereas others are reassured and amused, and many actually seek contact. It depends on how the patient interprets the voices. Where some people shout and swear at voices and resist commands, others may harm themselves or other people at the voices' behest (Chadwick & Birchwood, 1994, p. 190). Muhammad interpreted his Allah as a very fearful and cruel god, more satanic than divine. The liaison between Allah and Muhammad was neither friendly nor like father and son; it was purely that of a master and slave.

> "Narrated 'Umar: I heard the Prophet saying, 'Do not exaggerate in praising me as the Christians praised the son of Mary, for I am only a Slave. So, call me the 'Slave of Allah and His Apostle'". (Bukhari: 4.55.654)

> "And when the slave of Allah stood up in prayer to Him (Allah) ..." (Q: 72.19)

Muhammad had spent many years among Christians and Jews and adopted many of their customs and stories in his Qur'an, but he never adopted their "father and son" theological concept. He simply could not imagine that God could be loveable. Hence, the God-Prophet relationship was one of a slave to his master, with obedience, rather than love, being the primary impulse.

But there is a doubt – how are the content and form of the Allah's voice, and Muhammad's cognitive, affective and behavioral response, connected? Does there exist a well-established link between them? Romme and Escher (1989, pp. 209-16) used innovatory sampling methods to study hallucinations in clinical and non-clinical groups and showed how a person's ability to cope with voices varied according to his appraisal of the voices. Benjamin (1989, pp. 291-310) studied thirty patients and found that all had meaningful, integrated and interpersonally coherent relationships with their voices. These relationships are orderly and interpersonally "normal" for a schizophrenia patient but not always complimentary. These patients might claim that their voices liked them even though the content was hostile and attacking. Moreover, the content of the voice is "directly responsible" for the person's behavioral and affective response. Allah is "directly responsible" for Muhammad's actions.

"So you did not slay them, but it was Allah Who slew them, and you did not smite when you smote (the enemy), but it was Allah Who smote, and that He might confer upon the believers a good gift from Himself; surely Allah is Hearing, Knowing". (Q: 8.17)

In the above verse there is a very clear argument. The responsibility is on Allah for having started the fighting and in terrorizing others. Muhammad did not say that he terrorized others, but it was Allah who made him successful in terrorizing others. Muhammad made Allah the author of his vicious thoughts and pretended that it was not his goal to kill his opponents but it was the decision of Allah, who was commanding him. This way Muhammad did not take any responsibility because he did not "own" his actions. Over and above, he is conveniently implying that warfare is hateful to him, but he participated in it because it was ordained by Allah! He was just carrying out Allah's instruction. Anyone who wants to achieve victory by terrorizing others is simply called a terrorist. But Muhammad was not a terrorist by choice, but by compulsion. It was Allah, who wanted him to be a terrorist. Nobody could blame him for whatever misery he had caused to the unbelievers and their women and children. Such is the force and authority of the strange voices the schizophrenic hears.

"And that do not exalt yourselves against Allah, surely I will bring to you a clear authority". (Q: 44.19)

Where did the voices (Qur'anic revelations) come from that gave a clear authority to Muhammad? Ever since the birth of Islam, the skeptics are repeatedly asking this fascinating question. Many critics focus on either psychological or physiological aspects but in my opinion the two are closely linked in the formation of the revelations.

Using new techniques of functional brain imaging, the psychiatrists can show which part of the brain is active when normal people are doing various mental tasks, for example moving their hand (the motor area), or looking at a movie (the visual cortex). In a similar way, they can study the way the brain malfunctions when someone is experiencing psychotic symptoms. Modern brain imaging techniques have enabled us to demonstrate that the hallucinations (e.g. voices) and delusions (bizarre ideas) which characterize schizophrenia arise from malfunction of the brain. Lately with the development of positron emission tomography (PET) one can look at the function of the brain during auditory hallucinations and so obtain a more precise location of the areas responsible for the "voices". The studies show that, when patients experience auditory hallucinations (i.e. hear voices), activity is increased in that part of the brain which we normally use to generate our own inner "mental" speech. This indicates that the words which the schizophrenics hear as voices are self-generated in the same way that most of us would say the words of a rhythmic poem or favorite movie dialog, or part of a popular song, or a prayer silently to ourselves. For example, the opening Surah called the Fatiha,

"In the name of Allah, Most Gracious, Most Merciful. Praise be to Allah, the Cherisher and Sustainer of the worlds; Most Gracious, Most Merciful; Master

of the Day of Judgment. Thee do we worship, and Thine aid we seek. Show us the straight way, The way of those on whom Thou hast bestowed Thy Grace, those whose (portion) is not wrath, and who go not astray."

These words are addressed to Allah, in the form of a prayer. A god cannot pray to himself, or worship himself, or tell himself to show him the straightway – *"Thee do we worship, and Thine aid we seek. Show us the straightway".* (Q: 1.5, 6) – this is absurd. These are Muhammad's words of praise to Allah – the self-generated inner mental speech of a sincere but severely deluded hyper-religious schizophrenic – asking Allah's help and guidance. The silent prayer of the schizophrenic Prophet of Islam is recorded in the Qur'an in Allah's name. We have similar problem in the following verses.

*"Say: **I seek refuge in the Lord of the dawn**, from the evil of what He has created."* (Q: 113.1-2)

*"**For me, I have been commanded to serve the Lord of this city**, Him Who has sanctified it and to Whom (belong) all things: and **I am commanded to be of those who bow in Islam to Allah's Will**."* (Q: 27.91)

*"So verily **I call to witness the planets** - that recede,"* (Q: 81.15)

*"So **I do call to witness the ruddy glow of Sunset**."* (Q: 84.16)

*"Proofs have come unto you from your Lord, so whoso seeth, it is for his own good, and whoso is blind is blind to his own hurt. And **I am not a keeper over you**."* (Q: 6.104)

The speaker of the above verses is clearly Muhammad. In fact, Dawood in his translation of the verse 6.104 adds as a footnote that the "I" refers to Muhammad. This also explains why Allah and Muhammad command together. Allah gave blind support to his messenger because every single verse was actually coming from Muhammad's own diseased mind.

"Allah helped you at Badr when you were contemptible, so fear Allah. Fear Me." (Ishaq: 392).

" ... Obey Allah and His Messenger ..." (Muslim: 8.1, 8.20)

This particular instruction *"Obey Allah and His Messenger"* is repeated several times in the Islamic scriptures, as if Allah is in a constant panicky state. A real God cannot be in panic; the delusional Prophet was paranoid. The Surah 111 says,

"Perish the hands of the Father of Flame! Perish he! No profit to him from all his wealth, and all his gains! Burnt soon will he be in a Fire of Blazing Flame! His wife shall carry the (crackling) wood - As fuel! A twisted rope of palm-leaf fibre round her (own) neck!"

The complete Surah is a curse. Ali Dashti considers this Surah as the words of Muhammad on the grounds that these words are unworthy of God (cited Warraq, 1995, p. 106); "*It ill becomes the Sustainer of the Universe to curse an ignorant Arab and call his wife a firewood carrier.*" The short Surah refers to Abu Lahab, the uncle of Muhammad who was one of Muhammad's bitterest opponents. The evil Prophet of the Muslims could utter curses against his enemies, not the true God.

Any well-trained psychiatrist who makes an objective study of the Qur'an will find an unmistakable signature of a schizophrenic on every page of this supposed to be holy book. Qur'an contains only deception, lies and meaningless blabbering of a mentally sick person. Every single verse of the Qur'an directly or indirectly depicts the changing thought pattern of a severely confused author. Nothing is more foolish than dreaming of a paradise full of worldly pleasures as a reward for causing insult, injury and injustice to others. Not only every verse; but every letter and every word of every verse is the product of Muhammad's own sick imagination to achieve his own selfish needs. Hence, if Qur'an calls itself to be "mubeen", or clear, this is what it means – we have to study the book by the standard of a psychotic patient's sick judgment. Allah was Muhammad's own mental figment. When Muhammad claimed the title of Prophet of Allah, he really "felt" that way, more precisely, his self-generated voices confirmed his prophethood. If we say Muhammad was sincere in his claim it was on this delusion his sincerity based. He had lost touch with reality.

Allah spies on Muhammad's wives and alert him on various domestic issues.

"*The Prophet confided a certain matter to one of his wives but thereafter she disclosed it, then Allah revealed what she had done to him. He made part of it known and another part not. And when he acquainted her with it, she said: 'Who has told you this'? He replied: 'I was told of it by the Knower, the Aware'.*" (Q: 66.3)

"*If both of you (wives) turn to Allah in repentance, even though your hearts inclined; but if you support one another against him, (know that) Allah is his Guardian, and Gabriel, and the righteous among the believers; and thereafter the angels are his reinforcers*". (Q: 66.4).

We always wonder if God has nothing better job to do. A large portion of the Qur'an is preoccupied with the personal and political affairs of one man and his companions at one particular stage in the history. Most of these statements have no value to any other generation contrary to popular Muslim belief that Qur'an is eternal. In these two verses Muhammad was expressing his own concern. This schizophrenic never made the connection that he was hearing his own voice. In proper psychological term this is called "impaired monitoring of self-generated speech". Impaired self-monitoring, i.e., the cognitive ability to distinguish the products of self-generated actions or thoughts from those of other-generated actions or thoughts, is in fact the core symptom of schizophrenia. Similarly, the following verse is clearly a self-generated speech.

"*When you hear His verses being disbelieved or mocked, do not sit with them until they engage in other talk, or else you will surely be like them. Allah will surely gather the hypocrites and unbelievers altogether in Hell*". (Q: 4.140)

The question is, why do the schizophrenics not realize that they have generated the words themselves? Studies have shown that during hallucinations patients also activate their auditory cortex, the part of the brain which normally processes external speech. In short, when a patient is hearing voices, there is an activity involving two parts of the brain – first in the part that would normally be involved in generating inner speech, and next in the auditory cortex, the part that would normally be active while listening to another person speaking to them. This understanding is very important for us because human beings are the only species privileged to think in words. Hence, the schizophrenic first produces words in his brain but then mistakenly activates the auditory cortex, and this tricks the brain into thinking that there must be some external source for the words. Today, this new knowledge of how the voices are generated opens up new ways of assessing the most appropriate treatment for each hyper-religious patient.

With a schizophrenic, the nerve cells in part of the brain develop faulty connections with other cells. It results in a picture which can be likened to a computer with a minor problem in its "hard-wiring" – the machine works well most of the time but when it is overloaded it may malfunction. Similarly, when the schizophrenic is subject to stress, such as, examinations, or family problems, or paranoia, a part of his brain systems becomes overloaded, malfunctions, and fails to tell the difference between real and imaginary events. Just as crossed lines in a telephone exchange can cause one to overhear a conversation when dialing, so the misreading of signals within the brain can cause the schizophrenic to hear voices. Many other factors can also cause abnormal nerve cell wiring. Muhammad was paranoid. He used to see enemies everywhere.

> *"[Aisha recalled] Muhammad never failed to come by our house every day at the two ends of the day. ...Once he came during the heat of the day so we knew that it was because of something special. When he came in dad rose from his bed, and the Messenger sat down. Muhammad said, 'Send out those who are with you.' My father said, 'Prophet, these are my daughters [one of which is now your wife]; they can do you no harm, may my father and mother be your ransom.'"* (Ishaq: 223)

> *"Remember how the unbelievers [Meccans] plotted against you (Muhammad), to keep you in bonds, or slay you, or get you out (of your home). They plotted, and Allah too had arranged a plot; but Allah is the best schemer".* (Q: 8.30).

> *"And they (the disbelievers) schemed, and Allah schemed (against them); and Allah is the best of schemers".* (Q: 3.54)

Sadly, due to the underlying paranoia, the voice instructed Muhammad to do disagreeable tasks. Though Allah was directly responsible for Muhammad's own criminal actions, the question arises as to why Muhammad felt compelled to behave and respond affectively in such an apparently agreeable manner. The reason is, voices often have a very powerful impact on the lives of those who experience them (Falloon & Talbot, 1981, pp. 329-39). Muhammad was strongly influenced by his beliefs about Allah's authority and power, Allah's own degree of control and the presumed consequences of disobedience. The belief that a voice comes from a powerful and vengeful spirit may make the person terrified of the voice and comply with its commands to harm others; however, if the same voice were interpreted as self-generated, the behavior and affect might be quite different.

Interestingly, modern day psychiatrists follow an effective treatment approach that relies heavily on the disputing and testing of beliefs. The idea is, if beliefs about the voices could be weakened, this might reduce associated distress and problem behavior. For this, the patient is introduced to other people who hallucinate, and views videos of clients (those who have completed therapy successfully) discussing their voices. Information about voices is provided to back this up. These measures serve the purpose of preparing the patient for the later suggestion that the voices might be self-generated.

Visual hallucination is the second most common type with schizophrenia. Some seventy-three percent schizophrenics report visual hallucinations (Chadwick & Birchwood, 1994, p. 191). The images may be very clear, or vague or distorted. In spirituality, this is what we call vision. A vision is something seen in a dream, trance, or ecstasy, especially a supernatural appearance that conveys a revelation. Visionary experiences are so common in cults and religions that contemporary scholars have found spiritual and spirituality difficult to define without them. The visions are of two types – visionary spiritual experiences (dramatic, perceptual experiences involving spirit realities e.g., mystical experience, seeing a ghost, attack by an evil spirit), and interpretive spiritual experiences (ordinary experiences interpreted spiritually e.g., a beautiful sunset as evidence of God's love).

Visionary experiences have been discredited as symptoms of mental pathology in the scientific worldview and belief in such experiences is considered superstition from scientific points of view. Throughout the recorded history of mankind many people have reported visions, which later were passed on to the rest of humanity as symbols of faith. People who have undergone visions have been esteemed and enjoyed privileged status as shamans, prophets, or saints. Accounts range from Biblical Prophets and saints to shamans, as well as Socrates' famous Daemon voice. Psychiatrists have retroactively diagnosed all of them to have had mental disorders (Leuder & Thomas, 2000). The beloved Prophet of the Muslims is not an exception.

Muhammad's first experience of revelation in the cave was a vision. But the vision was so terrifying that Muhammad was not at all convinced at first that the vision was divinely commissioned. An account of his actual experience and immediate reaction reads as follows,

"The Apostle of Allah, was terrified. Whenever he raised his head towards the heaven he saw him; so he returned hastily to Khadijah and conveyed this information to her. He said; O Khadijah! By Allah, I never hated anything so much as idols and soothsayers, and I am afraid that I shall myself become a soothsayer ... O Khadijah! I hear sounds and see light and I fear I am mad".
(Ibn Sa'd, Kitab al-Tabaqat al-Kabir: Vol.1)

The images that the schizophrenic sees in his vision are often frightening. He thinks that the command comes from the devil by using telepathic power (Chadwick

& Birchwood, 1994, p. 198). At the first confrontation Muhammad was seized with anguish and, when the second similar vision occurred sometime later, he again came down in terror, crying to Khadija to cover him up, a sign that he feared he was being demonically assaulted. He was assured, however, that it was Allah himself, the one Supreme Being of the whole universe who had visited him, and, "... *after this the revelation was speeded up and followed rapidly.*" (Muslim: 1.305).

Over the next twenty-three years he never again had such a terrifying vision but the Qur'an consistently grew in content as the revelation came to him in dreams and other ways. Muhammad's visions and the process of Qur'anic revelations were part of a psychotic thought process, and slowly he developed a psychotic relationship with his Allah delusion.

In sum; Muhammad's hyper-religiosity was a unique case of false spiritual consciousness. There is a lesson to learn – without careful examination, our beliefs about who we are can easily slide into delusion. Our ideology can mask reality. Believing you have reached an elevated state of spiritual consciousness and enlightenment is particularly dangerous. This ideology of spiritual enlightenment works like a set of blinders. It conceals all those shadowy parts of ourselves that we like to keep in the periphery.

3.7: Conclusion

"It is not by delusion, however exalted, that mankind can prosper, but only by unswerving courage in the pursuit of truth."

Bertrand Russell

"It is far better to grasp the universe as it really is than to persist in delusion, however satisfying and reassuring".

Carl Sagan

Intellectual ideas always attract us because we are capable of thinking logically. But when an idea is the expression of so-called psychic experience which bears fruit in religious beliefs, it represents forces that are beyond logical justifications and moral sanctions. Jung (1933, p. 42) commented,

"They [the forces] are always stronger than man and his brain. Man believes indeed that he moulds these ideas, but in reality, they mould him and make him their unwitting mouthpiece".

For Muhammad (only for him) his hallucinations were real experiences. When he said that he was divinely commanded to preach in the name of Allah, he was telling the "truth" (only for him). His "honesty" in his prophetic claim and divine mission was based on this illusive "truth". His deceitful "sincerity" misled many Arabs to believe in him and to join his creed. This is how Islam started with a falsehood. And to quote from Freud (Strachey & Gay, 1966, p. 104),

"Doctors have observed cases in which a mental disease has started with a dream and in which a delusion originating in the dream has persisted; Historical figures are reported to have embarked on momentous enterprises in response to dreams".

Affirmation despite a total lack of evidence is the beginning of a delusion. When the illness is severe, the strength of belief increases. As Harris (2005, p. 12) commented,

"A belief is a lever that, once pulled, moves almost everything else in a person's life. Once believed, they become part of the very apparatus of your mind, determining your desires, fears, expectations, and subsequent behavior."

If there is any truth in Islam, it is this "deceptive truth" amidst a vast ocean of falsehood. Man has nothing to gain, emotionally or otherwise, by adhering to a falsehood, regardless of how comfortable or sacred that falsehood may appear. Muhammad needed psychoanalytic treatment. A lunatic Prophet and a god who evolves from his lunacy cannot bring anything real; they can only bring more delusion, deception and confusion. These are the gifts of Allah and Muhammad to the Muslims. Ignorance serves no one's interest. It is far better to accept the truth as it really is than to persist in delusion, however satisfying and reassuring.

3.8: The impact of command hallucinations on schizophrenics

"The possibility of truth has become a delusion to those who made their own disguise the truth."

Nema Al-Araby

Most people diagnosed with schizophrenia are not violent or a danger to other people. But those who experience delusions of persecution or have a command hallucination have a greater risk of acting violently to others (Bjorkly, 2002, pp. 617-31). The contents of the command hallucinations can range from the innocuous to commands to cause harm to the self or others. Various case studies had confirmed that patients with command hallucinations are most likely to be schizophrenic (Hellerstein et. al, 1987, pp. 219-21; Mitchell et. al, 1989, pp. 269-74; Junginger, 1995, pp. 911-4; Rogers et. al, 1988, pp. 251-8; Rogers et. al, 1990, pp. 1304-7). In command hallucination the voices tell the schizophrenic to do certain things that in some cases can cause significant problems. Allah commanded Muhammad to fight the infidels. According to Allah violence can be virtuous.

"O Prophet, exhort the believers to fight..." (Q: 8.65)

"O Prophet! Strive hard against the unbelievers and the hypocrites and be unyielding to them; and their abode is hell, and evil is destination" (Q: 9.73)

"Fighting is prescribed for you, and ye dislike it. But it is possible that ye dislike a thing which is good for you, and that ye love a thing which is bad for you. But Allah knoweth, and ye know not". (Q: 2.216)

"Fight in the way of Allah, and know that Allah is Hearer, Knower." (Q: 2.244)

"Then, when the sacred months have passed, slay the idolaters wherever ye find them, and take them (captive), and besiege them, and prepare for them each ambush. But if they repent and establish worship and pay the poor-due, then leave their way free. Lo! Allah is Forgiving, Merciful". (Q: 9.5).
"And be not weak hearted in pursuit of the enemy; if you suffer pain, then surely they (too) suffer pain as you suffer pain..." (Q: 4.104)

"O ye who believe! When ye meet those who disbelieve in battle, turn not your backs to them". (Q: 8.15)

"And fight with them until there is no more fitna (disorder, unbelief) and religion should be only for Allah ..." (Q: 8.39)

Muhammad's bizarre beliefs, incredible teachings, self-elevation and immense hate are well reflected in his Qur'an. The violent instructions of Allah in the Qur'an are mostly open-ended, meaning that they are not restrained by the historical context of the surrounding text. They are part of the eternal, unchanging word of Allah, and just as relevant or subjective as anything else in the Qur'an. The Prophet of Islam did not come to the world to bring something good like other great teachers. He came to this world to preach hatred, brutality and slaughter. Terrorism is not the problem with the Muslims, but with their militant god and the violent Prophet. Muhammad's own martial legacy – and that of his companions – along with the remarkable stress on violence found in the Qur'an have produced a trail of blood and tears across world history.

"Those who believe fight in the cause of Allah..." (Q: 4.76)

"I will cast terror into the hearts of those who disbelieve. Therefore strike off their heads and strike off every fingertip of them." (Q: 8.12)

A patient who gives an identity to a hallucinated voice should be considered at somewhat greater risk for compliance with the command than a patient who cannot identify the hallucinated voice. The voices may tell the schizophrenic to harm or kill himself or to harm someone else. Because the voices seem very real, they can be very compelling, making it difficult for the schizophrenic to resist acting on the command. Muhammad lived in Medina for only ten years (622-632 AD), but in this brief time, Allah compelled him to fight at least seventy-four raids, expeditions, or full-scale wars.

The following verse criticizes "peaceful" Muslims who do not join in the violence, letting them know that they are less worthy in Allah's eyes.

"Not equal are those believers who sit (at home) and receive no hurt, and those who strive and fight in the cause of Allah with their goods and their persons." (Q: 4.95)

Depp (1983) found in a study of inpatient assaults that nine of sixty (fifteen percent) violent incidents were preceded by command hallucinations. Patients are less likely to obey violent than nonviolent command. Here the command is clear and powerful from a mysterious voice that no one else could hear. People feel that they are being told what to do by an imposing or mythic figure with absolute obedience (Tardiff, 1998, pp. 567-76; Bjorkly, 2002a, pp. 605-15). Allah wrote,
"He cannot be questioned for His acts, but they will be questioned". (Q: 21.23)

Rogers et al (1990, pp. 1304-7) concluded that majority of the commands have criminal contents. Fifty-six percent of the patients had complied with a command hallucination *"with unquestioning obedience"* and forty-four percent patients have complied *"on a frequent or very frequent basis"*. The patients are sometimes ordered to assassinate a prominent personality, sacrifice a human being or a child, or harm themselves by the wish of God, or devil, or demons, or angels, or aliens (Sagan, 1997, p. 131). These voices compel the patient to obey them by making him helpless at the mercy of it. If he is reluctant to comply, dire penalties are threatened. Muhammad complied with the voice he heard.

"Narrated Jabir bin `Abdullah: The Prophet said: Allah made me victorious with terror". (Bukhari: 1.7.331).

"The Prophet said, 'Hear me. By Him who holds Muhammad's life in his hand, I will bring you slaughter '". (Ishaq: 130; Tabari: VI.101)

"Soon shall We cast terror into the hearts of the Unbelievers ..." (Q: 3.151)

Voices usually do not introduce themselves, e.g., "This is God speaking", is never heard. This leaves the patient wondering – Who would issue such a command? Who could speak inside my head? He assumes that it is God or Jesus or Satan or the Head of a covert spy agency, or criminals, or the leader of a gang. The voice Muhammad heard was a fearful voice. Allah ruled through fear. He wants us to submit to his will.

"Pronounce the Name of Allah, and fear Allah." (Q: 5.4)

"Allah warns you to be cautious of Him, the arrival is to Allah". (Q: 3.28).

"He who fears will obey". (Q: 87.10)

"What is the matter with you that you do not fear Allah?" (Muslim: 71.13)

"Fear Allah; Allah is Severe in Punishment". (Muslim: 59.6)

"Fear Allah as much as you can; listen and obey". (Q: 64.16)

"My (Allah) Anger should fall upon you, and upon whosoever My Anger falls has assuredly fallen". (Q: 20.81)

"So fear Allah, and keep straight the relations between yourselves: Obey Allah and His Messenger, if ye do believe". (Q: 8.1)

"And We did not send any messenger but that he should be obeyed by Allah's permission". (Q: 4.65)
"O ye who believe! Obey Allah and His Messenger, and turn not away from him when ye hear (him speak)." (Q: 8.20)

If there is a uniform theme throughout the Qur'an, it is that Allah must be obeyed, period. If Allah commands worship, man must worship. If Allah commands murder, man must murder. Command hallucinations may devastate a person turning him to a cold-blooded, conscienceless killer. Studies in forensic psychiatric settings have found that patients charged with crimes often report that voices told them to engage in the criminal acts (Rogers et. al, 1988, pp. 251-8; Thompson et. al, 1992, pp. 462-5). As example; Jeffrey Macdonald, who murdered his wife and two children in 1970, claimed that the "acid heads" had committed the crime. Macdonald was the subject of the book and movie *Fatal Vision* (McGinniss, 1989). Kenneth Bianchi, who raped, tortured and killed a dozen women, was mistakenly believed to have a multiple personality and crimes had been committed by "Steve" (O'Brien, 1985). Ted Bundy, a serial killer who killed several dozen of young women, claimed that a "malignant entity" had taken over his consciousness (Hare, 1993, p. 4). Very similar to Muhammad's hallucination, all these are some kind of delusional psychic experiences. Stout (2005, p. 54) concludes that when the human brain is impaired in this way, "The voices told me to do it" is not a joke but a horrifying reality and such a person can act on his delusional idea much against his conscience and will. If we want to assess the violent verses of the Qur'an we must read them from Muhammad's perspective. He had interpreted the hallucinatory commands based on his psychotic thinking.

Chapter 4: Human evil and dimensions of delusions

"Nothing happened to me ... I happened."
Dr. Hannibal Lecter (*The Silence of the Lambs*)

Dr. Hannibal "Cannibal" Lecter, the fictional character drawn from the profiles of real-life serial killers, has appeared in four novels and five films. Hannibal, a character with maroon eyes, six fingers on his left hand, superhuman strength, unnaturally sharp senses, and dominion over wild animals (Oleson, 2006, pp. 29-49), has been transformed into the kind of celebrity that at one time, as Skal (1993, p. 383) stated, *"was, arguably, the most publicized and recognizable personality (real or not) in America"*. In the film *The Silence of the Lambs*, the character of Hannibal Lecter dismisses the possibility that his crimes can be explained, defiantly boasting, *"You can't reduce me to a set of influences"* (Harris, 1988, p. 20). Yet in spite of all his existential bravado, a passage in one of Harris' subsequent books hints that something did happen to him, and he can be reduced to a set of influences.

Hannibal is indeed a set of influences and almost nothing else – there are biological predisposition, sociological influences and psychological factors. The character of Hannibal Lecter may be little more than the product of an acute childhood trauma. In *Hannibal* (Harris, 1999), Lecter falls asleep on an airplane. Dreaming, he recalls a terrible episode from World War II – his aristocrat parents were murdered by deserters from the wartime front. When the deserters depleted their food supply they slaughtered his younger sister Mischa and consumed her flesh. Her death formed the fantasy that shaped Hannibal Lecter, a revenge fantasy.

Hannibal is a delusional psychopath. He believes in a string theory through which he hopes to reverse time and restore Mischa to the world. Viewed through the lens of the Mischa story, Hannibal is not a monstrous killer – he is a hero, using his prodigious intellect and superhuman talents to seek a single goal: the restoration of his murdered sister to the world. Deep down, Hannibal Lecter is no monster, no vampire, and certainly not an incarnation of the devil; he is nothing more than a victim of his own delusion. Though he is a world-class psychiatrist with an immeasurably high IQ score, he is not aware of the parallels between his sister's death and his own crimes.

Not only is Hannibal a compelling paradox, but the character invites us to think about the nature of human evil. We should study this fictional serial killer because in doing so, we can understand his real-life counterparts in the world of crime.

4.1: Introduction

"The problem of evil is still with us ... except that of attributing evil to Satan, we look for the demonic figures in the world around us."
Shirley Guthrie

The relationship between psychotic delusional disorder, schizophrenia and criminal behavior has been well-documented by various researchers, but very few have investigated the link between them. Hodgins and Cote (1993, pp. 115-29) attempted to examine it and proposed that a psychotic with a co-occurring Antisocial Personality Disorder is more likely to commit criminal acts than persons with a singular major delusion. In Great Britain, Taylor et al (1998, pp. 218-26) had studied patient populations of three special psychiatric hospitals. The records of 1,750 patients were examined and the majority (fifty-three percent) was found to have schizophrenia and delusional disorder. Among all psychotic patients, both positive and negative symptoms were significantly present at the time of the crime.

They noticed that the main triggering factors for the crimes were delusional symptoms, which led more often to violent acts than to trivial acts. Hallucinations did not have the same effect when delusional activity was not present. Yet in another study, Link and Stueve (1994, pp. 137-59) reported that having delusions with paranoid content is strongly associated with acts of violence. Cheung et al (1997, pp. 181-90) reported similar findings. They investigated thirty-one patients and concluded that those in the violent group were more affected by persecutory delusions than were those in the nonviolent group. Appelbaum et al. (1999, pp. 1938-43) examined delusional patients with an evident history of violence and found a high degree of conviction in grandiose and religious delusions.

Though a serious act of violence committed by a psychotic is relatively a rare event (Monahan, 1992, pp. 511-21), there are cases where the disorder manifested as self-harm or harm to others in the name of God or Satan. Many of them are highly religious. Gary Ridgway, a serial murderer who holds the record for the most serial-murder convictions in US history with forty-eight victims, enjoyed doing missionary work to spread the Word of God. He watched religious television programs that often brought him to tears (Hickey, 2010, p. 24). Marron, in his book *Ritual Abuse* (1988), described the complexity of a case where parents allegedly performed ritualistic tortures on their children. By the time the courts, investigators, and social service agencies had all been involved, affixing blame and determining culpability had become extremely difficult. Such cases continue to surface and ignite public outrage, especially those that center on families and children.

Kahaner, in his book *Cults That Kill* (1988), noted that Satanism and murder are increasing and that an epidemic of youth violence is sweeping the country. The Robin Gecht case supports this claim. Robin Gecht and three other young men terrorized Chicago in the early 1980s by abducting, mutilating, and killing several young women. In a form of Satan worship, they were believed to have cut up animal and human body parts for sacrifice on a makeshift altar and then to have cannibalized some of the remains. In one case, Robert Berdella, a serial killer involved in the murders of several young men, was accused of Satan worship.

Also, there are cases where psychotic men had performed autocastration based on a literal, erroneous interpretation of a passage in the Bible (Matthew: 19.12). There are cases where, after performing self-enucleation, patients were often found with a copy of Matthew's Gospel open at 5.29, where it states, " ... *if the right eye offend thee, pluck it out and cast it from thee; for it is profitable for thee that one of thy members should perish and not that thy whole body should cast into hell.*"

People have also committed self-harm as per this Biblical passage,

"If your hand causes you to sin, cut it off; it is better for you to enter life maimed than with two hands to go to hell, to the unquenchable fire. And if your foot causes you to sin, cut it off; it is better for you to enter life lame than with two feet to be thrown into hell. And if your eye causes you to sin, pluck it out; it is better for you to enter the kingdom of God with one eye than with two eyes to be thrown into hell, where their worm does not die, and the fire is not quenched". (Mark: 9.43-48)

Today if the implications of this passage fail to sink in, it is probably because hardly any Christian of this scientific age takes its message literally. Such was not the case, however, with earlier and less sophisticated Christians who were moved to self-castration as a means of eliminating temptation. The enucleation represented a literal interpretation of the text. Also there are reports that deluded patients have committed rape and murder because they believed that the victims were antichrist. The notorious murderer Ed Gein's mother convinced her son that women were *"vessels of sin and caused disease"*. Ed Gein, in his twisted mind, misinterpreted this and literally made vessels out of women, by using their skulls for household items (Pokel, 2000, p. 27). This is the power of religious delusion. In every culture we find zealots who embrace hallucinatory confusion and aggressively proclaim it as moral and religious experience. They find "meaning" in their delusions.

4.2: The Allah delusion and the criminality of Muhammad

"Cruelty is the first of God's attributes."
Andre Gide

"The tragedy of life is what dies inside a man while he lives".
Albert Schweitzer

Evil comes in many shapes and forms. Most "normal" people have great difficulty in fathoming why someone would want to kill other people. However, in the mind of the killer the motivations are often very meaningful. If we examine the philosophical and psychological roots of moral evil (undeserved harm caused by human beings), we will see that some people demonstrate a seemingly insatiable appetite for crime, as the serial killer Alexander Pichushkin confessed, *". . . for me, a life without murder is like a life without food for you"* (Hickey, 2010, p. 328), as the well-known serial killer Ted Bundy, whose name was synonymous with terror, fear and brutality, once said, *"I just liked to kill, I wanted to kill"*. Charles Starkweather, after his killing spree, casually observed, *"Shooting people was, I guess, a kind of a thrill. It brought out something."* (Reinhardt, 1960, p. 78). But in the pantheon of infamy, the Prophet of Allah eclipses all in popularity. Muhammad took pleasure in harming and killing the innocents.

"It is not for any Prophet to have captives until he hath made slaughter in the land. You desire the lure of this world and Allah desires for you the hereafter and Allah is Mighty, Wise". (Q: 8.67)

"Now enjoy what you have won as lawful and good and keep your duty to Allah. Lo! Allah is forgiving, merciful". (Q: 8.69)

The above revelations were in reference to the prisoners that Muhammad held for ransom after the battle. Allah the "Merciful" is saying that they should all have been killed! In addition, Allah is conveniently commenting that whatever loot Muhammad had plundered is "lawful and good" because it was done in the service to Allah. Therefore; murder, rape, plunder and destruction are all perfectly fine with Allah as long as they are done in the name of Islam! Muhammad is also insidiously making himself seem very kind for having spared the lives of the prisoners, when in fact he only let them live so he could get more money from the ransom for them. In today's world this is called "terrorism" of the worst kind.

Muhammad's fanatic god and satanic religion were the ultimate expressions of moral evil, as if he had a hidden "evil" personality that lived for killing. If we are not very careful about moral evil then the idea of deserved harm can easily become a platform for justifying revenge and for all manner of disproportionate, undeserved harm – in other words, it can become a platform for evil – an evil which can be justified as we have seen in the case of Hannibal Lector. Margoliouth (cited Warraq, 1995, p. 103) commented,

"The character attributed to Mohammed in the biography of Ibn Ishaq is exceedingly unfavorable. In order to gain his ends he recoils from no expedient, and he approves of similar unscrupulousness on the part of his adherents, when exercised in his interest. He profits to the utmost from the chivalry of the Meccans, but rarely requites it with the like. He organises assassinations and wholesale massacres. His career as tyrant of Medina is that of a robber chief, whose political economy consists in securing and dividing plunder, the distribution of the latter being at times carried out on principles which fail to satisfy his follower's ideas of justice. He is himself an unbridled libertine and encourages the same passion in his followers. For whatever he does he is prepared to plead the express authorization of the deity".

The bloody stories of Muhammad's trail of violence, hatred, sexual exploitation and bloodshed that soon destroyed the once flourishing culture of Arabia were well-documented by his biographers and historians – surprise raids on merchant caravans and tribal settlements, use of plunder thus obtained for recruiting an ever growing army of greedy desperados, assassinations of opponents, beheading, torture, blackmail, expulsion and massacre of the Jews of Medina, attack and enslavement of the Jews of Khaybar, rape of women and children, sale of those victims after rape, burning alive, cruelty to animals, arson, robbery, destruction, trickery, treachery and bribery employed to their fullest extent to grow the numbers of his religion, Islam, which ironically was supposed to mean "Peace"! If we examine Muhammad through a theological lens, the evil is located within the external agent, i.e., the supernatural force, Allah, which caused him to act violently.

*"Narrated Aisha: Allah's Apostle never took revenge (over anybody) for his own sake but (he did) only when **Allah's Legal Bindings** were outraged in which case he would take revenge for Allah's sake"*. (Bukhari: 4.56.760).

Here the expression *"Allah's Legal Bindings"* needs to be noted. It raises two questions – Was Allah responsible for evil, or Muhammad? How to correlate our understanding of human nature to the nature of God?

Viewed from a psychological perspective, Muhammad's acts of violence were the products of his paranoid schizophrenia, not the fictitious Allah. It often appears that the serial killers and mass murderers have multiple personalities. Throughout the history, a number of serious offenders have insisted that evil forces are quite real, and are responsible for terrible crimes. Even high-profile offenders who have been deemed sane by psychiatrists have suggested that evil forces may play a role in explaining "inexplicable" crime. For example, Kenneth Bianchi, one of the "Hillside Stranglers" in California and Washington, claimed that he was involved in killing twelve women because he was controlled by multiple personalities. Convincing for a while, Bianchi's defense finally came apart under close scrutiny by psychiatric experts. Juan Chavez, who confessed to killing six white, middle-aged homosexuals, said he really did not know why he killed his victims, but believed the *"devil made me do it"*. David Richard Berkowitz, the "Son of Sam" or "44-Caliber Killer" who hunted thirteen victims over a period of thirteen months in New York, claimed that he did the killings since his neighbor's demonically possessed dogs commanded him to do so. Ted Bundy explained to the police using the third person, that he was eventually overcome by an internal force or an "entity" that constituted a "purely destructive power". Another criminal believed that the voice in his hallucinations was that of the devil, which possessed him (Hickey, 2010, pp. 37-8, 152, 358, 361). Notorious cannibal killer Jeffrey Dahmer told police officers that evil forces may have led him to commit his crimes. Speaking with police officers, Dahmer (cited Schwartz, 1992, pp. 200-01) mused,

*"I have to question whether or not there is an evil force in the world and whether or not I have been influenced by it…. Although I am not sure if there is a God, or if there is a devil, I know that of lately I've been doing a lot of thinking about both, and **I have to wonder what has influenced me in my life**"*.

There are four different types of serial killers – visionary, mission-oriented, hedonistic and control-oriented (Holmes & DeBurger, 1988, pp. 55-60; Pokel, 2000, pp. 14, 34). Visionary serial killers murder in response to voices, or visions urging them to kill (Hickey, 2010, p. 30). In cases, such as Manson, Lucas and Ramirez there was a satanic cult link. They strongly feel impelled to commit murder by visions or *"voices in my head."* Their quick, act-focused killings are seen as a job to be done. Some psychiatrists argue that a visionary killer cannot be included in the fantasy-addiction theory, but this is not true. Even though the killer is not in fully conscious control of his personal world, his mind still acts to preserve the fantasy, which in this case is the psychotic delusion.

The demonic evil, i.e., the evil for evil's sake, is nowhere to be found in reality, only in fiction. Also, the psychotic killers are not indestructible nor do they have special mystical powers. Psychiatrists have interviewed and researched enough serial killers to debunk such a myth. They are offenders with grotesquely distorted fantasy systems, and certainly not Hannibal Lecters. These people are average humans who have acquired certain skills and certain patterns of deviousness that permit some of them to elude police (Hickey, 2010, p. 388). Similar to Dahmer's belief, Allah, the internalized "judge" of Muhammad haunted him in every moment of his prophetic career. Given the tumultuous history of his prophetic career, with its raids, wars, and assassinations, it is undeniable that terror was Muhammad's legacy. For Muhammad, it was his divine duty to terrorize others.

> *"Warfare is ordained for you, though it is hateful unto you; but it may happen that you hate a thing which is good for you and it may happen that you love a thing which is bad for you. Allah knoweth, you knew not"*. (Q: 2.216).

> *"They question thee (O Muhammad) with regard to warfare in the sacred month. Say: Warfare therein is a great (transgression), but to turn (men) from the way of Allah, and to disbelieve in Him and in the Inviolable Place of Worship, and to expel His people thence, is a greater with Allah..."* (Q: 2.217)

> *"The Prophet said: Allah made me victorious with terror"*. (Bukhari: 1.7.331).

Here Muhammad is completely removing all the blame from himself for having started the fighting. The most insidious and devilish implication of this verse is that the evil force Allah is completely justifying the killing of innocent people. The mass murderers often deny responsibility. Bundy attempted to add a rational note to his murderous career by saying, *"Sitting there in a cell, I could convince myself that I was not guilty of anything"*. Another delusional murderer, who had killed twelve white female teenagers for no reason, had "justified" his crime by saying that he had killed only children because *"I like kids; I always did"* (Hickey, 2010, pp. 111, 154). This is the height of self-deception. Qur'an says,

> *"And We are not unjust to them, but they themselves were unjust"*. (Q: 43.76)

> *"It was not We that wronged them: They wronged their own souls"*. (Q: 11.101)

> *"Had it not been for an ordinance of Allah which had gone before, an awful doom had come upon you on account of what ye took"*. (Q: 8.68)

The words *"they themselves were unjust"*, *"they wronged their own souls"*, *"on account of what ye took"* need to be noted carefully. Religious persecution in that time was unheard of. The Arabs were polytheistic, and polytheistic societies are tolerant by nature. Though Muhammad insulted their Gods, they did not harm him; it was his paranoia. In persecutory delusions, the delusional distress increases the risk of delusions being acted upon (Wessely et al., 1993, pp. 69-76). Frequently, the association between delusion and aggressiveness persists throughout the course of the illness, so that violent behavior can be justified as the result of beliefs that others are attempting to, or have caused, harm (Junginger, 1996, pp. 91-103; Humphreys et al., 1992, pp. 501-5). In this case, violence appears as a forced choice in them associated with a strong conviction of being threatened and forced to defend himself (Bjorkly, 2002, pp. 617-31). Qur'an has no shortage of verses where Muhammad's paranoia is prominently reflected. Secondly, the schizophrenics tend to comply with hallucinations that are consistent with delusional beliefs (Junginger, 1990, pp. 245-7). In the absence of delusions, hallucinations have minimal violence-triggering effect (Taylor, 1998, pp. 47-54). If Muhammad had slightest doubt about himself, he would not have been violent. But he had a total loss of insight. Since violence in schizophrenics is correlated with lack of insight, it offers the possibility that violent behavior is not a direct result of the natural course of the illness.

Like Ted Bundy, Muhammad was "*not guilty of anything*". Though terror was his legacy he denied that he did harm to others. Another example is the Beat poet William S. Burroughs. In explaining how he had come to shoot his wife, Joan, in the head, Burroughs claimed that an evil force possessed him.

> "*Let's see, Joan was sitting in a chair, I was sitting in another chair across the room about six feet away, there was a table, there was a sofa. The gun was in the suitcase and I took it out, and it was loaded, and I was aiming it. I said to Joan, "I guess it's about time for our William Tell act." She took her highball glass and balanced it on top of her head. Why I did it, I don't know, something took over. **It was an utterly and completely insane thing to do**.... I fired one shot, aiming at the glass.*" (cited Morgan, 1988, p. 194).

Morgan (1988, p. 198) describes the evil force that Burroughs believed was responsible for Joan's death,

> "*The inimical force that had caused him to kill Joan, **Burroughs believed quite literally, was an evil spirit that had possessed him.** This was a concept more medieval than modern, although whether the evil spirit is seen as coming from within or without, the result is the same. **A divided personality with a capacity for wickedness can look for a psychological explanation, or can believe that he is possessed by malignant forces.** Both explanations are metaphors for the nature of evil, which religion and the 'ologies' do not satisfactorily define*".

Morgan makes an important point in the above statement that is necessary to understand Muhammad. Like Burroughs, the Prophet of Allah believed "quite literally" that he had divine authority to torture and murder those who did not believe his evil god. Bukhari (4.52.259) recorded.

> "*Narrated Abu Huraira: Allah's Apostle sent us (i.e. an army-unit) in a mission and said: I have ordered you to burn so-and-so and so-and-so, and **it is none but Allah who punishes with fire**, so, if you find them, kill them*".

In the history of mass murderers, one most infamous person was Joseph Kallinger. He claimed that a large, floating head with tentacles, which he refers to as "Charlie," instructed him to kill millions of people and cut up their genitals. Under severe delusion he killed his own son and many others in his community (Hickey, 2010, p. 63). Kallinger now resides in a psychiatric institution. The fact that he still has strong urges to kill again by carrying out those orders will likely require his permanent hospitalization.

The deluded killers often have great fascination for the corpses. They may even dig the graves. Denis Nilsen and Ed Gein both fulfilled some of their fantasies by grave robbing. After the first murder at the age eighteen, Dahmer visited graveyards in hopes of retrieving a corpse rather than killing another person. Muhammad loved corpses. He was a grave digger.

"Jabir reported, Allah's Apostle came to the grave of 'Abdullah b. Ubayy, brought him out from that, placed him on his knee and put his saliva in his mouth and shrouded him in his own shirt and Allah knows best." (Muslim: 38.6678)

Another offender robbed graves to have sex with the corpses and, as he noted, to have someone for "company". One murderer liked to share his bed with various corpses, some of which had been decapitated. Dennis Nilsen, a British serial killer and necrophile, had described how involved the murderer became with his victims after death. They were a source of company for him. In one instance, Nilsen stored the body of a boy under his floor and frequently would retrieve him for an evening's entertainment. This included propping the boy in a chair next to Nilsen, who carried on conversations with the corpse, bathing him, watching television "together," and performing sexual acts on the decomposing child (Hickey, 2010, pp. 114, 128, 184). Nilsen and others did not believe that the corpses are dead. Muhammad believed that the deceased is not actually "dead"; he can see and hear and can speak to the visiting angels.

"Anas b. Malik reported Allah's Apostle having said: When the servant is placed in his grave and his companions retrace their steps arid he hears the noise of the footsteps, then two angels come to him and make him sit and say to him: What you have to say about this person (Muhammad)? He would say: I bear testimony to the fact that he is a servant of Allah and His Messenger. Then it would be said to him: Look to your seat in the Hell−Fire, for Allah has substituted with a seat in Paradise. Allah's Messenger said: He would be shown both the seats. Qatada said: It was mentioned to us that his grave (the grave of a believer) expands to seventy cubits and is full with verdure until the Day when they would be resurrected." (Muslim: 40.6862)

"Narrated Al−Bara' bin `Azib : The Prophet said, "When a faithful believer is made to sit in his grave, then (the angels) come to him and he testifies that none has the right to be worshipped but Allah and Muhammad is Allah's Apostle. And that corresponds to Allah's statement: Allah will keep firm those who believe with the word that stands firm. (Q: 14.27)." (Bukhari: 2.23.450)

These two angels are Munkar and Nakir. As per Sunaan Tirmidhi (44), they have black faces and blue eyes. They will question a Muslim in his grave. When satisfied with the answers regarding Muhammad and Islam, these angels will increase the volume of the Muslim's grave, place light inside, and instruct the dead to have a peaceful sleep. But for a hypocrite his gravesides will be squeezed so much so that his bones are crushed. The dead Muslims will be raised in the same very state in which he had died. Allah will torment the Jews in their graves.

> *"Narrated Abi Aiyub: Once the Prophet went out after sunset and heard a dreadful voice, and said, 'The Jews are being punished in their graves'."* (Bukhari: 2.23.457)

Malik's Muwatta (16.6.18) says that even a non-Muslim child is liable to be tormented in his grave. Muhammad believed that the punishment of an unbeliever is that, in his grave ninety-nine serpents will be biting him and each serpent will have seven heads. This will continue up to the Day of Resurrection (Ghazali: 4.4150). These are satanic beliefs.

In Matamoros (Mexico), a mass grave was unearthed in April 11, 1989 that contained fifteen corpses, many of which appeared to have been ritualistically sacrificed. Cauldrons with animal remains mixed in a broth of human blood and boiled body parts were found not far from a bloodstained altar. Suspects arrested said the victims were "killed for protection." This group of drug smugglers was practicing a form of black magic in which sacrifices to the devil, both human and animal, were believed to provide protection from bullets and criminal prosecution (Fox & Levin, 1989, pp. 49-51). Muhammad's Allah delusion and a murderer's Satan delusion have no difference psychiatrically.

In the following verse, Allah says that to kill or to create warfare in the sacred month is a very grave offence, but to justify his own violation of Allah's rules, Muhammad came up with the idea that since the people killed were unbelievers, it was perfectly justified.

> *"They ask thee concerning fighting in the prohibited month. Say: "Fighting therein is a grave (offence); but graver is it in the sight of Allah to prevent access to the path of Allah, to deny Him, to prevent access to the Sacred Mosque, and drive out its members". Tumult and oppression are worse than slaughter. Nor will they cease fighting you until they turn you back from your faith if they can. And if any of you turn back from their faith and die in unbelief, their works will bear no fruit in this life and in the hereafter; they will be companions of the fire and will abide therein".* (Q: 2.217).

From this verse it is clear that Muhammad had absolutely no struggle with guilt and no remorse for his crimes. For Ted Bundy there was no guilt; once he declared, *"I don't feel guilty for anything . . . I feel sorry for people who feel guilt"* (Winn & Merrill, 1980, p. 313). Ted Bundy was deeply class conscious. In an interview he confessed; *"I didn't know what made people want to be friends. I didn't know what made people attractive to one another. I didn't know what underlay social interactions"* (Michaud & Aynesworth, 1983, p. 68). Muhammad had no friends in his group because he enjoyed privileged status as Prophet (Q: 33.50); he had only companions and partners in crime. Ted Bundy and Muhammad did not act under some irresponsible uncontrollable urge; rather, they consciously used their own free will, agency, to create the killer within themselves. On January 24, 1989, Ted Bundy died in the electric chair. His last words before a black hood was placed over his head were, *"Give my love to my family and friends."*

After initial hardship when Muhammad felt militarily strong at Medina, Allah gave him permission to fight the unbelievers. Qur'an says,

"To those against whom war is made, permission is given (to fight), because they are wronged;- and verily, Allah is most powerful for their aid." (Q: 22.39)

"Allah will certainly aid those who aid his (cause);- for verily Allah is full of Strength, Exalted in Might, (able to enforce His Will)." (Q: 22.40)

"Fight in the cause of Allah those who fight you, but do not transgress limits; for Allah loveth not transgressors." (Q: 2.190)

"And slay them wherever ye catch them, and turn them out from where they have turned you out ... But if they cease, Allah is Oft-forgiving, Most Merciful." (Q: 2.191-2)

"And fight them on until there is no more Tumult or oppression, and there prevail justice and faith in Allah; but if they cease, Let there be no hostility except to those who practice oppression." (Q: 2.193)

"The prohibited month for the prohibited month,- and so for all things prohibited,- there is the law of equality. If then any one transgresses the prohibition against you, Transgress ye likewise against him." (Q: 2.194)

If it is unscientific to explain the heinous crime of Burroughs or Dahmer as being caused by an evil spirit, then within the same logic it is equally unscientific to explain Muhammad's criminal acts as being caused by an evil god. Allah is certainly not a demonic "other" reality that can "possess" certain people and make them absolutely wicked for the very simple reason that Allah was his delusion. Neither an evil spirit nor a pathological personality can be empirically measured. Both evil forces and psychopathologies are, at some level, equivalent metaphors.

After initial success Muhammad ganged up all the criminals of Medina and set out to raid the caravan with 313 men. The Meccans got word of the raid and sent out an army for protection. Allah forbade Muslims from fleeing from the combat.

"O you who believe! when you meet those who disbelieve marching for war, then turn not your backs to them. And whoever shall turn his back to them on that day -- unless he turn aside for the sake of fighting or withdraws to a company -- then he, indeed, becomes deserving of Allah's wrath, and his abode is hell; and an evil destination shall it be." (Q: 8.15-6)

In the battle, the Muslims killed some seventy Meccans and took seventy prisoners (Bukhari: 4.52.276). All the prisoners were ransomed, and any prisoner who did not fetch a ransom had his head chopped off. In Islamic history this is known as battle of Badr. Allah revealed,

"O Prophet! Rouse the Believers to the fight. If there are twenty amongst you, patient and persevering, they will vanquish two hundred: if a hundred, they will vanquish a thousand of the Unbelievers: for these are a people without understanding." (Q: 8.65)

"For the present Allah has made light your burden, and He knows that there is weakness in you; so if there are a hundred patient ones of you they shall overcome two hundred, and if there are a thousand they shall overcome two thousand by Allah's permission, and Allah is with the patient." (Q: 8.66)

"It is not for any prophet to have captives until he hath made slaughter in the land. Ye desire the lure of this world and Allah desireth (for you) the Hereafter, and Allah is Mighty, Wise. Had it not been for an ordinance of Allah which had gone before, an awful doom had come upon you on account of what ye took." (Q: 8.67-8)

In these verses Allah not only encouraged violence but in fact made it a sacred duty for the Muslims to kill anyone who did not believe in Muhammad's creed. Also, whatever loot they had plundered was "lawful and good" as it was done in service to Allah. So murder, rape, plunder and destruction are all perfectly fine with Allah as long as they are done in the name of Islam. Yet another verse was revealed, where Allah demanded one-fifth booty for him and his dearest Prophet.

"And know that whatever thing you gain, a fifth of it is for Allah and for the Messenger and for the near of kin and the orphans and the needy and the wayfarer, if you believe in Allah and in that which We revealed to Our servant, on the day of distinction, the day on which the two parties met; and Allah has power over all things." (Q: 8.41)

Muhammad had difficulty in differentiating what was happening outside himself from what was happening within. His imaginary lord was speaking out his inner thoughts loudly. Like Ted Bundy Muhammad simply did not understand the pain of others. Even if he was able to recognize emotions in others, he was also able to disconnect that recognition from his own emotions. Hence he did not share the pain he inflicted on others. Our morality depends on our empathy, as Kluger (2007) commented, *"The deepest foundation on which morality is built is the phenomenon of empathy, the understanding that what hurts me would feel the same way to you"* – Muhammad was completely deprived of this. Since he did not have that foundation, he could not have a common morality.

After the battle of Badr, people of Medina were horrified that they had given shelter to such a bunch of criminals in their city. Many Jews feared that they might be Muhammad's next victims. On Muhammad's order two of his critics, Asma bt. Marwan and Abu Afak were brutally assassinated. Now Muhammad understood that to gain control of Medina he must get rid of all his rivals. The most prominent among these Jews were the Banu Quaynuqa, Banu Nadir and Banu Qurayza.

With some false excuses, Muhammad blockaded the fort of the Banu Qaynuqa for fifteen days until the starving Jews surrendered. Muhammad ordered that the Jews be driven out of their own homes. All their property was seized and looted, and many of their women were forced to sex-slavery. Muhammad took one-fifth of the enormous booty for himself. This was the way Muhammad repaid the kindness of the Jews of Medina, who had given him shelter and a refuge, when he had run away from Mecca in fear. Allah justified Muhammad's acts of planned terrorism against Banu Qaynuqa by revealing the following verses.

> "*For the worst of beasts in the sight of Allah are those who reject Him: They will not believe. They are those with whom thou didst make a covenant, but they break their covenant every time, and they have not the fear (of Allah). If ye gain the mastery over them in war, disperse, with them, those who follow them, that they may remember*". (Q: 8.55-7)

> "*And if you fear treachery on the part of a people, then throw back to them on terms of equality; surely Allah does not love the treacherous.*" (Q: 8.58)

Muhammad's most dreadful act of cruelty came in April 627, when he killed the entire adult male members (some 800 to 900 of them) of Qurayza tribe. Their adulthood was determined by the growth of pubic hair. The women and children were captured as slaves, their homes and properties were confiscated and distributed amongst Muslims. This beheading "ceremony" with heavy swords started in the morning and continued whole day long and then by torchlight into the following night (Khan, 2009, p. 48). Muhammad kept one-fifth of the captured property and the rest was distributed amongst other Muslims. Amongst the female captives, the young and pretty ones became his sex-slaves. Muhammad himself took a beautiful woman, Rayhana, as his own concubine and took her to bed on the same night he had killed her male relatives. No historical record has enlightened us as to her state of mind of being raped by the man responsible for the decapitation of her husband and other males of her family a few hours earlier. As usual, Muhammad did not "own" his actions. Allah revealed a verse to clear Muhammad from taking any blame for this wholesale slaughter of the humans,

> "*He brought those of the People of the Scripture who supported them down from their strongholds, and cast panic into their hearts. Some ye slew, and ye made captive some. And He caused you to inherit their land and their houses and their wealth, and land ye have not trodden. Allah is ever able to do all things*". (Q: 33.26, 27).

Now what should we say about this verse?

> "*... and those who have left their homes in Allah's cause: let them forgive and overlook, do you not wish that Allah should forgive you?*" (Q: 24.22)

If true nobility lay in forgiveness, why Muhammad failed to do that in his treatment of the Banu Qurayza? Complete denial to any injustice to the victims is a common ply used by many psychotic killers. Muhammad made Allah responsible for all the sufferings caused to the Jews. Hickey (2010, p. 93) observed,

"John Wayne Gacy, killer of 33 young males in Chicago, denied any involvement in the murders and suggested that someone else must have placed those 27 bodies in the crawlspace of his home while he was at work. Other serial killers have admitted murdering women, especially prostitutes, but insist there have been no real victims because they were, in the offenders' eyes, scum of the earth. Thomas N. Cream argued that he had aided society and ended the suffering of scores of prostitutes. In 1995, an offender who murdered five homosexuals in Los Angeles stated to me that his victims "deserved what they got" and that "they were asking for it because they kept trying to pick me up." Another offender, Robert Carr, explained that those who died by his hands "grew" a great deal during their brief stay with the killer. Others killed because they believed it was God's will or because of allegiance to their partners or to assist the survival of society."

Muhammad first neutralized his moral beliefs before drifting into violent behavior. For him the road to power is strewn with human sacrifices; power can be all-consuming and justifies every means and method to obtain it. His advantage was that he had a satanic god always ready at his service. Let us analyze the most hateful verse of the Qur'an – "The Verse of the Sword".

"When the sacred months are over, slay the idolaters wherever you find them. Take them and confine them, then lie in ambush everywhere for them. If they repent and establish the prayer and pay the obligatory charity, let them go their way. Allah is Forgiving and the Most Merciful". (Q: 9.5).

This verse is one of the most frequently quoted Qur'anic verses. This is both offensive and defensive and meant for worldwide application. Muslim terrorists cite this verse to justify their violent jihad. This verse appears to be self-contradictory – Allah is instructing the Muslims to slay the infidels, but at the same time Allah claims that he is "forgiving and the most merciful". But no; this verse should be judged from a psychotic's point of view, not according to our moral standard and intellect. Muhammad knew that his instructions were immoral and would cause great pain to others, but his way of viewing the world convinced him that though his actions were against society and humanity, he could "get away" with this, because whatever he is doing today is for a long term benefit to the civilization. In the future, people will accept him as a true Prophet, and his Allah as the most merciful and forgiving God. Muhammad's strength was his unshakable belief on Allah. He was capable to "*destroy a township*" and "*annihilate it with complete annihilation*" (Q: 17.16) without blinking an eye, and still could think himself sinless.

In history there is no shortage of delusional mass murderers. Some of the early European serial killers who were thought to have been vampires or other "creatures of the night", in reality, were nothing more than depraved murderers. As example; Gilles de Rais, who fought alongside Joan of Arc, convinced that he needed to make a pact with the devil himself in order to regain his fortunes. He murdered a young boy by slitting his throat, severing his wrist, cutting out his heart, and ripping out his eyes from their sockets. He then saved the boy's blood to write out his pact with the devil. Having discovered his enjoyment for torturing and killing children, he began

219

to recruit them in large numbers for his own murdering pleasure. Although proper documentation is not available, it is believed that he had killed several hundred children, drinking their blood and engaging in necrophilia.

Yet another such delusional mass murderer was Countess Elizabeth Bathory (fifteenth century Hungary). She was heavily involved in sorcery, witchcraft, and devil worship. Though she married and bore children, she maintained a predilection for young girls. With her husband off to the wars, she began to indulge herself in the torture and slaying of young girls and women. Stimulated by sado-eroticism, the countess bathed in the blood of her victims in order to maintain her fair complexion. She was believed to have been responsible for the deaths of more than a hundred victims. Muhammad's acts were no less disgusting or cruel than Gilles de Rais and Countess Elizabeth Bathory.

With the elimination of the Qurayza, Medina was cleansed of the Jews. Now Muhammad's attention turned to the Jewish community in Khaybar, another powerful Jewish stronghold in Arabian Peninsula. In May 628, he set upon an expedition against them with himself at the command of a strong army some 1,600 fighting men. Kinana, the young grandson of Abu Rafi, was the leader of the Jews. He was tortured for the information of the whereabouts of his treasure and then put to death. All the fighting-aged men were put to sword and their women and children were taken as captives (Bukhari: 2.14.68). Tabari and Ishaq recorded,

> *"May Allah's anger be intense against those who have bloodied the face of His Prophet"*. (Tabari: VII.120)

> *"So Muhammad began seizing their herds and their property bit by bit. He conquered home by home"*. (Tabari: VIII.116; Ishaq: 511)

Amongst the captured women there was Safiyyah, Kinana's seventeen years old beautiful wife and two cousins of hers. Muhammad took possession of Safiyyah and took her to a tent for sexual pleasure on the same day he had killed her husband and many other male relatives. Two years before Safiyyah's father was killed along with many male relatives of her when Muhammad – the mercy of God among mankind – butchered another important Jews' tribe, the Qurayza.

How could Muhammad show this type of monstrous brutality against Safiyyah? In a single day Safiyyah was the wife of a Jewish tribal chief, a widow, a captive and wife of Muhammad. No one should think that Muhammad fell in love with Safiyyah's beauty and therefore decided to marry her right away. He wanted to show his superiority over the Jews. Hickey (2010, p. 118) observed,

> *"In certain serial killings for the offender, the sexual attack is an integral part of the murder, both psychologically and physiologically. For other offenders the sexual attack may represent the best way to degrade, subjugate, and ultimately destroy their victim, but has little connection to the actual motive(s) for the killing."*

What greater crime exists than to deny another person his or her free agency, the right of self-determination? Dietz et al. (1990, p. 165) commented,

"The wish to inflict pain on others is not the essence of sadism. One essential impulse: to have complete mastery over another person, to make him/ her a helpless object of our will, to become the absolute ruler over her, to become her God, to do with her as one pleases. To humiliate her, to enslave her, are means to this end, and the most important radical aim is to make her suffer since there is no greater power over another person than that of inflicting pain on her to force her to undergo suffering without her being able to defend herself. The pleasure in the complete domination over another person is the very essence of the sadistic drive."

The questions of morality, i.e., concepts such as good and evil, right and wrong, virtue and vice, justice, etc., did not bother Muhammad. He was a complete evil creature. He felt that society's general morality does not apply to him and instead he preferred to form his own set of rules. He knew that looting and killing of innocents are evil deeds, but he did it. He knew that the orphans should not be oppressed, but how many orphans did he sell to the slave market after he devastated the Jewish tribes? He knew that one should speak kindly to a fellow human, but where those moral standards were when he declared,

"Hear me. By Him who holds Muhammad's life in his hand, I will bring you slaughter." (Ishaq: 130; Tabari: VI.101).

In his entire career, did he ever promote any ethical values; e.g., trust, honesty, good behavior, fairness, and kindness? He was typically a sociopathic personality. Muhammad's only message to the world was "I will bring you slaughter", and he had performed well as he had promised – efficiently and ruthlessly. These types of killers are generally *"cold, calculating and egotistically sadistic"* (DeRiver, 1949, p. 120). Moral evil results when people treat others as things or objects, or when there is a failure of concern for their welfare. Those people create the opportunities needed to live out their hero fantasies. Some of these offenders feel so inadequate that they are willing to jeopardize lives of others in order to be recognized. If we truly empathize with people, treating each person as a "Thou", rather than an "It", and if we simultaneously show them moral regard and concern, then personal moral evil is simply not possible. If either of these conditions is not met, then various kinds of moral evil can occur. Dr. Morrison, a practicing psychotherapist who has interviewed a number of serial murderers, concludes that the incidence of sadomasochistic sex is very common amongst them (cited McCarthy, 1984, p. 1). And to borrow words from Levin and Fox (1985, p. 230),

"He [the psychotic killer] lacks internal control, guilt or conscience to guide his own behavior but has an excessive need to control and dominate others. He definitely knows right from wrong, definitely realizes he has committed a sinful act, but simply doesn't care about his human prey."

Muhammad masterfully exploited the concept of prophethood with Qur'an as the only proof of his absolute authority. Theoretically, through Qur'anic revelations, Allah wants to guide the humans to save them from hell, and in return for the favor, he demands absolute submission that the humans should only worship him and live by his laws without ever questioning their purpose, validity and relevance. But there is a "catch" in this argument. Only a belief in Allah is not sufficient, they have to believe Muhammad as the only messenger of Allah. According to Qur'an,

> "Say: Obey Allah, and obey the Messenger." (Q: 24.54)

> "And obey Allah and the Messenger, that you may be shown mercy". (Q: 3.132).

> "If you love Allah, and follow me (Muhammad), God will love you, and forgive you your sins". (Q: 3.31)

> "And We did not send any messenger but that he should be obeyed by Allah's permission". (Q: 4.65)

Since Allah cannot be seen or contacted by anyone other than Muhammad, the words of Muhammad begin to rank as the words of Allah, and as time passes Allah recedes into the background. Muhammad, who (apparently) claimed to be Allah's most humble servant, now rises as the dominant force in the strange God-Prophet relationship. At this time, Muhammad holds the keys of paradise. Hence, a person must believe in Muhammad to qualify for paradise and the person who believes in Allah alone, cannot rank as a believer. He is an infidel and must go to hell, no matter how righteous he may be. This is the true nature and purpose of Muhammad's claim of prophethood. He wanted to elevate himself, as Sina (2008, p. 16) commented,

> "After 23 years of preaching, the core message of Muhammad remained the same. Islam's main message is that Muhammad is a messenger and that people must obey him. Beyond that, there is no other message. Failure to recognize him as such entails punishment, both in this world and the next. Monotheism, which is now the main argument of Islam, was not originally part of the message of Muhammad".

Through a legal lens, where evil and crime are synonymous, Muhammad was evil because he was a criminal. Of course, most criminologists do not explain crime in terms of evil. In fact less than one percent of all criminal cases use the insanity defense, and most of those are unsuccessful. Most people who commit crimes are sane, whereas those who truly are insane commit fewer crimes (Hickey, 2010, pp. 59, 62). Thus, "Criminal insanity" is more of a contradiction in terms, an oxymoron of sorts. Muhammad's capacity for violence was accelerated by his Allah-fantasy. He finally arrived at a point where he was so disconnected from society that violence became a viable option.

Typically, social scientists either ignore the concept of evil or reject it as a legitimate explanation for behavior. Muhammad's actions were condemned by society, but it was his culpable mental state – his "evil mind" that truly designated him as evil. The killing of a human being under some circumstances (e.g., in wartime or during a lawful execution) is non-criminal, but the killing of another human being with malice aforethought is murder. Female serial killer Jane Toppan, from the witness stand at her trial for murder, stated; *"This is my ambition - to have killed more people - more helpless people - than any man or woman has ever killed"* (Hickey, 2010, p. 273). For Muhammad and his companions, killing others was a very small matter.

"Killing disbelievers is a small matter to us". (Tabari: IX.69).

*"Allah said, 'A Prophet must slaughter before collecting captives. A slaughtered enemy is driven from the land. Muhammad, you craved the desires of this world, its goods and the ransom captives would bring. But **Allah desires killing them to manifest the religion** '"*. (Ishaq: 327)

*"Allah and Muhammad humiliated every coward and made our religion victorious. We were glorified and destroyed them all. By what our Apostle recites from the Book and by our swift horses, I liked the punishment the infidels received. **Killing them was sweeter than drink**"*. (Ishaq: 576)

The quest for power and control over the lives of others is exemplified by the case of Josef Mengele. He was a physician and geneticist recruited into the Nazi ranks to direct the processing of concentration camp prisoners at Birkenow and Auschwitz during World War II. Posner and Ware (1986), in their book *Mengele*, examine the depths to which one person is willing and able to descend, once given unbridled control over the lives of others. Under the guise of science he masqueraded as a medical researcher, but his rationalizations could not hide the truth – he loved torturing and killing innocents. Mengele's job was to identify which prisoners would or would not be immediately sent to the gas chambers. Though for other doctors this was a very stressful task that evoked severe anxiety, Mengele felt nothing. He had a strong faith in Nazi philosophy that it was possible through selection, refinement, and genetic engineering to create the ultimate "pure" race.

At the camps Mengele had an endless supply of human material on which to experiment. Those who were not deemed fit for experimentation, were usually gassed shortly after their arrival, except those prisoners who were forced to labor. Regarding Mengele's cruel experiments, Hickey (2010, p. 47) wrote in details,

"Mengele set himself apart from the other physicians and soon became known as the most feared man in Auschwitz. His "experiments" turned out to be ruthless, diabolical acts of torture that nearly always ended in death. Unlike many who simply followed orders, Mengele undertook his work with a passion. Witnesses reported having seen tables and walls in his laboratory lined with pairs of eyes from his experiments on dozens of victims. His obsession was to conduct comparative research on children, especially twins. He was constantly in search of identical twins. He often performed surgery on the children without anesthetics. In one case he took two children, one of them a hunchback, and surgically sewed them back to back.

223

Mengele never tired of his work and killed hundreds of children simply to dissect them. In one instance he had a hunchback father and his 15-year-old son, who had a deformed foot, executed, then had all the flesh boiled off their frames. After bleaching their skeletons, Mengele displayed the victims' bones for his colleagues to see. He also ordered several adult female prisoners to be shot and their breasts and muscles from their thighs extracted to be used as "cultivating material" for future experiments. According to the West German indictment, Mengele was reported to have jumped on pregnant women's stomachs until the fetuses were expelled and even dissected a 1-year-old child while it was still alive.

His indifference to suffering was immense. He was charged with having 300 children, most under the age of 5 years, burned alive. Witnesses recount the night when several dump trucks arrived and parked near a large pit fire that had been started earlier by soldiers. One by one the trucks backed up and emptied their load of screaming children into the roaring fire. Some of the burning children managed to crawl up to the top of the inferno. Under the direct supervision of Mengele, soldiers with sticks pushed the little girls and boys back into the pit.

Mengele went to great lengths to care for children who developed various diseases. Once they were cured, he sent them to be gassed. His goal was not to relieve misery but to succeed at his task. One survivor reported how sometimes he would calm frightened children whom he had ordered killed by making their last walk into a game he called 'on the way to the chimney'."

Mengele's strong faith in Nazi philosophy of creating a "pure" German race and Muhammad's belief in Arab supremacy had something in common. Both of them were self-deceptive and displayed an unrelenting will to promote their own wants and needs over everyone else's. They thought they would achieve their goal by mass killing. Peck (1983, pp. 66-75, 78) refers to these people as the "*people of the lie*" – people of self-deception and the deception of others. Peck concluded,

"The lie is designed not so much to deceive others as to deceive themselves. They cannot or will not tolerate the pain of self-reproach. The decorum with which they lead their lives is maintained as a mirror in which they can see themselves reflected righteously. ... They are men and women of obviously strong will, determined to have their own way. There is remarkable power in the manner in which they attempt to control others."

Islam is a slap in the face of morality. Muhammad's deliberate crimes were first-degree murder – the most culpable (most evil) variety of murder. Because his crimes involve the willful and intentional killing of others, he exhibits the most serious kind of evil recognized by the law. He was a terrible villain because he deliberately chooses to defy law and morality. His crimes are born of knowing choice, not ignorance. Therefore, his belief that a spiritual force such as Allah was responsible for crime is not acceptable. As Robinson (1963, p. 98) puts it,

"Complete submission to an authority, far from being commendable, is a grave irresponsibility. We are responsible for all our opinions, however ignorant we may be in the field, because we are responsible for our choice of any authorities on whom we rely. All submission to an authority should be based on, and revocable by, our own judgement whether he is an authority; and this judgement should be revised from time to time in the light of the best considerations then available".

In order to claim the sphere of authority for faith, nobody can deny it to reason. Even a layman judges between doctors and quacks, competent and incompetent lawyers, journalists and storytellers – there is nothing called absolute authority or authoritative trust without rational justification. Blind, unthinking commitment is complete fanaticism, and the fanatics of this world have left millions of dead in their wake.

Muhammad perceived himself as almost godlike beings. But whenever he faced the hard reality all of a sudden, he had a psychological fall, and it was very debilitating, very disorienting, confusing, and harrowing. It was a very scary feeling. This time he switched into a retaliatory mode – I am going to fight this, I am going to stand up for my self-importance. The way to deal with that was simply to prove it. His means of being someone important was violence. Violence to him had been reinforced as a means of taking control by victimizing, brutalizing of another human being. It was his proof, a seal of approval – self-approval. With violence in the name of Allah Muhammad was restored.

Criminologists disagree about what causes crime. Introductory textbooks identify a number of competing theories, but most of the criminologists and social scientists, agree on at least one fundamental axiom: crime is caused by knowable influences. The etiology of crime can be known (Hergenhahn, 1997). In sum; crime does not simply occur – something causes it – and it is not caused by immeasurable and unobservable forces like "evil" or Allah.

Heinous crimes such as those committed by Hannibal Lecter or Muhammad often defy explanation because it is still a mystery of how human physiology, and more specifically the brain, can be linked to aggression and violence. But an empirical study of evil may eventually allow criminologists to understand the causes of their violent actions. Hannibal Lecter is attractive because he is both man and monster, devil and avenging angel, villain and victim. The public's fascination with Hannibal Lecter says as much about the public as it does about Lecter. Similarly, Muhammad was a man of contradiction. Muslims are so obsessed with Muhammad that they have lost their ability to recognize real face of the evil, even when it stands directly before them.

4.3: Conclusion

"Our own wills become the demons, and it is this which attacks us."
Abba Poemen

Evil is a part of the human equation. It is as familiar to us as our own face. It exists because we exist. The notion of evil gods or demons are overpowering people to act against their wish can be traced back to early civilizations. Socrates described his philosophical inspiration as the work of a personal, benign demon. Plato, Socrates' most celebrated student assigned a high role to the demons. Aristotle, Plato's most famous student, believed that dreams are scripted by demons (Sagan, 1997, pp. 115-6). In the past, explanations for mass and serial murders were often derived from demonology or the belief that life events were controlled by external forces or spirits. In many past cultures mental illness was generally viewed as a distinct form of possession, the controlling of a human by an evil spirit. Often the mentally ill or possessed people were revered as the oracle of a deity or a soothsayer.

Critics often ask one question; was Muhammad a knowing fraud or he genuinely believed that the revelations were coming from a God? No matter whatever is the truth, it simply does not make much sense. Even if he was sincere, it does not relieve him from the criminal charges that are put on him. If a racially prejudiced white man "sincerely" believes that blacks should not get equal rights in the civilized society, his "sincerity" does not affect our moral condemnation of his belief. Similarly, Muhammad cannot get away in any case. If he was not a knowing fraud, then we can say that he was capable of self-deception. He used to bring messages freely from his god to justify political murders, assassinations, raid, booty, pedophilia, abundant sex even to solve his domestic problems which are clear evidences that he was an absolute fake; his sincerity means nothing. In fact, his sincerity defense plays a similar role to the "insanity plea" made in courtrooms.

What is important is truth, not sincerity. Qur'an is Muhammad's own terrorist manual; it ultimately tells us more of his complex personality and convictions than any other record we have of his remarkable life and assumed prophetic mission. Muhammad was perfectly capable of distinguishing right from wrong and anticipating the results of his actions and their influence on the society. Though he caused great misery to others, he hardly felt responsible for them. Therefore, he should be held liable for his own deeds and exploits – the cause of Allah and the punishment of Allah are lame excuses.

In the end, the man is responsible for his own actions and inactions.

Chapter 5: Allah: The virus of the mind

[Note: "Virus" here is a metaphor for Allah. The comparison is that viruses are nasty things that make us sick, and multiply and infiltrate places where they are not wanted. Allah is the mental equivalent of a virus that poisons the mind. It is certainly not a physical thing; it is just an idea. Here I chose to use the "virus" concept because viruses are well known to most people, and the biology of viruses creates a useful parallel for our discussion.]

There are hundreds of examples in popular science fictions of invading aliens taking over mind and bodies of the humans to further their own end, as example, the famous novel by Robert Heinlein *The Puppet Masters* and the movie by the same title (1994) directed by Stuart Orme, and also another movie *Invasion of the Body Snatchers* (1956) based on a novel *The Body Snatchers* by Jack Finney (Kay, 2008, p. 330). These two heart-pounding horror films often leave the audience wondering – Where did science fiction get the idea? Fiction cannot be stranger than truth. In the biology of pathogens, parasites and viruses there are many examples of such infections. Certain parasites can literally take over parts of the brain and control the host by reprogramming the organism in the best interest of parasite and to the determent of the host (Alford & Hill, 2000, p. 82). In biology we find,

1. Parasitic viruses can make their hosts suicidal to further own reproduction. Grasshoppers infected with hairworm (Spinochordodes tellinii) are more likely to jump into water where the hairworm reproduces. This death drive has an excellent parallel with the Jihadi suicide terrorism – *al-jihad fi sabil Allah*, means striving in the cause of Allah. Once in the water the mature hairworms, which are three to four times longer that their hosts when extended, emerge and swim away to find a mate, leaving their host dead or dying in the water. When the suicide bomber sacrifices his life, it is Allah-virus that gains.

2. The rabies virus is a neurotropic virus that causes fatal disease in human and animals. It infects very specific neurons in the brain of the mammal host to create aggressive behavior. This induces the host to attack and bite animals it might otherwise avoid or ignore. The virus takes over the brain for its own purposes without regard for the well-being of the host, who usually dies. What an extraordinary parallel – remember the motivating jihadi statement of Ayatollah Khomeini "*The purest joy in Islam is to kill and be killed for Allah*" (Hagee, 2007, p. 68). Allah-virus can program us to think and behave in ways that are destructive to our lives. As a result of it, a well-educated man like Osama bin Laden could leave his home, family, business, and wealth in Saudi Arabia and travel to Afghanistan to fight the infidels, the enemies of his Prophet. Flinging his affluence away, he chose a life of deprivation solely to increase the pleasure of Allah.

3. The lancet fluke (Dicrocoelium) infects the brain of ants by taking control and driving them to climb to the top of a blade of grass where they can be eaten by cattle. The ingested fluke then lays eggs in the cattle gut. Eventually, the eggs exit the cattle, and hungry snails eat the dung (and fluke eggs). The fluke enters the snail's digestive gland and gets excreted in sticky slime full of a seething mass of flukes to be drunk by ants as a source of moisture (Ray, 2009, p. 22). Is not this how the religion of Allah self-propagates? The Mullahs, terrorists, preachers, so-called peaceful Muslims – every Muslim plays an important role in propagating Islam once they are infected by Allah-virus.

4. The parasitic protozoa Toxiplasma gondii causes infected rodents to lose their inborn aversion to cat smells. Toxiplasma reproduces in cats that have eaten infected mice and rats. Infected cats in turn spread Toxiplasma through their droppings. The infected rodents can still distinguish between all other kinds of smells but selectively lose their fear of cat pheromones, making them much easier for the cat to catch. When the Allah virus infects the mind, Muslims become lifelong zombies that they cannot apply minimum logic and reason to discover the true nature of Islam. Even if he spends his entire life studying Qur'an, ahadith (plural of hadith) and Muhammad's biography, he will never detect a single error in the Qur'an though he will easily find similar type of errors in other scriptures. He will never notice that Muhammad was a criminal, a liar, a pedophile, a shameless womanizer, a mass-murderer and a ruthless tyrant, though minor character flaws of some Catholic Priests and their sex-scandals will never go unnoticed. They can still distinguish between all other kinds of absurdities in other religions but selectively lose their capacities to define what is logical or illogical when Islam is concerned.

There is no shortage of examples; we see that parasites, viruses and many other pathogens literally take over parts of the brain by causing a chemical imbalance, and "control" the host. Similarly, the Allah-virus reprograms the human mind in the best interest of his parasite selfishness, to the detriment of the host. By this argument, Islam is a parasite-induced fatal attraction. While the parasite virus takes over the perceptions of the ant, Allah takes over the perceptions of those it infects.

5.1: Introduction

"Men are disturbed not by things, but by the views they take of things."
                                                                    Epictetus

Often we wonder what makes Allah so powerful. What makes Muslims profess deep faith in Allah and his messenger though Allah was too immoral to be divine and the Prophet was an extremely cruel man? We also want to know what makes Muslims blind to the irrationalities of their own faith yet see clearly the problems of other religions. Ever since the birth of Islam, the Allah delusion had penetrated the

Muslim mind – largely unexplained and unchallenged. This demonic god simply existed like a deadly virus to corrupt the Muslim mind and deteriorate the society. Those who attempted to question or expose Allah were often persecuted mercilessly – their books were burned, they were imprisoned, tortured even executed.

Various philosophers – starting from Spinoza to Voltaire, Feuerbach to Marx – blazed a path toward understanding religious faith and its role in the society, but it was not until Dawkins' idea of "viruses of the mind" that we gained a ready-made way to examine religion as closely as we look at the epidemiology of the flu virus. The idea is, when minds are friendly environments to parasitic, self-replicating ideas or information a typical massive infection takes place. As Brodie commented,

> *"You catch thoughts—you get infected with them, both directly from other people and indirectly from viruses of the mind. People don't seem to like the idea that they aren't in control of their thoughts. The reluctance of people to even consider this notion is probably the main reason the scientific work done so far is not better known. As we'll see, ideas people don't like have a hard time catching on."* (Brodie, 2009, p. xiv)

Once created, the mind virus gains a life independent of its creator and evolves quickly to infect as many people as possible. Like computer viruses, successful mind viruses will tend to be hard for their victims to detect. When a person is victim of one, the chances are that he won't know it, and may even vigorously deny it. When Allah virus infects the mind the person typically finds himself impelled by some deep, inner conviction that something is true, or right, or virtuous in Islamic faith – this is such a conviction that does not seem to owe anything to evidence or reason, but which, nevertheless, he feels as totally compelling and convincing. He may feel that the less evidence there is, the more virtuous the belief. This paradoxical idea that lack of evidence is a positive virtue when Allah is concerned is self-sustaining because it is self-referential. And once the proposition is believed, it automatically undermines opposition to itself. A related symptom of Allah-infection is the conviction that "mystery" is not only a good thing but also divine. It is not virtuous for a Muslim to solve the mysteries of Allah; rather he should enjoy them, even protect the mystery from being investigated in a scholarly manner.

Any desire to solve the mysteries of Allah could be a serious challenge to the spread of Allah-virus – *"It is by all means to be believed, because it is absurd"*. Mysteries are not meant to be solved, they are meant to strike awe. In fact, the very mysteriousness of Allah moves a believing Muslim to perpetuate the mystery.

This chapter will show how Allah does fit in the natural world, how he functions and propagates in the Muslim minds and culture and how similar he is to the germs, parasites and viruses that inhabit our bodies.

5.2: How Allah-virus infects the Muslims?

The parasitic virus programs the host to replicate the virus. Once infected, the virus makes copies of itself. Similarly, the Allah-virus uses the Muslim mind as its laboratory for making copies of itself, frequently leaving a mess behind. It is more than a parasite, more than an infiltrator, more than an unchecked self-copier. For the biological virus, the copying equipment it commands is in the cells of the organism being attacked. Cells use that equipment in the normal course of their affairs to manufacture proteins, duplicate nucleic acids, and prepare to divide into two. The virus infiltrates the cell and fools the copying equipment into copying the virus in addition to, or instead of its usual workload (Brodie, 2009, p. 39). The Allah-virus activates some special programs for replication in the Muslims. This is either done by childhood indoctrination or by alienating from an individual's own power.

5.2.1: Childhood indoctrination

"Those who will not reason, are bigots, those who cannot, are fools, and those who dare not, are slaves."

George Gordon Byron

Childhood indoctrination is the prime infection strategy of Allah-virus. In Islam certain behaviors are programmed to ensure that the Allah-virus is passed onto others specially their children. Islamization of the Muslim mind starts from the birth and continues throughout his life. It is the most extensive brainwashing process a human can ever be subjected to. After birth, an adult holds the newborn and recites the azan (the call for prayers) directly into its ears. This way, the newborn hears the blessed names of Allah and Muhammad before he hears anything else. As the child grows up, he reads and hears more about Qur'an and Sunna. He sees people performing prayers and walls are decorated with posters of Arabic calligraphy of some Qur'anic verses. He also hears the azan repeated five times a day through loudspeaker (though loud azans are prohibited – Q: 17.110) in every mosque in the area. The call for prayers soon becomes the most frequently heard sound by him. His ears soon get used to hearing the endless recitations of the Qur'an that go on almost continuously. Brodie (2009, p. 188) explains,

"The more we repeat an action, idea, or belief, the more comfortable we get with it and the less we question it: we become conditioned or programmed by it. Successful religions have evolved to embody what any advertising executive would tell you: repetition sells."

If the kid goes to Madrassah (Islamic school) indoctrination continues. Both Hurgronje and Guillaume point to the mindless way children are forced to learn either parts of or the entire Qur'an (some 6,200 odd verses) by heart at the expense of teaching them critical thought. Guillaume (1956, p. 74) observed,

"[The children] accomplish this prodigious feat at the expense of their reasoning faculty, for often their minds are so stretched by the effort of memory that they are little good for serious thought".

Hurgronje (cited Zwemer, 2012, p. 25) concluded,

"This book now serves but to be chanted by teachers and laymen according to definite rules. The rules are not difficult but not a thought is ever given to the meaning of the words; the Quran is chanted simply because its recital is believed to be a meritorious work. The inspired code of the universal conquerors of thirteen centuries ago has grown to be no more than a mere text-book of sacred music, in the practice of which a valuable portion of the youth of well-educated Muslims is wasted."

The fear of Allah, paradise and hellfire etc are systematically programmed in him. This is coupled with illogical thoughts and twisted logic to make the child to believe that Muhammad is the best man Allah ever created, or will ever create to the end of time. Allah (like the Big Brother) is watching every Muslim, and he should behave strictly according to Allah's will. Intelligence and critical thinking seem to disappear at the Mosque door.

Even if the Madrassah teaches other subjects, it does so "in its own way" – the school presents all subjects only from an Islamic point of view, and requiring all teachers, supervisors, and assistants to agree with the religion's doctrinal position. The fear factor starts working and soon the innocent mind of the child gets the message that there is something very special about the Qur'an which he is destined to read hundreds of times without ever understanding it, and, except Allah no other God to be worshipped.

Slowly a sacred cosmos is established and the reality is replaced with sacred mystery and power of Allah. The child tries to 'locate' every human phenomenon within a cosmic frame of reference. Once fully indoctrinated, he fails in his 'reality test' – the ability to distinguish the actual from the imagined. Neither he can confront the truth nor can he admit it even to himself. His sick mind fervently believes in Allah's mercy, power, hell, paradise etc. Slowly; Islam becomes his drug and the Allah delusion becomes his addiction. Without Allah, it is a world of black and white. With Allah it is a colorful show complete with drama, thrills, fun and full of excitement. Now he is in the mental prison of Allah and the key is with Muhammad. He simply cannot dare to cross the narrow limits specified by Allah. Now he can see things only through the spectacles of Islam. For him to live outside the religiously legitimated world is to *"make a deal with the devil."* (Berger, 1990, p. 39). This continues for throughout his life. Children are easiest to hook because they experience insecurity and anxiety as they pass through puberty. Also they have fewer intellectual tools with which to resist Allah infection.

5.2.2: Alienation from an individual's own powers

"The chains men bear they forged themselves. Strike off their chains and they will weep for their lost security."

John Passmore

"We fear things in proportion to our ignorance of them".

Titus Livius

231

Islam is a dictatorial religion. Ideologies that place divine law above civil law are inherently authoritarian. In this religion, man is controlled by a higher power. Allah is entitled to obedience, reverence, worship and praises. But the reason for worship, praise, reverence and obedience lies not in the moral qualities of the deity, not in love or justice, but in the fact that the deity has control, i.e., has power over man. Allah, the higher power, has the right to force man to worship him and that lack of reverence and obedience constitutes sin. So, Allah is the sole possessor of what was originally belonged to man. The more perfect Allah becomes, the more imperfect becomes the man. Qur'an says,

"Praise be to Allah, the Cherisher and Sustainer of the worlds." (Q: 1.2)

"He is Allah, than Whom there is no other Allah, the Sovereign Lord, the Holy One, Peace, the Keeper of Faith, the Guardian, the Majestic, the Compeller, the Superb. Glorified be Allah from all that they ascribe as partner (unto Him)." (Q: 59.23)

"… Allah is the Absolute, Owner of praise" (Q: 2.267)

"In order that ye may believe in Allah and His Messenger, that ye may assist and honour Him, and celebrate His praise morning and evening". (Q: 48.9).

A Muslim projects the best he has unto Allah and thus impoverishes himself. Now, Allah has all love, all wisdom and all justice. Man is deprived of these qualities; he is now empty, poor and completely powerless. The more he transfers his own powers to Allah, the poorer he himself becomes, and the more dependent on Allah. Ultimately the man is alienated from himself. His only access to himself is through Allah. Having lost his own he is completely at Allah's mercy.

For a better understanding let us look at the Marx's theory of alienation. Marx was a true Humanist, and nothing was more attractive to him than human beings themselves. Alienation, for Marx, is the estrangement of humans from the aspects of their human nature. The man does not experience himself as the acting agent in his grasp of the world, but that the world and he himself remain alien to him. They stand above and against him as objects, even though they may be objects of his own creation. Alienation is essentially experiencing the world and oneself passively, receptively, as the subject separated from the object. When man bows down to an imaginary power he often transforms himself into a "lifeless object". He transfers to this imaginary power the attributes of his own life, and instead of experiencing himself as the creating person, he is in touch with himself only by the worship or slavery of that power.

This mechanism is the very same which can be observed in interpersonal relationships of a masochistic, submissive character where one person is awed by another and attributes his own powers and aspirations to the other person. When he has thus projected his own valuable power to God, his relationship to his own power is ruined – he has become alienated from himself. The alienation from his own powers makes the Muslim slavishly dependent on Allah. Slowly he becomes a man without self-confidence. That is why everything is *Insha'Allah* (if Allah wills it –

fatalism) for a Muslim. His religious experience is always authoritarian, never blissful. What an extraordinary parallel to those famous words of Dostoyevsky! (cited Felty, 1997, p. 258), *"In the end they will lay their freedom at our feet and say to us, 'make us your slaves, but feed us'"*. In his famous discussion of the alienation of labor in 1844, Marx (cited Elster, 1986, p. 40) compared material alienation with spiritual alienation and wrote;

> *"Just as in religion the spontaneous activity of the human imagination, of the human brain and the human heart, operates independently of the individual— that is, operates on him as an alien, divine or diabolical activity -- in the same way ..."*

This is a trap – for a Muslim self-realization is possible only in an external manner. He has become estranged from his own life forces, from the wealth of his own potentialities, and is in touch with himself only in the indirect way of submission to life frozen in the Allah. Science cannot save him, logic cannot save him, knowledge cannot save him, medicine cannot save him – only his Allah can save him. Deprived of everything, such a person's only hope is Muhammad. Only through Muhammad, a Muslim can "beg" Allah to return some of his humanity and for this he is ready to reserve his full life for Islam. This is one main reason why there is no humanity in Allah's religion.

> *"Surely Allah has bought of the believers their persons and their property ..."* (Q: 9.111)

The delusion of helplessness in turn acts on him. He always feels himself to be a sinner (living without humanity is obviously sinful). The more he praises Allah, the emptier he becomes. The emptier he becomes, the more sinful he feels. The more sinful he feels, the more he praises Allah – and less he is able to regain himself. The less he is able to regain himself, the more he comes within the evil grip of Muhammad. This is the same mechanism that makes people endow the leaders of even the most inhuman systems with qualities of super wisdom and kindness. Whether the people worship a punishing, awesome god or a similarly conceived leader makes little difference.

In sum; what a Muslim does not understand is that his own spiritual forces were robbed from him by his Prophet, and subsequently, the same forces were erected into autonomous power to act against him, to enslave him. The power that enslaves the Muslims and makes them helpless actually belongs to them, not to Muhammad or Allah. The strength of Allah is an externalized expression of the potential spiritual power of the individual Muslims. In worshipping Allah and Muhammad, a Muslim does not affirm himself but actually denies himself.

5.3: How Allah-virus survives and dominates?

A parasitic virus creates antibodies or strong defenses against other viruses (Sompayrac, 2002, p. 14). When Allah-virus infects a person (a "host" in biological terms), it immediately begins creating "antibodies" against other rivaling religions. Simultaneously, it effectively blocks curiosity and questioning in one area that might be a threat to its survival. It also disables the ability to think critically about one's own religion. Now the infected person can see and hear what Allah-virus wants. Throughout his life he will view non-Muslims only through the lens of Allah-virus. Any verbal denial of any principle of Muslim belief is considered apostasy, and apostasy is punishable by death. Allah instructed,

> *"If anyone desires a religion other than Islam (submission to Allah), never will it be accepted of him; and in the Hereafter He will be in the ranks of those who have lost (All spiritual good)."* (Q: 3.85)

> *"The Religion before Allah is Islam (submission to His Will)."* (Q: 3.19).

> *"Whosoever disbelieves in Allah after believing except he who is forced while his heart remains in his belief but he who opens his chest for disbelief, shall receive the Anger of Allah and for such awaits a mighty punishment."* (Q: 16.106).

> *"... take them (apostates) and kill them wherever you find them. Do not take them for guides or helpers."* (Q: 4.89).

> *"Say: 'Flight will not avail you (apostates), if you flee from death or slaughter, you would enjoy (this world) only for a little (time)'."* (Q: 33.15, 16)

The Allah-virus ensures that Muslims get absolute immunity from other religions. In the society people of different race, color and religion are expected to live together. Since the Allah-virus cannot control the Muslims from coming in contact in day-to-day life, it takes preventive measures to keep the Muslims blind and unreceptive to other human beings. Allah has isolated the Muslims from the rest of the human society by dividing the Humankind into two perpetually hostile groups Dar al-Islam (the house of Islam), and Dar al-harb (the house of war), i.e., Muslims and Kafirs, and has implanted the concept of jihad in the minds of the Muslims. Deprived of contact with others and starved for human interactions, the Muslims bond with their predator. The more helpless a Muslim is, the more he is a dependant on the Allah-virus. Ultimately he offers himself as a sacrificial animal to Allah.

The parasitic viruses take over certain mental and physical functions and hide itself within the individual in such a way that it is not detectable by the individual. When a normal healthy human being is infected by Allah-virus, his attitude towards others and worldview significantly changes. He, willingly and submissively, self-denigrates to become a partner of Arab imperialism.

This tendency has a devastating affect on the national character of the non-Arab Muslims. When a non-Arab person accepts Islam, he is forced to love Arabia and its traditions at the expense of the culture, honor and pride of his own motherland. Mecca is now more favorite than his birthplace, Arabic more than his mother-tongue and the Arab heroes more than the heroes of his nation. Since Allah hates the infidels, a non-Arab Muslim must hate his own people of his own nation who are following the faith of their ancestors. Some biological viruses take over the machinery of the cell for its own purposes and kill it (The world book encyclopedia, 2005, p. 335). In Egypt, the glorious land of ancient Pharaohs; the people do not call themselves Egyptians any more. All of them had become Arabs. As Naipaul wrote,

"Islam is not simply a matter of conscience or private belief. It makes imperial demands. A convert's worldview alters. His holy places are in Arab lands. His sacred language is Arabic. His idea of history alters. He rejects his own: he becomes, whether he likes it or not, a part of the Arab story. The convert has to turn away from everything that is his. The disturbance for societies is immense, and even after a thousand years can remain unsolved. The turning away has to be done again and again. People develop fantasies about who and what they are." (Naipaul, 1998, p. 1)

In sum; the Allah-virus grooms the Muslim minds in such a way that they become lifelong slaves of the Arabs. They will 'sincerely' deceive themselves into believing that non-Muslims either know that Islam is truth and reject it out of pure unreasonableness or else are simply ignorant of it. Ray (2009, p. 25) commented,

"Once infected, the individual cannot detect major contradiction in his beliefs and behavior. Belief systems become self-evident to him and no amount of logical discourse will move him from his belief."

When the parasitic Allah-virus takes over some functions of the Muslim minds it modifies them like aliens snatch the bodies of the victims by controlling their minds. This is the time the Muslims fail the reality test. From the very deep bottom of their heart, they know that hatred towards a fellow human being is wrong but still they have to 'sincerely' hate the nonbelievers because Allah wants them to hate. As Shaikh (1998, p. 161) lamented, *"The only relationship between a Muslim and a non-Muslim is that of ill-will, hatred and animosity"*. Today an Islamic nation does not require any particular reason to attack a non-Muslim nation. According to Allah, all religions except Islam are false.

Today, Jews and Christians are the most advanced people in the world in every field and Muslims are at the bottom, but they have to 'sincerely' believe that monkeys and pigs are descendent of Jews and Christians because Allah wants them to believe. The Pakistani, Afghan, Bangladeshi and Indian Muslims immensely hate their Hindu counterpart. They understand well that their Hindu forefathers were forced to accept Islam under sword and through deception. Every Asian Muslim is a blood relative in the direct line of descent of Hindu parents. Scratch the surface of a Muslim and you will obviously find an Infidel Hindu, but they have to 'immensely' hate the Hindus, because it pleases Allah. This type of self-contradiction is not there in any other religion.

5.4: How Allah-virus spreads?

The parasitic viruses use specific methods for spreading the virus. In biology, the organism that spreads disease is called a vector. Mosquito is a vector for malaria. Common vectors of the Allah-virus are Imams, Mullahs, Moulavi, Ulemas and preachers (e.g. Zakir Naik). The clerics program the common Muslims, even reengineer them so that they become effective careers of Allah virus.

In viral terms, it means that Muslims are so deeply infected that they are immune to influence and generally ignore any evidence that contradicts their beliefs. It gives rise to Islamic fundamentalism. When Muslims see themselves as the only true believers or at least more righteous and accurate in behavior and beliefs they seek to impose their Islamic belief through means of force, coercion, ostracism or political power, even at the expense of lost or ruined individual lives. The Arabs and other Islamic Nations spend in billions to keep this parasitic Allah-virus survives through jihadi terrorism. To ensure its own survival, Allah instructed,

"Go forth, light-armed and heavy-armed, and strive with your wealth and your lives in the way of Allah! That is best for you if ye but knew." (Q: 9.41)

"Those who believe, and have left their homes and striven with their wealth and their lives in Allah's way are of much greater worth in Allah's sight. These are they who are triumphant." (Q: 9.20)

"O ye who believe! Shall I show you a commerce that will save you from a painful doom? Ye should believe in Allah and His messenger, and should strive for the cause of Allah with your wealth and your lives. That is better for you, if ye did but know." (Q: 61.10, 11).

"The (true) believers are only those who . . . strive with their wealth and their lives for the cause of Allah." (Q: 49.15)

"… Pay the zakat. Those saved from covetousness prosper. If you loan to Allah a beautiful loan, He will double it. He will grant Forgiveness: for Allah is most ready to appreciate" (Q: 64.16).

Some vectors can actually be more efficient when dead. Just as the rabies virus takes over the brain of the raccoon and reprograms it to bite other animals – even at the cost of its own life – the Allah-virus directs few programmed Muslims to go on suicide mission to propagate the cause of Allah. No doubt, a suicide is the ultimate act which ends the person, but when a bomber kills himself in the name of Allah, Allah's religion gets a powerful tool for propagation. Umm Nidal, a Muslim mother whose only claim to fame was that she proudly sent three of her sons to die for Allah in terrorist attacks against Israeli targets, is reported to have said (Spencer, 2005, p. 102), *"Because I love my son, I encouraged him to die a martyr's death for the sake of Allah ... jihad is a religious obligation incumbent upon us, and we must carry it out."* And elsewhere, *"I prayed from the depths of my heart that Allah would cause the success of his operation... I encouraged all my sons to die a martyr's death, and I wish this even for myself".* When the operation was over, the media broadcast the news and Umm Nidal was informed of her son's death, she began to cry. Tears of joy rolled down from her eyes on her son's death.

Also the Muslim family itself is a vehicle for the propagation of the virus. Allah has no problem disbanding a family if it does not meet his need. Islam supports divorce if one falls away from the Allah-virus or wants to live a virus-free life (apostasy). Often the children of the apostate are taken away from him to be brought up by Muslims and the apostate forfeits his rights of inheritance. Sometimes, the family will take matters into its own hands and simply kill the apostate. It means a typical Muslim family consists of virally infected parents only. In recent years in the news media there is no shortage of cases of Muslim girls being killed by their parents and relatives for merely wanting to marry a non-Muslim. This is how Allah-virus seeks to create an environment that makes it easy to propagate. As the family expands, so goes the virus. Allah-virus makes sure that the infection is passed on to the next generation. It creates an environment which can ensure that the young will be infected as efficiently as possible.

5.5: Sex and Allah-virus

Allah loves large families with full of children. Large family means more spreading of the Allah-virus. Here the control of reproduction is the fundamental strategy, and when the strategy is undermined, the Allah-virus is weakened. It is only concerned with propagation.

"*Narrated by Said bin Jubair: Ibn 'Abbas asked me, 'Are you married?' I replied, 'No'. He said, 'Marry, for the best person of this (Muslim) nation (i.e., Prophet Muhammad) of all other Muslims, had the largest number of wives'.*" (Bukhari: 7.62.7)

"*And We gave him back his people (family), and doubled their number, as a grace from Ourselves.*" (Q: 38.43)

Allah-virus is highly threatened by low birth-rates. Ghazali (2.28) confirms that prayer, a big family and poverty will ensure paradise. Children are viewed as a source of mercy and a gift given by Allah. Muslims have a responsibility to inhabit and develop the earth, and in order to do this people are ordained to multiply. Thus, according to Allah, one of the principal purposes of marriage is procreation.

"*He brought you forth from the earth and delegated you to inhabit and develop it.*" (Q: 11.61)

"*O mankind! Be careful of your duty to your Allah who created you from a single soul, and from it created its mate, and from them twain, has spread a multitude of men and women.*" (Q: 4.1)

Because of this, the concept of family planning has raised some concerns in its acceptability within certain Muslim populations. While some Muslim states and organizations have adopted a rather cautious approach to the issue, others have gone to the extent of inviting religious leaders to present religious verdicts, i.e., fatwas on the subjects. Moreover, as the Muslim mass is generally poor and uneducated (in Islam higher education is not encouraged) the level of awareness remains low, and there are many misconceptions related to family planning.

Additionally, within Muslim communities, there is a common concern that the family planning is deemed to be a Western ideology or "conspiracy", which aims to limit the size of the Muslim population. An Indonesian religious group, namely *Young Muslims, Save Indonesia with Sharia and the Caliphate*, denounced family planning methods and the government family planning programme as being part of a "genocide conspiracy" to weaken the country's population (Wisnu, 2009). Among Muslims in Kashmir there is a belief that large families are good, as it is in line with Islamic teachings. The men, though aware of family planning methods, felt it would be un-Islamic to reduce the size of the family. One individual had ten children, whom he felt were gifts from Allah (Hamri, 2010). In the rural areas of Pakistan, the 'religious factor' is extremely important in the decision by men not to make use of contraceptive method (Ali & Ushijima, 2005, pp. 115-22). The majority of married men believe that Muslim leaders are against fertility control, twenty-nine percent cited religion as a reason for their non-use of modern contraceptives, which illustrates the ability of Muslim leaders to influence the attitudes of the community towards family planning. As a result, the population of Pakistan is growing at a rate of three percent which is among the highest in the world (Aziz, 1991).

Sadly, such views are not restricted to men in Islam. A high percentage of Yemeni women believe that Islam is against family planning. A survey in 1997 found that two-thirds of Yemeni women who were not using contraception did not intend to use it in the future, with seventeen percent of those interviewed stating that religion did not permit family planning at all (Roudi-Fahimi, 2004). This is the height of religious influence on family planning among Muslims.

5.6: Intelligence, personality and Allah-virus
"Most people would rather die than think; in fact, they do so."
                                                            Bertrand Russell

"To really be free, you need to be free in the mind."
                                                            Alexander Loutsis

Islam is a painful mental disease. By a million roots, all of them with strict religious significance, the Allah-virus penetrates every phase of a Muslim's life and makes him a zombie. When the Allah-virus infects a person, most of the mental functions, as example; logic, reason, study, learning and critical thinking, creative imagination etc are disabled. Therefore, in spite of having fully functioning brain, Muslims cannot prosper. Though they live in the twenty-first century, they are still hardwired for the caveman days. The Allah-virus originated from Mecca and it keeps the infected persons focused on Mecca through rituals and actions that reinforce their faith on a daily basis.

The religious vectors (Imam, Mullah etc) are experts in playing the authority figure. Their pronouncements (fatwa – religious verdicts) are made with strong conviction and accompanied with all the trappings of religio-political power.

Regardless of a Muslim's personality characteristics, the fear and need for security are the key areas the Allah-virus uses to infect. That is why fear of hellfire, Satan and evil are all used to a great extent by the clerics. The Qur'an has 695 references to death and 537 to dead (Ray, 2009, p. 187). Death is the most powerful tool of Allah-virus. If the cleric can evoke a sufficient fear response in the potential host there are better chances of infection. The fear response and need for security pushes the Muslims to seek relief and protection that the cleric offers. This is clear manipulation, but when the logic and reason are suspended, Muslims cannot see the game-plan. They feel a sense of relief when the clerics tell them that only Allah can save them. For the cleric, Allah is a very useful word. Whenever he faces a difficult situation, he offers his "Allah" as his readymade explanation.

Once a person comes within the evil grip of Islam, the Allah-virus sets about making his mind a friendly place for Islam. It systematically shuns off the areas of potential threat and enhances ideas and behaviors that support the faith of Islam. The rituals, prayers, monotonous recitation of the Qur'anic verses – all create behavioral feedback loop that makes the person "feel good" about his infection and creates a safe passage for the Allah-virus.

Muslims tend to imagine that they see more clearly than the non-believers. They see the hand of Allah at work and feel the power of their god within them. That is why they have to invoke Allah in every few sentences. Allah seems to infest even the most ordinary events. This makes Muslims highly defensive people when Allah is concerned. Defensive people do not want to learn or change because they cannot listen. Creating defensiveness does not help the cause of rational discussion and positive change. Being self-aware means learning to observe not just ourselves, but the way others react to us. Others often mirror our impact. Muslims cannot see their lifelong viral programming because the Allah-virus has rendered them blind to anything that would threaten it. Hence, trying to convince a Muslim of his Allah-infection will often have the opposite effect. A Muslim goes through a huge emotional struggle before he gathers the confidence to say – I have been fooled by Islam my whole life. Deep childhood programming is not easy to overcome.

Islam evolves not toward truth, not even toward the betterment of its adherents, but toward more effective ways of virus replication. This is the most crucial point in this entire chapter. The belief systems are not guaranteed to be good ways to live life. The Allah-virus is concerned more about his own existence than about Muslims' quality of life.

5.7: The sacred violence

"*One of the most noticeable things about the Prophet Muhammad as described by the Koran is that he spoke of mercy for humankind*".
Mohammad Ahmadullah Siddiqi, (cited Spencer, 2006, p. 183)

"*Don't forget that killing [unbelievers] is also a form of mercy.*"
Khomeini (cited Bjorgo, 2005, p. 58)

Muslim violence is religiously motivated violence, because the mandate is from the highest power – the Islamic god and the perpetrators are in their own minds immune from the normal laws governing us, and can commit acts of atrocity that would normally be reviled. The goal is simply to lash out at the "enemies of Allah" in such a brutal way which is harmful enough to be noticed throughout the world. Al-Qaeda's goal is simply to "strike at the West". USA is called "The Great Satan" (Sproul & Saleeb, 2003, p. 90; Razzaque, 2008, p. 170) and "The Bigger Terrorist" (Cohen, 2007, p. 21). Terrorism has long brought to mind visions of bombs and hostage-taking, but the events of 9/11 showed the world that planes with no bombs or chemicals aboard could still serve as weapons of enormous destruction.

When the members of al-Qaeda, Islamic jihad, al-Aqsa Martyrs' Brigade, and Hamas were asked why they were killing the non-Muslims, they said, "*Islam. We are following Muhammad's orders*" (Winn, 2004, letter to the reader). Habis al Saoub quoted in his Arabic document, entitled *A Martyr's will* (Spencer, 2003, p. 23), "*The Prophet Muhammad's seventh-century assertion that abandoning the cause of jihad is a disgraceful act tantamount to leaving the Islamic religion*". Mahmood Ghazi, Pakistan's Minister for Religious Affairs, openly supported Kashmir jihad stating that it was "*in accordance with the teachings of Prophet Muhammad*" (Spencer, 2003, p. 45). This is how Muhammad is directly responsible for today's Islamic terrorist attacks.

When Muhammad killed his opponents he justified it by Allah's name, "*Allah made me victorious with terror*". After 9/11 attack, Laden claimed that the terrorist attack was in defense of own people and was the will of Allah (Lachkar, 2008, p. 30). He called the Muslims "*to comply with God's order to kill the Americans and plunder their money, whenever and wherever they find them*" (Bjorgo, 2005, p. 59). It was as if Laden was the new messenger of Allah, only relaying the commands of Allah which were justified with verses from the Qur'an. The distorted thinking pattern is mirrored in this quote from Brigadier S.K. Malik's (Pakistani Army) controversial book, *The Qur'anic Concept of War* (2008, p. 57),

"*We see that, on all the occasions when God wishes to impose His will upon His enemies, He chooses to do so by casting terror into their hearts*".

During 1995, The Armed Islamic Group of Algeria (GIA) commented in a press release, "*Everyone should know that the killing, massacring, slaughtering, expulsion, burning, taking of captives that we do, these are sacrifices for the sake of Allah*" (Cook, 2005, p. 171). Where from these destructive thoughts are coming? This is what Muhammad had convinced the Muslims in the Qur'an.

"*Say: Truly, my prayer and my service of sacrifice, my life and my death, are (all) for Allah, the Cherisher of the Worlds*". (Q: 6.162)

GIA collapsed in 1998 and the dissidents formed a new terrorist group – Jama'a al-Salaffiya. Its first communiqué tells the tale, "*[Those who] grasp the tails of cattle, are satisfied with farming, and [if you] have left Jihad, then God will cause humiliation to overtake you that will not leave you until you return to your religion*" (Cook, 2005, p. 120). Who is uttering these words? It is not the terrorists, but the

Allah-virus is talking through them. Muhammad had no experience with farming. His livelihood was totally dependent upon raids and plunder. According to Bukhari (3.39.514), Allah had a great disdain for agriculture and agricultural implements.

A pan-Arab daily newspaper published an article on February 23, 1998, where some advice was given to all Muslims and a Qur'anic verse was cited. The advice was, "*The ruling of killing Americans and their allies whether civilian or military is incumbent upon every Muslim who is able and in whichever country is easiest for him*" (Cook, 2005, p. 175), and the relevant verse was, "*And fight them until persecution is no more, and religion is for Allah...*" (Q: 2.193)

The words "*Allah wishes*" and "*sacrifices for the sake of Allah*" need particular attention. Muhammad had never sacrificed any worldly pleasure for the sake of Allah, his followers did it for him during his lifetime and present day Muslims are still doing it. Malik (2008, pp. 59, 60) wrote, "*Terror struck in the hearts of the enemies is not only a means, it is the end in itself ... Terror is not a means of imposing decision upon the enemy; it is the decision we wish to impose upon him*".

Allah is only an ancient myth. Belief in Allah, or identification with the Islamic religious ideology, does not give the right to impose that belief on others. Where did Malik get such destructive ideas? He was simply repeating Muhammad's words. Did Muhammad not say in his Qur'an (8.12), "*I will instill terror into the hearts of disbelievers*"? Malik continued,

"*It [terror] can be instilled only if the opponent's faith is destroyed. Psychological dislocation is temporary, spiritual dislocation is permanent ... to instill terror into the hearts of the enemy, it is essential, in the ultimate analysis, to dislocate his faith*".

From the above examples it is very clear that the Allah-virus plays a crucial role in a Muslim terrorist's target selection, and the Qur'an functions as the central terrorist manual that urges them to slaughter, rape, torture, pillage, mutilate and molest all the non-Muslims. While some teachings of the Qur'an appear to have benevolent implications, this benevolence disappears when they are considered within the context of their wider ethical framework. Through the Qur'an the Allah-virus supplies them an initial motive for action and provides a prism through which they view events and the actions of the non-Muslims. Very few Muslims are able to separate their belief in Allah from their other beliefs, particularly in the area of ethics. For Muslim terrorists, the confirmed beliefs of Islam provides them the moral and political vision that inspires their violence, shapes the way in which they see the world, and defines how they judge the actions of people and the society.

Muslim ethics is based throughout on falsehood – and this alone is sufficient to guarantee its failure. Muslim ethics is more conducive to misery than to happiness, and it prescribes moral principles that are more accurately described as a code of death rather than a code of life. While ostensibly offering man a reprieve from the suffering in life, Muslim ethics, like Muslim theology, creates many of the problems that it later offers to solve, but fails miserably in its attempt to find a solution.

Terrorism is there in every cell of Islam. Allah and his Islam cannot survive without terrorism because terrorism is the life-giving force of Islam. Those who are against terrorism have no place in Islam; they are infidels. The Muslim terrorists are not "hijacking" Islam; they are actually restoring it. Without terrorism Allah will suffocate and collapse. The peaceful face of Islam is the political Islam and it is the mask of violent Islam. Islam is the only religion born of war and established by war, and terrorism is the blood brother of Islam.

5.8: The excellent defenses of Allah-virus

In biology, we saw that the rabies virus works its way very quickly through the peripheral nervous system. It uses nerve pathways that are hidden from the immune system. When the virus weaves its way to the brain it takes over the central nervous system in service of its own propagation. Allah-virus works in the same manner.

The Allah-virus searches for a pathway to the power centers of the state. Having the powers of state is by far the most efficient method of propagation and defense against other competing religions. In the Islamic states, Muslims have strong control over the political power systems. In non-Muslim states the Allah-virus constantly put pressure on the state to infect the political central nervous system for legislating the Islamic beliefs. Once the Allah-virus invades the political power center of the state it disables the ability to have reasonable and rational discussion of national issues. Remember that famous statement of Khomeini. Early in 1984, Ayatollah Khomeini declared to the entire world,

"In order to achieve the victory of Islam in the world, we need to provoke repeated crises, restore value to the idea of death and martyrdom. ***If Iran has to vanish, that is not important. The important thing is to engulf the world in crises"***. (cited Mitchell, 1991, p. 146)

Islam is constitutionally incapable of separating religion and politics. It is one of the first religions to successfully combine religious and political controls into a single belief system. Muhammad fought battles more for political purposes than spiritual. Allah-virus always had the justification for military methods of infection.

Allah's strong political defenses were written into the Qur'an and subsequent traditions. This separation of religion and politics is nonexistent in Islam. There is no word in classical Arabic for the distinctions between lay and ecclesiastical, sacred and profane, spiritual and temporal (Warraq, 1995, p. 164). The early Islamic scriptures were based on what Muhammad had learned from the Jewish, Christian and Polytheists of Arabia and, to certain extent, from the Zoroastrians of Persia (Ray, 2009, p. 42). Both Judaism and Islam began as political/military movements, but Judaism was not a parasitic religion while Islam had the potential to be more parasitically aggressive when consolidating political power with a society. From the very beginning Islam's writings were well-designed guides to survive as a minority religion in a large and powerful emperor. The Allah-virus more focused on the ability to survive in a hostile religious and political environment, and for this the Allah-virus took guidance from Judaism and from the patriarchs and rulers of ancient Israel, as example, Isaiah, Jeremiah, David and Solomon – all saw the religion as inseparable from the political (Ray, 2009, p. 43). The ancient Judaism gave Muhammad great material on which to build his cult.

Also, Islam developed in a fragmented society where Polytheistic Gods were weak and the Christian faith was slowly coming out of the religious orthodoxy. As the grip of the Orthodox Church was relaxed, there was a wave of theological deviants and the contemporaneous Christians evaluated Muhammad and his sect as yet another such group which had gone astray. It was unthinkable to them that Islam might be "a new religion" in the strict sense of the term.

The Allah-virus sometimes attacks stealthily similar to the HIV that attacks the immune system itself. By disabling key components of the immune system, the HIV can propagate unnoticed and unimpeded. Similarly the Allah-virus can hide or stay for long periods and then break out in an epidemic. This is very similar to the reservoirs of biological viruses. Bats are a reservoir for rabies virus. In West Africa, the Ebola virus stays hidden and occasionally breaks out (Ray, 2009, p. 46). Muslims migrate to the Western Nations for better living standard. When their number grows by birth or immigration, they want to impose the Sharia rule. When they become majority, they start bringing death and destruction to the host nation and start ethnic cleansing in Allah's name. Today Europe is finding itself in a new struggle with the Allah-virus as the Muslim population grows in an alarming rate. British Muslims demand the recognition of Sharia law, veils being worn by government female employees, and a demand for Islamic creationism be taught – Allah-virus has started to corrupt a rather civilized society. Everywhere in the Western Nations, Muslims are demanding recognition of their religious practices and beliefs in the public domain without respect for the secular law. This is the worst kind of hypocrisy as if the Allah-virus is lurking inside every Muslim and waiting for a suitable chance to come out.

5.9: Sometimes Allah-virus fails

"Abstractly and absolutely speaking, where reason is able to understand, faith has no further role to play. In other words, we cannot both know and believe [on faith] the same thing at the same time under the same aspect. ..."
Etienne Gilson

"Sometimes people want to believe but find they can't."
John Ortberg (2008, p. 20)

Happily, biological viruses do not win every time. Sometimes the vectors fail. If a Muslim expands the sphere of reason, he diminishes the boundaries of his faith in Allah. Though Muslims have the notion "apostasy = Allah's wrath = hellfire" drilled into their head since childhood, today we can see that many Muslims, even hardcore Islamic terrorists and radical Imams, have left the cult of Islam. Biological viruses mutate. A mutation is an error in copying. When Allah-virus mutates, Islam divides into different sects – Sunni, Shiaa, Sufi etc. In biology, occasionally the mutations are so powerful that they smash even the strongest defenses of the virus. It happens when mutation produces an improved copy instead of an exact duplicate or a defective copy of the original. This mutation goes out of control. They are the ex-Muslims and freethinkers of Islam who have finally eliminated their infection.

Though apostasy is a punishable act, there was large scale apostasy during Muhammad's lifetime and after his death. Many early Arabs, who took him as a Prophet, could not remain quiet by seeing the irrationalities of his supposed to be revealed doctrine and the contradictions in his behavior. They had no genuine inclination towards Islam, its dogma and ritual. Goldziher (1971, p. 43) pointed out,

"There are countless stories, unmistakably taken from true life, which describe the indifference of the desert Arabs to prayer, their ignorance of the elements of Muslim rites, and even their indifference towards the sacred book of God itself and their ignorance of its most important parts. The Arabs always preferred to hear the songs of the heroes of paganism rather than holy utterances of the Koran".

Therefore, from the very beginning, Islam had no shortage of apostates. It is estimated that at the time of Muhammad's death, the total number of people who really believed in Muhammad's prophethood did not exceed a thousand (Warraq, 2003, p. 41). In spite of that Islam survived.

When the Jihadi Muslims are painting the world with blood almost everyday, the ex-Muslims are my biggest hope. According to me, the ex-Muslims are those people whose Islam disease is cured. They have fully re-activated their brain, which was previously disabled by the deadly Allah-virus. As a result they can draw their own conclusions about Islam without any priestly interpretation. As Ray (2009, p. 32) commented,

"When people were able to read for themselves, inevitably some of them concluded that the whole enterprise was a house of cards. Most kept their mouths shut to avoid losing their heads, but others made the leap to open to openly criticize..."

Today these ex-Muslims should convince their brethren that loss of Islamic faith represents, not a degeneration, but a step forward – faithlessness does not lead to disastrous consequences. When a Muslim discovers the rules of thought and the laws of logic, he can direct his thinking toward enlightenment. Muslims only need critical thinking skills to resist Allah-virus, but there has to be a place to practice those skills. The Muslim child growing up in a small tribal village of Pakistan or Afghanistan has very little opportunity to practice critical thinking skills as he has hardly any exposure to alternative ways of thinking. Also, man's ability to think and question the orthodox Islamic belief system can become his most dangerous liability in these nations, and the intellectually frightened, docile, unquestioning believer is presented as the exemplification of moral perfection.

5.10: Conclusion

"There are no misunderstandings in nature; they are only to be found in the realms that man calls 'understanding'."

Carl Jung

The faith of the Muslims is based on certain presuppositions. Muslims simply assume (as if they "know" from their birth) that Muhammad was a true Prophet and Qur'an is purely God's instructions. These two presuppositions are so strongly embedded in their minds that they completely obliterate the facts and accounts for no aspect of the authenticity of Muhammad's prophethood. For this reason Muslims fail to identify Muhammad's so-called divine experiences as delusion. If a person changes his concept of reality in such a way as to admit that all psychic happenings are real and no other concept is valid, then he will never find any contradiction in his views. Such a person with "voluntary blindness", no matter whatever his conscious development, or education, or social status, is still an archaic man at the deeper levels of his mind. On every opportunity, he will take every painful effort to falsify reality and uphold Muhammad's neurotic disorder as spiritual.

Today there are many powerful threats to Allah-virus. The ex-Muslim and freethinking websites have awakened many Muslims to take a hard look at their cherished faith. The recent developments in communications technology, mainly satellite television and the Internet in even the remotest harems of Islamic Nations, is profoundly altering the mental climate in the Muslim world. Slowly Islam will phase out like communism (Desai, 2007, pp. 15-8). Another threat of Allah-virus is the continual march of science. Yet another threat is the Psychology. Many psychologists can clearly see what Islam does to Muslims; how it destroys healthy relationships and families, forces people into self-defeating beliefs, and generates unjust hate. Religion is a major contributor to mental illness. But for Islam, it by itself is a mental illness. Humanity's worst scourge, the Allah-virus must be completely eliminated from the earth like the smallpox virus which was eradicated in the 1970s from human populations. Otherwise, the Allah-virus if survives will happily take us back to Stone Age.

5.11: As Science gets bigger, Allah gets smaller

"That's one small step for man, one giant leap for mankind."
Neil Armstrong

Throughout the history of Islam, the Allah-virus has opposed science to a great extent. Allah cannot exist without "believers" but science can, because belief plays no role in a scientific analysis. Science is in no way dependent upon Allah. The tremendous expansion of scientific knowledge in the modern era has had a profound influence upon the belief of Allah's religion. Since the beginning of twentieth century, scientific information about the world has steadily expended in fields such as astronomy, geology, chemistry and physics. Contradicting assertions in the same fields derived from the Qur'an rather than from direct observation and experiment, have increasingly been discarded. In each of the great battles between scientists and the Islamic clerics the validity of the scientific method was vindicated by its practical fruitfulness. Warraq (1995, p. 7) wrote,

"Every Muslim will have to face the challenge of the scientific developments of the last hundred and fifty years. Scientific knowledge directly conflicts with

Muslim religious beliefs on a number of issues. But the more fundamental difference is a question of methodology—Islam relies on blind faith and the uncritical acceptance of texts on which the religion is based, whereas science depends on critical thought, observation, deduction, and results that are internally coherent and correspond to reality. We can no longer leave religious thought uncriticized: all the sacred texts must be scrutinized in a scientific manner. Only then will we stop gazing back and only then will religion stop being an obscurantist justification for the intellectual and political status quo."

Today it had become apparent that the author of the Qur'an inevitably clothed his testimony in his own contemporary pre-scientific understanding of the world. Advancing knowledge has made it necessary to distinguish between Muhammad's understanding of divine presence and calling and the primitive worldview that formed the framework of his thinking. Once we make this distinction, we can easily recognize the aspects of the Islamic scriptures in general and Qur'an in particular that reflect the pre-scientific Arab Bedouin culture prevailing at the seventh century. Allah's science is no longer credible in the light of modern knowledge. The flat-earth theory can no longer be regarded as a reasonable belief. In the Qur'an there is no shortage of Allah's statements on Astronomy, but today Astronomy can be studied without any reference to Allah. Qur'an says,

"(Non-believers are) deaf, dumb, and blind, they will not return (to the path of Allah)." (Q: 2.18)

"... deaf, dumb and blind, so they do not understand." (Q: 2.171)

"For the worst of beasts in the sight of Allah are the deaf and the dumb - those who understand not." (Q: 8.22)

Allah may call non-believers "deaf dumb and blind" but the fact is that all the science and technology in the Muslim world is almost exclusively purchased from the non-Muslim world. Allah repeatedly cursed the infidels, but the infidel world is progressing well; it is Muslims who are the lowest people in a multicultural society.

Advances in non-Muslim medicine and technology have vastly saved more lives than have been lost in all the jihads in history. Two-thirds of world's poorest people live in Muslim countries. With all their oil-wealth, there is no Muslim Nation among the top thirty of the world's richest nations. Democracy and rule of law is practically non-existent (Trifkovic, 2002, p. 3). In the recent years there has been increased education and increased literacy in some Muslim Nations. But in Muslim societies, more education means more Islamic education, and more literacy means more reading of the Qur'an and Sunna. Hence, practically nothing changes. The perception of a golden era of Islam, which can be achieved by stricter enforcement of religion, produces an endless reversion to historical failure. Today most of the Muslim Nations are like living hell which is one of the reasons Muslims immigrate to more civilized Western Nations. Some Muslim Nations are so poor that their people will simply die from starvation if USA stops financial aid to them.

Islam's golden age was a clever myth. This is self-deception in the face of distressing truth. It is infidel's education, science, technology and endurance, based on which the human civilization had spread everywhere including Islamic world itself on which the Ummah has no contribution. The sheikhs of Islam could not do anything better than stand silently as spectators to infidel's prosperity. Islamic art and architecture owes an enormous debt to the rich and ancient traditions of the Near East with which the Arabs came into contact after the rapid conquests of seventh century (Warraq, 1995, p. 194). As Trifkovic (2002, p. 196) concluded, "*Whatever flourished, it was not by reason of Islam, it was in spite of Islam.*" The glorious past of Ummah is a wishful thinking of the Muslims. Arabia, at the rise of Islam, possessed nothing worthy of which Muslims can be proud. It is hard to look forward with clear vision when we try to locate something that never existed. When Muslims look at the infidel prosperity, it is their challenge to find a way to stay pumped up inside in order to hold these harsh realities at bay. But facts are independent of one's desires, fears and hopes.

In this scientific age we can safely assume that all the credentials of Allah should be put to question without any fear of Allah's wrath. And if we do so, we will either accuse Allah of lying or to deny that Qur'an is divinely inspired. If Allah is a scientific hypothesis, then Muslim clerics must let him submit to the same judgment as any other scientific hypothesis, or they should admit that Allah's status is no higher than that of fairies and river sprites.

While Muslim commentators have no problem in reconciling the apparent contradictions, a modern, scientifically literate reader will not even bother to look for scientific truths in Allah's book. The author of the Qur'an was an ignorant god. Instead of accepting the mistakes about unscientific Qur'anic cosmology, the Islamists try to cover it by silly explanations which further make them a laughing stock. These explanations to protect the Qur'an from a divine downfall do not bring prestige either to Qur'an, or Muhammad, or Allah. Shourie (2002, p. 468) wrote,

"*Instead of studying the heaven and earth, we are taught how perverse and distorted interpretations can be put on everything. And how what is being done amounts to calumny upon the Holy Book because what is being proposed is nothing but adding clauses to the Word of God. **The duty incumbent upon a Muslim is to make science accept Islam**"*.

Some apologists quote this verse to prove that Islam encourages science.

"*Say (unto them, O Muhammad): Are those who know equal with those who know not? But only men of understanding will pay heed*". (Q: 39.9)

But this is not true because the knowledge advocated in this quote is religious knowledge. There is a clear distinction between Islamic science and Infidel science. The study of the Infidel sciences was always looked upon with suspicion and even animosity. Intellectual inquiry is deemed dangerous to the Islamic faith. In the words of Nicholson (1930, p. 284),

"*There was little room in Islam for independent thought. The populace regarded philosophy and natural science as a species of infidelity. Authors of works on these subjects ran a serious risk unless they disguised their true opinions and brought the results of their investigations into apparent conformity with the text of the Koran".*

As Alexis de Tocqueville (French thinker/historian) commented (cited Spencer, 2005, p. 25),

"I studied the Quran a great deal. I came away from that study with the conviction that by and large there have been few religions in the world as deadly to men as that of Muhammad. So far as I can see, it is the principal cause of the decadence so visible today in the Muslim world."

Inhibiting progress is a recipe for disaster. In Islam, inhibiting progress is endemic. Islam is a human rights and humanitarian disaster for its believers. We see the cost in terms of the economic and social welfare forgone.

In sum; what historians throughout the world are unable to find, even in this twenty-first century, is a name more hateful than Muhammad, a religious book more intolerable and unholy than Qur'an, a god more demonic than Allah and a belief more dangerous than Islam. As Muir (1992, p. 522) commented;

"The sword of Mohammad and the Koran are the most stubborn enemies of civilization, liberty and truth which the world has yet known".

Islam considered the main task and aim of man is to serve Allah. Infidel science does not help acting rightly towards Allah. Warraq (1995, p. 171) concluded,

"As long as we continue to regard the Koran as eternally true, with an answer for all the problems of the modern world, we will have no progress. The principles enshrined in the Koran are inimical to moral progress."

Scientific advance of human civilization and the theological retreat of Allah are interlocked. And science has many advantages over Allah's science. Science represents man's attempt to systematize given aspects of reality into a coherent framework of knowledge. Since science is dedicated to understanding reality, it rests on the premise that reality can be understood. Islam, on the other hand, is dedicated to the proposition that an important segment of reality (in fact, its ultimate form) is forever unknowable. In real science there is a built-in error-correcting machinery. There are no forbidden questions, no matters too sensitive or delicate to probe, and above all, no sacred "truth-claims". Opinions are encouraged to contend – substantively and in depth. The scientists are open to new ideas, and diversity and debates are valued. All ideas must pass through the acid-test of most rigorous and skeptical scrutiny, and if an idea does not work, it is thrown away instantly. Even though science had not specifically disproved the existence of a supernatural power, science has thrown such a flood of light upon Allah and his religion that now Allah can be regarded as a paper tiger – a harmless, spineless scarecrow – a figment of Muhammad's private fantasy. Islam is clearly a losing cause.

Chapter 6: The cost of Allah delusion

"The lie I tell ten times gradually becomes a half-truth to me, and as I continue to tell my half-truth to others, it becomes my cherished delusion."

A. M. Meerloo

"Sometimes, when you don't ask questions, it's not because you are afraid that someone will lie to your face. It's because you're afraid they'll tell you the truth."

Jodi Picoult

In this section, I wish to probe deep into the superstitious beliefs and irrational acts in Islam. The superstitions that encompass practically every aspect of a Muslim's life are mostly based on Arab Bedouins' society of Muhammad's time. But most of what the Muslims believe to be supernatural, divine and pure have neither scientific nor rational basis. These superstitions have detrimental effects on the Muslims; it hampers their ability to think and comprehend. Allah demands blind faith. Qur'an says,

"Say: Obey Allah and the Messenger; but if they turn back, then surely Allah does not love the unbelievers." (Q: 3.32)

Allah needs blind faith because Islam is stagnated in unlimited superstitions, irrationality, mind-boggling, meaningless rituals and customs. Due to totalitarian nature of Islam, a Muslim cannot escape Islamic superstitions – he will have to live with them and die with them. For a Muslim Islam is the 'complete' code of life as per Allah's dicta and as per Muhammad's traditions and acts (Sunna). Curiosity is no longer necessary after Muhammad nor inquiry after the Qur'an. In many Muslim Nations this is enforced with full force of law and defectors are punished severely.

Tabari (6.75) recorded that two angels visited Muhammad somewhere in the valley of Mecca, They opened Muhammad's chest, took out the heart, cleaned it and placed a white cat-face like object in his heart. The angels then sewed up his chest and placed the seal of prophethood between his shoulders.

"It is reported on the authority of Malik b. Sa'sa' that the Messenger of Allah narrated: I was brought a gold basin full of wisdom and faith, and then the (part of the body) right from the upper end of the chest to the lower part of the abdomen was opened and it was washed with the water of Zamzam and then filled with wisdom and faith." (Muslim: 1.315)

"Narrated Abu Dhar: Allah's Apostle said, 'While I was at Mecca the roof of my house was opened and Gabriel descended, opened my chest, and washed it with Zamzam water. Then he brought a golden tray full of wisdom and faith and having poured its contents into my chest, he closed it'." (Bukhari: 1.8.345)

"Narrated Malik bin Sasaa: The Prophet said, 'While I was at the House in a

state midway between sleep and wakefulness, (an angel recognized me) as the man lying between two men. A golden tray full of wisdom and belief was brought to me and my body was cut open from the throat to the lower part of the `Abdomen and then my `Abdomen was washed with Zamzam water and (my heart was) filled with wisdom and belief". " (Bukhari: 4.54.429)

Elsewhere Muhammad mentioned religious guidance of Allah and his angels as wisdom (Bukhari: 2.24.490) and Qur'an as a source of wisdom (Bukhari: 9.89.255). Now we will discuss some Islamic wisdom that the Prophet of Islam had received from Allah and the angels.

The fancy of pious Muslims was largely occupied with devising myths on the subject of the Friday (Margoliouth, 1914, p. 165). Muslim (4.1856-7) recorded, Friday is the best day because Allah created Adam on a Friday, he entered paradise on a Friday and he was booted out from paradise on a Friday, and the last hour will take place on a Friday. But no Muslim has the courage to ask – so many important events have taken place on other days as well, but why Allah preferred the Friday only? Moreover, Adam, if ever existed, certainly he did not have seven day week calculation system.

Allah instructs Muslims not to doubt the Qur'an and to believe in the unseen.

*"This Book, **there is no doubt in it**, is a guide to those who guard (against evil). **Those who believe in the unseen and keep up prayer** and spend out of what we have given them."* (Q: 2.2-3)

The "unseens" are angels and jinns. These are the two most important elements of Allah's wisdom that Muhammad had received.

"The messenger believes in what has been revealed to him from his Lord, and (so do) the believers; they all believe in Allah and His angels and His books and His messengers; We make no difference between any of His messengers; and they say: We hear and obey, our Lord!" (Q: 2.285)

"O you who have been given the Book! Believe that which we have revealed, verifying what you have, before we alter faces then turn them on their backs, or curse them as We cursed the violators of the Sabbath, and the command of Allah shall be executed." (Q: 4.47)

These verses indicate, if a Muslim does not believe in angels and jinns, he at once loses his Islamic faith. Allah has reserved stiff penalty for such disobedience. Qur'an has a chapter exclusively for the jinns (Surah 72) and one named Malaika (Surah 35) exclusively for the angels. But no Muslim ever asked – if it is so important to have belief in jinns and angels then why Allah made them "unseen"? The limiting of reason is a necessary ingredient for the concept of faith; it is what makes the concept of faith possible. Qur'an says,

"Praise be to Allah ... Who made the angels, messengers with wings, -- two, or three or four (pairs): He adds to Creation as He pleases: for Allah has power over all things." (Q: 35.1)

From this verse we understand that Allah has appointed angels as couriers of his dicta and the angels have two, three or four wings. But Bukhari (4.54.455) noted, Muhammad saw Gabriel with 600 wings. Why there is a contradiction, unless we conclude that Muhammad had hallucinated. Islam induces blindness to facts and reason. Another important angel is Azazil – the angel of death. When the time of death approaches to someone, Allah sends Azazil to take his life and he ends the lives of the non-Muslims in a very cruel manner.

> *"Say: 'The Angel of Death, put in charge of you, will (duly) take your souls: then shall ye be brought back to your Lord.'"* (Q: 32.11)

> *"And had you seen when the angels will cause to die those who disbelieve, smiting their faces and their backs, and (saying): Taste the punishment of burning."* (Q: 8.51)

> *"But how (will it be) when the angels take their souls at death, and smite their faces and their backs?"* (Q: 47.27)

The Islamic angels do not come near an unbeliever's dead body, anything perfumed with saffron, and sexually defiled people (Sunan Abu Dawud: 33.4168). Though the angels are unseen, the cocks can see them. It crows when it sees an angel (Sunaan Abu Dawud: 3.41.5083). Angels do not enter a house in which there is a bell (Sunaan Abu Dawud: 3.34.4219), or there is a dog, or there are pictures (Bukhari: 7.72.833). Every Friday the angels stand at the gates of mosques and take attendances in the chronological order (Bukhari: 4.54.433). Every Friday the devils go to the markets with their flags to prevent the people from Friday prayers, and the angels sit at the mosque-doors in the morning and record the attendance time of the Muslims until the Imam comes out from the mosque (Sunaan Abu Dawud: 3.1046). Islam is a well-protected nursery of superstitions. It played that role because science does not support the Allah delusion, but superstition and pseudoscience do. As a result Muslims view science with suspicion.

The verse 7.79 says that many men and jinns are destined for hell because they are worse than cattle. But if some men and jinns are worse than cattle, why Allah created them? The jinns have special magical power. Some people sought power through jinns but the jinns brought adversity to them.

> *"And those persons from among men used to seek refuge with persons from among jinn, so they increased them in wrongdoing. And that they thought as you think, that Allah would not raise anyone."* (Q: 72.6-7)

The jinns are of four types – serpents, scorpion, worms and those roaming the sky like free air (Ghazali: 3.43). Some jinns are righteous (Q: 72.11), and only they will enter paradise. In verse 72.14 Allah says that only the jinns who embrace Islam are on the right track. Some evil jinns attempt to eavesdrop on the conversation of Allah, but Allah punishes them.

"And (the Jinn who had listened to the Qur'an said) we sought to reach heaven, but we found it filled with strong guards and flaming stars. And that we used to sit in some of the sitting-places thereof to steal a hearing, but he who (try to) listen now would find a flame lying in wait for him. And we know not whether harm is boded unto all who are in the earth, or whether their Lord intends guidance for them." (Q: 72.8-10)

"And there are among us some (Jinns) who have surrendered (to Allah) and there are among us some who are unjust. And whoso hath surrendered to Allah, such have taken the right path purposefully." (Q: 72.14)

"And as for those (Jinns) who are unjust, they are firewood for hell." (Q: 72.15)

Muhammad's seventh century wisdom confirms that the meteorites are Allah's projectiles to annihilate the disobedient or non-Muslim jinns. Bukhari (4.55.634) wrote that once Muhammad caught a jinn also. In the mosque jinns used to gather around Muhammad to listen to his prayer.

"And when the slave of Allah stood up in prayer to Him, they (jinns) crowded on him, almost stifling." (Q: 72.19)

Many jinns have awesome power. Some devils, in the form of jinns, worked for Solomon by diving into the water, but Allah protected Solomon (Q: 21.82). Some jinns fought for Solomon (Q: 27.17). Once a mysterious man competed with a jinn of Solomon to bring the mansion of Queen of Sheba. In the end, Solomon gave the job to this mysterious, pious person. This man brought the glittering edifice of Queen of Sheba to Solomon before Solomon blinked his eyes (Q: 27.39-40). These Islamic jinns eat bones, charcoal and animal dung. They often visit private toilets of the Muslims (Sunaan Abu Dawud: 1.6). Once Muhammad met a delegation of jinns in the city of Nasibin (Bukhari: 5.58.200; Sunaan Abu Dawud: 1.1.39; Mishkat: 1.186). Iraq is the place of rebellious jinns and disease with no cure (Malik's Muwatta: 54.11.30). Allah's most obedient jinn is Iblis (Satan). But Allah banished Iblis from paradise because he disobeyed to prostrate before the newly created Adam. The common view is that knowledge comes first and that faith comes afterward. But in Islam faith precedes knowledge and makes knowledge possible. Here science rests upon acts of faith. Warraq (1995, p. 48) commented,

"Given all the gross superstitious elements in Islam, already described, one wonders how eighteenth-century philosophers ever came to regard it as a rational religion. Had they delved a little deeper into Muslim ideas of jinn, demons, and evil spirits, they would have been even more embarrassed at their own naiveté."

Though the belief in angels and demons is said to have been acquired from the Persians, this belief is sanctioned and officially fully recognized by the Qur'an, and the full consequences of their existence has been worked out in Sharia law. Since demons frequently assume human shape, the clerics assess the consequences of such transformations for Sharia law, and serious arguments and counterarguments are urged. To quote from Warraq (1995, p. 168),

"Popular superstition, too, furnishes the jurists with material for such exercises. Since . . . demons frequently assume human shape, the jurists assess the consequences of such transformations for religious law; serious arguments and counterarguments are urged, for example, whether such beings can be numbered among the participants necessary for the Friday service. Another problematic case that the divine law must clarify: how is one to deal with progeny from a marriage between a human being and a demon in human form. . . . What are the consequences in family law of such marriages? Indeed, the problem of (marriages with the jinn) is treated in such circles with the same seriousness as any important point of the religious law."

Allah often equates nonbelievers with animals.

"They (few Jinns and men) are like cattle,- nay more misguided: for they are heedless (of warning)." (Q: 7.179)

"For the worst of beasts in the sight of Allah are the deaf and the dumb - those who understand not." (Q: 8.22)

"The similitude of those who were charged with the (obligations of the) Mosaic Law, but who subsequently failed in those (obligations), is that of a donkey which carries huge tomes (but understands them not)." (Q: 62.5)

"Or do you think that most of them do hear or understand? They are nothing but as cattle; nay, they are straying farther off from the path." (Q: 25.44)

Qur'an (27.19) says that Solomon had the ability to understand the languages of animals, insects and ants. Ants sing glory of Allah, so ants are not to be killed except those that bite (Muslim: 26.5567-8). Some snakes are believers of Islam, so they should not be killed; only killing of non-Muslim snakes is allowed (Muslim: 26.5558). Snakes with two stripes are bad snakes because they cause miscarriage and blindness in a woman; so those need to be killed. (Sunaan ibn Majah: 5.3534-5). Monkeys even follow the Sharia law. For example, in Bukhari (5.58.118), we read that a group of monkeys stoned a she-monkey for committing illegal sexual intercourse. Some animals are, however, breakers of Sharia laws. In ibn Majah (4.3230) we read that lizards are adulterous.

Muhammad believed that some animals could talk like humans.

"Narrated Abu Huraira: The Prophet said, "While a man was riding a cow, it turned towards him and said, 'I have not been created for this purpose (i.e. carrying), I have been created for sloughing." The Prophet added, "I, Abu Bakr and `Umar believe in the story." The Prophet went on, "A wolf caught a sheep, and when the shepherd chased it, the wolf said, 'Who will be its guard on the day of wild beasts, when there will be no shepherd for it except me?' "After

narrating it, the Prophet said, "I, Abu Bakr and `Umar too believe it." Ahban bin Aus said, "I was amongst my sheep. Suddenly a wolf caught a sheep and I shouted at it. The wolf sat on its tail and addressed me, saying, 'Who will look after it (i.e. the sheep) when you will be busy and not able to look after it? Do you forbid me the provision which Allah has provided me?' " Ahban added, "I clapped my hands and said, 'By Allah, I have never seen anything more curious and wonderful than this!' On that the wolf said, 'There is something (more curious) and wonderful than this; that is, Allah's Apostle in those palm trees, inviting people to Allah.'" (Bukhari: 3.39.517)

"Abu Huraira reported Prophet as saying: A person was driving an ox loaded with luggage. The ox looked towards him and said: I have not been created for this but for lands (i. e. for ploughing the land and for drawing out water from the wells for the purpose of irrigating the lands). The people said with surprise and awe: Hallowed be Allah, does the ox speak? Allah's Messenger said: I believe it and so do Abu Bakr and 'Umar." (Muslim: 31.5881).

Allah will use his talking animals to extract zakat (Islamic income tax) from those Muslims who refuse to pay. On the Day of Resurrection the camels and sheep will come to their owner, far bigger and fatter than before, and if he had not paid zakat then they would tread him with their feet, or with their hooves and would butt him with their horns (Bukhari: 2.24.485, 539). According to Muslim (5.2166-7, 2170), Allah will make the owner of the camels to sit on a soft sandy ground and they would trample him with their feet and hooves. The owner of the sheep and goats would be gored by their horns and trampled under their feet.

On the Resurrection Day the human organs will speak like humans. Our own organs may turn to be our enemies. Qur'an says,

"... their hands will speak to us, and their feet bear witness, to all that they did." (Q: 36.65).

"On the Day when their tongues, their hands, and their feet will bear witness against them as to their actions Allah will pay them back (all) their just dues." (Q: 24.24, 25)

"... their hearing, their sight, and their skins will bear witness against them, as to (all) their deeds. They will say to their skins: "Why bear ye witness against us?" They will say: "Allah hath given us speech,- (He) Who gave speech to everything." (Q: 41.20, 21)

Muhammad believed in the effect of an evil eye (Sunaan ibn Majah: 5.3506-7; Bukhari: 7.71.636), and advised that if anyone is caught by an evil eye then he should take a bath (Muslim: 26.5427). Elsewhere, he said that Truffle juice is a medicine for the spell of evil eye (Tirmidhi: 1194). Once he put some hair in a pot of water and claimed that it has miraculous power to cure an evil eye.

"Narrated Israil: `Uthman said, "My people sent me with a bowl of water to Um Salama." Isra'il approximated three fingers ('indicating the small size of the container in which there was some hair of the Prophet). `Uthman added, "If any person suffered from evil eye or some other disease, he would send a vessel (containing water) to Um Salama. I looked into the container (that held the hair of the Prophet) and saw a few red hairs in it,"'" (Bukhari: 7.72.784)

Muhammad thought that incantation can be used against every kind of poison, and snake and scorpion bite, and Sura Fateha (Surah 1) can be recited and spittle should be applied at the bitten part. (Muslim: 26.5442-3, 52). Once he saw black stains on the face of a little girl and thought that that was due to the influence of an evil eye, and advised incantation (Muslim: 26.5450). The lunacy can be cured by reciting the Surah Fateha in the morning and in the evening, and spitting on the lunatic for three days (Sunaan Abu Dawud: 2.23.3413). Elsewhere Muhammad claimed that Surah Fateha is a cure for all diseases. The effect of evil eyes can be removed if the last two Surahs are recited (Sunaan ibn Majah: 5.3511). By reciting Sura an-Nas and Fateha a fatal illness can be cured. (Bukhari: 7.71.631). For some severe pain, the affected part to be washed seven times with right hand and Muhammad's prayer of casting spell should be said (Sunaan Abu Dawud: 3.28.3882). Incantation of Qur'anic verses was like cheap insurance against something bad happening. It might sound just implausible and weird, but that is the way Allah's medical science works. We cannot advance even a single step closer toward real science by following the Qur'an and Hadith.

Rational thought had little to do with Muhammad's superstitious beliefs. Wrong harmful suggestions of various kinds and crude fantastic superstitions were rooted deeply in his mind. He believed that Allah sends eclipse to frighten the believers (Bukhari: 2.18.167). If the Muslim lifts his eyes towards sky during prayer he may lose his eyesight (Muslim: 4.862-3). Allah will change the face of a man to an ass's face if he lifts his head before the Imam (Muslim: 4.859-61). Fear is a strong brain mechanism because it is wired so directly into our brains. Fear pushes the "buttons" very fast. This is how Allah keeps the Muslims in Islam, example; Ghazali (1.67) wrote if anyone searches for this world instead of Islamic religious knowledge, he will be turned into a pig. Anyone who advocates Allah's science simultaneously advocates irrationalism.

Muhammad had many absurd claims about himself. Once he called a tree and it came to him (Ishaq: 179). Whenever Muhammad went about to attend his business (defecation), every stone and every tree he passed by would say, "Praise be upon you". (Tabari: 6.63). Once a Lote tree split in reverence of Muhammad (Ash Shifa: 167). Trees shaded him when he defecated (Ash Shifa: 165). A tree talked to him (Ash Shifa: 168; ibn Sa'd: 195). Food talked with him and pebbles glorified him (Ash Shifa: 169). Allah has ordered heaven, earth and mountains to obey him (Ash Shifa: 165). The black stone in Mecca paid him regular salutation.

"Jabir b. Samura reported Allah's Messenger as saying: I recognize the stone in Mecca which used to pay me salutations before my advent as a Prophet and I recognize that even now." (Muslim: 30.5654)

Muslims believe that Islam has the perfect solution for all the human problems – in this world, as well as in the next world. Thus there is no field of knowledge where Islam does not have a say. Everything is possible when we leave the domain of science and enter the realm of faith. For a Muslim to accept science is ideological suicide. With Allah's excellent guidance, Muhammad had much contributed in medical science.

> "*Narrated Ibn `Abbas: (The Prophet said), 'Healing is in three things: A gulp of honey, cupping, and branding with fire (cauterizing)." But I forbid my followers to use (cauterization) branding with fire.*'" (Bukhari: 7.71.584)

Cupping was a surgical technique in which, using a sharp object such as a needle, an incision was made on certain part of the body, usually on the neck or on scalp. Then an experienced cupper would suck the incision to draw out the blood from the body. The Arabs believed that cupping would heal headache. In ibn Majah (5.3478) Muhammad said that cupping softens the backbone and improves the eyesight. Also, for pain in the legs we should dye them with henna (Sunaan Abu Dawud: 3.3849). This is Allah's divine medical guidance.

Cauterizing is a technique of burning the skin with fire to stop bleeding. This was a prevalent practice among the Bedouin Arabs. When a wound became infected the desert surgeons would heat a piece of metal rod, and burn the affected part. This was a very crude, extremely painful, and often dangerous practice. Elsewhere Muhammad claimed that pouring out blood without medical treatment is all right (Sunaan Abu Dawud: 3.3850). Cupping and cauterizing are very unhygienic, unscientific, and lethal. Some Muslim socities still follow these practices because these are Allah's surgery. In Sunaan Tirmidhi (1197) Muhammad recommended that Thursday is the best day for cupping before eating any food. He also believed that cupping increases intelligence, improves memory, and lowers blood pressure. Faith is, for a Muslim, not subjective whim or believing simply because one feels like it, rather it is a method of acquiring knowledge. Ibn Kathir explains; honey is hot so it is a cure for all cold diseases, because a disease should be treated with its opposite. In ibn Majah (5.3452) and Tirmidhi (1196) Muhammad said honey and Qur'an are the remedies for all disease.

> "*Narrated 'Aisha: Whenever Allah's Apostle went to bed, he used to recite al−Ikhlas, al−Falaq and an−Nas and then blow on his palms and pass them over his face and those parts of his body that his hands could reach. And when he fell ill, he used to order me to do like that for him.*" (Bukhari: 7.71.644)

> "*Narrated 'Aisha: The Prophet, during his fatal ailment used to blow (on his hands and pass them) over his body while reciting the an-Nas and al-Falaq. When his disease got aggravated, I used to recite them for him and blow (on his hands) and let him pass his hands over his body because of its blessing.*" (Bukhari: 7.71.647)

Allah's wisdom in herbal medicines fascinates us. As example; the water of Kama (a kind of fungus) is a cure for eye trouble (Bukhari: 6.60.5), Indian incense heals throat trouble, pleurisy, and inflammation of lungs (Bukhari: 7.71.596), the black cumin and Nigella seed heal all diseases except death (Bukhari: 7.71.591-2; Muslim: 26.5489-90), Talbina gives comfort to the aggrieved heart and lessens grief (Muslim: 26.5491), Sea incense is the best medicine if used along with cupping (Bukhari: 7.71.599), Truffles (underground fungus) heals eye diseases (Bukhari: 7.71.609), Ajwah dates are from paradise; it is a cure for poison. Truffle juice is a medicine for the eye (Sunaan Tirmidhi: 1127, 1194). Probably the funniest hadith is this, where Muhammad prescribed honey for loose motion. But if this does not work, then the abdomen must have told a lie.

> "*Narrated Abu Sa`id: A man came to the prophet and said, 'My brother has got loose motions. The Prophet said, Let him drink honey." The man again (came) and said, 'I made him drink (honey) but that made him worse.' The Prophet said, 'Allah has said the Truth, and the `Abdomen of your brother has told a lie.*" (Bukhari: 7.71.614)

Then there are many Islamic natural techniques to cure or avoid illnesses, as example; four things reduce eye-sight – to look at unclean and impure objects, to see one being hanged, to look at female private parts and to sit keeping the Ka'ba behind (Ghazali: 2.19). Four acts improve sexual power – to eat the meat of sparrows, to eat big Atri fruit, to eat pistachio, and to eat water-fruit (Ghazali: 2.20). Insomnia makes the heart bright, pure, and radiant (Ghazali: 3.67). Diseases compensate sins – fever of one day expiates the sins of a year (Ghazali: 4.239), if a person loves any material object it will cause him blindness and deafness (Sunaan Abu Dawud: 41.5111). The most fascinating Islamic medicine is the healing power of a housefly. One wing of a fly has a disease, and the other has the cure. Hence, if a fly falls in a drink, dip it in the drink, and gulp the water. Allah's wisdom has easy answer for everything.

> "*Narrated Abu Huraira: Allah's Apostle said, "If a fly falls in the vessel of any of you, let him dip all of it (into the vessel) and then throw the fly away, for in one of its wings there is a disease and in the other there is healing (antidote for it) i e. the treatment for that disease'.*" (Bukhari: 7.71.673)

According to Allah, camel urine, horses' dung, human saliva, dust and ash are also medicines. Horses' dung and urine are pure and it is Allah's reward for keeping the horse ready for Jihad (Bukhari: 4.52.105). Camel's milk and urine are medicines (Bukhari: 7.71.589, 590, 623; Sunaan ibn Majah: 5.3503). The burnt ashes of palm leave can stop excessive bleeding (Bukhari: 7.71.618). Mix saliva with dust, and then apply on the affected part for reducing pain (Sunaan Abu Dawud: 3.28.3886). Once Muhammad spat in the eye of a blind man; the blind man regained his sight. During the battle of Khaybar Muhammad spat on the thigh-wound of Salam ibn al-Akwa' and it healed him (Ash Shifa: 178). Muhammad spat in a well of Medina and the water became the sweetest among all (Ash Shifa: 183). Although, to the medical mind Allah's wisdom signifies nothing, for a believing Muslim these are very meaningful. Hence, superstition and pseudoscience keep getting in his way every moment in his life. Slowly Allah's wisdom becomes his obsession.

Superstition and pseudoscience are easier to contrive than real science and it is much easier to present them to the general public because they cater to fantasies. This makes them "feel good". Superstitions speak to powerful emotional needs that real science often leaves unfulfilled. But ignorance has a cost. Yes, the world would be more interesting place, if all the illnesses could be cured by chanting the Surah Fateha. How satisfying it would be if Muslims really had a paradise package that is promised in the Qur'an. How fascinating it would be if everything were *Insha'allah*. But in reality these do not work because this "feel good" factor is based on delusion, more precisely the Allah delusion. Though the Allah delusion presses their awe buttons and makes them very comfortable in the air-tight cocoon of Allah's world, it also makes them victim of credulity – the emperor must not be told that he does not have cloths. Unable to distinguish between what feels good and what is true, they slide, almost without noticing, into the darkness of endless superstitions.

Muhammad, his numerous wives and companions lived in terrible unhygienic conditions. They had little regard for a healthy, clean and disease-free environment. Muhammad had developed lice on his head (Bukhari: 4.52.47; 9.87.130). Some jihadist's lice fell from their heads on their faces. Most of them had stinky body odor because they used to take infrequent bath.

"Narrated Kab bin Ujra: The Prophet came to me at the time of Al-Hudaibiya Pledge while lice were falling on my face. He said, 'Are the lice of your head troubling you?' I said, 'Yes'. He said, 'Shave your head and fast for three days, or feed six poor persons, or slaughter a sheep as sacrifice'." (Bukhari: 5.59.503)

"Narrated Aisha: The companions of Allah's Apostle used to practice manual labor, so their sweat used to smell, and they were advised to take a bath." (Bukhari: 3.34.285)

Imam Nasai (1.316) writes that a Muslim can bathe in dirt and dust simply by rolling his body as a camel or a beast does. Also, after sexual intercourse no need for proper washing. Just clean the private parts with hand, rub the hand in wall, and then wash the hand.

"Narrated Maimuna: The Prophet took the bath of Janaba. (sexual relation or wet dream). He first cleaned his private parts with his hand, and then rubbed it (that hand) on the wall (earth) and washed it. Then he performed ablution like that for the prayer, and after the bath he washed his feet." (Bukhari: 1.5.260)

Since every Muslim is expected to emulate Muhammad in all aspects, including his personal hygiene habits, they have no problem to live in a horrifying unhygienic condition either in public places or in the privacy of their homes. They often spit anywhere they like, urinate and defecate in public places whenever opportunity permits oblivious to the fact that saliva and excrement are potential carriers of deadly germs and viruses. In Allah's wisdom, if a cat drinks from a vessel, the water still remains clean (Sunaan Nasai: 1.69, 343). The water polluted by dead dogs, menstruating clothes and human excrement is suitable for use for anything.

"Narrated Abu Sa'id al-Khudri: I heard that the people asked the Prophet of Allah; Water is brought for you from the well of Buda'ah. It is a well in which dead dogs, menstrual clothes and excrement of people are thrown. The Messenger of Allah replied: Verily water is pure and is not defiled by anything." (Sunaan Abu Dawud: 1.67)

Faith is required only if reason is inadequate. If reason can tell us anything there is to know, there is no longer a job for faith. The entire notion of faith rests upon and presupposes the inadequacy of reason. Reason is fine as far as it goes, but it is limited. Here faith makes its grand entrance. Human reason is very deficient in things concerning Allah.

A fasting person often develops terrible stench in his mouth. In Islam, it is considered quite a healthy habit to possess such a bad breath. Bukhari (7.72.811) states that bad-breathe of a fasting person is better to Allah than the smell of musk. This means, a Muslim is not obliged to resort to good oral hygiene during the month of Ramadan. Elsewhere, Muhammad suggested that a tooth pick can be shared between two persons (Sunaan Abu Dawud: 1.50), and if a person touches a carcass, no need to wash hands (Sunaan Abu Dawud: 1.186). Also, polluted water can be used for ablution (Sunaan Abu Dawud: 1.66). Muhammad had a dirty habit of spitting in the mouth of the suckling babies. He also gave his tongue to a baby to suck (Ash Shifa: 184). It was believed that his spittle had some divine power.

There is no shortage of endless, incoherent, and superstitious rituals in Islam. It starts in the dawn, before the sunrise, with the call for prayer to Allah. These rituals are not voluntary; they are forced imposition upon Muslims. Muhammad instructed his followers to burn the houses of those Muslims who do not present themselves for the Islamic prayers.

"Narrated Abu Huraira: Allah's Apostle said, "By Him in Whose Hand my soul is I was about to order for collecting firewood (fuel) and then order someone to pronounce the Adhan for the prayer and then order someone to lead the prayer then I would go from behind and burn the houses of men who did not present themselves for the (compulsory congregational) prayer. By Him, in Whose Hands my soul is, if anyone of them had known that he would get a bone covered with good meat or two (small) pieces of meat present in between two ribs, he would have turned up for the `Isha' prayer."' (Bukhari: 1.11.617)

If the spouse does not wake up for the morning prayer, it is permitted to throw water on his/her face (Ghazali: 1.261). Also, the Muslims should say their prayers in a dramatic manner because Allah loves it. When the Muslim stands for prayer, his head should perspire, his limbs should tremble and his face should change (Ghazali: 1.145). If he also wears turban, he will receive the blessings of Allah and his angels (Ghazali: 1.152). This is why fanatic Muslims, as we watch on televisions, wear turbans. Also, Qur'an should be recited in a dramatic way. The true believers should weep when they recite it (Ghazali: 2.176), and if they cannot weep then they must pretend to do so (Ghazali: 1.213). Muslims should not pass wind during prayer. Because Allah will not accept his prayer (Bukhari: 1.4.137). But if he passes wind silently or without smell he may continue with the prayer (Bukhari: 1.4.139). Islam has strict rules for everything, even for passing wind.

Allah does not like Muslims to sit on dining chair and eat on the table. Devout Muslims eat sitting on floor, and with their hands, making sure the plate of food is resting on the floor. Also he should eat with the right hand and eat of the dish that is nearer to him (Bukhari: 7.65.288). After eating, he should lick the fingers by himself, or someone else may lick on his behalf (Muslim: 23.5037-8; Bukhari: 7.65.366; Sunaan ibn Majah: 4.3270). After licking his fingers he should lick the dish. The dish will ask Allah for his forgiveness (Sunaan ibn Majah: 4.3271; Sunaan Tirmidhi: 1121). When he drinks, he must drink in three gulps (Muslim: 23.5029-30). He should not drink from a silver or gold vessel, otherwise he drinks fire in his belly (Muslim: 24.5126, 5128). Sometimes I wonder; how many Muslims really know about Hippocrates of Cos, who is considered the father of the medicine and his efforts in the fourth century – much before Allah's medical science was known to us – to bring medicine out of the pall of superstition and into the light of science. Allah is a spoof – a self-caricature.

Allah does not like a Muslim to sleep on his stomach. He can send a Muslim to hell fire for this (Tirmidhi: 1226). Ghazali (2.20) writes that to lie with belly up is to sleep like the Prophets. Also, when he goes to bed he should lie on his right side and then recite Allah's name and glorify him. If he dies in this state then he dies in Islam (Muslim: 35.6544).

The standard of Muslims' toilet habits is nasty. It is full of indecent and uncivil manners, and customs. Muhammad and his wives used open field to answer call of nature (Bukhari: 1.4.148-9). Muhammad prayed to Allah when he was answering the call of nature (Bukhari: 1.4.144). When Muslims enter a toilet they should pray to Allah (Muslim: 3.0729; Sunaan Nasai: 1.19). Muslims also should say Bismillah when visiting toilet (Tirmidhi: 130). Urinating in a hole is prohibited (Sunaan Nasai: 1.34). Also, a Muslim should not face or back Qibla (direction for prayer) or Baitul–Maqdis (Jerusalem) during defecation (Bukhari: 1.4.146; Muslim: 2.504). This rule applies whether he is defecating in his latrine or in an open field. However Muhammad did not follow the Allah's rule.

"Narrated `Abdullah bin `Umar: People say, 'Whenever you sit for answering the call of nature, you should not face the Qibla or Baitul–Maqdis (Jerusalem)." I told them. "Once I went up the roof of our house and I saw Allah's Apostle answering the call of nature while sitting on two bricks facing Baitul–Maqdis (Jerusalem)'." (Bukhari: 1.4.147)

*"Narrated `Abdullah bin `Umar: I went up to the roof of Hafsa's house for some job and I saw Allah's Apostle answering the call of nature facing Sham (Syria, Jordan, Palestine and Lebanon regarded as one country) **with his back towards the Qibla**".* (Bukhari: 1.4.150)

After defecating a Muslim should use stones to cleanse himself, and he should use odd number (preferably three) stones.

"Narrated Abu Huraira: I followed the Prophet while he was going out to answer the call of nature. When I approached near him he said to me, 'Fetch for me some stones for cleaning the private parts, and do not bring a bone or a piece of dung'. So I brought the stones in the corner of my garment and placed them by his side and I then went away from him. When he finished (from answering the call of nature) he used them." (Bukhari: 1.4.157)

"Narrated Abu Huraira: The Prophet said, "Whoever performs ablution should clean his nose with water by putting the water in it and then blowing it out, and whoever cleans his private parts with stones should do it with odd number of stones'." (Bukhari: 1.4.162)

There are many superstitions for bath also. Females cannot use the leftover water by males, but the males can use the leftover water by females (Sunaan Abu Dawud: 1.81). In Allah's wisdom, leprosy is caused by taking bath in water exposed to the sun (Mishkat: 1.245). Allah believes that a woman ejaculates sperm during her orgasm like a man and she should take a bath (Sunaan Nasai: 1.197-9). Men's sperm is white and women's sperm is yellow (Sunaan Nasai: 1.202).

"Narrated Um Salama: Sulaim came to Allah's Apostle and said, 'Verily, Allah is not shy of (telling) the truth. Is it necessary for a woman to take a bath after she has a wet dream (nocturnal sexual discharge?) The Prophet replied, 'Yes, if she notices a discharge'. Um Salama, then covered her face and asked, 'O Allah's Apostle! Does a woman get a discharge?' He replied, 'Yes, let your right hand be in dust (An Arabic expression, meaning 'you will not achieve goodness'), and that is why the son resembles his mother'." (Bukhari: 1.34.132)

The monthly period of a woman is a disease, unholy, and impure. Qur'an says,

"They question thee (O Muhammad) concerning menstruation. Say: It is an illness, so let women alone at such times and go not in unto them till they are cleansed. And when they have purified themselves, then go in unto them as Allah hath enjoined upon you." (Q: 2.222)

Science says, there is nothing impure, ugly, reprehensible, or sinful in this biological cycle of a woman; its certainly not an illness. Monthly period of a woman is the basis of survival of human species. Bukhari says,

"Narrated Abu Sa`id: The Prophet said, 'Isn't it true that a woman does not pray and does not fast on menstruating? And that is the defect (a loss) in her religion'." (Bukhari: 3.31.172)

In Sunaan Abu Dawud (1.1.287) we read that excessive blood-flow during a woman's period is from Satan. In Sunaan ibn Majah (1.595, 596) Muhammad said that a sexually defiled man and a menstruating woman cannot recite the Qur'an. He also advised to use saliva and nails to rub off bloodstains from period (Bukhari: 1.6.309). In Allah's view, a woman ranks as a household chattel. She is just a man's

261

sexual toy – total subjection of the wife. Her total slavery includes her husband's right to beat her, whip her, cane her and abuse her morally and physically (Fallaci, 2006, p. 107). Her body is a machine to produce babies.

"*Your wives are as a tilth unto you; so approach your tilth when or how ye will; but do some good act for your souls beforehand; and fear Allah. And know that ye are to meet Him (in the Hereafter), and give (these) good tidings to those who believe.*" (Q: 2.223)

We should make no mistake about this verse. It includes sexual positions. In Allah's views, the man controls his wife's body. She must have sex when he wants and whatever position he wants including anal intercourse. Allah considers women as crocked and blameworthy.

"*Abu Huraira reported: Woman has been created from a rib and will in no way be straightened for you; so if you wish to benefit by her, benefit by her while crookedness remains in her.*" (Muslim: 8.3467)

Daughters are such burdensome that a man will go to paradise for having the burden of one or two or three daughters (Ghazali: 2.41). In fact, women's lives are so cheap that in many Islamic countries 'honour killing' of women is not considered a serious crime. Ghazali (2.43; 2.24) wrote,

"*A woman has ten private parts. When she gets married, her husband covers one private part; when she dies the grave covers other nine private parts.*"

"*A prison in the corner of a house is better than a childless woman.*"

Allah considers women truly evil. A nation ruled by a woman will never be successful (Bukhari: 5.59.709, 9.88.219). The evil omens are: the horse, the women and the house (Bukhari: 4.52.110-1). A woman is an evil omen, a mat in the house is better than a barren woman (Abu Dawud: 3.29.3911). Allah discourages women to beautify their looks to appear presentable and charming. He curses those women who wear false hair (Muslim: 24.5295). In his farewell sermon Muhammad equated women to cattle. Tabari recorded,

"*Treat women well for they are like domestic animals and they possess nothing themselves. Allah has made the enjoyment of their bodies lawful in his Qur'an.*" (Tabari: IX.113)

This is the royal status of women in Islam. Since women are domestic animals, logically, the old stock can be replaced by new one.

"*Ali [Muhammad's adopted son, son-in-law, and future Caliph] said, 'Prophet, women are plentiful. You can get a replacement, easily changing one for another'.*" (Tabari: VIII.62; Ishaq: 496)

These ideas are so deep-rooted in a Muslim mind that from birth to death, in every phase and stages of his life, he will be hunted down with Islamic superstitions – this is the cost of Allah delusion. Every action he does, he must ensure that it conforms to Allah's divine wisdom. He must not question Allah's likes and dislikes, he must not doubt even a word of the Qur'an, and he must not deviate even an inch from the Islamic specifications. Under the (mis)guidance of the Qur'anic revelations and sunna, Muslims live in a ghostly world of fearful piety, surrounded by devils, jinns crossing themselves a hundred times a day, imploring the intercession of Muhammad for afterlife, prostrating five compulsory prayers, awed by miracles performed by Muhammad, trembling over Allah's fury and selling everything to perform Hajj. A non-Arab Muslim family is a poor imitation of an Arab family within the principled confines of Islam.

The entire Islamic belief system is purely based on blind faith; obedience is the major virtue, disobedience the major vice. Now, what should we conclude about the following verse where Allah attests that Muhammad's knowledge is from Allah?

"But Allah bears witness by what He has revealed to you that He has revealed it with His knowledge, and the angels bear witness (also); and Allah is sufficient as a witness." (Q: 4.166)

The Muslims regard the humility of unquestioning obedience as a virtue. When they identify ignorance of worldly affairs with spiritual grace it hardly matters what their minds may still remain capable of learning, because they themselves will have made certain they never again use this capacity. As long as the Allah delusion persists, the Muslims will have to live with these superstitions and die with them. They live in such a society where most adults – not just a few crazies, but most adults – subscribe to a whole variety of weird and nonsensical beliefs, that in one way or another they shamelessly impose upon their children.

When there is a lack of logical thinking, it is difficult to distinguish between falsehood and truth. Since truth cannot be changed, Muslims have to change their mindset to remain in the "logic-tight" compartment of Islam. Thus lying becomes a second nature, and Allah-delusion soon takes over. Muslims make themselves what they want to be and not what they actually are. The typical Muslim mindset is, *"I do not seek to understand in order to believe. I believe in order to understand. We should not aim to understand what we have believed after we are confirmed of our Islamic faith."* (Durant, 1950, p. 932, quote modified by present Author). With this mindset, a Muslim cannot think anything beyond Allah, Qur'an and Muhammad. He lives in a constant dream-like state. Smith (1981, p. 291) commented,

"Muslims do not read the Qur'an to understand whether it is divine; rather, they believe it to be divine, and then they read it. This makes a great deal of difference, and I urge upon Christian and secular students of the Qur'an that if they wish to understand it as a religious document, they must approach it in this spirit. If an outsider picks up the book and goes through it even asking himself, 'What is there here that has led Muslims to suppose this from God?' he will miss the reverberating impact. If, on the other hand, he picks up the book and asks himself, what would these sentences convey to me if I believe them to

be God's word? Then he can much more effectively understand what has been happening these many centuries in the Muslim world."

It is not that Muslims do not want to know about science. Like other people they have a natural appetite for science, but only for Qur'anic science. This is the reason Muslims are nervous about modern science and technology.

"Narrated Ibn `Abbas: Once the Prophet embraced me (pressed me to his chest) and said, "O Allah, teach him wisdom (i.e. the understanding of the knowledge of Qur'an)." (Bukhari: 5.5.100)

Today, who will tell them that diseases that once tragically carried off countless infants and children have been progressively mitigated and cured by science? Who will tell them that it is science that had wiped out smallpox worldwide, not Allah? In this scientific age should we pray to Allah for cholera victims, or should we give them 500 milligrams of tetracycline every twelve hours? Their cultural tradition, educational system and the Islamic communication media had failed them – all the real science had gotten filtered out before it reaches them. To conform Allah's science, the faithful Muslims have to deny germ theory of disease, and if prayer fails, they should rather see their children die than rather give them antibiotics. There is no one who can teach them how to distinguish real science from Allah's pseudoscience. As a result, a religious Muslim who puts his trust on Allah's wisdom knows nothing about how real science works. And since he knows nothing how real science works, he can hardly be aware he is embracing pseudoscience and superstition.

Allah's science is even less than a cheap imitation of real science. There is so much in real science that is more exiting and more mysterious than Allah's science; a greater intellectual challenge – as well as being a lot closer to the truth. In this scientific era Muslims will have to knock them down by reason, sublime suggestions and right thinking. To live a healthy life, Muslims must abandon Allah's wisdom. Allah is a delusion, and what scientific wisdom can we learn from a fantasy superhero?

Muslims' superstitious beliefs seem relatively harmless but they are not. The reason is that if someone is willing to accept such absurd claims as divine wisdom, what else are they willing to believe? The clerics pass these superstitions around freely and these superstitions when believed as divine wisdom strengthen the Allah-virus; it diverts the common Muslims' attention from real science, affect their behavior, and program them to spread these superstitions to others. If these clerics knew how magnificent the real science is, their jaws would drop through the floor.

Chapter 7: The final conclusion

"Truth can never be told so as to be understood and not be believed".
William Blake

"While man must recognize his limitations, he must also become aware of the power in himself – the power to make use of his own reason and see the truth".
Eric Fromm (quote modified by the present Author)

Looking for evidence is fatal for certain kinds of ideas. Allah is one such idea whose life-support system is blind faith. Therefore, Allah has a great psychological appeal. A real god does not need a life-support system in order to survive. Muslims fall on their knees five times a day to beg an imaginary god for a little mercy on their tormented souls. But all those prayers are in vain. The reflection of a god that Muhammad had placed in front of the Muslims has no life – Allah is not matter, neither is nonexistence; Allah does not have limitations, neither does nonexistence; Allah is not visible, neither is nonexistence; Allah does not change, neither does nonexistence; Allah cannot be described, neither can nonexistence, and so on down the list. If Muslims wish to distinguish their belief in Allah from the belief in nothing at all, they must give some positive substance to the concept of Allah. When Muhammad was frustrated since he had no power to solve his own problems, he turned to Allah, expecting to find a solution in a supernatural force. Hence, the vision of Allah is an abnormal perception of reality created by his fear and anxiety. Allah is the negation, the exact reversal of how man perceives reality. He exists only as a superstitious idea with infective power, but high survival value that depends on Muslims' blind faith on him. Their faith is so strong that it itself is taken as the evidence of truth.

A Muslim who demands scientific evidence of Allah's existence is discredited. But there is no Ayatollah or Grand Mufti who can create an Allah with the force of his religious faith, even if when he shares his belief with the entire Muslim Ummah. Nobody can alter the nature of reality with the power of his blind faith. Religious faith does not make humans infallible; extraordinary claims require extraordinary proof. You cannot claim that Allah exists only because you have a blind faith that Allah exists. A blind belief in Allah and his Qur'an cannot flatten the earth or cause the sun to revolve around earth to conform Allah's wisdom. Science can prove that the universe is billions of years old. Consequently, divine creation is a fantasy; the hypothesis of divine creation is based on the superstitious beliefs of the primitive mentality. Why then would an Allah delusion cause the existence of Allah? Allah is like a doctor's placebo, which is, however, effective in spite of being pretended. To state that "Allah exists" is to communicate nothing at all; it is as if nothing has been said. The label of "Allah" serves no function, except, perhaps, to create confusion.

A blind faith in Allah can drive Muslims to such dangerous rage and insanity that it qualifies as a severe mental illness. Blind faith can make people believe so strongly that they are willing to kill and die for their faith without any further justification. It is so powerful that it immunizes people against all appeals to pity, forgiveness, and decent human feelings. It even immunizes them against fear as they think they will go to paradise. This pattern of behavior is passed from one generation to another by imitation. The Allah delusion is so much deep-rooted in their minds that they have Allah always uppermost in their minds – so much so that they cannot make any division between secular and sacred. If the evidence seems to contradict Allah, it is the evidence that must be thrown out, not the belief in Allah. It is a human tragedy that so many people have been misguided by ignorance, superstition, greed, and madness, while dedicating their entire lives to the pursuit and promotion of a false and evil idea. No other individuals have ever reached more eminence on the basis of ignorance than the Muslim theologians. Blind faith can justify anything. Hence it can propagate in a ruthless way.

The achievements of Islam during the history have been bloody wars against non-believers and mass-murdering them, torturing inquisitions, culture-destroying missionaries, and legally enforced resistance to each new piece of scientific truth – all done in the name of a god who only existed in the sick mind of a seventh century epileptic schizophrenic. Muslims are brainwashed from birth to believe in Allah and they are simply not open-minded enough to ever seriously and honestly question their god. Many Muslims, in contrast, were raised as theists but were open-minded enough to question what they were taught, and the result is disbelief.

Muhammad suffered from religious delusion that caused his mind to perceive unreal and imaginary objects as if they were real. That is why there is no scientific evidence of Allah because science does not support or explain a delusion. How a religious delusion can be the creative source of life and the world? The strength of a religious faith cannot materialize or give life to the creature of a fantasy. Now we know why Allah is so miserable when looked through the spectacle of science and logic. There is no observable evidence in the behavior of nature to support the claim that Allah exists. As Luther (cited Kaufmann, 1972, pp. 305-7) wrote, "*Faith must trample under foot all reason, sense, and understanding, and whatever it sees it must put out of sight, and wish to know nothing but the word of God*". There is also no scientific evidence of miraculous Qur'an being revealed from a divine source. A real Almighty God does not need to speak through a schizophrenia criminal. The people who are under the influence of drugs can also claim to communicate with God. What if the behaviors recorded 1400 years ago that has been the basis for so much religious zealotry is simply better understood in the context of mental illness? Our commonsense says if it walks like a duck, looks like a duck and swims like a duck, there is hardly any doubt we are dealing with a duck. When it comes to Allah's religion, however, we change our perceptions. If it behaves like a hardcore criminal, if it talks like a schizophrenic and if it has all the symptoms of Temporal Lobe Epilepsy, it must be the Prophet of Allah!

The discovery that all living organisms evolve by a process of natural selection gave Muslims a difficult dilemma. According to Allah, earth was created in six or eight days. But the new scientific evidence proved that the earth is billions of years old. Since the Islamic theologians were not able to contradict science, they had no choice but to accept the evidence, but argued that Qur'an gives many scientific explanations. But, if Allah created evolution why did not he reveal evolution to man, rather than wait for scientific discoveries to be made? It is clear that Allah never knows anything until humans make new scientific discoveries. If there are no new scientific discoveries made, the Muslim theologians cannot reveal any new divine plan. This is irrefutable evidence that only science can explain everything, not Allah. If an omniscient Allah really existed, Muhammad would be the first to know his plans, and would have known about evolution and the real age of the earth long before scientists did, since he had communicated with such a god. Why would a real god choose to reveal the mysteries of the universe to scientists first, rather than to his believers? If Qur'an is full of science why no well-known scientist has ever looked at the Qur'an for scientific enlightenment? This proves that knowledge can only be gained through human investigation and has never been provided by the Allah. This is irrefutable evidence that the Muslim scholars are compelled to change their dogmas when they are challenged by new scientific discoveries.

The *insha'allah* theory is equally absurd since there is no god with a personal interest in Muslims' behavior or wellbeing. Moral distinctions do not depend on god. Ethics is autonomous and can be studied and discussed without reference to Allah. We cannot escape our moral responsibility that our independent moral understanding gives us. Also, a god who has no existence cannot grant miracles. The ineffectiveness of their prayer proves there is no Allah. Muslims are not able to cope with the problems of life and seek to invoke an almighty being that will solve their troubles with magic. They turn to religion, expecting to find a solution in a supernatural force. Therefore, the idea of an ungodly god like Allah is an abnormal perception of reality created by fear and anxiety. Islam thus serves to provide an escape from reality to the mentally disturbed.

The great majority of the believing Muslims are unwilling to reexamine their beliefs. They are quite sure that their faith is correct, and to start questioning it would be an outright condemnation of themselves. They would lose their chance of salvation and the expectation of life in heaven at the end of this experience. Muslims find it difficult to accept the truth because of their fear to lose the false moral support that is founded in the belief of Allah. They are afraid to lose the delusion that an omnipotent Allah protects them at all times and takes care of them. They live in constant fear and insecurity. The belief and desire for a constant guardian is a psychological trauma; it is more than a simple philosophical problem.

Delusion is one of the main characteristics of psychosis. Science is impossible under such circumstances. Indeed, it is both irrelevant and dangerous. Irrelevant because what matters in the world is not how the material world interacts, but the Allah that inhabits it, and dangerous, because systematic inquiry may offend Allah. Therefore, their thinking goes like this – so what if Muhammad had temporal lobe epilepsy and schizophrenia! If Allah wants to use that mechanism to transmit his revelation, then so be it. If the choice must be made between the comfort of Allah delusion and the truth of science, they will sacrifice the latter without hesitation. For them schizophrenia is not an illness but a shortcut to spiritual enlightenment. Any further healthy discussion with such people is a complete waste of time.

The solution to the problems of life does not depend on imaginary perceptions. Where was Allah while millions of Muslim children died from starvation and disease in the Middle East? Where was Allah while a cyclone killed 266,000 Pakistanis in 1970? As per the verse 7.57, – "... *make rain to descend thereon, and produce every kind of harvest therewith*" – rain is the mercy of Allah, yet devastating floods claim the lives of thousands of people in, ironically, a Muslim country, namely, Bangladesh. The cyclone of 1991, with winds of 200 kilometers per hour, resulted in floods that left 100,000 dead and 10,000,000 without shelter. All these must be the works of Allah, as the verse 57.22 tells us – *"No misfortune can happen on earth or in your souls but is recorded in a decree before we bring it into existence: That is truly easy for Allah"*. Muslims have prayed for the total destruction of the Jewish ever since the time of Muhammad without a single result. There was no Allah to save the hundreds of thousands of children who died from starvation and disease in Afghanistan, Bangladesh and Sudan. This is clear evidence that the power of blind faith in Allah is a hideous instrument of forged reality that confronts every faithful Muslim at every waking hour and can convince even the most educated of them.

Allah does not create history, because a delusion has no power to change anything. If science is true, Muslims are alone in this world and thereafter. There is no Allah to think for them, to watch out for them, to guarantee their happiness in the paradise. It would be fortunate if the attainment of happiness were that simple, but it is not. These are the sole responsibility of man. If Muslims want knowledge, they must think of themselves, if they want success, they must work. If they want happiness, they must strive to achieve it. All power belongs to men; they are the history creators. From one generation to another, men learn from history, develop and transform themselves. As Fromm (1991, p. 26) commented,

> *"History is the history of man's self-realization; it is nothing but the self-creation of man through the process of his work and his production"*.

Muslims will never be free without this self-realization. Self-realization is a maturing of the personality to allow the soul to grow and to reveal itself. To achieve self-realization, first the Muslims have to liberate themselves from their own belief, and true freedom can only be realized in that state. When I speak of freedom, I mean absolute freedom – freedom of the soul. As Mosab Hassan Yousef, the son of Sheikh Hassan Yousef (a founder and leader of the Palestinian terrorist group Hamas), said;

> *"The problem is not in Muslims. The problem is with their God. They need to be liberated from their God. He is their biggest enemy. It has been 1,400 years they have been lied to"*. (cited Bishara, 2011, p. 177)

If Muslims could only see that Allah is nothing more than a lie that had been used to enslave them they would walk away from this evil cult of Islam within no time. Then only they will become fully and truly human. A world without Allah delusion is not a terrifying prospect; it is a refreshing, exhilarating challenge. How a Muslim will react to an Islam-free world depends only on himself and the extent to which he is willing to assume responsibility for his own choices and actions. There is no glory in the slavery of the Allah delusion; it is a disgrace.

ADDENDUM 1: The delusion of Dr. Richard Dawkins

"Psychology, since its founding roughly a century ago, has often focused on the opposite topic - namely the psychology of religious belief. Indeed, in many respects the origins of modern psychology are intimately bound up with the psychologists who explicitly proposed interpretations of belief in God."

Professor Paul C. Vitz

Richard Dawkins proved himself a gifted thinker. Soon after the publication of his world-famous book *The Selfish Gene* in 1976 in which he established a shockingly original account of life on the planet, in other words, a new version of what it means to be human, he has established himself as one of the most successful and skillful science popularizers. In this book he has presented the evolutionary biology (gene-centered view of evolution) in a very interesting manner and introduced the term *meme* (the behavioral equivalent of a gene). The term *meme* was coined as a way to encourage readers to think about how Darwinian principles might be extended beyond the realm of genes (Dawkins, 1989, p. 11). Though he invented the specific term *meme* independently, he has not claimed that the idea itself was entirely novel, and there have been other expressions for similar ideas in the past. For instance, Laurent (1999, pp. 14-19) has suggested that the term may have derived from the work of the little-known German biologist Richard Semon. Nevertheless, there is much truth in Dawkins' observation. As Gleick (2011, p. 269) describes Dawkins' concept of the *meme* as *"his most famous memorable invention, far more influential than his selfish genes or his later proselytizing against religiosity"*.

The Selfish Gene is one of his best books – his scientific analysis is bold and original and his emerging antireligious bias is kept under tight leash. I long envy his clarity, beautiful use of helpful analogies and entertaining style. Most of his questions and insights are certainly worthy of contemplation. However his 2006 book *The God Delusion* marks a significant departure. This book has established Dawkins as the world's most high-profile atheist polemicist. Here Dawkins contends that a supernatural creator almost certainly does not exist and that religious faith is a delusion (2006, p. 5) – *"a persistent false belief held in the face of strong contradictory evidence"*. Dawkins hurls an arrogant criticism against all the religions and repeatedly argues (2006, pp. 5, 6, 20, 23, 34, 176, 186, 188, 193-4, 262-272, 282, 374), he is not a fundamentalist because he does not prescribe violence against his opponents and his hostility towards religion is limited to words – *"I am not going to bomb anybody, behead them, stone them, burn them at the stake, crucify them, or fly planes into their skyscrapers, just because of a theological disagreement"*.

Yet he believes ridicule is a valid form of discourse and uses disease imagery to describe the religious. His language is therefore divisive, painting the world in hues of black and white, good or evil. As opposed to "irrational" religion, which is a "vice" and a "poison" (its followers are delusional if not insane), science and reason are unlimited in their potential to discern the truth and set the human race in a moral direction. Using such rhetoric, *The God Delusion* resembles a religious tract in its intent to convert its reader to atheism,

> *"If this book works as I intend, religious readers who open it will be atheists when they put it down ... Of course, dyed-in-the-wool faith-heads are immune to argument, their resistance built up over years of childhood indoctrination using methods that took centuries to mature (whether by evolution or design). Among the more effective immunological devices is a dire warning to avoid even opening a book like this, which is surely a work of Satan. But I believe there are plenty of open-minded people out there: people whose childhood indoctrination was not too insidious, or for other reasons didn't 'take', or whose native intelligence is strong enough to overcome it. Such free spirits should need only a little encouragement to break free of the vice of religion altogether. At very least I hope that nobody who reads this book will be able to say, 'I didn't know I could'".*

In the 1960s (in those days we have all heard the mantras such as "science has disproved God" and "religion is superstition"), it had been predicted with confidence that atheism would be the future of the world, and our future generation would live in a god-less society. Wilson, one of the most outstanding biologists of 1970s, cheerfully announced that evolution has triumphed over supernaturalism of any sort. He strongly concluded (1978, p. 192),

> *"The final decisive edge enjoyed by scientific naturalism will come from its capacity to explain traditional religion, its chief competition, as a wholly material phenomenon. Theology is not likely to survive as an independent intellectual discipline."*

The oversimplified thinking was – if we can get rid of the God and religion, violence would be eradicated. Yet, with much disappointment, religion has made a comeback. As Michael Shermer, the famous humanist writer, the director of the *Skeptics Society* and publisher of *Skeptic* magazine, pointed out (2000, pp. 16-31) that never in history have so many, and such a high percentage of Americans believed in God. Polls suggest that approximately ninety-five percent of the population of the United States believe they will survive their own death (Dawkins, 2006, p. 356). Recent pools confirm (Collins, 2007, p. 4) that ninety-three percent of Americans profess some form of belief in God. On April 7, 1980 Time ran a major story entitled *Modernizing the Case for God*, which described the movement among contemporary philosophers to refurbish the traditional arguments for God's existence. Time marveled (cited Martin, 2006, p. 84, footnote 2),

> *"In a quiet revolution in thought and argument that hardly anybody could have foreseen only two decades ago, God is making a comeback. Most intriguingly, this is happening not among theologians or ordinary believers, but in the crisp intellectual circles of academic philosophers, where the consensus had long banished the Almighty from fruitful discourse".*

In this article, the noted American philosopher Roderick Chisholm opined that the reason atheism was so influential in the previous generation is that the brightest philosophers were atheists; but today, he observes, many of the brightest philosophers are theists, using a tough-minded intellectualism in defense of that belief. Although religious beliefs vary widely across the world, the most prevalent beliefs involve "God" and the "afterlife". In North American surveys, ninety-five percent of all persons stated a belief in God, seventy-one percent a belief in the afterlife, but only fifty-three in the existence of hell (Kroll & Sheehan, 1989, pp. 67-72). Another opinion poll confirmed that a full ninety-eight percent of the US population say they believe in God, seventy percent believe in life after death (Humphrey, 1997). In 1992, historian of science Frederic Burnham stated (cited Briggs, 1992, p. B6) that the God hypothesis is now a more respectable hypothesis than at any time in the last one hundred years.

Religion is not only anathema for scientists; according to Dawkins (2006, p. 16), religion should not even be considered a *"proper field, in which one might claim expertise,"* and that it is no better than *"fairyology"*. He speculates that real scientists reject belief in God because science has wrecked their religious faith (McGrath & McGrath, 2007, p. 12), but the statistics points us to the opposite conclusion – a lot of scientists and intellectual geniuses do sincerely believe in God.

The God Delusion was published in 2006 and in the same year three other books were published by leading research scientists – Owen Gingerich, a noted Harvard Astronomer wrote *God's Universe,* declaring (2006, p. 7)*, "the universe has been created with intention and purpose, and that this belief does not interfere with the scientific enterprise"*, Francis Collins (Director of the Human Genome Project, the project which spent several decades mapping the human DNA) published his *The Language of God*, which argues that the wonder and ordering of nature points to a Creator God very much along the lines of traditional conception. In this book Collins described (2007, pp. 7, 198) his conversion from atheism to a believer – *"I had reached the conclusion that faith in God was much more compelling than the atheism I had previously embraced"*. A few months later the cosmologist Paul Davies published his *Goldilocks Enigma*, arguing for the existence of "fine-tuning" in the universe. According to him, the bio-friendliness of the universe points to an overarching principle that somehow pushes the universe towards the development of life and mind. Davies does not subscribe to a traditional Christian notion of God but he strongly believes that there is something Divine out there (or, may be in there). Another distinguished cosmologist and science expositor James Jeans supports his view (cited Cornwell, 2008, p. 57) – *"The universe begins to look more like a great thought than a great machine"*.

Another book was written by Dr. Mani Lal Bhaumik, an Indian-born American physicist, *Code Name God: The Spiritual Odyssey of a Man of Science.* In this autobiographical meditation a world-renowned physicist examines the hidden links between science and spirituality revealed by recent breakthroughs in quantum physics and cosmology. Bhaumik argues,

"The surprising discovery of quantum physics that the primary source of everything in the universe is present in each minutest stitch of the fabric of space of this immensely vast cosmos empowers us to ponder the One Source of

all creation. It is not merely a blind faith anymore. This ought to enable us to feel ourselves as an inextricable part of the One Source, which would significantly improve the quality of our lives."

Professor Walter Thirring, the former director and head of the theory division at European Organization for Nuclear Research (also known as CERN), Geneva, asserts in the foreword to its German edition,

"Dr. Bhaumik's portrayal of a higher power embedded in the fabric of the universe and responsible for its continuing existence and operation is consistent with his reliance on the highly technical and mathematical intricacies of the Quantum Field Theory, an area of study to which I had the opportunity of making some significant contributions."

Thirring and Bhaumik are two "hard scientists" who have openly accepted the spiritual implications of quantum physics and cosmology. Today several hundred PhDs in religious studies are awarded each year! Is Dawkins seriously suggesting that the contributions of all these intellectuals are not "real"? This type of poor judgment is not only intellectual nonsense but personally offensive as well. What honest academic in any field would make the self-serving claim that another entire field of study is illegitimate? It is precisely for these reasons that so many books have been written in response to *The God Delusion* by religious and non-religious authors alike.

Dawkins may find hard to agree, but today a large number of intellectuals who clearly do think – and even think within the same discipline of science as Dawkins does – have seen reason to commit their lives to God. Dawkins' assertion that belief in God and religion is just does not make sense in a logical and orderly world of facts and reason, is just that – an assertion; it is not based on evidence. Theism is emerging as a worldview with extraordinary explanatory scope and power. God is certainly not dying; in fact He never seems to be more alive. The evident truth is that the religious beliefs and behavior, no matter how absurd and harmful they are, will not fossilize so easily; we have to live with them. In today's world, when the majorities are guided by one or another religious belief system, we cannot simply ignore the religions and live in a society amongst the religious people.

In his earlier book, *The Selfish Gene*, Dawkins gave us a wonderful definition of religion– *"[Faith is] blind trust in the absence of evidence, even in the teeth of evidence."* (1989, p. 198). Faith is voluntary blindness and it is *"an evil precisely because it requires no justification and brooks no argument."* (2006, p. 308). These basic statements are deeply rooted in his mind as if he is obsessed with them. From this standpoint, obviously the definition of a theist is that a person who is deluded or has lost touch with reality. Dawkins (2006, p. 5) quotes from Robert Pirsig, *"When one person suffers from a delusion, it is called insanity. When many people suffer from a delusion it is called Religion"*.

If believing in God is just like believing in the Tooth Fairy, Santa Claus or similar many, then obviously the theists are severely deluded. Delusions need to be exposed and only then we can remove them. However, this analogy is flawed. How many people believe in Santa Claus in adulthood? Who found belief in Tooth Fairy is consoling in old age? There is no harm in it for children because they are in a growing stage. They create imaginary worlds while playing and start knowing the differences between fantasy and reality by the age three or four. But there are thousands of normal, sane and non-religious people who discover God in later life. Others do not regard this as delusion, or some kind of mental perversion, regression or degeneration. We can make a very long list of highly intelligent people, including many scientists, who were atheists in their youth, but who have since turned to a belief in God. What should we say about the famous atheist philosopher Antony Flew (11 February 1923 – 8 April 2010) who became a theist in his eighties?

For over fifty years this British philosopher Antony Flew was the English-speaking world's most intellectually serious public atheist. He started writing on atheism in 1950s and continued to pursue scholarly defenses of atheism for over five decades. Flew was the Dawkins of his day, and cast arguments with sufficient weight to remain important for a long time. He was the author of over thirty professional philosophical works that helped set the agenda for atheism for so long. His basic argument was always the same – there just was not enough evidence to believe in God. Then, at age eighty-one, he changed his mind and became a staunch believer of God.

On 1st November 2007, Antony Flew published his book *There is a God: How the World's Most Notorious Atheist Changed his Mind* where he recounts how he has come to believe in a Creator God as a result of the scientific evidence and philosophical argument. Flew explained repeatedly that he simply had to go where the evidence leads, and made it clear that it is possible for an omnipotent being to choose to reveal himself to human beings, or to act in the world in other ways (Flew & Varghese, 2007, p. 213). In an exclusive interview Flew (Flew & Habermas, 2004, p. 201) commented on Dawkins as;

> "*It seems to me that Richard Dawkins constantly overlooks the fact that Darwin himself, in the fourteenth chapter of The Origin of Species, pointed out that his whole argument began with a being which already possessed reproductive powers. This is the creature the evolution of which a truly comprehensive theory of evolution must give some account. Darwin himself was well aware that he had not produced such an account. It now seems to me that the findings of more than fifty years of DNA research have provided materials for a new and enormously powerful argument to design.*"

In Flew's assessment, the scientific data indicates that one cannot argue (as he used to argue), that there is not "*any good evidence [to] postulate anything behind or beyond this natural universe*". The caricature of God and religions that Dawkins presents is easy for him to attack, but this is not the real thing. Many of his analogies have been constructed with a specific agenda in mind. In his attacks on all religions, regardless of individual philosophies, as being the source of all ills in the world, Dawkins goes too far; he wants to leave no quarter open for the religionists, and his book reads like a declaration of war upon mainstream religions and theists.

> "*Imagine, with John Lennon, a world with no religion. Imagine no suicide bombers, no 9/11, no 7/7, no Crusades, no witch-hunts, no Gunpowder Plot, no Indian partition, no Israeli/Palestinian wars, no Serb/Croat/Muslim massacres,*

273

no persecution of Jews as 'Christ-killers', no Northern Ireland 'troubles', no 'honour killings', no shiny-suited bouffant-haired televangelists fleecing gullible people of their money ('God wants you to give till it hurts'). Imagine no Taliban to blow up ancient statues, no public beheadings of blasphemers, no flogging of female skin for the crime of showing an inch of it."

"The fact that religion is ubiquitous probably means that it has worked to the benefit of something, but it may not be us or our genes. It may be to the benefit of only the religious ideas themselves, to the extent that they behave in a somewhat gene-like way, as replicators."

"Faith is an evil precisely because it requires no justification and brooks no argument."

"Even if religion did no other harm in itself, its wanton and carefully nurtured divisiveness - its deliberate and cultivated pandering to humanity's natural tendency to favour in-groups and shun outgroups - would be enough to make it a significant force for evil in the world."

His attack singles out every worst element of religion, e.g., fundamentalist, non-thinking faith, and intolerance of others outside the 'flock', while ignoring the large-scale charity work carried out by many religions, both large and small, as well as the profound morality teachings found in each, from the parables of Jesus Christ through to the Buddhist doctrine of protecting all life. Many critics (including die hard atheists) point out this massive flaw in *The God Delusion*. In a book of almost four hundred pages, Dawkins can hardly bring himself to concede that a single human benefit has flowed from religious faith. This biased view is not only improbable but empirically false as well. It is not that there are no difficult points for faith. Of course there are. But his blanket statement that religion produces violence is hard to accept. The worlds of business and commerce, sport and leisure, art and music, even of academia, all have their stories to tell of human violence. Cruelty accompanies human interaction in every known sphere, including religion. But we cannot forget that in the recorded history of mankind there are millions of people who have devoted their entire lives selflessly to the service of others in the name of Christ or Buddha or Mahavira Jain. They are certainly not deranged, deluded, deceived and deceiving. Gandhi, Mother Teresa and Dalai Lama were deeply religious, but I cannot see any reason to ridicule them by naming "faith-heads" (Dawkins's own word). Elsewhere Dawkins calls Mother Teresa a hypocrite and implies that she is somehow dishonest and worse because she obeys the Pope in condemning abortion. No one who agrees with Mother Teresa about the sanctity of life should *"be taken seriously on any topic, let alone be thought seriously worthy of a Nobel Prize"* (2006, p. 292). But not for a single time Dawkins mentioned Teresa's work among lepers and the desperately poor. She spent her life bathing, washing, and comforting poor people, taking them off the streets, and giving them a place to live out their final days, asking for nothing for herself, and giving those the world cast away love. A better question would be why Yasser Arafat – who had no objection to the destruction of young life – won the Nobel Prize. Most people have the sense to recognize that the Nobel committee honored itself by their association with Mother Teresa, not the other way around. The more Dawkins defames Teresa, the more ill-informed his criticisms of her tend to be.

Dawkins argues that it is the gene and its relentless drive for survival that explains the existence of all living things. He also agrees that we humans are at last far enough advanced to be able to rebel against our genetic imperatives. Dawkins (1989, pp. 200-1) wrote, "*We can even discuss ways of deliberately cultivating and nurturing pure, disinterested altruism – something that has no place in nature, something that has never existed before in the whole history of the world.*" But there is a paradox – apparently Dawkins is a subscriber to the moral law. Where might this rush of good feelings have come from if we believe in a godless evolution?

According to Dawkins (2006, pp. 237, 247),

> "*Much of the Bible is not systematically evil but just plain weird ... Those who wish to base their morality literally on the Bible have either not read it or not understood it. ... Modern morality, wherever else it comes from, does not come from the Bible.*"

But the history says, the Christians led the fights against slavery, child labor, and oppressions of many kinds. Admittedly, the Church of the day did not always support them, but those at the forefront of many peaceful and peace-making movements were often people driven by their Christian convictions. The Red Cross was originally a Christian organization, hence its name. Dawkins' *The God delusion* can easily be used to delude or destructively mislead people. He has been attacked for this by his colleagues in scholarly circles, but the ordinary reader assumes his "stories of faith" as real science assuming it is really a "scientific and reasonable conclusion". Because of this lack of depth and blanket generalization, many atheists are somewhat embarrassed about Dawkins' book.

Dawkins offers atheist equivalent of religious fundamentalism. He assumes that his readers will share his prejudices and ignorance about religion unquestionably. He has little interest in engaging religious believers, and that is why he fails to see that every established religion has a certain core noble message. Jainism is the only religion which has the principle of *Kathora Ahimsa* (strict nonviolence) as its central doctrine. Hinduism talks about *Sarva dharma sambhava* (equal respect for all religions). Hinduism is also known as *Sanatana Dharma* (eternal religion) and the five principal virtues prescribed by all the schools of *Sanatana Dharma* are, nonviolence, chastity, truthfulness, non-stealing and non-covetousness. Traditional Hinduism has adopted an ancient Sanskrit phrase *Vasudha eva kutumbakam* – The world is one family. Buddhism speaks about toleration, kindness, humbleness, peace and *Pancha Sila* (the five rules of morality – killing any living being, stealing, adultery, lying, drinking intoxicating drinks). Sikhism advises us to restrain from *Punj Chor* (five cardinal vices – ego, lust, greed, attachment, anger) which should be fought with the weapons of wisdom and knowledge. Christianity teaches us love, brotherhood and forgiveness. The teachings of Christianity are based on four essentials – humbleness or faith and trust in God, communication with God through prayer and self-denial, observance of the law which is written in Scripture and in the hearts of those who love the truth, and the offering of sacrifice to God and partaking of the sacrificial offering. The Jews believe that God appointed them to be His chosen people in order to set an example of holiness and ethical behavior to the world, and peace is seen as something that comes from God, which would only be fully realized when there is justice and harmony not just between peoples but within individual communities. Dawkins also does not probe into the worldwide mystical traditions closely tied to the religions, e.g., Jewish Kabbalah and Hindu teachings of yoga. These traditions speak more to a personal, wondrous gnosis than the blind worship of an autocratic, vengeful god that Dawkins appears to take umbrage with.

There is little scientific analysis in *The God Delusion.* In his arguments often Dawkins is clearly out of his depth, and his authority is much under question. As example; when Dawkins offered an account of the origins of religion based on an alleged *"near-universal tendency to let belief be coloured by desire"* (2006, p. 190), he did not mention Ludwig Feuerbach, Sigmund Freud or any of the works of their critics. His authority at this point was William Shakespeare! The admirers trumpet the fact that Dawkins was recently voted one of the world's three leading intellectuals by a survey that took place among the readers of *Prospect* magazine in November 2005, but in a review, the famous cultural and literary critic Terry Eagleton (2006) pointed out, *"Imagine someone holding forth on biology whose only knowledge of the subject is the Book of British Birds, and you have a rough idea of what it feels like to read Richard Dawkins on theology.*" McGrath and McGrath (2007, p. 62) commented,

> *"The God Delusion is a wonderful case study exactly this kind [a built-in resistance to change position according to new information that is inconsistent to our views – even if the change is in positive direction] of unconscious bias. Without full awareness that he is doing so Dawkins foregrounds evidence that fits his own views and discounts or distorts evidence that does not... [In a scientific investigation it is very important to minimize the effects of cognitive bias] ... The entire point of the scientific method is to reduce, and where possible to eliminate, such bias, to strive to give as objective and fair an account as possible. Dawkins does not apply this method to his consideration of religion."*

In *The God Delusion* there is too much pseudo-scientific speculation, linked with hateful criticism of religions – these are mostly borrowed from the stereotyped older atheist writings. I believe in evidenced-based thinking and being a Humanist, I can operate in a godless atmosphere, but can Dawkins, being a die-hard atheist, operate outside his "non-God" way of thinking? If not, then what wrong it is to call him an atheist-fundamentalist? He has a low view of the religionists; as example, once he refused (2004, p. 218) to participate in formal debates with creationists because *"What they seek is the oxygen of respectability"*, and doing so would *"give them this oxygen by the mere act of engaging with them at all"*. He suggests that creationists *"don't mind being beaten in an argument. What matters is that we give them recognition by bothering to argue with them in public"*. McGrath and McGrath (2007, p. 14) commented;

"When some leading scientists write in support of religion, Dawkins retorts that they simply cannot mean what they say. Dawkins clearly feels deeply threatened by the possibility of his readers encountering religious ideas or people that they might actually like – or even worse, respect and regard as worthy of serious attention."

God to Dawkins is like a red flag to an angry bull – *"I am not attacking any particular version of God or gods. I am attacking God, all gods, anything and everything supernatural, wherever and whenever they have been or will be invented."* (2006, p. 36). Quite simple; he would rather believe in anything but God. When Dawkins is so transparent about his dislike for God, he opens himself to the charge of *"theophobia"*, that is, a fear of (or revulsion against) God. According to him (2006, p. 38), God is a *"psychotic delinquent"*. This is the core message of *The God Delusion*. Dawkins continued,

"The deist God is a physicist to end all physics, the alpha and omega of mathematicians, the apotheosis of designers; a hyper-engineer who set up the laws and constants of the universe, fine-tuned them with exquisite precision and foreknowledge, detonated what we would now call the hot big bang, retired and was never heard from again."

Any serious theologian agrees that no one can prove for certainty that God exists. Dawkins, however, pretends that the reverse is true – that he can prove that God does not exist. According to him all Gods are unnecessary; even agnosticism is flawed because it assumes that the probability that God exists is equal to the probability that God does not exist. Dawkins is deaf to theology, and discredits all the theologians in just one argument (2006, p. 56),

"What expertise can theologians bring to deep cosmological questions that scientists cannot? Why are scientists so cravenly respectful towards the ambitions of theologians, over questions that theologians are certainly no more qualified to answer than scientists themselves?"

Dawkins is simply unable and unwilling to understand God outside of his "Atheistic Theory of Everything". For him, God is a delusion because (2006, p. 31),

"Any creative intelligence, of sufficient complexity to design anything, comes into existence only as the end product of an extended process of gradual evolution. Creative intelligences, being evolved, necessarily arrive late in the universe, and therefore cannot be responsible for designing it".

Such a Creator, capable of designing our universe to lead to our evolution must be extremely complex and supremely improbable and demand an even bigger explanation than the one he is supposed to fulfill. One of his main arguments against God, then, is that as an explanation God is a "magic spell" which has been rendered redundant and unnecessary by a growing knowledge of the powers of natural selection.

Dawkins suggests that God is a hypothesis proposed by man as an answer to questions about the universe that were, at one time, unanswerable, but which science is now answering. This definition is irrelevant and incorrect because this certainly does not conform to the thought of those who believe that religion and science are separate but compatible sources of knowledge. Yet it is exactly the definition Dawkins needed in order to accomplish his conclusion. In attacking God, Dawkins writes (2006, p. 31),

> *"The God is arguably the most unpleasant character in all fiction: jealous and proud of it; a petty, unjust, unforgiving control-freak; a vindictive, bloodthirsty ethnic cleanser; a misogynistic, homophobic, racist, infanticidal, genocidal, filicidal, pestilential, megalomaniacal, sadomasochistic, capriciously malevolent bully."*

I fully agree with Dawkins – I do not believe in a God like that either because such is the description of a demonic creature, not a God. We have an entirely different conception of God that Dawkins would probably never understand. As the Christian author Walsch (2007) writes *"The God of which [Dawkins] speaks ... does not exist. ... the God of which he does not speak ... does exist"*. We comprehend God as a *"symbol for the love and the good between people"* (Hutsebaut & Verhoeven, 1995, p. 53). The God whom the Christians believe is a loveable God. The face, will and the character of the Christian God are fully disclosed in Jesus of Nazareth. Dawkins agrees that Jesus did no violence to anyone. The worst thing he did was to tip over tables, twice, to protest against unfair profiteering (John: 2.15; Matthew: 21.12). His whole life was given to doing good. He was at the receiving end of much violence, but he himself was a man of peace and was universally acclaimed as being such. He encouraged his followers to copy his example.

Dawkins mostly argued against the God of Christians but brushes off roughly half of the world's religions, Hinduism and Buddhism, with hardly a word – perhaps because he does not want to wrestle with the uncomfortable fact that neither Brahman in Hinduism, nor the Buddha is ultimately theistic.

Dawkins is right to express his concern about the religious indoctrination of the children without their consent by their parents and religious teachers. Priests, for centuries, have irrevocably transformed children into the religion of their faith without allowing them to decide for themselves – *"children are too young to know where they stand on such issues, just as they are too young to know where they stand on economics or politics"*. We should not teach children about religious dogma until their brains have developed the ability to understand religious concepts.

> *"It is about abuse of trust; it is about denying the child the right to feel free and open and able to relate to the world in the normal way . . . it's a form of denigration; it's a form of denial of the true self in both cases.... Children, I'll argue, have a human right not to have their minds crippled by exposure to other people's bad ideas - no matter who these other people are. Parents, correspondingly, have no God-given license to enculturate their children in whatever ways they personally choose: no right to limit the horizons of their children's knowledge, to bring them up in an atmosphere of dogma and superstition, or to insist they follow the straight and narrow paths of their own faith"*. (2006, pp. 325-6)

I wholeheartedly support Dawkins' views. Indoctrination and brainwashing of children with dogmatic religious doctrines is a grievous wrong; it is religion-motivated child abuse, and I believe with the psychologist Humphrey (1997) that children *"have a human right not to have their minds crippled by exposure to other people's bad ideas – no matter who these other people are"*. But would not it also be "child abuse" to tell children that no matter what they do, at the end of their lives they just die and fall to pieces and the universe has no purpose? Both are harsh lessons. The religious story of the possibility of a happy ending at least leaves a way out. Should atheists be charged with child abuse? According to Dawkins, faith is passed on from parents to children like a virus or as religious *memes*, i.e., cultural genes that injures the impressionable child for life. The remedy is to see to it that they are given no religious instruction at all. Here I cannot agree with him. This whole approach sounds uncomfortably like an antireligious fundamentalism. There is no harm if, instead of intensive religious indoctrination, children are taught the certain core messages of their religion.

Dawkins complains about how confusing the word 'God' can be, but then it is because he does not converse with the believers. If the world was more like Jesus of Nazarath, or Buddha, or the Masters of Vedanta Philosophy, or, spiritual leaders of Sikh Philosophy violence might indeed be a thing of the past. There would be no religious rivalry, revenge, suicide bombing – only love, toleration, brotherhood, kindness and unconditional charity. Dawkins asks us to imagine a world without any religion, but what wrong it is if we hope for a world free from, not all the religions, but imposter Prophets, killer faiths, revengeful God and a holy book, that, in his own words (2006, p. 278), *"explicitly condemns all heretics and followers of rival religions to death, and explicitly promises that the soldiers of God will go straight to a martyrs' heaven"*? True religions promote morality and bring harmony in the society, and that is why religions have persisted so long after the scientific revolution, and indeed are staging a global comeback of terrifying proportions.

Though *The God Delusion* has many flaws, this book is easy to criticize but hard to ignore. Despite the fact that he has written, perhaps, the most powerful set of arguments against the alleged supernatural God ever written with bravery, integrity, humor and explanatory skill, there is a fundamental problem with his approach. He divides the world into two camps – good, tolerant atheists who believe in science and logic; and evil-minded, intolerant theists who try to counteract science and logic. People who fall outside this pattern have no room in his view of the world. In that way, he is weakening his chances of establishing a constructive dialogue with his opponents, who feel that he is unfair to them or does not even make an effort to understand them. In a world where we more than ever need a sensible dialogue between different cultures and philosophies of life, marked by respect and willingness to understand the other party, Dawkins resorts to stereotypes and provocations. In his urge to liberate the world from all fundamentalists and intolerant dogmatists he is dangerously close to becoming one of them.

Dawkins had devoted a complete chapter (Chapter Ten: A Much Needed Gap) to describe how to fill unexplained gaps in our knowledge with scientific thinking instead of fantasy filled Gods and spirits which only serve to stop our thinking about real world problems. He talks about how creationists eagerly look for any gap in our present-day scientific knowledge. They then try to fill that gap with an explanation involving God. Dawkins is absolutely right – if we try to use pure unrestrained cosmic chaos to explain the gaps in cosmological evolution then anything becomes possible. We do not need gradual evolution anymore because our universe could have sprung directly from pure cosmic chaos. Even a personal God could conceivably spring from cosmic chaos. If there was any chaos at all in our origin, then we could not trust our laws of nature to be fail-proof. Dawkins's criticism of those who "worship the gaps" is clearly appropriate and valid.

> *"If the scientist fails to give an immediate and comprehensive answer, the creationist draws a default conclusion: 'Right then, the alternative theory, 'intelligent design', wins by default ... There is, then, an unfortunate hook-up between science's methodological need to seek out areas of ignorance in order to target research, and ID's need to seek out areas of ignorance in order to claim victory by default. It is precisely the fact that ID has no evidence of its own, but thrives like a weed in gaps left by scientific knowledge, that sits uneasily with science's need to identify and proclaim the very same gaps as a prelude to researching them."*

But, sadly, having made such a good point, Dawkins weakens his excellent argument by suggesting that all religionists try to stop the scientists from exploring those gaps (2006, p. 126) – "*one of the truly bad effects of religion is that it teaches us that it is a virtue to be satisfied with not understanding.*" It is a ridiculous generalization that ruins a perfectly interesting discussion. Mainstream Christianity, Hinduism and Buddhism do not support blind faith. Buddha, the great teacher, did not speak in the name of a supernatural power but in the name of reason, who called upon every man to make use of his own reason to see the truth (Fromm, 1978, p. 38). Bible teaches, you will know the truth, and the truth will set you free.

In Dawkins's worldview (2006, pp. 279-86) science and God are locked into a battle to the death. Only one can emerge victorious and it must be science. But how can we polarize the world into two factions? The relationship between science and God is complex and variegated, but we cannot represent it as a state of total war. We should have a more optimistic view. Instead of God versus science, it should be all about truth versus falsehood, good versus evil, justice versus injustice, perversion versus righteousness, rationalism versus superstition and delusion versus reality – and at the end; the truth, good, reality, justice and righteousness must triumph. And to achieve this we have to eliminate all the false gods, demi-gods and the ungodly gods from the face of the earth. Instead of declaring total war against all the Gods, we should single out those false gods and the fake prophets – and that would be the real war, a holy battle to save the humankind and freedom. Militant atheism is not a solution to religious fundamentalism because it is equally flawed and skewed as its religious counterparts. Therefore, within the same logic atheism is also a blind faith because it adopts a belief system that cannot be defended on the basis of pure reason and science. Dawkins himself has confessed that his atheistic view of the universe is based on faith. When asked by the Edge Foundation, "*What do you believe is true even though you cannot prove it?*" Dawkins replied;

"I believe that all life, all intelligence, all creativity and all 'design' anywhere in the universe, is the direct or indirect product of Darwinian natural selection. It follows that design comes late in the universe, after a period of Darwinian evolution. Design cannot precede evolution and therefore cannot underlie the universe." (cited Flew and Varghese, 2007, p. xvii)

At bottom, then, Dawkins's rejection of an ultimate intelligence is a matter of "belief" without proof. This is as much as to say that metaphysical naturalism is something Dawkins believes even though he cannot prove it. And like many whose beliefs are based on blind faith, he cannot tolerate dissent or defection. Though Dawkins insists that he is not an atheist fundamentalist, clearly he is part of the problem here, not its solution.

The false gods and the charlatan prophets often ensure that science is seen in a negative light within its communities. They dread the advance of science as witches do the approach of daylight. If the scientific evidence seems to contradict their holy book, it is the evidence that must be thrown out, not the book. Nothing will budge them from their belief. These people are dangerous because they can be just as delusional and self-serving as the worst that religion has to offer. They will neither look at science nor ever apply logic and conclude – This is better than we thought! The world is much bigger than what those Prophets envisioned.

A false delusional faith which promotes violence has no right to carry on; it is only ethics that makes a religion eligible for survival. The real God of Humankind, as the designer of the universe, has to be a scientist. Such a God must reward kindness, generosity and humility, and regard honest seeking after truth as the supreme virtue. Bertrand Russell was not open to any serious discussion of God's existence or of any organized religion, but in an emotional passage, this great philosopher and Nobel Prize winner Russell once said (cited Flew and Varghese, 2007, p. xviii, xix); *"Nothing can penetrate the loneliness of the human heart except the highest intensity of the sort of love the religious teachers have preached."* We cannot find any passage that remotely resembles this in Dawkins. Time changes, science develops and our understanding grows. Along with this, the true religions evolve and grow spiritually. Only for this reason many very intelligent men and women, though fully committed to the world of reason and with a firm belief in truth-finding power of science, are also deeply religious.

Religions go back to the very beginnings of humanity. Before our ancestors had learned to speak they were dancing sacred dances and almost certainly drawing sacred drawings to demonstrate the beauty and significance of birth, life, and the horror of death that they deeply felt but could not yet explain in words. Religion is a system of mimetic acts, symbolic, mythological stories, and more recently rationally argued theoretic propositions – all of these go together to create a community. It is one system of acts and principles among many such systems, from monetary to military and literary systems. The religious community is not bound together by pure theory, or purely rational argument. They always rely ultimately on faith. In spite of Dawkins' arguments against Aquinas' "proofs" for God's existence, both Aquinas and the leaders of every other major faith all acknowledged that religion is never based on reason alone. And this faith is always grounded in the very highest moral ideals available to the community where a religion is born and thrives. They are by no means the same but they have a core of sameness – love-compassion, mercy, and help for the poor, sick, aged and downtrodden. These highest of moral ideals and the nature of the Ultimate always support each other; the musical rituals, meditation and the like elicit moods and motivations that wed moral ideals and the notions of the Ultimate together in a very believable fashion.

Let me conclude this chapter with a wise comment from Michael Shermer. Shermer agrees that religions were implicated in some human tragedies, such as wars in the name of God, suicide terrorism or intersect violence, but he goes on to make a point that most rationalists would endorse. According to him (2000, p. 71), there is a clearly significant positive point of the religions.

> *"However, for every one of these grand tragedies there are ten thousand acts of personal kindness and social good that go unreported. ... Religion, like all social institutions of such historical depth and cultural impact, cannot be reduced to an unambiguous good or evil."*

True religions and true Gods are certainly not evil, but false religions and fake gods are. Dawkins, in his various writings, clearly regards Shermer as a competent and sympathetic authority, but he is unwilling to adopt the balanced and judicious analysis that Shermer presents. It is very clear that Dawkins is not interested in the truth as such but is primarily concerned to defeat an ideological opponent by any available means. There are enough reasons for suspecting that the whole enterprise of *The God Delusion* was not, as it at least pretended to be, an attempt to discover and spread knowledge of the existence or non-existence of God; rather an attempt – an extremely successful one – to spread the author's own convictions in this area. Gross generalizations and careless statements about religion, exclusion and violence will simply delay and defer a solution of humanity's real problems. Any social scientist will agree that religion can cause problems, but it also has the capacity to transform, creating a deep sense of personal identity and value, and bringing social cohesion that Dawkins cannot see. The whole premise on which *The God Delusion* rests is therefore a delusion itself.

ADDENDUM 2: Closing thoughts: Militant Islam and Militant Atheism – both failed

"A philosophy whose principle is so incommensurate with our most intimate feelings as to deny them all relevancy in universal affairs, as to annihilate their motives at one blow, will be even more unpopular than pessimism – that is why materialism will always fail of universal adoption".

William James

"To know a person's religion we need not listen to his profession of faith but must find his brand of intolerance."

Eric Hoffer

"If power corrupts, then absolute power corrupts absolutely."

Ibn Warraq

Dr. Dawkins may not agree with me but his type of militant atheism will never be able to sweep God from the public arena. A god of terror like Allah and Dawkins' aggressive godlessness – both failed. Dawkins writes with erudition and sophistication on issues of evolutionary biology, but when he comes to deal with anything to do with God careful evidence-based reasoning seems to be left behind, and be displaced by rather heated, enthusiastic overstatements. Throughout Dawkins' writings, religious people are demonized as dishonest, liars, fools and knaves, incapable of responding honestly to the real world, and preferring to invent a false, pernicious and delusory world into which to entice the unwary, the young and the naive. But this is very similar how militant Muslims discredit the Infidels in a pure Islamic way. Dawkins believes that all the religions lead to evil. But this is not strictly a scientific judgment, in that, as Dawkins often points out, the sciences cannot determine what is good or evil. Elsewhere Dawkins himself said (2004, p. 34), *"Science has no methods for deciding what is ethical."* This raises my concern, because he is determined to replace religion with science and uncompromising atheism in spite of knowing the limitation of science.

In the Darwinian world that Dawkins inhabits and commends God has no entry. Certainly we theists are "faith-heads" in such a "scientific" world. But if such a "scientific" world cannot be described as evil, at least it cannot be described as good either, because science cannot decide what is ethical. Secondly, Dawkins fails to demonstrate the scientific necessity of aggressive atheism. It means militant atheism and militant Islam have something in common – both emerge as a blind faith, both impair human judgment. Dawkins (2006, p. 249) wrote,

"I do not believe there is an atheist in the world who would bulldoze Mecca - or Chartres, York Minster or Notre Dame, the Shwe Dagon, the temples of Kyoto or, of course, the Buddhas of Bamiyan".

Does Dawkins really believe every word he says? To believe that atheism had "nothing to do" with all this, is either ignorant or delusional. Mao Zedong, Joseph Stalin and their followers murdered millions in the name of an ideology that excluded God. In fact Joseph Stalin was one of millions, not only in Russia but in China, Cambodia, North Korea, Romania, Albania, Vietnam, Taiwan, Cuba, and other countries also, who put a third of the human race behind barbed wire and mines, destroyed great art, transformed great cities into endless, soulless stretches of grey concrete, turned children against their parents, taught citizens to distrust and hate one another, and tortured and murdered tens of millions of innocent people – all in the name of a "sacred" godlessness. Dawkins should get the error right. Though moral values can be separated from the belief in a God and atheism does not necessarily lead to moral bankruptcy, atheists are just as capable of moral atrocities as are theists. And it is equally clear that atheism is no safeguard against misery, anxiety and neurosis. This is something that Dawkins always overlooks. Let me direct the readers to twentieth century of Russia and China where the militant atheists did their best to destroy thousands of years of cultural wealth.

Militant atheism, as advocated by Lenin and the Russian Bolsheviks, treats religion as the dangerous opium and narcotic of the people, a wrong political ideology serving the interests of antirevolutionary forces; thus counter-force may be necessary to control or eliminate religion. The League of Militant Atheists (also known as Society of the Godless and Union of the Godless) was an atheistic and antireligious organization of workers and intelligentsia that developed in Soviet Russia under the influence of the ideological and cultural views and policies of the Communist Party in 1925–1947. Guided by Bolshevik principles of antireligious propaganda it propagated atheism in a militant way. By 1928 some 15,000 Russian Orthodox Churches were officially shut down, Church properties were seized through coercive tactics and were converted into buildings for Communist offices or activities. By 1941, less than eight percent churches were functioning (Froese, 2004, p. 41). In the 1930s, all church bells were confiscated and melted down for their precious metal (Luukkanen, 1997, p. 181). No longer would Soviet citizens hear the bells chiming a call to worship. Often the members conducted "individual work", that means sending atheist tutors to meet with individual believers to convince them of atheism, which could be followed up with public harassment if they failed to comply.

In 1929, society's name was changed to *The Union of Belligerent Atheists* (Ramet, 1993, p. 5). Now the society called for the extermination of religion "*at the tip of the bayonet*" (Koehler, 2009, p. 6). Emelian Yaroslavsky, Stalin's loyal aide in the secretariat, the leader of the union said that "*several hundred reactionary zealots of religion*" ("faith-heads" in Dawkins language) needed to be exterminated (Pospielovsky, 1987, p. 65). Elsewhere Yaroslavsky made the following declaration (Lee & Lee, 1972, p. 90),

> "*It is our duty to destroy every religious world-concept... If the destruction of ten million human beings, as happened in the last war, should be necessary for the triumph of one definite class, then that must be done and it will be done*".

In 1932 an antireligious five-year plan was adopted with the intention of annihilating religion in the USSR by force (Pospielovsky, 1987, p. 64). With the support and funding of the Soviet regime, the League of Militant Atheists launched an atheistic crusade that was intended to totally secularize Soviet society by 1937 (Froese, 2004, p. 37). The society took a violent approach to those who would not accept its message; example, *"bishops, priests, and lay believers"* were *"arrested, shot, and sent to labour camps"* (Ramet, 2005, p. 15). It was also demanded that no holidays should be allowed to coincide with important Church feast days and this policy was carried out immediately. Soon work schedules were created in such a way that always conflicted with religious holidays and the seven-day week was replaced with a six-day one (Pospielovsky, 1987, p. 56) – *"five days of work, the sixth off. The anti-religious propaganda believed this would be a most effective means of preventing believers from attending the Sunday liturgy. In addition, the 25th and 26th of December were proclaimed the Days of Industrialization with obligatory presence at work."*

The society also called on antireligious education to be instituted from the first-grade up. Two years later, further calls would be made to institute antireligious education among pre-school children – *"the bringing up of children in the atheist spirit"* as one of its primary missions (Van den Bercken, 1989, p. 138). Many schools daily ran through anti-religious lessons. The society also took advantage of rifts between different sects, including that between the orthodox and reformists, in order to get either side to vote for the closure of each other's religious structures (Pospielovsky, 1987, p. 59). In 1934, the leader (Yaroslavsky, 1934, p. 59) proudly declared,

> *"There can be no doubt that the fact that the new state of the USSR led by the communist party, with a program permeated by the spirit of militant atheism, gives the reason why this state is successfully surmounting the great difficulties that stand in its way - that neither 'heavenly powers' nor the exhortations of all the priests in all the world can prevent its attaining its aims it has set itself."*

Very similar to Dawkins, the leader of the society Yaroslavsky in 1937 claimed that all scholars and scientists who believe in God were insincere deceivers and swindlers (Pospielovsky, 1987, p. 63). The society aided the Soviet Government in killing clergy and committed theists on a regular basis, and made it a priority to remove religious icons from the homes of believers under the slogan, *"the Storming of Heaven"* (Stearns, 2008, p. 278). It also pressed for *"resolute action against religious peasants"* leading to the mass arrest and exile of many theists, especially village priests. Some clergymen and bishops even turned KGB informers and some became atheist proselytizers for the society (Ramet, 1998, pp. 229-30). By 1940 (Weeks, 2011, p. 167), *"over 100 bishops, tens of thousands of orthodox clergy, and thousands of monks and lay believers had been killed or had died in Soviet prisons and the Gulag"*.

In the late 1930s and early 40s, the climate of the campaign was changing and the society slowly became more moderate in its approach to religion. Yaroslavsky, in 1941, warned against condemning all religionists, but said that there were many loyal Soviet citizens still possessing religious beliefs. He called for patient and tactful individual work without offending the theists, but "re-educating" them. He claimed that religion had disappeared in some parts of the country but in other parts it was strong, and he warned against starting brutal offensives in those areas (Pospielovsky, 1987, p. 66). In spite of his threat, society's own figures (based on the 1937 census) found fifty-six percent of the population still held religious beliefs, even if they had no structures to worship in any longer and they could no longer openly express their theism (Fletcher, 1981, p. 211; Corley 1996, p. 76; Froese, 2004, p. 38). All the atheist journals of the society ceased to publish by September 1941. Though the official disbandment date is unknown, it is traced somewhere between 1941 and '47 and widespread killings of the theists by militant atheists nearly ended. During the final months of the Great Terror the *"personnel and cadres of the League of Militant Atheists movement were under heavy fire"* (Luukkanen, 1997, p. 161). Yaroslavsky and Stalin viewed the number of atheist converts (even with probable inflation) as utterly unsuccessful (Pospielovsky, 1987, pp. 65-7). Yaroslavsky turned his attention to other pursuits when he understood that his aggressive atheism propaganda had miserably failed even after so much brutality.

Communists expected individuals to abandon religion with fervor. As it turns out, though Russians had to stay away from the Russian Orthodox Church, they did not abandon religion as it was expected. Sectarian religious groups continued to flourish through the Soviet era and after the fall of the Soviet Union. In fact, the end of communism was greeted with religious revivals throughout Russia due to the activities of newly allowed religious movements (Greeley, 1994, pp. 253-73). To add salt to injury by mid century and toward the end of the Soviet era, Hare Krishnas, Jehovah's Witnesses, Seventh Day Adventists, and various "charismatic" sects entered the religious landscape. One could interpret the religious revivals throughout the former Soviet Union as a reflection of the degree to which Soviet citizens hid their true religious beliefs under militant atheism.

In the seventy-year old war on God in the Soviet Union, thousands of ancient churches, monasteries, temples and historical buildings were destroyed and many religious leaders were executed or sentenced to decades of hard labor. Religious groups were the victims of extreme violence and schools were flooded with militant atheist propaganda, but majority of older Soviet citizens retained their belief in God. Bolsheviks targeted Orthodox Churches and Monasteries, and clerics as potential sources of anti-religious activity. Church property was seized and religious leaders, monks, and nuns were often killed in the process. The terror of the Civil War sometimes spun out of control as murderous gangs took advantage of the fight: *"in many cases the tortures, murders and vandalism were the autonomous initiative of local anarchistic bands of army and naval deserters calling themselves Bolsheviks"* (Pospielovsky, 1988, p. 1). In addition to liquidating religious advocates, the Soviets also spread false information concerning religious activities. Many orthodox theists fill a corner of their home with the religious symbols and pray to them daily. The militant atheists composed various lies to justify their destruction. In one especially fierce effort to eradicate religious possessions, they *"claimed that an epidemic of syphilis in the countryside was being spread through the practice of kissing icons"* (Peris, 1998, p. 85). In contrast, the writings of Lenin were treated as sacred text from a Prophet and became the final justification of any act (Froese, 2004, p. 43). When Yugoslavian Vice-President Milovan Djilas visited Lenin's tomb in 1940s, he observed – "*as we descended into the Mausoleum, I saw how simple women in shawls were crossing themselves as though approaching the reliquary of a saint*" (Bourdeaux, 1965, p. 124). The most generous estimates of atheistic belief show that less than one-quarter of Russians were atheists and this number dramatically drops to around five percent of the population after the fall of communism.

Militant atheism equally failed in China. During the '70s China appeared to be the most secularized country in the world – people appeared to believe wholeheartedly in atheism. An American observer reported,

"*During our visit [to China in 1974] we saw almost no evidence of surviving religious practice. . . . We saw no functioning Buddhist temples. Some of those we visited had been converted to use as tea houses, hostels or assembly halls; others were maintained as museums*" (MacInnis, 1975, pp. 249, 251)

But what he saw was only on the surface, which was maintained by a terrifying godless dictatorship. At the turn of the twenty-first century, China may have become one of the most religious countries in the world. All kinds of religions, old or new, conventional or eccentric, are thriving in spite of atheist ideology and repressive religious policy of the government. Scholarship has shifted away from ideological atheism (mostly militant atheism) – a radical form of secularization theories – to a more scientific, objective approach that affirms both the positive and negative functions of religion.

Almost as soon as the Chinese Communist Party (CCP) took power in 1949, it followed the hard line of militant atheism. Within a decade all religions were brought under the iron control of the Party. The Religious Affairs Administration was dissolved, religious cadres were censured for their crime of following the wrong political line and all religious venues were closed (Dai, 2001, p. 43). Folk religious practices were vigorously suppressed or banned, foreign missionaries, considered part of Western imperialism, were expelled, and major world religions were coerced into patriotic national associations under close supervision of the Party, and academic research on religion was replaced by hardcore atheist propaganda. From 1967 to 1974, not a single article on religion was published in popular journals, magazines or newspapers in the People's Republic of China (Huang, 1998, p. 102). Scholarly research on religion completely ceased to exist. The authors, who wrote about religion in the past, were muted, and many of them suffered physical and psychological tortures, as did many religious believers. Many religionists who dared to challenge these policies were mercilessly banished to labor camps, jails, or execution grounds.

In spite of this, militant atheism and merciless suppression failed to eradicate religion in Chinese society. Many believers went underground – keeping one's faith to oneself or gathering in homes amidst vigilant secrecy. Instead of declining, religions persisted and resurfaced as soon as the suppression policy relaxed. Soon after 1978, the CPP changed religious policy from complete eradication to limited toleration, and a limited number of Christian churches, Buddhist temples and other religious sites were allowed to reopen, bringing religious life back to the public scene. CPP also acknowledged the mistakes of militant atheism. Within another few years books about religion began to be published, including introductions or general surveys of various religions. The overall tone of the publications gradually changed from completely negative criticism of religion to a more balanced evaluation. In the 1990s, several new religious journals were launched. A newly established publisher was even named, *Religious Culture Press*. Many "confirmed" atheists openly took Christian or Buddhist faith, though some of them had also advocated reformation in theology and religious organizations.

In sum; religious research in China has changed from virtual nonexistence from the 1950s to the 1970s to flourishing in the 1990s. Once the suppressive policy relaxed religious revivals burst through the vast land. In 2000, there were over sixty institutes focusing on religious research and over sixty journals on or of religion. This marks complete failure of militant atheism in China.

In Russia and China the dramatic increase of religious research and general inclination of the common citizen towards the God hypothesis has developed independently with its own internal dynamics in spite of state-sponsored atheistic terrorism. In less than one century theism ran the gamut from being thought dead, absolutely nonsensical, and irrational, to being found by many philosophers to be perfectly rational and intellectually fulfilling. In the era of increasing globalization, religious research in China and Russia is poised to expand and destined to merge into the global streams of religious scholarship. Certainly all these people who give priority to religion and God are not "faith-heads". Any form of atheism, even the initially well intentioned, if becomes an ideology constricts, shrinks and enslaves the atheist within and against himself and, eventually, as it reaches plague proportions among men, goes on to enslave and murder society. Those godless Communists taught us that once a man becomes ideologically dogmatic, he makes his tools the goal. A mere belief in god or godlessness has little psychological influence, but the belief in a system of doctrines structured around this belief more often claims a heavy psychological toll. Militant atheism is an intellectually bankrupt fallacy very similar to Islamic theocracy.

It is not the business of the democratic state to interfere with the freedom of religious belief or unbelief of its citizens. The state cannot make people spiritual or unspiritual by force, or by influence – this is an utter noncompliance of Article 18 of Universal Declaration of Human Rights of 1948. Citizens should be free to enter or leave any particular creed at any time as they want according to his conviction and conscience. Regretfully, neither militant Islam nor militant atheism had ever favored democratic tendencies. Article 18 (Melden, 1970, appendix) says,

> *"Everyone has the right to freedom of thought, conscience and religion; this right includes freedom to change his religion or belief, and freedom, either alone or in community with others and in public or private, to manifest his religion or belief in teaching, practice, worship and observance"*.

Terrorism in the name of godless is an almost exact mirror image of the Islamic terrorism in the name of Allah. Both are based on the quicksand of grand delusion, and therefore both often seem exotic or even extreme in the modern civilized world. Atheists proclaimed that religion was based on ignorance, but they repeatedly demonstrated their own incapacity to address the most basic questions from the theists.

Today, dozens of books are published every year that promote the atheist ideology. The chief target of these books is, without question, organized religion of any kind. Paradoxically, the books themselves read like fundamentalist sermons of the Qur'an. The authors, for the most part, sound like hellfire-and-brimstone preachers warning us of dire retribution, even of apocalypse, if we do not repent of our wayward beliefs and associated practices. There is no room for ambiguity or subtlety; it's black and white. Either you are with us all the way or one with the enemy. Even eminent thinkers who express some sympathy for the other side are denounced as traitors. This is the same mindset of the militant Muslims. But most of these books refuse to engage the real issues that involved the question of God's existence. Many of these authors even fail to address the central grounds for positing a divine reality. Flew and Varghese (2007, p. xv) wrote,

> "Dennett spends seven pages on the arguments for God's existence; Harris none. They fail to address the issue of the origins of the rationality embedded in the fabric of the universe, of life understood as autonomous agency, and of consciousness, conceptual thought, and the self. Dawkins talks of the origins of life and consciousness as "one-off" events triggered by an "initial stroke of luck." Wolpert writes: 'I have purposely [!] avoided any discussion of consciousness, which still remains mostly poorly understood.' About the origin of consciousness, Dennett, a die-hard physicalist, once wrote, "and then a miracle [!] happens. Neither do any of these writers present a plausible worldview that accounts for the existence of a "law-abiding," life-supporting, and rationally accessible universe."

When Antony Flew explained to Habermas that he was considering becoming a theist because certain philosophical and scientific considerations were causing him to do some serious rethinking and he characterized his position as that of atheism standing in tension with several huge question marks – "*the most impressive arguments for God's existence are those that are supported by recent scientific discoveries*" and that "*the argument to Intelligent Design is enormously stronger than it was when I first met it.*" (Flew & Habermas, 2004, p. 200), his fellow atheists verged on hysteria.

> "One atheist Web site tasked a correspondent with giving monthly updates on Flew's falling away from the true faith. Inane insults and juvenile caricatures were common in the freethinking blogosphere. The same people who complained about the Inquisition and witches being burned at the stake were now enjoying a little heresy hunting of their own. The advocates of tolerance were not themselves very tolerant. And, apparently, religious zealots don't have a monopoly on dogmatism, incivility, fanaticism, and paranoia." (Flew & Varghese, 2007, p. vi)

Richard Dawkins has made it clear that he argues against God on the basis of a generalized evolutionary assumption which he believes although he cannot prove it, while Antony Flew has made it clear that he now argues for God on the basis of scientific evidence that evolution is in principle unable to explain. Dawkins gives the impression that God belongs in a box marked "Things people believe even though they cannot prove it", but unconsciously he placed his militant atheism in the very same box, just as Flew took God out. On Flew's new conversion from atheism to theism, Dawkins commented,

> *"We might be seeing something similar today in the over-publicized tergiversation of the philosopher Antony Flew, who announced in his old age that he had been converted to belief in some sort of deity (triggering a frenzy of eager repetition all around the Internet)."* (2006, p. 82 footnote)

Dawkins's "old age" argument (if it can be called that) is a strange variation of the ad hominem fallacy. It has no place in an academic debate among the academicians. Ad hominem attack has no place in civilized discourse. True thinkers evaluate arguments and weigh the evidence without regard to the proponent's race, sex, or age. Also, history cannot be re-written by the raging mobs, and true thinkers cannot be silenced by ad-hominem attacks. Flew's position in the history of atheism transcends anything that today's militant atheists have on offer.

If we say atheism is scientific then it leads to another difficulty, as actual scientists avoid the topic of belief/disbelief in God in their scientific investigation. In the end, "scientific" atheism becomes an ideology, akin to Islamic ideology, that avoids the scientific methods altogether. Though scientific atheists may have initially discussed evidence for atheism, they soon fell into an ideological stance that did not allow for any actual discourse. The slaves of atheistic ideology and the slaves of Allah have come to accept that a realm lacking in factual reality is more real than their collective experience. Both wreak terror calling it peacekeeping and label the other's belief as absurd. Both call their followers holy while opponents are called evil. Both destroy but do not rebuild.

If it is not fair to judge all of atheism by what the disciples of Karl Marx made of it, then by the same reason it is foolishness of Dawkins to try to correlate God, religion and violence the way he does. We know that "religion" is an abstract term; it cannot be treated as a single, concrete entity. The way all of atheism is not violent, in the same way all of theism is not a significant force for evil in the world. I know of no evidence that religious people are more violent than people who lack faith in God, and Dawkins does not offer any. Allah is certainly a delusion, but not all the Gods. All the religions are not based on ignorance. Only a fake religion like Islam wants to keep the "slaves" in ignorance for keeping them in bondage.

A true religion instills ethical behavior, promotes human values, fraternity, respect, integrity, and the moral guidelines required for the construction of a better human society. Also, it tries to give a meaning, a purpose to life. In Hinduism; the guiding principles of the Vedas are truthfulness and nonviolence. Traditionally Hinduism (more specifically, Vedanta philosophy) is known to be Universalist and accepts all other religions to be true and valid. According to the authority of Bhagavad-Gita, the Absolute Truth is the objective of devotional sacrifice, which continues through many incarnations. As example; those who are devotees of other Gods and who worship them with faith actually worship only me (Lord Krishna) (Bhagavad-Gita: 9.23) and, I am the source of all spiritual and material worlds. Everything emanates from Me (Bhagavad-Gita: 10.8). In the Vedanta philosophy, the Supreme God teaches, *"Do not injure another. Love everyone as your own self, because the whole universe is one. In injuring another, I am injuring myself; in loving another, I love myself"*. The purpose of life is to develop, to grow, *abhudaya* (means, spiritual growth) in Sanskrit (Lokeswarananda, 2003, p. 3). In Buddhism, the peaceful way of life taught by Lord Buddha is a Universal Way – a way to personal, and collective (family, social and global) peace and happiness that everyone can cultivate, irrespective of his life situation. Buddha's teaching does not contradict the teaching of other great teachers. In Sikhism, we find similar wisdom – follow the Guru's (enlightened master) teachings and dwell in truth. Practice truth, and only truth, and merge in the true word of the Shabad (a sacred song) (Siri Guru Granth Sahib). Jains are followers of Jina (the conqueror of inner enemies). These inner enemies (Kashay) are anger (Krodh), greed (lobh), ego (man) and deceit (maya). They arise out of attachment (rag) – leading to greed and pride and aversion (dvesh) – leading to deceit and anger. Any activity of body, speech or mind that helps us eliminate our inner weaknesses; like anger, ego, deceit, greed (Kashay) is a Jain activity. There is no blind faith, no authoritative absolutism, and no biased dogma.

Great teachers, such as Socrates, Gandhi, Confucius, Lao Tze, Buddha and Jesus, opposed the control of the human spirit by the external forces of oppressive religions. They reminded individuals of the great potential power within the individual consciousness. Thus, Jesus taught that the kingdom of heaven is within each individual, not the property of a separate temple or church. Lao Tze reminded his followers of the original harmony of the individual with the natural and social totality, thereby pointing to limitless potential power for the individual who reconnects with species life. Spiritual quest should be a spontaneous activity; it cannot be imposed upon the individual by a satanic god or fanatic Prophet in the name of a revealed ideology. Anyone who claims, on the one hand, that he is concerned with human welfare, and who demands, on the other hand, that man must suspend or renounce the use of his reason, is contradicting himself. There can be no knowledge of what is good for man apart from knowledge of reality and human nature, and there is no manner in which this knowledge can be acquired except through reason. Buddha called upon every man to make use of his own reason to see the truth (Fromm, 1978, p. 38). The teachings of Buddha have changed millions of lives for the better. If everyone followed the Buddha's advice there would be no wars, no violence or crime, we could trust other people more, and feel much safer anywhere we live and anywhere we go. Jainism is a religion of self-help without any outside agency, not even the God. The soul is its own destroyer or liberator. Mahavira Jain said,

"Accept not what I say as truth because it is backed by tradition, or because it is the law of the land, or because it sounds good, or because it comes from your teacher. Accept as truth only that which is sagaciously acceptable to reason as well as sentiment."

These great teachers did not bring down any revelation in the name of a proud god, yet they had contributed much in the growth of the civilization. All of them were first rated moral philosophers. They are the pride of the humanity as a whole.

True religions are like water for our soul and our spirit; we need them. They teach us that revealing the true nature of our soul and the inherent qualities of our soul is *Dharma* (righteousness). The capacity to reach our goal is within us. Hindu seers repeatedly tell us that man can grow to the point of infinity, not physically but morally and spiritually. You and me are really one; if I hurt you I hurt myself. It is from this sense of unity that the ideas of love, compassion and non-violence have come (Lokeswarananda, 2003, p. 11). But Islam and militant atheism are two evil ideologies that endanger the lives of the masses, disturb the stability of the society and monopolize power. The common philosophical message of these two ideologies is crystal clear – reason and criticism must succumb to faith, blind obedience and threats of violence. Mankind will not lose a single moral precept if Islam and militant atheism are not there tomorrow.

The question of the future role of the religion in the society is far too important to leave to the religious fundamentalists or to atheist fundamentalists. If religious fundamentalism is a severe delusion about God, within the same logic might atheist fundamentalism be a delusion about God as well. Both live by faith not by reason, and wish the faith to rule, not through negotiation, but through brutal conquest and purposeful deception. None of them can raise the moral standard; in fact, the contrary seems to have been the case. They make us selfish, force us to hate others and make us think of ourselves only. Perfection comes when we identify ourselves with others, when we are able to share the fortunes and misfortunes of others – "*See yourself in others and see others in yourself*" – this is the essence of every true religion.

The world belongs to Human beings who consider all on its rational merits. The contingency of this life should make us aware of its beauty and preciousness, and we should try and improve it for as many people as possible. In this world, freedom is the birth-right of every Human being and no free man can conform his freedom to the dictates of another. This is the primary concern of every true religion. The pawns to the dead hands of evil ideologies cannot be the master of Human fate. There is no vacancy for "faith-heads" of a cruel god and the godless cruelty in our beautiful world. Both, disguised in morality, are profoundly anti-life, especially in terms of its psychological effects. Human misery is a sad spectacle, but it is still sad when disguised as moral righteousness.

References

Doctoral theses and Master's dissertations

1. Ahmed, Shahab (1999); *The Satanic Verses Incident in the Memory of the Early Muslim Community - An Analysis of the Early Riwayahs and their Isnads*. A dissertation presented at Princeton University.
2. Alvarez, Javier (1998); *Mysticism and Epilepsy*. A doctoral thesis submitted in May 1998. Faculty of Medicine. University of Murcia.
3. Arimbi, Diah Ariani (2006); *Reading the Writings of Contemporary Indonesian Muslim Women Writers: Representation, Identity and Religion of Muslim Women in Indonesian Fictions*. Ph.D thesis submitted in Sept. 2006, Women's and Gender Studies, Faculty of Arts and Social Sciences. University of New South Wales.
4. Bouman, Danielle (2011); *The neurobiological basis of hyper-religiosity*. Bachelor thesis in Cognitive Neuroscience. Department Psychology and Health. Submitted in June 2011. Section Cognitive Neuroscience. Tilburg University
5. Drane, Emma (2012); *Accelerated long-term forgetting of verbal material in adults with late-onset temporal lobe epilepsy*. Ph.D Thesis. Harris Manchester College, Trinity Term 2012. University of Oxford.
6. Lippincott, Cynthia E. (2010); *An Investigation of Extra-Temporal Deficits in Temporal Lobe Epilepsy*. Ph.D Thesis, submitted in Feb., 2010. Drexel University.
7. Pokel, Cindy A. (2000); *A critical analysis of research related to the criminal mind of serial killers*. Master's dissertation submitted in Aug. 2000. The Graduate College University of Wisconsin-Stout.

Journals

1. Adler Matthew (1997); *Where do voices come from?* J R Soc Med. Vol. 90.
2. Ahmed, Shahab (1998); *Ibn Taymiyyah and the Satanic Verses*. Studia Islamica, no. 87.
3. Ali M. and Ushijima H. (2005); *Perceptions of men's role of Muslim leaders in reproductive health issues in rural Pakistan*. J Biosoc Sci. Issue 37.
4. Andoh O, Tomizuka O, Sekiguchi H, Iimori M (1994); *A consideration on the meaning of invocation psychosis in today*. Seishinka Chiryougaku, volume 9. (Original in Japanese)
5. Appelbaum PS, Robbins PC, Roth LH (1999); *Dimensional approach to delusions: comparison across types and diagnoses*. Am J Psychiatry. Vol. 156, no. 12.
6. Bassetti, C.L; Bischof M; Valko P (2005); *Dreaming: a neurological view*. Schweiz Arch Neurol Psychiatr. Issue 8.
7. Bateson Gregory, Don D. Jackson, Jay Haley, and John Weakland (1956); *Toward a theory of schizophrenia*. Veterans Administration Hospital, Palo Alto, California; and Stanford University. Behavioral Science. Vol. 1, Issue 4.
8. Bayley, R. (1996); *First person account: Schizophrenia*. Schizophrenia Bulletin, Issue 22.

9. Bear, D. M., & Fedio, P. (1977); *Quantitative analysis of interictal behavior in temporal lobe epilepsy*. Archives of Neurology, Issue 34.

10. Bear, D., Levin, K., Blumer, D., Chetham, D., & Reider, J. (1982); *Interictal behavior in hospitalized temporal lobe epileptics: Relationship to idiopathic psychiatric syndromes*. Journal of Neurology Neurosurgery & Psychiatry, Issue 45.

11. Beard AW (1963); *The schizophrenia-like psychoses of epilepsy, (ii) Physical aspects*. Brit J Psychiat Issue 109.

12. Bearden, C. W., Hoffman, K. M., & Cannon, T. D. (2001); *The neuropsychology and neuroanatomy of bipolar affective disorder: A critical review*. Bipolar Disorder, Vol. 3.

13. Benjamin L. S. (1989); *Is chronicity a function of the relationship between the person and the auditory hallucination?* Schizophrenia Bulletin. Vol. 15

14. Bjorkly S. (2002); *Psychotic symptoms and violence toward others - a literature review of some preliminary findings*. Part 1. Delusions. Aggressive Violence Behavior. Issue 7

15. Bjorkly S. (2002a); *Psychotic symptoms and violence toward others - a literature review of some preliminary findings. Part 2.* Hallucinations. Aggressive Violent Behavior. Issue 7.

16. Boven W (1919); *Religiosite et epilepsie*. Schweiz Arch Neurol u Psychiat. Issue 4.

17. Brewerton, T. D. (1994); *Hyperreligiosity in psychotic disorders*. Journal of Nervous and Mental Disease, Issue 182.

18. Brugger, P., & Graves, R. E. (1997); *Testing vs. believing hypotheses: Magical ideation in the judgment of contingencies.* Cognitive Neuropsychiatry, Issue 2

19. Buckley, P. (1981); *Mystical experience and schizophrenia*. Schizophrenia Bulletin, Issue 7.

20. Cannon, B. J., & Kramer, L, M. (2012); Delusion content across the 20th century in an American psychiatric hospital. Int. Journal of Social Psychiatry. Vol. 58

21. Carrazana, E, DeToledo, J, Tatum, W, Rivas-Vasquez, R, Rey, G, and Wheeler, S. (1999); *Epilepsy and religious experiences: voodoo possession*. Epilepsia, Vol. 40

22. Castillo, R. (2003); *Trance, functional psychosis, and culture*. Psychiatry, Issue 66.

23. Chadwick, P. and Birchwood, M. (1994); *The Omnipotence of Voices: A Cognitive Approach to Auditory Hallucinations*. British Journal of Psychiatry .Vol. 164.

24. Chen E, Berrios G.E. (1996*); Recognition of hallucinations: a multidimensional model and methodology.* Psychopathology. Issue 29.

25. Cheng, WW; Otsubo, H and Snead, O. E (2001); *Surgery for intractable epilepsy in a 14-year-old girl*. HKMJ. Vol. 7 no. 1 (March issue). Department of Paediatrics, Caritas Medical Centre. Hong Kong.

26. Cheung P, Schweitzer I, Crowley K, Tuckwell V (1997); *Violence in schizophrenia: role of hallucinations and delusions*. Schizophr Res. Issue 26.

27. Coid J. (1996); *Dangerous patients with mental illness: increased risks warrant new policies, adequate resources and appropriate legislation*. Br Med J Issue 312.

28. Cothran, M. M., and Harvey, P. D. (1986); *Delusional thinking in psychotics: Correlates of religious content*. Psychological Reports, Issue 58.

29. Covington Michael A.; T, Congzhou He; Cati Brown; Lorina Naci; Jonathan T. McClain; Bess Sirmon Fjordbak; James Semple, John Brown (2005); *Schizophrenia and the structure of language: The linguist's view*. Schizophrenia Research, Vol. 77

30. Crow, T. J., Cross A. J, Johnstone E.C , Owen F, Owens D. G. C, and Waddington J. L. (1982); *Abnormal involuntary movements in schizophrenia: Are they related to the disease process or its treatment? Are they associated with changes in dopamine receptors?* Journal of Clinical Psychopharmacology. Issue 2.

31. Currie S, Heathfield K. , and Henson R. A, (1971); *Clinical course and prognosis*

of temporal lobe epilepsy. A survey of 666 patients. Brain; Issue 94 suppl. 1.

32. Davidson, L., & Strauss, J. S. (1992); *Sense of self in recovery from severe mental illness.* British Journal of Medical Psychology, Issue 65.

33. Davies, M. and Coltheart, M. (2000); *Introduction: pathologies of belief. Mind & Language.* Vol. 15. suppl.1.

34. Davies, M., Coltheart, M., Langdon, R. and Breen, N. (2001); *Monothematic delusions: towards a two-factor account.* Philosophy, Psychiatry, and Psychology Volume 8, Number 2/3, June/September 2001.

35. Devinsky O (2003); *Religious experiences and epilepsy.* Epilepsy Behavior. Vol. 4.

36. Devinsky, O., and Lai, G. (2008); *Spirituality and religion in epilepsy.* Epilepsy & Behavior, Issue 12

37. Dewhursta, Kenneth and Beard A.W. (1970); *Sudden religious conversions in temporal lobe epilepsy.* British Journal of Psychiatry. Issue 117.

38. Diederen, K., Neggers, S., Daalman, K., Blom, J., Goekoop, R., Kahn, R., et al. (2010); *Deactivation of the parahippocampal gyrus preceding auditory hallucinations in schizophrenia.* The American Journal of Psychiatry, Issue 167 suppl. 4.

39. Docherty N, Schnur M, Harvey PD. (1988); *Reference performance and positive and negative thought disorder: a follow-up study of maniacs and schizophrenics.* J Abnorm Psychol. Vol. 97

40. Dodrill, C. B. (1992); *Neuropsychological aspects of epilepsy.* Psychiatric Clinics of North America, Vol. 15, Issue 2.

41. Falloon I. R and Talbot (1981); *Persistent auditory hallucinations: coping mechanisms and implications for management.* Psychological Medicine. Vol. 11.

42. Feldman, J., and Rust, J. (1989); *Religiosity, schizotypal thinking, and schizophrenia.* Psychological Reports, Issue 65.

43. Fisher, R. S., Emde Boas, W., Blume, W., Elger, C., Genton, P., Lee, P., & Engel, J., Jr. (2005); *Epileptic seizures and epilepsy: Definitions proposed by the International League Against Epilepsy (ILAE) and the International Bureau for Epilepsy (IBE).* Epilepsia, Vol. 46, Issue 4.

44. Foote-Smith E., and L. Bayne (1991); *Joan of Arc.* Epilepsia. Issue 32.6 (Nov-Dec, 1991).

45. Francis, L. J., & Wilcox, C. (1996); *Prayer, church attendance, and personality revisited: A study among 16- to 19-yr-old girls.* Psychological Reports, Issue 79.

46. Gearing, R. E., Alonzo, D., Smolak, A., McHugh, K., Harmon, S., & Baldwin, S. (2011); *Association of religion with delusions and hallucinations in the context of schizophrenia: Implications for engagement and adherence.* Schizophrenia Research. Vol. 126, Issue 1.

47. Geschwind N (1983); *Interictal behavioralchangesin epilepsy.* Epilepsia. Vol. 24, Suppl. 1.

48. Geschwind, N. (1979); *Behavioural changes in temporal lobe epilepsy.* Psychological Medicine, Issue 9.

49. Getz, G. , Fleck, D., and Strakowski, S. (2001); *Frequency and severity of religious delusions in Christian patients with psychosis.* Psychiatry Research, Issue 103.

50. Glaser GH (1964); *The problem of psychosis in psychomotor temporal lobe epileptics.* Epilepsia. Issue 5.

51. Goldwert, M. (1993); *The messiah-complex in schizophrenia.* Psychological Reports, Issue 73.

52. Gould LN (1948); *Verbal hallucinations and activity of vocal musculature.* AmJ Psychiat. Issue 105.

53. Hall R.C.W, Popkin M.K, Devaul R.A, Faillace L.A and Stickney S.K (1978); *Physical illness presenting as psychiatric disease.* Arch Gen Psychiatry. Vol. 35.

54. Hamri, Najat El (2010); *Approaches to family planning in Muslim communities*. J Family Planning Reproduction. Health Care. Vol. 36, issue1.
55. Hellerstein D, Frosch W, Koenigsberg H (1987); *The clinical significance of command hallucinations*. Am J Psychiatry. Vol. 144.
56. Helmstaedter C, Elger CE, Lendt M. (1994); *Postictal courses of cognitive deficits in focal epilepsies*. Epilepsia. Vol. 35, issue 5.
57. Hermann, B. P., Seidenberg, M., Schoenfeld, M. A., & Davies, K. (1997); *Neuropsychological characteristics of the syndrome of mesial temporal lobe epilepsy*. Archives of Neurology, Vol. 54,
58. Hodgins, S. and Cote, G. (1993); *The criminality of mentally disordered offenders*. Criminal Justice and Behavior, Vol. 2, Issue 2.
59. Humphreys M, Johnstone E, MacMillan J, and Taylor P. (1992); *Dangerous behavior preceding first admissions for schizophrenia*. Br J Psychiatry. Issue 161
60. Hutsebaut, D. and Verhoeven D. (1995); *Studying Dimensions of God Representation: Choosing Closed or Open-ended Research Questions*. The International Journal for the Psychology of Religion. Westmont College.
61. Hyde, T. M., and Weinberger, D. R. (1997); *Seizures and schizophrenia*. Schizophrenia Bulletin, Issue 23.
62. Junginger J. (1990); *Predicting compliance with command hallucinations*. Am J Psychiatry. Issue 147
63. Junginger J (1995); *Command hallucinations and the prediction of dangerousness*. Psychiatry Serv. Vol. 46
64. Junginger J. (1996); *Psychosis and violence: the case for a content analysis of psychotic experience*. Schizophr Bull. Issue 22
65. Kanemoto, K., Kawasaki, K., & Kawai, I. (1996); *Postictal psychosis: A comparison with acute interictal and chronic psychoses*. Epilepsia, Issue 37.
66. Kanner AM (2004); *Recognition of the various expressions of anxiety, psychosis, and aggression in epilepsy*. Epilepsia. Issue 45 (suppl. 2).
67. Karagulla S. and Robertson EE (1955); *Physical phenomena in temporal lobe epilepsy and the psychoses*. British Medical Journal. Issue 1.
68. Kroll, J., and Sheehan, W. (1989); *Religious beliefs and practices among fifty-two psychiatric patients in Minnesota*. American Journal of Psychiatry, Issue 146.
69. Langfeldt, John A., (1994); *Recently Discovered Early Christian Monuments in Northeastern Arabia*. Arabian Archaeology and Epigraphy, Vol. 1. Issue. 5
70. Langfitt, J. T (1995); *Comparison of the Psychometric Characteristics of Three Quality of Life Measures in Intractable Epilepsy*. Quality of Life Research. Issue 4.2. (April, 1995). JSTOR.
71. Laurent, John (1999); *A Note on the Origin of 'Memes'/'Mnemes'*. Journal of Memetics. Evolutionary models of information transwmiswsion, Vol. 3, Issue 1.
72. Loo, C., Sainsbury, K., Mitchel, P., Hadzi-Pavlovic, D., and Sachdev, P. (2010); *A sham-controlled trial of left and right temporal rTMS for the treatment of auditory hallucinations*. Psychological Medicine: A Journal of Research in Psychiatry and the Allied Sciences, Issue 40 (suppl. 4)
73. MacInnis, Donald (1975); *The Secular Vision of a New Humanity in People's China*. Christian Century. Issue March 12.
74. Magiorkinis, E.; Sidiropoulou, K. & Diamantis, A. (2010); *Hallmarks in the history of epilepsy: epilepsy in antiquity*. Epilepsy Behavior, Vol. 17
75. Maltby, J. (1997); *Personality correlates of religiosity among adults in the Republic of Ireland*. Psychological Reports, Issue 81.
76. McAllister, T. W. (1998); *Traumatic brain injury and psychosis: What is the connection?* Seminars in Clinical Neuropsychiatry, Issue 3.
77. McGuigan FJ (1966); *Covert oral behaviour and auditory hallucinations*.

Psychophysiology. Issue 3.
78. Mellor, C. H. (1970); *First rank symptoms of schizophrenia.* British Journal of Psychiatry. Issue. 117.
79. Mendez, M.F, Cherrier M. M and Perryman K.M (1996); *Epileptic forced thinking from left frontal lesions,* Neurology. Issue. 47.
80. Mitchell J, and Vierkant A. D (1989); *Delusions and hallucinations as a reflection of the subcultural milieu among psychotic patients of the 1930's and 1980's.* J. Pers. Soc. Psychol, Vol. 125.
81. Miyamoto T and Oda S (1965); *Religious psychopathology.* In Imura *et al.* (eds) Lectures of abnormal psychology. Misuzu Press; Tokyo. (Original in Japanese).
82. Modestin J, and Ammann R. (1996); *Mental disorder and criminality: male schizophrenia.* Schizophr Bull. Issue 22.
83. Mohr S, Borras L and Betrisey C. (2010); *Delusions with religious content in patients with psychosis: how they interact with spiritual coping.* Psychiatry. Vol. 73, Issue. 2.
84. Monahan J (1992); *Mental disorder and violent behavior: perceptions and evidence.* Am Psychol. Issue 47.
85. Monahan, J. (1992a); *A terror to their neighbors: Beliefs about mental disorder and violence in historical and cultural perspective.* Bulletin of the American Academy of Psychiatry and the Law, Vol. 20 (Suppl. 2).
86. Morita S (1915); *So-called psychosis induced by invocation.* Psychiat Neurol Jap (Original n Japanese). Vol. 14.
87. Nakaya, Makoto and Ohmori , Kenich (2010); *Psychosis Induced by Spiritual Practice and Resolution of Pre-Morbid Inner Conflicts.* The German Journal of Psychiatry, Dept. of Psychiatry. The University of Gottingen, Germany.
88. Nakayama K (2008); *Significance of "psychosis induced by invocation" study to precede conclusion of Morita therapy.* Japanese Journal of Morita Therapy. Vol. 19 (Original in Japanese)
89. Nawata H and Nishimura R (2005); *A case of invocations psychosis induced by baptism in a religious organization.* Seishinka. Vol. 7 (Original in Japanese)
90. Nayani T.H and David A.S (1996); *The auditory hallucination: a phenomenologic survey.* Psychol Med. Vol. 26
91. Nielsen, M. E. (2000); *Descriptions of religious experience using trait and affect adjectives.* Psychological Reports. Issue 86.
92. Nozaki Y, Okada Y, Arai M and Nagata T (1992); *A case of brief reactive psychosis induced by self-improvement seminar: an aspect of invocations psychosis in Japan.* Japanese Journal of Clinical Psychiatry. Vol. 21(Original in Japanese).
93. Ogata, A., and Miyakawa, T. (1998); *Religious experiences in epileptic patients with a focus on ictus-related episodes.* Psychiatry and Clinical Neurosciences. On-line journal. Issue 52.
94. Oleson, J. C. (2006); *Contemporary demonology: The criminological theories of Hannibal Lecter,* (Part two). Journal of Criminal Justice and Popular Culture (The School of Criminal Justice, University at Albany). Issue 13.
95. Owens, D. G. C., Johnstone E. C and Frith C. D (1982); *Spontaneous involuntary disorders of movement.* Archives of General Psychiatry. Issue 39.
96. Panayiotopoulos CP (1999); *Elementary visual hallucinations, blindness, and headache in idiopathic occipital epilepsy: differentiation from migraine.* J Neurol Neurosurg Psychiatry. Vol. 66 (Suppl. 4).
97. Persinger, M. A. (1993); *Vectorial cerebral hemisphericity as differential sources for the sensed presence, mystical experiences and religious conversions.* Perceptual and Motor Skills, Issue 76.
98. Persinger, M. A. (1994); *Sense of a presence and suicidal ideation following*

traumatic brain injury: Indications of right-hemispheric intrusions from neuropsychological profiles. Psychological Reports, Issue 75.

99. Persinger, M. A., & Makarec, K. (1987); *Temporal lobe epileptic signs and correlative behaviors displayed by normal populations.* Journal of General Psychology, Vol. 114.

100. Peters, E., Day, S., McKenna, J., and Orbach, G. (1999); *Delusional ideation in religious and psychotic populations.* British Journal of Clinical Psychology (British Psychological Society, published by Wiley-Blackwell). Issue 38.

101. Pickard, Hanna (2010); *Schizophrenia and the Epistemology of self-knowledge.* EuJAP. Vol. 6, no. 1. Oxford Centre for Neuroethics and All Souls College, University of Oxford.

102. Pirkner, E. H. (1929); *Epilepsy in the light of history.* Ann Med Hist, Vol. 1.

103. Rescher, Nicholas (1985); *The strife of systems: An essay on the grounds and implications of philosophical diversity.* University of Pittsburg press. Pittsburg.

104. Roberts, G., and Owen, J. (1988); *The near-death experience.* British Journal of Psychiatry. Issue 153.

105. Roberts G.W, Done D.J, Bruton C, and Crow TJ (1990); *A "mock up" of schizophrenia: temporal lobe epilepsy and schizophrenia-like psychosis.* Biol Psychiatry. Issue 28.

106. Rogers R, Gillis J.R, Turner R.E, Frise-Smith T. (1990); *The clinical presentation of command hallucinations in a forensic population.* Am J Psychiatry. Vol. 147.

107. Rogers R, Nussbaum D, Gillis R (1988); *Command hallucinations and criminality: a clinical quandary.* Bulletin of the American Academy of Psychiatry and the Law. (Published by the American Academy of Psychiatry and the Law). Vol. 16.

108. Roman, R. E., and Lester, D. (1999); *Religiosity and mental health.* Psychological Reports, Issue 85.

109. Romme A. J. and Escher, A D. (1989); *Hearing voices.* Schizophrenia Bulletin (Oxford Journals on Medicine). Vol. 15, Issue. 2.

110. Runions, J. E. (1979); *The mystic experience: A psychiatric reflection.* Canadian Journal of Psychiatry, Issue 24.

111. Roudi-Fahimi F (2004); *Islam and family planning.* Population Reference Bureau. Washington, DC

112. Sachdev, P. (1998); *Schizophrenia-like psychosis and epilepsy: The status of the association.* American Journal of Psychiatry, Issue 155.

113. Sakurai T (1938); *Four cases of invocation psychosis.* Rinshoujikken. Vol 16 (Original in Japanese).

114. Saver, J. L., & Rabin, J. (1997); *The neural substrates of religious experience.* Journal of Neuropsychiatry and Clinical Neurosciences, Issue 9.

115. Sedman G. (1966); *Being an epileptic: a phenomenological study of epileptic experiences.* Psychiat Neurol Issue 152.

116. Shaner, A., and Eth, S. (1989); *Can schizophrenia cause posttraumatic stress disorder?* American Journal of Psychotherapy, Issue 4.

117. Shehadeh, Imad (2004); *Do Muslims and Christians Believe in the Same God?* Bibliotheca sacra. Vol. 161, number 641.

118. Sherwin, I. (1984); *Differential psychiatric features in epilepsy; relationship to lesion laterality.* Acta Psychiatrica Scandinavica, Volume 70 (Suppl. 313).

119. Siddle R, Haddock G, Tarrier N (2002); *Religious delusions in patients admitted to hospital with schizophrenia.* Soc Psychiatry Psychiatr Epidemiol. Vol. 37, no. 3.

120. Slater E and Beard A.W (1963); *The schizophrenia-like psychoses of epilepsy.* Brit J Psychiat. Issue 109.

121. Slater E, Glithero E and Beard AW (1963); *The schizophrenia-like psychosis of epilepsy.* Br J Psychiatry Vol. 109.

122. Spence, Sean (1996); *Free will in the light of neuropsychiatry*. Philosophy, Psychiatry, and Psychology, Vol, 3, number 2.

123. Spencer, J. (1975); *The mental health of Jehovah's Witnesses*. British Journal of Psychiatry, Issue 126.

124. Stinson, K., Valmaggia, L., Antley, A., Slater, M., & Freeman, D. (2010); *Cognitive triggers of auditory hallucinations: An experimental investigation*. Journal of Behavior Therapy and Experimental Psychiatry, Issue 41 (suppli. 3).

125. Stompe T., Friedmann A., Ortwein G., Strobl R., Chaudhry H.R, Najam N., (1999); *Comparison of delusions among schizophrenics in Austria and Pakistan*. Psychopathology. Vol. 32.

126. Stueve A, and Link B. (1997); *Violence and psychiatric disorders: results from an epidemiological study in Israel*. Psychiatry Quarterly Issue 68.

127. Swanson J, Holzer C, Ganju V, and Jono R. (1990); *Violence and psychiatric disorder in the community: evidence from the Epidemiologic Catchment Area surveys*. Hosp Community Psychiatry. Issue 41.

128. Tardiff K. (1998); *Unusual diagnoses among violent patients*. Diagnostic Dilemmas. Issue 21.

129. Tateyama, M., Asai, M., Hashimoto, M., Bartels, M., Kasper, S., (1998); *Transcultural study of schizophrenic delusions: Tokyo versus Vienna versus Tubingen (Germany)*. Psychopathology. Vol. 31. Issue 2

130. Taylor P. (1998); *When symptoms of psychosis drive serious violence*. Soc Psychiatry Psychiatr Epidemiol Suppl. 1.

131. Taylor PJ, Leese M, Williams D (1998); *Mental disorder and violence: a special (high security) hospital study*. Br J Psychiatry. Issue 172

132. Temkin, O. (1942); *A medieval translation of rhaze's clinical observations*. Bull Hist Med, Vol. 12.

133. Thomas, Kenneth, (2006); *Allah in the Translation of the Bible*. International Journal of Frontier Missions. Vol. 4. Issue 23.

134. Thompson JS, Stuart GL, Holden CE (1992); *Command hallucinations and legal insanity*. Forensic Reports. Vol. 5.

135. Trimble, M., and Freeman, A. (2006); *An investigation of religiosity and the Gastaut-Geschwind syndrome in patients with temporal lobe epilepsy*. Epilepsy & Behavior, Issue 9.

136. Wessely S., Buchanan A., and Reed A., (1993); *Acting on delusions. I: Prevalence*. Br J Psychiatry Issue 163.

137. Willis, John Ralph (1967); *Jihad fi Sabil Allah- Its Doctrinal Basis in Islam and Some Aspects of Evolution in Nineteenth-Century West Africa*. The Journal of African History. Volume 8, no. 3.

138. Winnett, Frederick V. (1938); *Allah before Islam*. The Muslim World. Vol. 28. Issue 3.

139. Woodberry, J. Dudley (1996); *Contextualization Among Muslims: Reusing Common Pillars*. International Journal of Frontier Missions, Vol.4. Issue 13.

140. Yasuda M., Ohsawa T., Kobayashi S. and Katoh S. (2008); *A 30-aged woman of invocations psychosis with childcare stress*. Tochigi Seishinigaku. Vol. 28 (Original in Japanese)

Newspapers

1. Aziz, Q. (1991); *Pakistan and the Demographic Challenge*. The Pakistan Times, April 26 Issue, 1991.

2. Briggs, David (1992); *Science, Religion Are Discovering Commonality in Big Bang Theory*. Los Angeles Times. 2nd May Issue, 1992

3. Wisnu A. (2009); *Population control: 'a weapon of the West'*. The Jakarta Post, 27 July 2009 issue.

Books, Magazines and Reports

1. (Brig.) Malik, S. K (2008); *The Qur'anic Concept of War*. Adam Publishers and Distributors. New Delhi. India.
2. (Dr.) Bhaumik, Mani Lal (2005); *Code Name God: The Spiritual Odyssey of a Man of Science*. The Crossroad Publishing Company, NY.
3. (Dr) Joseph, Rhawn (2002); *NeuroTheology: Brain, Science, Spirituality, Religious Experience*. University Press, San Jose, California
4. (Dr.) Ayoub, Mahmoud (1992); *The Qur'an and Its Interpreters, Vol. II The House of Imran*. State University of New York Press, Albany.
5. (Dr.) Razzaque, Russell (2008); *Human Being to Human Bomb*. Icon Books Ltd. Cambridge.
6. (Dr.) Bishara, Safwat (2011); *A Journey of Faith: Moving from the Middle East to the West*. iUniverse. Bloomington
7. (Ed.) Bjorgo, Tore (2005); *Root Causes of Terrorism; Myths, Reality and Ways Forward*. Routledge. Taylor and Francis Group. Abingdon. UK.
8. (Ed.) Broome M and Bortolotti L. (2009); *Psychiatry as Cognitive Neuroscience: Philosophical Perspectives*. Oxford University Press.
9. (Ed.) Foyaca-Sibat, Humberto (2011); *Novel Aspects on Epilepsy*. InTech. Croatia.
10. (Ed) Ramet, Sabrina Petra (1993); *Religious Policy in the Soviet Union*. Cambridge University Press
11. (Eds) Shienbaum Kim and Hasan Jamal (2006); *Beyond Jihad, Critical Voices from the Inside*. Academica Press, LLC. Bethesda.
12. (ed. & trans) Barrett, W.P. (1932); *The Trial of Joan of Arc*. Medieval Sourcebook. Gotham House.
13. (ed.) Felty, David (1997); *Faith and Morals*. University Press of America. Maryland.
14. (ed.) Momigliano, A. (1963); *The Conflict between Paganism and Christianity in the 4th Century*. The Clarendon Press. Oxford.
15. (eds.) Beeston A., Johnstone T.M; Serjeant R.B and Smith R.B (1983); *Arabic Literature to the End of the Umayyad Period*. Cambridge University Press. Cambridge and New York.
16. (Ed.) Temkin O. (1971); *The falling sickness: A history of epilepsy from the Greeks to the beginnings of modern neurology*, 105, The John Hopkins University Press, Ltd, London.
17. (Sir) Muir William (1992); *The Life of Muhammad* (first published in London in 1894). Reprinted by Voice of India. Delhi. India.
18. Adil, Hajjah Amina (2002); *Muhammad, the messenger of Islam: his life & prophecy*. Islamic Supreme Council of America. Washington DC.
19. Adler, Mortimer J. (1967); *The Difference of Man and the Difference it Makes*. Holt, Rinehart and Winston. NY
20. Ahmad, Mahmood bin (2006); *The magnificence of the Qur'an*. Maktaba Dar-us-Salam. Riyadh.
21. Alford, Diane and Hill, Jennifer (2008); *Excel HSC biology*. Pascal Press. Sydney.
22. Ali, Abdullah Yusuf (1983); *The Holy Qur'an: Translation and Commentary*. Amana Corp., Brentwood, Maryland.
23. Armstrong, Karen (2001); *Islam: A Short History*. Phoenix Press. A division of the Orion Publishing Group Ltd. London

24. Asad, Muhammad (1993); *The Message of the Qur'an*. Dar al-Andalus Limited, 3 Library Ramp Gibraltar.
25. Batchelor, Stephen (1994); *The awakening of the west: the encounter of Buddhism and Western culture*. Parallax Press. California.
26. Bell, R, and Watt W. M. (1977); *Introduction to the Quran*. Edinburgh.
27. Berger, Peter L. (1990); *The sacred canopy: elements of a sociological theory of religion*. Anchor Press. NY.
28. Bourdeaux, M. (1965); *Opium of the people: The Christian religion in the USSR*. Faber and Faber. London
29. Brodie, Richard (2009); *Virus of the mind: The New Science of the Meme*. Hay House UK Ltd. London
30. Buber, M. (1995); *Ecstatic Confessions*, Editions Grasse & Fasquelle. Paris.
31. Caird, John (1956); *An introduction to the philosophy of religion*. Chakravarti and Chatterjee Publishers. Calcutta. India.
32. Carlyle T (1973); *Sartor Resartus: On Heroes and Hero Worship*. J. M Dent and sons. London,
33. Celestine N. Bittle (1936); *Reality and the Mind*. The Bruce Publishing Co., NY.
34. Charles R. H. (1999); *The Book of the Secrets of Enoch*. Book Tree. USA.
35. Claridge, G.S., Pryor, R. and Watkins, G. (1990); *Sounds from the Bell Jar: Ten Psychotic Authors*. The Macmillan Press Ltd. London.
36. Clifford W.K (1897); *The ethics of belief, in Lectures and Essays*. Macmillan. London.
37. Cohen, Jared (2007); *Children of Jihad*. Gotham Books. Penguin Group. NY.
38. Collins, Francis (2007); *The Language of God*. Simon Schuster. London.
39. Cook, M, and Crone, P, (1977); *Hagarism: The Making of the Muslim World*. Cambridge.
40. Cook, David (2005); *Understanding Jihad*. University of California Press. USA.
41. Corley, F. (1996); *Religion in the Soviet Union*. McMillian Press. London.
42. Cornwell, John (2008); *Darwin's angel*. Profile books. London
43. Cragg, Kenneth, (1991); *The Arab Christian: A History in the Middle East*. John Knox Press Lousiville: Westminster.
44. Dai, Kangsheng (2001); *Xin zhongguo zongjiao yanjiu 50 nian (50 Years of Religious Research in New China)*. Annual of Religious Research in China, 1999–2000. Religious Culture Press. Beijing.
45. Dasti, Ali (1985); *Twenty-Three Years: A study of the Prophetic Career of Mohammad*. Allen and Unwin, London
46. Dawkins, Richard (1989); *The Selfish Gene*. Oxford University Press.
47. Dawkins, Richard (1996); *The Blind Watchmaker: Why the Evidence of Evolution Reveals a Universe without Design*. Norton, NY.
48. Dawkins, Richard (2004); *A Devil's Chaplain: Reflections on Hope, Lies, Science, and Love*. Houghton Mifflin Harcourt.
49. Dawkins, Richard (2006); *The God Delusion*. Bantam Press (a division of Transworld Publishers). London
50. Depp FC (1983); *Assaults in a public mental hospital*. In "Assaults Within Psychiatric Facilities". Edited by Lion JR, Reid WH. Grune and Stratton. NY.
51. DeRiver, J.P. (1949); *Crime and the sexual psychopaths*. Charles C. Thomas. Springfield, IL.
52. Desai, Meghnad (2007); *Rethinking Islamism – The Ideology of the New Terror*. T.J International Ltd. Padstow. Cornwall. GB.
53. Dodds E R (1951); *The Greeks and the Irrational*. University of California Press. Berkeley.

54. DSM-IV-TR (2000); *Diagnostic and Statistical Manual for Mental Disorders.* (Fourth edition). The American Psychiatric Association.
55. Durant, Will (1950); *The story of civilization – The age of faith.* Simon and Schuster. NY.
56. Elster Jon (1986); *Karl Marx: A Reader.* Cambridge University Press. UK.
57. Encyclopedia Britannica (1993), Vol. 3.
58. Fallaci, Oriana (2006); *The Force of Reason.* Rizzoli Int. Publication Inc. NY.
59. Fletcher, W. C. (1981); *Soviet believers: The religious sector of the population.* Regents Press. Lawrence, KS:
60. Flew, Antony (1984); *God, Freedom and Immortality.* Amherst, NY.
61. Flew, Antony, Roy Abraham Varghese (2007); *There Is A God: How the World's Most Notorious Atheist Changed His Mind.* HarperCollins. NY
62. Fox, J. A., and J. Levin. (1989); *Satanism and Mass Murders.* Celebrity Plus.
63. Freud, Sigmund (1939); *Moses and Monotheism.* Vintage Books.
64. Frith, Christopher (1992); *The cognitive neuropsychology of schizophrenia.* Lawrence Erlbaum Associates. Hillsdale, NJ.
65. Frith, Christopher (1992a); *Cognitive Neuropsychology of Schizophrenia.* Taylor & Francis. Hove: Erlbaum. UK.
66. Froese, Paul (2004); *Forced Secularization in Soviet Russia: Why an Atheistic Monopoly Failed.* Journal for the Scientific Study of Religion, Vol. 43, No. 1 Issue March 2004.
67. Fromm (1978); *Psychoanalysis and Religion.* Yale University Press. London.
68. Fromm, Erich (1991); *Marx's concept of man.* Continuum. NY
69. Gatje, Helmut (1996); *The Qur'an and Its Exegesis: Selected Texts with Classical and Modern Muslim Interpretations.* Oneworld Publishers.
70. Geisler, Norman. L and Saleeb, Abdul (2002); *Answering Islam – the Crescent in the light of Cross.* BakerBooks. Michigan. USA.
71. Gibb H.A.R (1953); *Islam.* Oxford.
72. Gingerich, Owen (2006); *God's Universe.* Harvard University Press. Cambridge.
73. Gleick, James (2011); *The Information: A History, a Theory, a Flood.* Pantheon Books. NY
74. Goldziher, Ignaz (1971); *Muslim Studies. Vol. 1.* Translated by C. R. Barber and S. M. Stern. London.
75. Goldziher, Ignaz. (1981); *Introduction to Islamic Theology and Law.* Translated by Andras and Ruth Hamori. Princeton
76. Greeley, A. (1994); A religious revival in Russia? Journal for the Scientific Study of Religion. Volume 33. Issue 3.
77. Green, C.E. (1968). *Lucid Dreams.* Hamish Hamilton. London.
78. Guillaume, Alfred (1978); *Islam.* Harmondsworth. UK.
79. Guillaume, Alfred (1956); *Islam.* Penguin Books Inc., Baltimore.
80. Guillaume, Alfred (2002); *The Life of Muhammad: A Translation of Ishaq's Sirat Rasul Allah with Introduction and Notes.* Oxford University Press. NY
81. Hagee, John (2007); *Jerusalem Countdown.* Front Line. Lake Mary. Florida
82. Haleem, M A S Abdel (1992); *Grammatical Shift For The Rhetorical Purposes: Iltifat And Related Features In The Qur'an.* Bulletin of the School of Oriental and African Studies, Islamic Awareness, Volume LV, part 3.
83. Halm, Heinz (2004); *Shi'ism* (2nd ed.). Columbia University Press.
84. Hare, Robert D. (1993); *Without Conscience: The Disturbing World of the Psychopaths Among Us.* The Guilford Press. A Division of Guilford Publications. Inc. NY.
85. Harris, Sam (2005); *The End of Faith: Religion, Terror, and the future of reason.* Simon & Schuster UK Ltd. London.

86. Harris, T. (1988); *The silence of the lambs.* St. Martin's Press. NY
87. Harris, T. (1999); *Hannibal.* Delacorte Press. NY
88. Hartshorne, Charles (1984); *Omnipotence and Other Theological Mistakes.* State university of New York Press. Albany. US
89. Haykal, Muhammad Husayn (1976); *The Life of Muhammad,* translated by Isma'il Razi A. al-Faruqi (from eighth edition). Chapter 5: From the beginning of Revelation to the Conversion of Umar; Chapter 8: From the Violation of the Boycott to al Isra'. American Trust Publications. Plainfield. USA.
90. Henri Ey (1954); *Psychiatric Studies III,* Desclée de Brouwer, Paris
91. Hergenhahn, B. R. (1997); *An introduction to the history of psychology.* Pacific Grove, CA: Brooks/Cole.
92. Hickey, Eric W. (2010); *Serial Murderers and Their Victims.* Wadsworth, Cengage Learning. Belmont, USA.
93. Hippocrates (1983): *Tratados hipocraticos I* [Hippocratic Treatises I], Gredos, Madrid. Spain.
94. Hippocrates (1849); *On the sacred disease* (De la maladie sacree), Oeuvres completes d' hippocrate, J-B. Baillere, Paris.
95. Hitchens, Christopher (2007); *The Portable Atheist: Essential Readings for the Nonbeliever.* Da Capo Press. Cambridge.
96. Hitti, Philip K (2002); *History of the Arabs,* First published in 1937, revised tenth edition, Palgrave Macmillion, Basingstoke, UK.
97. Holldobler, Bert and Wilson Edward O. (1990); *The Ants.* Belknap Press of Harvard University Press. Cambridge.
98. Holmes, Ronald M. & De Burger, James. (1988); *Serial Murder.* Newbury Park: Sage.
99. Howell Smith, A. D (1943); *In Search of the Real Bible.* Watts & Co, London.
100. Huang, Xianian. (1998); 20 shiji de zhongguo foxue yanjiu (Buddhist Studies in 20th Century China). Annual of Religious Research in China. China Social Sciences Press. Beijing.
101. Hurgronje Snouck, C (1951); *La Légende qoranique d'Abraham et la politique religieuse du prophète Mohammad in Revue Africaine.* Vol. 95, translated by Bousquet.
102. Iyer, Meena (2009); *Faith & Philosophy of Zoroastrianism.* Kalpaz Publications. Delhi.
103. Jeffery, Arthur (1938); *The Foreign Vocabulary of the Qur'an.* Oriental Institute. Baroda.
104. Johnson F.H (1978); *The Anatomy of Hallucinations.* Nelson-Hall. Chicago.
105. Jung, C.G (1933); *Modern Man in Search of A Soul.* A Harvest Book. Houghton Mifflin Harcourt Publishing Company. NY.
106. Kahaner, L. (1988); *Cults That Kill: Probing the Underworld of Occult Crime.* Warner Books. NY.
107. Kaufmann, Walter (1972); *Critique of Religion and Philosophy.* Harper Torchbooks, NY
108. Kay, Glenn (2008); *Zombie Movies: The Ultimate Guide.* Chicago Review Press. USA.
109. Keller, Nuh Ha Mim (1999); *Reliance of the Traveller, A Classic Manual of Islamic Sacred Law.* Amana Publications. Beltsville, Maryland.
110. Khalid, Muhammad Khalid (2005); *Successors of the Messenger* (English Translation of al Khulafa al Rasool: Biographies of the Five Rightly Guided Caliphs of Islam). Dar Al-Kotob Al-Ilmiyah Publishing House. Beirut. Lebanon.
111. Khan, M.A (2009); *Islamic Jihad: A Legacy of Forced Conversion, Imperialism, and Slavery.* iUniverse, Inc. NY.

112. Khan, Muhammad Zafrulla (1980); *Muhammad: Seal of the Prophets*. Routledge & Kegan Paul Books. London.
113. Kimball, Charles (2002); *When Religion Becomes Evil*. Harper, San Francisco.
114. Kingdon, D. G., & Turkington, D. (1993); *Cognitive behavioural therapy of schizophrenia*. Guilford. NY
115. Kluger, Jeffrey (2007); *What Makes Us Moral*. Time Magazine. November 21, 2007
116. Koehler, John (2009); *The Soviet Union's Cold War against the Catholic Church*. Pegasus Books.
117. Lachkar, Joan (2008); *How to Talk to a Narcissist*. Routledge. Taylor and Francis Group. USA
118. Lee, Alfred McClung and Lee, Elizabeth Briant (1972); *The Fine Art of Propaganda*. Octagon Books.
119. Leuder I. and Thomas P (2000); *Voices of Reason, Voices of Insanity: Studies of Verbal Hallucinations*. Routledge, Philadelphia.
120. Levin, J. and Fox, J.A. (1985); *Mass murder*. Plenum. NY.
121. Lewis, Bernard (2003); *The Assassins*. Phoenix. London.
122. Lings, Martin (1975); *What is Sufism?* George Allen & Unwin, London.
123. Link BG and Stueve A (1994); *Psychotic symptoms and the violent/illegal behavior of mental patients compared to community*, in Violence and Mental Disorder: Developments in Risk Assessment. University of Chicago Press.
124. Lokeswarananda, Swami (2003); *Science and religion*. The Ramakrishna Mission Institute of Culture. Kolkata. India.
125. Lovecraft, H. P (1973); *Supernatural horror in literature*. Dover Publications, Inc. NY.
126. Luukkanen, A. (1997); *The religious policy of the Stalinist state*. Helsinki: SHS.
127. Margoliouth, David Samuel (1914); *The Early Development of Mohammedanism*. Charles Scribner's Sons. NY.
128. Marron, K. (1988); *Ritual Abuse*. McClelland-Bantam. Toronto.
129. Martin, Michael (2006); *The Cambridge Companion to Atheism*. Cambridge University Press.
130. McCarthy, K. (1984); *Serial killers: their deadly bent may be set in cradle*. Los Angeles Times. 7th July 1984.
131. McGinniss, Joe (1989); *Fatal Vision*. New American Library. NY.
132. McGrath, Alister and McGrath, Joanna Collicutt (2007); *The Dawkins Delusion: Atheist Fundamentalism and the Denial of Divine*. InterVarsity Press. Illinois. US.
133. Melden, A. I (1970); *Human Rights*. Belmont.
134. Michaud, S. G., and Aynesworth H. (1983); *The Only Living Witness: A True Account of Homicidal Insanity*. Linden Press, Simon and Schuster. NY
135. Mill, John Stuart (1874); *Three Essays on Religion*. H. Holt and Co. NY.
136. Miller, Judith (1997); *God Has Ninety-nine Names: Reporting From a Militant Middle East*. Touchstone. Simon & Schuster. USA.
137. Mitchell, Edwin (1991); *The two headed dragon of Africa*. Josiah Pub
138. Morgan, T. (1988); *Literary outlaw: The life and times of William S. Burroughs*. Henry Holt & Co. NY.
139. Naipaul, V. S (1998); *Beyond Belief: Islamic Excursions Among the Converted People*. Abacus. London.
140. Nasr, Vali (2007); The Shia Revival: How Conflicts within Islam will shape the Future. W. W Norton. NY
141. Newberg A, D'Aquili E and Rause V. (2001); *Brain Science and the Biology of Belief: Why God Won't Go Away*. Ballantine Books, NY
142. Nicholson, R. A. (1930); *Literary History of the Arabs*. Cambridge.

143. O'Brien, Darcy (1985); *Two of a kind, the Hillside Stranglers*. New American Library. NY.
144. Ortberg, John (2008); *Faith and Doubt*. Zondervan Books. Michigan. US
145. Paine, Thomas (1974); *The Age of Reason*. Secaucus
146. Peck, M. S. (1983); *People of the Lie.* Simon and Schuster. NY.
147. Peris, D. (1998); *Storming the heavens: The Soviet league of the militant godless.* Cornell University Press. Ithaca, NY.
148. Posner, G. L., and Ware J. (1986); *Mengele*. Dell. NY.
149. Pospielovsky, D (1988); *Soviet anti-religious campaigns and persecutions*. St. Martin's Press. NY.
150. Pospielovsky, Dimitry V. (1987); *A history of Soviet atheism in theory and practice, and the true believer.* St Martin's Press. NY
151. Rahman, Afzalur (1979); *Muhammad: Blessing for Mankind.* The Muslim Schools Trust, London.
152. Ramet, S. P. (1998); *Nihil obstat: Religion, politics, and social change in east-central Europe and Russia.* Duke University Press. Durham, NC.
153. Ramet, Sabrina (2005); *Religious Policy in the Soviet Union.* A report published on 10th Nov 2005. University of Cambridge.
154. Ray, Darrel W. (2009); *The God Virus: How Religion Infects Our Lives and Culture.* IPC Press, Bonner Springs, Kansas
155. Reinhardt, J. M. (1960); *The Murderer's Trail of Charles Starkweather.* Springfield, IL: Charles C Thomas.
156. Reyes, Christopher (2010); *In His Name*. AuthorHouse. Bloomington.
157. Richardson, Joel (2006); *Antichrist: Islam's Awaited Messiah*. Pleasant Word. A division of WinePress Publishing. Enumclaw.
158. Robinson, John A. T. (1963); *Honest to God*. The Westminster Press. Philadelphia.
159. Rodinson, Maxime (1980); *Muhammad* (Original in French, translated to English by Anne Carter). The New Press. NY.
160. Sagan, Carl (1997); *The Demon Haunted World: Science as a Candle in the Dark.* Ballantine Books. Random House Inc. USA.
161. Saks, E. (2007); *The Centre Cannot Hold: A Memoir of my Schizophrenia*. Virago. London.
162. Schneider K (1957); *Primary and secondary symptoms in schizophrenia.* Fortschrift für Neurologie und Psychiatrie, trans. by Marshall H, in Hirsch S & Shepherd M (1974) Themes and Variations in European Psychiatry: An Anthology, John Wright & Sons. Bristol.
163. Schwartz, A. E. (1992); *The man who could not kill enough*. Birch Lane Press. NY.
164. Shahid, Irfan, (1989); *Byzantium and the Arabs in the Fifth Century.* Harvard University Press. Cambridge.
165. Shaikh, Anwar (1995); *Islam: The Arab National Movement*. The Principality Publisher. Cardiff. UK.
166. Shaikh, Anwar (1998); *Islam and Human Rights and Other Essays,* Published by A. Ghosh, Houston, USA.
167. Shaikh, Anwar (1998a); *ISLAM: The Arab Imperialism*. The Principality Publishers. Cardiff. GB. (Re-published by Hindu Writers Forum. New Delhi. India)
168. Shermer, Michael (2000); *How we believe: science, skepticism and the search for God.* Freeman. NY.
169. Shourie, Arun (2002); *The World of Fatwas*. Rupa & Co. New Delhi. India.
170. Sina, Ali (2008); *Understanding Muhammad, a Psychobiography of Allah's Prophet*. Felibri.com. USA
171. Skal, D. (1993); *The monster show: A cultural history of horror*. W.W. Norton and Co. NY

172. Smith, P. (1999); *A Concise Encyclopedia of the Bahai Faith*. Oneworld Publications. Oxford.
173. Smith, Wilfred Cantwell (1981); *On understanding Islam: selected studies.* Mouton publishers. The Hague. The Netherlands
174. Snow, Robert L. (2003); *Deadly Cults: The Crimes of True Believers.* Praeger Publishers. CT. USA.
175. Sompayrac, Lauren (2002); *How pathogenic viruses work.* Jones and Barelett Publishers. Sudbury. USA.
176. Spencer, Robert (2003); *Onward Muslim Soldiers: How Jihad still threatens America and the West.* Regnery Publishing. Washington DC.
177. Spencer, Robert (2005); *The politically incorrect guide to Islam (and the crusades).* Regnery Publishing. Washington DC.
178. Spencer, Robert (2006); *The Truth about Muhammad.* Regnery Publishing. Washington DC
179. Sproul R. C and Saleeb, Abdul (2003); *The Dark Side of Islam.* Crossway Books (a division of Good News Publishers). Wheaton. Illinois.
180. Stanford, Edward V. (1960); *Foundations of Christian Belief.* The Newman Press. Westminster.
181. Stearns, Peter N. (2008); *The Oxford Encyclopedia of the Modern World.* Oxford University Press.
182. Stewart, Charles (1907); *A Response to An Urgent Testimony.* Liberty Missionary Society. Seventh-Day Adventists.
183. Stout, Martha (2005); *The Sociopath Next Door.* Broadway Books (a division of Random House. Inc). NY.
184. Strachey, James and Gay, Peter (1966); *Sigmund Freud: Introductory Lectures on Psycho-analysis.* W.W Norton & Company. NY.
185. Stutley, M. J (1977); *A Dictionary of Hinduism.* London.
186. Tauler, J. (1990); *Institutions. Matters for Prayer*, SIgueme, Salamanca.
187. The world book encyclopedia (2005), Volume 5, World Book, Inc.
188. Torrey, C. C (1933); *The Jewish Foundation of Islam.* Jewish Institute of Religion Press, NY.
189. Trifkovic, Serge (2002); *The Sword of the Prophet.* Regina Orthodox Press. Boston.
190. Trimingham, J. Spencer, (1979); *Christianity Among the Arabs in Pre-Islamic Times.* Longman. London.
191. Van den Bercken, W (1989); *Ideology and atheism in the Soviet Union.* Mounton de Gruyter. NY
192. Voltaire (1971); *Dictionnaire philosophique.* Translated by Besterman. London.
193. Walker, Benjamin (2002); *Foundation of Islam, the Making of a World Faith.* Rupa & Co. New Delhi. India.
194. Warraq, Ibn (1995); *Why I am not a Muslim.* Prometheus books. NY.
195. Warraq, Ibn (1998); *The Origins of the Koran, Classic Essays on Islam's Holy Book.* Prometheus Books. NY.
196. Warraq, Ibn (2000); *The Quest for the Historical Muhammad.* Prometheus Books. NY.
197. Warraq, Ibn (2003); *Leaving Islam, Apostates Speak Out.* Prometheus Books. NY.
198. Warraq, Ibn (2011); *Which Qur'an? Variants, Manuscripts, Linguistics.* Prometheus Books. NY.
199. Weeks, Theodore R (2011); *Across the Revolutionary Divide: Russia and the USSR, 1861-1945.* John Wiley & Sons.
200. Weston, Mark (2008); *Prophets and Princes: Saudi Arabia from Muhammad to the Present.* John Wiley and Sons. USA and Canada.

201. White, Arthur L. (1981); *The Early Elmshaven Years Volume 5 (1900-1905)*. Herald Publishing Association. Washington, D.C.
202. Wilson, Edward (1978); *On human nature*. Harvard University Press. Cambridge
203. Winn, Craig (2004); *Prophet of Doom. Islam's terrorist Dogma in Muhammad's own Words*. Cricketsong books. A division of Virginia publishers. Canada.
204. Winn, S. and D Merrill (1980); *Ted Bundy: The Killer Next Door*. Bantam Books. NY.
205. Wrobel, J., (1990); *Language and Schizophrenia*. Benjamins, Linguistic and Literary Studies in Eastern Europe. Amsterdam.
206. Yaroslavsky, Emelian (1934); *Religion in the U.S.S.R.* International Publishers. NY
207. Zwemer, S. (2011); *Islam: A Challenge to Faith*. (Classic reprint). Nabu Press. NY
208. Zwemer, S. (2012); *The Influence of Animism on Islam -- An Account of Popular Superstitions* (classic reprint). Forgotten Books. London.

Public lectures, interviews

1. Humphrey, Nicholas (1997); *What shall we tell the children?* Amnesty Lecture, 21st February, Oxford.
2. Flew, Antony and Habermas, Gary (2004); *My Pilgrimage from Atheism to Theism: An Exclusive Interview with Former British Atheist Professor Antony Flew'*. Philosophia Christi. Vol. 6, no.2

Internet

1. Eagleton, Terry (2006); *Lunging, flailing, mispunching: A review of Richard Dawkins' The God Delusion*. London review of books. Published on October 19, 2006 URL: http://www.lrb.co.uk/v28/n20/terry-eagleton/lunging-flailing-mispunching (Last accessed Apr. 19, 2013)
2. Ghamidi J. A, Zaheer K., Sina, A (2007); *Probing Islam*. Faith Freedom International. URL: http://www.news.faithfreedom.org/downloads/probing-islam.pdf (Last accessed October 19, 2012).
3. Glazov, Jamie, Warner (2007); *The Study of Political Islam. An interview of Bill Warner* published on February 05, 2007. FrontPageMagazine.com. URL: http://97.74.65.51/readArticle.aspx?ARTID=297 (Last accessed Apr. 19 / 2013)
4. Islam-Watch (2007); *Twenty Three Years: A Study of the Prophetic Career of Mohammad*. Published on February 18, 2007. URL: http://www.islam-watch.org/Ali_Dasti/Twenty-Three-Years-of-Muhammad1.htm (Last accessed March 02, 2013)
5. Walsch, Neale Donald (2007); *In Response to Richard Dawkins*. BeliefNet. URL: http://blog.beliefnet.com/conversationswithgod/2007/10/in-response-to-richard-dawkins.html (Last accessed June 07, 2012)